Sustainable Tourism XI

WITPRESS

WIT Press publishes leading books in Science and Technology.
Visit our website for the current list of titles.
www.witpress.com

WITeLibrary

Home of the Transactions of the Wessex Institute.
Papers contained in this volume are archived in the WIT eLibrary in volume 263 of WIT Transactions on Ecology and the Environment (ISSN 1743-3541).
The WIT eLibrary provides the international scientific community with immediate and permanent access to individual papers presented at WIT conferences.
Visit the WIT eLibrary at www.witpress.com.

ELEVENTH INTERNATIONAL CONFERENCE ON
SUSTAINABLE TOURISM

Sustainable Tourism 2024

CONFERENCE CHAIRMAN

Stavros Syngellakis
Wessex Institute, UK
Member of WIT Board of Directors

INTERNATIONAL SCIENTIFIC ADVISORY COMMITTEE

Alma Bojorquez-Vargas
Joao-Manuel Carvalho
Pablo Diaz Rodriguez
Eleni Didaskalou
Mauro Dujmovic
Hiroshi Kato
Robert Mahler
Jose Luis Miralles i Garcia
Yasuo Ohe
Marko Peric
Lorenz Poggendorf
Meng-Cong Zheng

Organised by
Wessex Institute, UK

Sponsored by
WIT Transactions on Ecology and the Environment

WIT Transactions

Wessex Institute
Ashurst Lodge, Ashurst
Southampton SO40 7AA, UK

We would like to express our thanks to the conference Chairs and members of the International Scientific Advisory Committees for their efforts during the 2024 conference season.

Conference Chairs

Alexander Cheng
University of Mississippi, USA
(Member of WIT Board of Directors)

Stavros Syngellakis
Wessex Institute, UK
(Member of WIT Board of Directors)

International Scientific Advisory Committee Members 2024

Socrates Basbas Aristotle University of Thessaloniki, Greece
João Batista de Paiva University of São Paulo, Brasil
Alma Bojórquez-Vargas Universidad Autonoma De San Luis Potosi, Mexico
Colin Booth University of the West of England, UK
Carlos Borrego University of Aveiro, Portugal
Roman Brandtweiner Vienna Universiy of Economics and Business, Austria
André Buchau University of Stuttgart, Germany
Paúl Carrión Mero Higher Polytechnic School of the Litoral, Ecuador
João Manuel Carvalho University of Lisbon, Portugal
Weiqiu Chen Zhejiang University, China
Jeng-Tzong Chen National Taiwan Ocean University, Taiwan
Mario Cvetković University of Split, Croatia
Maria da Conceição Cunha University of Coimbra, Portugal
Luca D'Acierno University of Naples Federico II, Italy
Pablo Díaz Rodríguez University of La Laguna, Spain
Eleni Didaskalou University of Piraeus, Greece
Petia Dineva Bulgarian Academy of Sciences, Bulgaria
Eduardo Divo Embry-Riddle Aeronautical University, USA
Hrvoje Dodig University of Split, Croatia
Chunying Dong Beijing Insitute of Technology, China
Mauro Dujmović Juraj Dobrila University of Pula, Croatia
Ney Dumont Pontifical Catholic University of Rio de Janeiro, Brazil
Siyabulela Fobosi University of Fort Hare, South Africa
Zhuo Jia Fu Hohai University, China
Alexander Galybin Schmidt Institute of Physics of the Earth, Russia

Xiao-Wei Gao Dalian University of Technology, China
Eric Gielen Universitat Politècnica de València, Spain
Emanuele Giorgi Tecnologico de Monterrey, Mexico
Luis Godinho University of Coimbra, Portugal
Andreas Karageorghis University of Cyprus, Cyprus
Alain Kassab University of Central Florida, USA
Hiroshi Kato Hokkaido University, Japan
John Katsikadelis National Technical University of Athens, Greece
Dima Legeyda, Newcastle University, UK
Edson Leonel University of São Paulo, Brazil
Daniel Lesnic University of Leeds, UK
Danila Longo University of Bologna, Italy
Isabel Madaleno University of Lisbon, Portugal
Robert Mahler University of Idaho, USA
Irina Malkina-Pykh St Petersburg State Institute of Psychology and Social Work, Russia
George Manolis Aristotle University of Thessaloniki, Greece
Ilia Marchevsky Bauman Moscow State Technical University, Russia
Liviu Marin University of Bucharest, Romania
José Luis Miralles i Garcia Polytechnic University of Valencia, Spain
Juraj Mužík University of Žilina, Slovakia
Yasuo Ohe Tokyo University of Agriculture, Japan
Özlem Özçevik Istanbul Technical University, Turkey
Leandro Palermo Jr State University of Campinas, Brazil
Ernian Pan National Yang Ming Chiao Tung University, Taiwan
Marilena Papageorgiou Aristotle University of Thessaloniki, Greece
Marko Perić University of Rijeka, Croatia
Filomena Pietrapertosa National Research Council of Italy, Italy

Lorenz Poggendorf Toyo University, Japan
Dragan Poljak University of Split, Croatia
Dimitris Prokopiou University of Piraeus, Greece
Elena Cristina Rada Insubria University of Varese, Italy
Marco Ragazzi University of Trento, Italy
Jure Ravnik University of Maribor, Slovenia
Antonio Romero Ordóñez University of Sevilla, Spain
Francesco Russo Mediterranea University of Reggio Calabria, Italy
Monica Salvia National Research Council of Italy, Italy
Božidar Šarler University of Ljubljana, Slovenia
Marco Schiavon, University of Padova, Italy
Marichela Sepe DICEA-Sapienza Università di Roma, Italy
Vladimír Sládek Slovak Academy of Sciences, Slovakia
Elena Strelnikova National Academy of Sciences of Ukraine, Ukraine
Antonio Tadeu University of Coimbra, Portugal
Carlo Trozzi Teche Consulting srl, Italy
Sirma Turgut Yildiz Technical University, Turkey
Wolf Yeigh University of Washington, USA
Jianming Zhang Hunan University, China
Meng-Cong Zheng National Taipei University of Technology, Taiwan

Sustainable Tourism XI

Editor

Stavros Syngellakis
Wessex Institute, UK
Member of WIT Board of Directors

WITPRESS Southampton, Boston

Editor:

Stavros Syngellakis
Wessex Institute, UK
Member of WIT Board of Directors

Published by

WIT Press
Ashurst Lodge, Ashurst, Southampton, SO40 7AA, UK
Tel: 44 (0) 238 029 3223; Fax: 44 (0) 238 029 2853
E-Mail: witpress@witpress.com
http://www.witpress.com

For USA, Canada and Mexico

Computational Mechanics International Inc
25 Bridge Street, Billerica, MA 01821, USA
Tel: 978 667 5841; Fax: 978 667 7582
E-Mail: infousa@witpress.com
http://www.witpress.com

British Library Cataloguing-in-Publication Data

A Catalogue record for this book is available
from the British Library

ISBN: 978-1-78466-491-6
eISBN: 978-1-78466-492-3
ISSN: 1746-448X (print)
ISSN: 1743-3541 (on-line)

The texts of the papers in this volume were set individually by the authors or under their supervision. Only minor corrections to the text may have been carried out by the publisher.

No responsibility is assumed by the Publisher, the Editors and Authors for any injury and/or damage to persons or property as a matter of products liability, negligence or otherwise, or from any use or operation of any methods, products, instructions or ideas contained in the material herein. The Publisher does not necessarily endorse the ideas held, or views expressed by the Editors or Authors of the material contained in its publications.

© WIT Press 2024

Open Access: All of the papers published in this volume are freely available, without charge, for users to read, download, copy, distribute, print, search, link to the full text, or use for any other lawful purpose, without asking prior permission from the publisher or the author as long as the author/copyright holder is attributed. This is in accordance with the BOAI definition of open access.

Creative Commons content: The CC BY 4.0 licence allows users to copy, distribute and transmit an article, and adapt the article as long as the author is attributed. The CC BY licence permits commercial and non-commercial reuse.

Preface

This book contains a selection of papers among those presented at the 11th International Conference on Sustainable Tourism, organised by the Wessex Institute of Technology, UK, in Seville, Spain, from 24 to 26 September 2024. The meeting was sponsored by the WIT Transactions on Ecology and the Environment.

The contributors of this volume address a wide range of issues covering several important areas of research. In the field of policies and management practices, there is a discussion on how UN member states consider promoting decent work and economic growth as well as responsible consumption and production as crucial policy areas and actions to boost the development of sustainable tourism in their territory. It is also argued that there is a need for new products and services to account for recent contradictory socio-economic developments. Practical policy options, based on the use of sustainability indicators, should be explored towards a holistic management that addresses the consequences of neglected or undervalued services.

Environmental, social and governance principles and practices should guide the tourist industry towards more eco-friendly and socially responsible products and services. The potential value of other economic activities, such as agriculture, may be explored and sustainable programmes can be developed or improved to ensure that they contribute to a country's tourism industry. Research on short-term rentals (STR) has shown spatial distribution patterns aligning closely with traditional accommodations, leading to increased tourist pressure in densely populated neighbourhoods, underscoring the need for measures to regulate the STR. Public transport can be considered as an opportunity to promote tourist homes in urban peripheries.

Destination management includes SWOT analysis for the development of strategies to design sustainable tourism indicators; research on the effects of local planting on the urban microclimate; a bibliometric examination of tourism versus sustainable destinations; investigation on tourism carrying capacity of geosites; transformation design for local community empowerment and well-being in destination; the effect of service learning on university tourism students' social skills.

Indigenous culture can be cultivated and promoted by developing sustainable tourism based on education; assessing the impact of modern construction on urban heritage sites is an essential step towards the protection of such sites; the attraction of local food markets to visitors and their conversion into a tourist destination should be explored.

Several cases on tourism's strong impact on the environment are included in this volume. Mitigation case studies in major ports are explored; air pollution from cruise ships during hotelling in ports is studied; integrated strategies for coastal management in emerging tourist destinations is proposed; the ocean literacy of recreationists and tourists as ocean users is studied. Ecotourism can be the mechanism for green development transformation in urban borderland and the exploration of untouched lands as a consequence of a war thus playing a key role in building a lasting peace in a war-ravaged country.

This volume is part of the WIT Transactions on Ecology and the Environment. The digital version of the papers, as well as those presented in the previous conferences are archived in Open Access format in the eLibrary of the Wessex Institute (https://www.witpress.com/elibrary) where they are freely available to the international community.

The editor is grateful to all authors for the quality of their contributions as well as to the members of the International Scientific Advisory Committee and other colleagues who helped to review the papers and hence ensure the quality of this volume.

Stavros Syngellakis
Editor, 2024

Contents

Section 1: Sustainable tourism implementation

Changing faces of Croatian tourism
Mauro Dujmović & Aljoša Vitasović 3

The place of tourism in the implementation of the Sustainable Development
Goals at national level
Giulio Pattanaro 13

Management of sustainable tourism in tourist destination ports:
The use of sustainable indicators in the case study of Piraeus Port, Greece
*Ioannis Anastasopoulos, Nikolaos Georgopoulos, Ioannis Katsanakis,
Nikoletta Klada, Chryssoula Konstantopoulou, Evangelia Kopanaki,
Asterios Stroumpoulis, Georgios Tsoupros & Sotirios Varelas* 23

Section 2: Strategies and sustainable business models

The future of competitive advantage in the hotel industry:
ESG initiatives as a key differentiator
*Konstantina K. Agoraki, Alexandra Alexandropoulou, Eleni Didaskalou
& Dimitrios A. Georgakellos* 39

Using agriculture to improve and increase the sustainable tourism
industry in Idaho, USA
Robert L. Mahler, Nav Ghimire, Brad Stokes & Iris Mayes 49

Characterisation of short-term rentals in Granada, Spain: Spatial analysis
*Sofía Mendoza de Miguel, Rubén Villar Navascués, Manuel de la Calle,
Patricia Valenzuela, Begoña Guirao, Armando Ortuño, Daniel Gálvez-Pérez,
Fernando de Mingo & Jairo Casares* 63

Public transport as an opportunity to promote tourist homes in urban
peripheries: The case of Madrid, Spain
*Daniel Gálvez-Pérez, Begoña Guirao, Patricia Valenzuela, Armando Ortuño,
Inmaculada Mohíno, Fernando de Mingo & Manuel de la Calle* 77

Section 3: Destination management

SWOT analysis for the development of strategies to design sustainable tourism indicators in Galapagos, Ecuador
Lady Soto-Navarrete, Óscar Saladié, María Jaya-Montalvo, Maribel Aguilar-Aguilar & Paúl Carrión-Mero 93

Effects of local planting on the urban microclimate: A case study in a touristic city in Italy
Alessandra Chiappini, Umberto Rizza, Diletta Bevilacqua & Giorgio Passerini 107

Tourism and sustainable destinations: A bibliometric examination
Mehmet Bahadir Kalipçi 119

Tourism carrying capacity of geosites on Santa Cruz Island, Galapagos, for its sustainability
María Jaya-Montalvo, Josué Briones-Bitar, Lady Soto-Navarrete, Ramón Espinel & Paúl Carrión-Mero 127

Transformation design for responsible tourism: A paradigm shift for local community empowerment and well-being in destination
Valentina Facoetti & Laura Galluzzo 139

Service learning: A technique that enhances university students' social skills
Denise Rodríguez-Zurita & Humberto Morán-Rodríguez 153

Section 4: Cultural, heritage and gastronomic tourism

Developing sustainable indigenous tourism based on education: A comparison between Japan and Canada
Lorenz Poggendorf, Takeshi Kurihara & Miho Hamazaki 167

Impact assessment of urban heritage sites: The case of Khor Dubai, UAE
Eman Assi 181

Converting a local market into a tourist destination: The case of Plaza de Mercado Las Ferias, Bogotá, Colombia
Maricela I. Montes-Guerra, Natalia Zapata-Cuervo, Maria Paula Deaza, Felipe Castilla Corzo, Maria Catalina Gonzalez Forero & Annamaria Filomena-Ambrossio 193

Section 5: Tourism and the environment

Environmental impact of cruise tourism: Exploring mitigation case studies in major ports
Alexandra Alexandropoulou, Natalia Chatzifoti, Konstantina K. Agoraki, Andreas Fousteris & Dimitrios A. Georgakellos 209

Air pollution from cruise ships during hotelling in ports:
A case study in Ancona harbour, Italy
*Simone Virgili, Umberto Rizza, Martina Tommasi, Silvia Di Nisio
& Giorgio Passerini* 221

Green dreams in urban borderland: The ecotourism development
transformation under the context of policy in Xishuangbanna,
Yunnan Province, China
Min Liu & Thanapauge Chamaratana 229

Integrated coastal management in emerging tourist destinations on the
Mexican Caribbean coast
*Mónica Ariadna Chargoy Rosas, Óscar Frausto Martínez
& José Alfredo Cabrera Hernández*.. 243

The end of a war = the exploration of untouched lands: An investigation
into how ecotourism can play a key role in building a lasting peace
in Colombia
Rachel Germanier & Sofia Vargas Sourdis... 257

Are ocean users ocean literate? A case study of recreationists and tourists
in Cape Town, South Africa
Serena Lucrezi... 269

Author index 281

SECTION 1
SUSTAINABLE TOURISM IMPLEMENTATION

CHANGING FACES OF CROATIAN TOURISM

MAURO DUJMOVIĆ & ALJOŠA VITASOVIĆ
Faculty of Economics and Tourism, Juraj Dobrila University of Pula, Croatia

ABSTRACT

The present and future of the Croatian tourism are once again certain and no one is interested in its further improvement. It seems today as if the COVID-19 pandemic never took place. Contrary to suggestions and desires, the pandemic period was not utilised for the redefinition of Croatian tourism or the modernisation of its development. Croatian tourism, apart from the sea and sun, has failed to introduce anything new. Tourism development continues to rely on circumstances that work in its favour, such as the fact that Croatia is still a safe country relatively close to the emissive markets that guests decide to visit out of inertia. Croatia is in desperate need to change the course of its tourism development and create new products and services instead of just building numerous new accommodation capacities which only contribute to the uniformity of the tourism offer. The central argument of this paper is that the traditional notions of Croatian tourism development and practices have to be modified because of a range of contradictory socio-economic developments occurring in the field of contemporary tourism. The article outlines the nature of such changes and points out that Croatia needs tourism on a smaller scale which involves the growth of quality tourist services and offers in order to attract fewer tourists with higher purchasing power which would put a stop to the devastation of space and resources and achieve the preservation of the quality of life of local communities.

Keywords: Croatian tourism, capacities, devastation, prices, sustainable tourism, uniformity of offer, quality, value for money.

1 INTRODUCTION

Tourism is of central importance to social, cultural and economic lives in the 21st century and it is one of the most exciting and relevant phenomena in today's times of great mobility. As a social, economic and cultural phenomenon, tourism is in the process of permanent and powerful changes. Due to the increase in both standards of living and free time, tourism has developed into a mass phenomenon and directing of a large number of people towards tourist destinations led to specific ecological, cultural and social consequences. In the context of a fast-changing world and forces of geographical transformation, globalisation and international migration, tourism undoubtedly acquires new dimensions, properties and directions. By utilising the sociological social action theory, it is our aim to reveal and indicate new trends and tendencies in Croatian tourism and encourage readers not just to understand contemporary tourism from the binary of supply and demand perspectives, but also to encourage them to begin to think critically and question the assumptions inherent in much writing and talking about tourism. As Franklin and Crang argue: 'tourism has broken away from its beginnings as a relatively minor and ephemeral ritual of modern national life to become a significant modality through which transnational modern life is organised' [1]. Writers such as Lash and Urry [2] argue that a significant change has taken place within contemporary societies, involving a shift from organised to disorganised capitalism or from Fordism to post-Fordism, that is a shift from mass consumption to more individuated patterns of consumption. These changes have been characterised by Poon [3] as involving the shift from old tourism, which involved packaging and standardisation, to new tourism, which is segmented, flexible and customised.

The mass tourism of cheap package tours, which characterised escape from the modern economy of Fordist industrial production, has given way to tourism based on the consumption of a broad palette of sights, attractions and, above all, experiences. The paradigm has shifted from the modern notion of mass tourism to the post-modern notion of lifestyle experience tourism.

Tourism has become a key element of national development strategies and a very important tool in hands of many governments as the initiator of economic renovation. However, tourism is much more than this. It is a complex activity including much more than the commonly simplified understanding of this industry as a relatively simple source of revenue.

This article is the authors' independent attempt to review the contemporary nature of Croatian tourism and trends from the sociological point of view. This critical analysis is based on information collected from various resources and sites including publications of the Institute of Economics in Zagreb, Croatian National Tourist Board's publications and well-established sociological literature, which have all been used by the authors to identify the most important social and cultural features or consequences related to the development of contemporary tourism in the Republic of Croatia. It begins by reviewing the most prominent features of the contemporary tourism development in general and the common characteristics of the contemporary Croatian tourism in particular. Subsequently the article considers the nature of a large-scale Croatian tourism development in order to reveal the inadequate quality of the Croatian tourism offer and to state that Croatia has failed to redefine its tourism or modernise its development. The last section of the article highlights Croatia's efforts to tackle overtourism and develop sustainable tourism that preserves rather than consumes spaces and resources contributing to the preservation of destination's natural and social capital.

2 POSTMODERN TOURISM

Early sociological conceptualisations of the tourist experience emphasise its distinctiveness from everyday life. For example, Cohen [4] describes tourism as a quest for novelty and a temporary reversal of everyday activities. Similarly, Smith [5] sees the tourist as a person who visits a place away from home for the purpose of experiencing change. The differentiation between everyday life and tourist experience was also highlighted by MacCannell [6], who argues that tourism is a modern form of the religious quest for authenticity in which process authentic experiences are believed to be available only to those people who try to break the bonds of their everyday experiences and by Turner and Ash [7] who suggested that the temporary distance of tourists from their regular environments allows them to suspend the power of norms and values that govern their daily lives.

The notion of the tourist experience as disparate from the routine of everyday life has been challenged since the 1990s by scholars who introduced the perspective of postmodern tourism [2], [8], [9]. Mowforth and Munt [10] describe occurred changes in the field of tourism in several different levels. First, the Fordist production model has been turned into post-Fordist model. Secondly, modern has changed to postmodern. Thirdly, the change has occurred from readily packed tourism towards individual and flexible tourism. Postmodern tourism is characterised by the multiplicity of tourist motivations, experiences, and environments. In this respect, the notion of a diverse and plural realm of postmodern tourism goes one step beyond Cohen's [11] proposition regarding the variety of tourist experiences. While Cohen proclaimed that different people perform different tourist activities, Feifer [12] characterised the 'post-tourist' by his/her enjoyment of moving across the different types of tourist experiences. Such conceptualisations which emphasise the multiplicity and flexibility of postmodern tourist experiences react against the tendency of modernist theories to view societies as totalities [13]. Bauman [14] describes tourism by stating that it is a substitute to genuine needs, the real, which cannot be reached. Therefore, unlike Rojek's [15] claims, tourism can be seen to represent a larger scale of motivation than just escapism. Tourism is a practice which is more complex than the one concentrated on simple need satisfaction [16].

In the context of tourism, it means that the mass tourism of cheap package tours, which characterised escape from the modern economy of Fordist industrial production, has given way to tourism based on the consumption of a broad palette of sights, attractions and, above all, experiences. The paradigm has shifted from the modern notion of mass tourism to the post-modern notion of lifestyle experience tourism. Tourism has become highly diverse; a miscellany of different interests involving visits to sacred, informative, broadening, beautiful, uplifting or simply different sites. The whole phenomenon is based on consumption although the product itself is immaterial. The development of differentiated products and services has become unavoidable in tourism as well as the creation of experiences in all tourism products. Tourists are no longer passive consumers but they actively participate in the process of creation of the tourist experience. Increased market saturation, educated and conscious consumers, with higher income and more free time have determined the viability of those who offer services in the tourism industry. Consumers have numerous choices and possibilities, and often undertake seemingly incompatible activities simultaneously in order to capitalise on this array of opportunities. Therefore, the number of overnight stays and the profit of a destination have long ceased to be the main criteria and more emphasis has been given to the quality, diversity and particularities of the tourism offer.

The next section elaborates the nature of the Croatian tourism development by briefly analysing some of its prominent features bringing to the forefront the issue of the over-dependence on tourism.

3 KEY FEATURES OF THE CROATIAN TOURISM DEVELOPMENT

One of the significant characteristics of Croatian tourism is the marked concentration of tourist facilities along the Adriatic coast, which indicates that the tourism industry is more developed along the coast than in the continental parts of the country. Another prominent feature of Croatian tourism is its seasonal nature [17]. Additionally, excessive increase of tourism capacities especially private accommodation at the expense of living space and the normal way of life of the local population has been the dominant feature of Croatian tourism development for the whole decade and without a wise approach to the solution of these issues, the real price could be paid in the years to come.

For decades, these have been the key features of Croatian tourism, which has been growing in size year by year with breaking records in the number of tourist arrivals, overnight stays, revenues generated and direct and indirect earnings from tourism. Tourism has been Croatia's modus operandi and modus vivendi, the main response to all economic and existential problems. Croatia, known as a safe country (last year out of 128 countries worldwide, Croatia was ranked 22nd [18]), became one of the most desirable destinations for numerous tourists from around the world. Numerous world media reported on Croatia, its cities, coastline, sea, and natural beauty. In such conditions, little thought was given to the future and how to further improve Croatian tourism.

According to the Croatian Tourist Board data, in the last two pre-pandemic years, the number of beds in family accommodation increased by 14.8%, and the number of overnight stays increased by 9.3%, indicating that capacity growth is nowhere near matching demand growth. In those two years, commercial accommodation capacities in Croatia increased by 10.5%, while the number of overnight stays in them was only half of that, a mere 5.7% [19]. Year after year, we witnessed other, mostly negative and very concerning phenomena such as unreal price increases of goods and services alongside a decline in their quality, rising prices for parking and beach lounger rentals, a lack of qualified workforce, discrepancies between infrastructure and the intensity of tourist traffic (problems with waste, increasing release of sewage in the sea, etc.), and similar problems that have been swept under the rug for years and have increasingly tarnished the reputation of Croatian tourism. This was largely and still is a consequence of the imperative of quick and easy earnings from tourism, which accounts for one-sixth of Croatia's gross domestic product and is the only crucial and almost only relevant industry in Croatia [20]. Renting out accommodation has become the main weapon in tackling the existential problems of the local community, ignoring the fact that tourism is a highly unstable product subject to seasonality, unpredictable external influences, heterogeneity of tourist motives and expectations, and very elastic in terms of price and earnings.

Before the final part of the article the nature of a large-scale tourism development is debated in the next two sections in order to reveal the inadequate quality of the Croatian tourism offer.

4 THE PRESENT AND THE FUTURE OF THE CROATIAN TOURISM

The year 2020 was one of the worst tourism seasons ever in Croatia, as was in the rest of the world. The colonisation of the coast by hordes of mostly foreign tourists during the summer months suddenly came to an end, at least for a while, as did the dependence of Croatian tourism on developed countries that were the main generators of tourism revenue and tourists coming from those countries. In early 2020, almost all countries introduced epidemiological measures, and travel bans and border closures were among the first measures to prevent the spread of the pandemic. According to the Croatian Tourist Board, 2019 was a record year for Croatian tourism with almost 21 million arrivals and 108.6 million overnight stays. According to all predictions from January 2020, the revenue in 2020 was expected to exceed that of 2019. However, only 53% of arrivals and 61% of overnight stays were recorded in July 2020 in comparison to the same period the previous year [21].

Krešić and Mikulić [22] concluded that the pandemic threatened the very foundations of the tourism economy. Part of the income spent on tourism and travel was decreasing due to the global economic crisis and the decline in GDP of most developed countries. Due to protectionist measures and border closures, traffic connections between emitting and receptive tourist regions were on a decline. Additionally, the virus posed the greatest threat to older age groups, which had been one of the most important market segments for extending the tourism season.

2021 showed the first signs of recovery in tourism traffic. In Croatia, during 2021, there were 13.8 million arrivals and 84.1 million overnight stays, which represented 77% more arrivals and 55% more overnight stays compared to the same period in 2020. Foreign tourists accounted for 71.9 million overnight stays, while domestic tourists accounted for 12.3 million overnight stays. In 2021 67% of arrivals and 77% of overnight stays were achieved in comparison to 2019 [23].

Measures to prevent the spread of the COVID-19 pandemic affected tourist behaviour in terms of fewer arrivals but more overnight stays, i.e., prolonging their stay in the destination and their higher average spending [24]. Among other trends tourists' desire for higher levels of safety and more sustainable travel offer became evident. More and more tourists were looking for value for money, and there was an increasing demand for promotional offers and savings with such behavioural patterns expected to last for years [24], [25]. Due to maintaining physical distance, traveling by car or camper and staying in private accommodation with the popularisation of accommodation with a refund option and flexibility for booking changes without additional fees continued for many to be a safer option than staying in large hotels [26]. In addition to sun and sea, there was a significant increase in the number of visitors to national parks, rural areas and visitors spending time with family outdoors, indicating a shift in priorities when it comes to travel and the desire of tourists to enjoy the natural resources available to them.

It is a fact that the tourism sector in Croatia suffered greatly compared to other sectors and activities in Croatia during the pandemic. Therefore, much has been written about how the pandemic has revealed the need to find ways to stimulate and develop domestic agriculture and other forms of production and generally stimulate the development of small and medium-sized entrepreneurs and producers of all kinds as drivers of future development and that the state should establish a legislative framework, devise a strategy, and encourage reforms and changes [27]. It was believed that the crisis should be used to find ways to emerge from it in the best possible way and to leave it to the relevant and capable people of this country to devise a new economic model and a new model of tourism development [21].

Contrary to all expectations, the year 2022 was significantly marked by a trend of recovery in tourist traffic and approaching tourism figures from 2019. In Croatia, during 2022, there were 18.9 million arrivals and 104.8 million overnight stays, i.e., 37% more arrivals and 25% more overnight stays compared to 2021. Foreign tourists accounted for 92.3 million overnight stays, while domestic tourists accounted for 12.5 million overnight stays. 91% of arrivals and 96% of overnight stays were achieved in comparison to 2019. Revenues from foreign tourists amounted to €11.6 billion, higher by 23% compared to the same period in the record-breaking 2019 [28].

In a relatively short time, there was a return to the old ways, as if the pandemic had never happened. Contrary to suggestions and desires, the pandemic period was not used to redefine tourism or modernise its development, which would have been necessary to redefine or assign a new development role to every part of Croatia. The present and future of Croatian tourism were again certain, and no one was interested in further improving Croatian tourism. Instead of apocalyptic predictions about the political and economic impact of the pandemic usual topics such as prices of services and products in tourism and occupancy rates of accommodation dominated again the media space.

The year 2022 and especially 2023, were also marked by a much more intense media campaign against private renters, which was only partially justified. It might have been justified in the part where it said that the tax revenue per bed in collective accommodation was about 10 times higher compared to private accommodation, i.e., tax payments for private accommodation did not exceed 800 Croatian kunas per bed annually, while research conducted with companies with mixed accommodation portfolios (hotels and campsites) showed that the total burden of taxes and other levies amounted to 8,200 kunas per bed [29]. It was certainly justified in the part where it talked and wrote about the uncontrolled growth of accommodation capacities at the expense of space, infrastructure, and the normal life of the local population. And in this context, what is still worrying is the fact that the growth of supply does not cease although it is clear that the offer has already exceeded the demand and it is certain that it will be increasingly difficult to fill accommodation capacities in the coming years.

However, this media frenzy was not justified in the part where the hotel industry advocated for the construction of new hotel capacities. In that context, a key part of the story of the coastal devastation and overtourism in Croatia have been large hotel consortia and investors backed up by major banks and reputable architects who act only in favour of maximising their market monopoly and profit protecting their own interests, that is the interests of large foreign-owned capital and hotel companies. Nevertheless, the fact is that in the total tourist accommodation in Croatia, apartments account for a huge 61%, while the number of beds in hotel accommodation is almost the same (13%). In tourist countries like

Italy, Spain, Greece, and Portugal, between 19% and 35% of tourist accommodation is accounted for by apartments [30]. Therefore, it is clear that it is necessary to stop the growth of private accommodation and limit it, primarily for the sake of private renters themselves. Otherwise, due to the large number of accommodation capacities, prices will drop to the point where it will no longer be profitable for anyone.

For this purpose, a new tourism legislation has also been announced [31] in order to extend the power of the local government to restrict the construction and building of new accommodation units, restaurants and catering facilities. However, it is unlikely that this measure will solve the problem of overtourism created by the state itself by discouraging the manufacturing industry and encouraging overtourism primarily through small rental taxes. In addition, it should be emphasised that foreign investors, speculators, builders, real estate agencies, etc., still have the main say in the tourism industry, and all of them operate in cooperation with members of local authorities which enables individuals and groups to enrich themselves by selling land or building new accommodation capacities and thus further ruining and disfiguring space, which is considerably losing its value and attractiveness.

The fact is that no laws without adequate alteration of the existing tax system will stop excessive construction. If private accommodation is part of Croatian tradition and its key distinguishing feature compared to our competitors, then family accommodation should be tax-protected (small renters whose income represents additional earnings for patching household budgets in comparison to owners of a large number of accommodation units who have distributed their ownership among family members and relatives to avoid higher tax payments). In doing so, the state should find tools for much more efficient control of the so-called non-commercial accommodation, which is becoming a sore spot of Croatian tourism and which is currently growing rapidly. Such accommodation is mostly in the hands of foreigners, non-residents who rent out their uncategorised property and usually charge in cash. Such accommodation represents unfair competition to everyone working legally and investing in their properties. It has become a big issue that has exploded especially since 2016. Croatia will hardly restore the space to its original state, but we need to do everything to prevent the space from permanently losing its attractiveness and atmosphere and to avoid the situation where we are selling something that we ourselves would often not buy.

5 CONSEQUENCES OF A LARGE-SCALE TOURISM DEVELOMENT IN CROATIA

The Sustainable Travel Index 2020 shows that countries that are more committed to sustainable tourism development have a better chance of attracting new tourists [32].

In Croatia, 2022 was also marked by the adoption of the Sustainable Tourism Development Strategy. The most important feature of this strategic document is the absolute determination to permanently abandon haphazard, mass tourism and position Croatia as an authentic destination, with historic city centres protected against tourist devastation, knowing how to manage its space and hordes of tourists, with people at quality, safe, and well-paying jobs in the tourism industry [33].

Although spectacularly presented, the new Development Strategy does not present anything new. Namely, creators of development strategies and policies seize every opportunity to emphasise the importance of fighting against mass tourism and advocate for the development of sustainable tourism, while simultaneously battling for every inch of free space at the local level. Beaches continue to be overcrowded, roads and parking spaces are still inadequate to meet the demands of numerous visitors, the electricity and water supply systems are problematic, and there is a shortage of tourism labour [29]. According to spatial plans, additional 210 tourist zones shall be built on top of the existing 206 covering an area of nearly five thousand hectares or fifty million square meters along the Croatian Adriatic coast. Furthermore, 38 new marinas with 6,861 moorings are planned alongside the existing 16 marinas with a total of 3,049 moorings. Seven hundred kilometres of Croatian coastline has been filled, paved, and covered with concrete with plans for concreting almost one thousand six hundred kilometres more (or one quarter of the coastline) [34]. In such circumstances, the logical question to ask is whether such a tourism development strategy makes any sense and what is the limit to the growth of accommodation capacities and tourism infrastructure in Croatia. Excessive and uncontrolled construction creates the basis for mass arrivals and leads to exceeding the threshold of destination carrying capacities (physical, economic, and social) and the development of the so-called overtourism. Is there any sense in investing in the construction of new hotel capacities, regardless of the fact that according to data from the Ministry of Tourism and Sports, hotels account for only 13% of the total structure of accommodation capacities, while over 60% of capacities are in private accommodation and are steadily increasing [35].

6 DISCUSSION AND REMARKS

At the beginning of 2023, optimistic forecasts for the upcoming tourist season due to the introduction of the euro and the entry into the Schengen area predicted a record tourist season and based on such predictions and largely due to inflation raging in Europe since the beginning of the conflict in Ukraine, landlords, hoteliers, restaurateurs, and merchants raised prices. All of them blamed high food prices and the increase in energy prices as justification for raising prices. However, despite numerous complaints about high prices crowds continued to pour into Croatian coastal destinations.

According to recently published e-visitor data, in Croatia during the first 8 months, there were 16.2 million arrivals and 88.5 million overnight stays, which compared to the same period last year represents an 8% increase in arrivals and 2% increase in overnight stays, and compared to 2019, it equals the results. Why are prices the main topic? The problem partly lies in the fact that Croatia is still perceived as a cheap destination, and partly in the fact that on account of its offer, it attracts tourists with medium or lower purchasing power who generally do not want to spend a large amount during their stay in our country. All previous research has shown that the average daily spending of tourists in Croatia amounts to €98. Even half of that amount is related to accommodation services, and less than 20% to food and beverages outside the accommodation facility [28].

However, what is really worrying is the fact that Croatian tourism has become too expensive for a large number of Croatian citizens, for whom a stay at the sea during the peak season has become simply impossible. When it comes to supply, it should be noted that apart from some exceptions, Croatian tourism, besides sea and sun, has not offered anything new. Croatian tourism has been saved, as always, by circumstances that favour it, such as the fact that it is still a safe country relatively close to the emitting markets, and last year's statistics were good not because Croatian tourism has progressed, but because guests arrive out of inertia.

In this context, the story about sustainable tourism seems out of place, and the purpose of developing modern tourism should be to make mass tourism destinations attractive to all types of consumers, both deep-pocketed and shallow-pocketed ones. This is the formula for success of the world's largest tourist destinations, so why not Croatia's. The most popular destinations such as Paris, Barcelona, Venice, and even Dubrovnik, by combining various cultural, gastronomic, commercial, natural, and other attractions, attract a large number of tourists. Such destinations, while respecting the principles of sustainability of their urban structure and infrastructure capacities, offer the widest range of accommodation to their guests, restaurants, cultural attractions, and shops in all price categories with the best accommodation and restaurants playing a distinguishing role in the destination's overall portfolio.

Instead of counting overnight stays and arrivals, the focus should be on tourists' consumption, in which process Croatian tourism industry should be creating content, services, and experiences that will coerce tourists into spending based on the value for money principle. It is necessary to create conditions for high-quality and content-rich holidays during which guests will feel comfortable and satisfied without feeling cheated for the money they spent. Therefore, the answer lies in the development of quality tourism with quality service for all guests. Only in this way discussions about how expensive Croatia is as a destination should give way to discussions about Croatia as a quality tourist destination.

7 CONCLUSION

Over the past 50 years of intensive global tourism growth, tourism has often faced various types of crises. The reaction has usually been tumultuous, with almost immediate and dramatic declines in demand. This time was no exception. Undoubtedly, tourism worldwide was one of the hardest-hit economic activities by the pandemic, which, given its importance in the global economy, left no country immune, especially not those, like Croatia, that are highly dependent on international tourism flows. After the discovery of the vaccine against the coronavirus, with sufficient levels of vaccination and population immunity, the safety of travel was guaranteed, and tourism began to recover very quickly. It seems that, apart from a short-term recession and the halt of several years of growth, the experience with the pandemic did not significantly impact our values and bring about significant changes in aspects of our lives. It seems that tourism after the era of COVID-19 is not much different and better than before, and it seems that we eagerly awaited a return to the status quo.

Croatia is a country of exceptional natural beauty, and tourism emerges as a logical, but not the only choice and a natural source of socio-cultural and economic growth and development. However, we must use this period ahead of us to make a certain leap in tourism offer and work on creating new products and services instead of building accommodation capacities and apartments whose surplus significantly contributes to the monotony of the tourist offer. In this way, we would preserve space and its atmosphere and prevent its further devastation. Tourism needs to be freed from commercial shackles and protected from the imperatives of consumer society and it should be tailored to human and humane needs. Just as COVID-19 forced us to slow down our lives, we should also consider a more balanced and thoughtful approach to tourism. No one in this country would object to tourism numbers decreasing while the quality of tourism improves. Croatia needs tourism on a smaller scale that valorises spaces and resources rather than consumes them and contributes to a meaningful understanding of local residents, local culture, and natural beauties.

If we want to develop sustainable tourism that fully considers the economic, social, and environmental impacts and meets the needs of visitors, industry, the environment, and the local community, then we want the development which involves the growth of quality tourist services and offer in order to attract fewer tourists with higher purchasing power which would put a stop to the devastation of space and resources and achieve the preservation of the quality of life of local communities. Achieving all of the above requires primarily political will, followed by a general social consensus about the need to reinvent the existing model of tourism development. In sustainable tourism that considers the specifics of the destination and the interests of the local community and preserves the economic, social, and spatial resources of the destination, and which we all strive for at least declaratively, there is no easy profit. It is important to emphasise that sustainable tourism does not mean the development of selective forms of tourism, such as nautical or cultural tourism; the essence lies in the fact that every form of tourism should strive for sustainable development. The fundamental question of sustainability in tourism is to establish a balance between visitor demand, consumption and the destination and system's ability to provide tourism experiences without diminishing the destination's natural and social capital.

REFERENCES

[1] Franklin, A. & Crang, The trouble with tourism and travel theory. *Tourist Studies*, **1**, pp. 5–22, 2001.
[2] Lash, S. & Urry, J., *Economies of Signs and Space*, SAGE: London, 1994.
[3] Poon, A., *Tourism, Technology and Competitive Strategies*, CAB International: Wallingford, Oxon, 1993.
[4] Cohen, E., Towards a sociology of international tourism. *Social Research*, **39**(1), pp. 164–182, 1972.
[5] Smith, V.L. (ed.), *Hosts and Guests: The Anthropology of Tourism*, Blackwell: Oxford, 1977.
[6] MacCannell, D., Staged authenticity: Arrangements of social space in tourist settings. *American Journal of Sociology*, **79**, pp. 589–603, 1973.
[7] Turner, L. & Ash, J., *The Golden Hordes*, Constable: London, 1975.
[8] Munt, I., The 'other' postmodern tourism: Culture, travel and the new middle class. *Theory, Culture and Society*, **11**, pp. 101–123, 1994.
[9] Urry, J., *The Tourist Gaze*, SAGE: London, 1990.
[10] Mowforth, M. & Munt, I., *Tourism and Sustainability: New Tourism in the Third World*, Routledge, 1998.
[11] Cohen, E., A phenomenology of tourist experiences. *The Sociology of Tourism: Theoretical and Empirical Investigations*, eds Y. Apostopoulos, S. Leivadi & A. Yiannakis, Routledge: London, pp. 90–111, 1979.
[12] Feifer, M., *Going Places*, Macmillan: London, 1985.
[13] Uriely, N., Theories of modern and postmodern tourism. *Annals of Tourism Research*, **24**(4), pp. 982–985, 1997.
[14] Bauman, Z., *Legislators and Interpretators*, Polity Press: Cambridge, 1987.
[15] Rojek, C., *Ways of Escape: Modern Transformations in Leisure and Travel*, Macmillan: London, 1993.
[16] Sharpley, R., *The Tourist Business: An Introduction*, Business Education Publishers: Sunderland, 2002.
[17] Vukonić, B., The 'new old' tourist destination: Croatia. *Mediterranean Tourism: Facets of Socioeconomic Development and Cultural Change*, ed. Y. Apostolopoulos, L. Leontidou & P. Loukissas, Routledge: London and New York, pp. 64–72, 2001.
[18] Weforum.org, 2019. https://www.weforum.org/publications/the-travel-tourism-competitiveness-report-2019/. Accessed on: 1 Dec. 2023.
[19] HTZ, Turizam u brojkama, 2020. Ministarstvo turizma RH: Zagreb, 2021. https://www.htz.hr/sites/default/files/202106/HTZ%20TUB%20HR_%202020_0.pdf Accessed on: 28 Nov. 2023.
[20] Ekonomski Institut Zagreb, *Sektorske analize: turizam*, Ekonomski institut Zagreb: Zagreb, 2020.
[21] Benko, L., Krstanović, K. & Sovulj, L., Procjena učinaka pandemije koronavirusa na turističke dolaske i noćenja u Republici Hrvatskoj te na vrijednost CROBEXturist indeksa Zagrebačke burze. *EFZG serija članaka u nastajanju*, **2022**(01), p. 4. https://hrcak.srce.hr/clanak/397392

[22] Krešić, D. & Mikulić, J., Scenarij faznog pristupa oporavku turističkog tržišta nakon COVID-19 pandemije, Institut za turizam, Zagreb, pp. 2–3, 2020. http://www.iztzg.hr/UserFiles/file/novosti/2020/COVID19%20radovi/Kre%C5%A1i%C4%87D_Mikuli%C4%87-J_2020.pdf.
[23] HTZ, U 2021.g. Hrvatsku posjetilo gotovo 14 milijuna turista, 2022. https://www.htz.hr/hr-HR/press/objave-za-medije/u-2021-godini-hrvatsku-posjetilo-gotovo-14-milijuna-turista. Accessed on: 28 Nov. 2023.
[24] Šerić, N., Jakšić Stojanović, A. & Bagarić, L., Model kreiranja specijaliziranog turističkog proizvoda za post covid vrijeme. *Zbornik radova X. Jahorinski poslovni forum. Naučne konferencije sa međunarodnim učešćem*, ed. R. Božić, pp. 85–98, 2021.
[25] Payne, J., Gil-Alana, L. & Mervar, A., Persistence in Croatian tourism: The impact of COVID-19. *Tourism Economics*, **28**(6), pp. 1676–1682, 2021.
[26] Jakšić Stojanović, A. & Šerić N., Sports and health as corner stones of tourism development: Case study of Montenegro. *Sports Science and Human Health: Different Approaches*, eds D.A. Marinho, H.P. Neiwa, C.P. Johnson & N. Mohamudally, IntechOpen: London, pp. 119–128, 2019.
[27] Vuković, V., Riding a high: 3 reasons why the market is hitting new records in a recession. Seeking Alpha, 2020. https://seekingalpha.com/article/4370736-riding-high-3-reasons-why-market-is-hitting-new-records-in-recession.
[28] HTZ. U 2022. g. ostvareno više od 104 milijuna noćenja, 2023. https://www.htz.hr/hr-HR/press/objave-za-medije/u-2022-godini-ostvareno-vise-od-104-milijuna-nocenja. Accessed on: 28 Nov. 2023.
[29] Bogunović, B., Turizam u Istri je automobil koji juri prema zidu. Treba zaustaviti loše trendove i odrediti nove. Glas Istre. https://www.glasistre.hr/istra/2022/12/01/bogunovic-turizam-u-istri-je-automobil-koji-juri-prema-zidu-treba-zaustaviti-lose-trendove-i-odred-832968. Accessed on: 29 Nov. 2023.
[30] HTZ, U 2022. g. ostvareno više od 104 milijuna noćenja. 2023. https://www.htz.hr/hr-HR/press/objave-za-medije/u-2022-godini-ostvareno-vise-od-104-milijuna-nocenja, Accessed on: 28 Nov. 2023.
[31] Vlada, R.H., Zakon o turizmu na snazi od iduće godine, fokus na održivom upravljanju destinacijama. https://vlada.gov.hr/vijesti/zakon-o-turizmu-na-snazi-od-iduce-godine-fokus-na-odrzivom-upravljanju-destinacijama/38762. Accessed on: 1 Dec. 2023.
[32] Bremner & Dutton, Top countries for sustainable tourism. Euromonitor International, 2021. https://forumnatura.org/wpcontent/uploads/2021/07/SustainableTravelIndex-v0.3.pdf.
[33] NN 2/2023 Strategija razvoja održivog turizma do 2030. https://narodne-novine.nn.hr/clanci/sluzbeni/full/2023_01_2_18.html.
[34] Rudež, Z. & Marić, J., Prostorno planiranje u funkciji održivog razvoja turizma Dubrovačko-Neretvanske županije. *Zbornik Sveučilišta u Dubrovniku*, **1**, pp.155–174, 2014. https://hrcak.srce.hr/clanak/201315.
[35] Brozović, I. & Perko, J., *Dolasci i noćenja turista u 2022*. Državni zavod za statistiku RH: Zagreb, 2023.

THE PLACE OF TOURISM IN THE IMPLEMENTATION OF THE SUSTAINABLE DEVELOPMENT GOALS AT NATIONAL LEVEL

GIULIO PATTANARO
Independent Researcher

ABSTRACT
Tourism can play a significant role in achieving the objectives of the United Nations' 2030 Agenda for Sustainable Development (UN Agenda 2030) and its 17 Sustainable Development Goals (SDGs). Tourism has been explicitly mentioned in only three out of the 17 SDGs: SDG 8 (promoting decent work and economic growth), SDG 12 (promoting responsible consumption and production) and SDG 14 (protecting marine resources). However, as the United Nations World Tourism Organization and the United Nations Development Programme underline, tourism has the potential to contribute, directly or indirectly, to all 17 SDGs. In the context of the annual United Nations High-Level Political Forum on Sustainable Development, on a voluntary basis the Member States of the United Nations (UN Member States) have carried Voluntary National Reviews (VNRs) of their progress in the implementation of the UN Agenda 2030 and of its 17 SDGs. The present paper explores the place currently dedicated to tourism in the most recent VNRs, identifying the SDGs that UN Member States most frequently associate to tourism. A review of the most relevant literature on the relation between SDGs and tourism is followed by the analysis of the VNRs which were submitted by 38 UN Member States in 2023, as well as of the VNRs submitted by the same UN Member States in the previous years. The results show a growing relevance of tourism in the implementation of the SDGs at national level; it also emerges that promoting decent work and economic growth as well as responsible consumption and production are considered by the UN Member States as crucial policy areas and actions to boost the development of sustainable tourism in their territory. Further research also looking at the VNRs which will be submitted in the coming years is finally recommended.
Keywords: SDGs, sustainable tourism, Agenda 2030.

1 INTRODUCTION
The 17 Sustainable Development Goals (SDGs) are at the very heart of the United Nations' 2030 Agenda for Sustainable Development (hereinafter, UN Agenda 2030). They apply to both developing and developed countries and target different but interconnected areas: poverty, hunger, health, education, gender equality, clean water and energy, decent work and economic growth, just to mention the first half of the list.

With the adoption of UN Agenda 2030, the Member States of the United Nations (hereinafter, UN Member States) have committed to implement the SDGs at national level; on a voluntary basis, they are reporting on their progress through Voluntary National Reviews (VNRs).

As highlighted among the others by the United Nations World Tourism Organization (UNWTO) and the United Nations Development Programme (UNDP) [1], tourism can provide a major contribution to the achievement of the SDGs, given that it relates to all the areas that the SDGs are addressing.

By starting from a review of the most recent VNRs, the present paper explores the relevance currently given to tourism in the implementation of the SDGs at national level. Through the identification of the most frequent SDGs associated to tourism, the paper aims to point out the policy areas and actions which UN Member States regard as crucial to boost the development of sustainable tourism in their territory. A review of the most relevant literature on the relation between SDGs and tourism is followed by the analysis of the VNRs which were submitted by 38 UN Member States in 2023, as well as of the VNRs submitted by the same UN Member States in the previous years. The findings from each VNR are reviewed and compared and some general conclusions are drawn.

2 LITERATURE REVIEW

After a brief overview of the process that led to the definition and adoption of the SDGs, the literature review will focus on the content of the SDGs and on the opportunities and challenges that their implementation brings about for the tourism sector. Particular attention will be paid to how the UN Member States have been reporting on the implementation of the SDGs at national level, notably through the VNRs.

2.1 The SDGs

The process that led to the definition and adoption of the SDGs started in 2012 at the Rio+20 Conference on Sustainable Development. The conference was organised 20 years after the 1992 United Nations Conference on Environment and Development, which promoted through Agenda 21 the three pillars – i.e., the social, the economic and the environmental one – of sustainable development. Three years after the Millenium Development Goals (MDGs) would have also reached their end, and it was therefore time for the international community to start defining their successors [2].

To be achieved by 2015, the eight MDGs were intended to guide development cooperation and development aid towards eradicating extreme poverty and hunger, reducing child mortality, improving maternal health, combating diseases like HIV or malaria, ensuring environmental sustainability and establishing a global partnership for development [3]–[5]. Although underscoring that 'the Millennium Development Goals are a useful tool in focusing achievement of specific development gains as part of a broad development vision and framework for the development activities of the United Nations, for national priority-setting and for mobilisation of stakeholders and resources towards common goals' [6, V.B.245], the Rio+20 Conference on Sustainable Development underlined the need to strengthen the environmental component in a broader and more global agenda for sustainable development. This approach led to the identification and approval, during the 2015 United Nations Summit on Sustainable Development, of the SDGs. The SDGs are at the hearth of the United Nations' 2030 Agenda for Sustainable Development and their scope and ambition apply to both developing and developed countries, with connections and implications for all the sectors of the economy [2], [3].

The 17 SDGs and their 169 targets address different but interconnected areas and challenges: ending poverty (SDG 1) and hunger (SDG 2), ensuring healthy lives (SDG 3) quality education (SDG 4) and gender equality (SDG 5), promoting clean water (SDG 6) clean energy (SDG 7) and decent work and economic growth (SDG 8), building resilient infrastructure and promoting a sustainable industrialisation through innovation (SDG 9), reducing inequality (SDG 10), making cities and communities inclusive and sustainable (SDG 11), promoting responsible consumption and production (SDG 12), fighting climate change (SDG 13), protecting marine resources (SDG 14) as well as terrestrial ones (SDG 15), and promoting peace and justice (SDG 16). By working in partnership (SDG 17), governments, the private sector and the civil society from both developed and developed countries are asked to take actions to implement these goals, fully acknowledging their strong interdependence [2], [7], [8].

2.2 The SDGs and tourism

The UNWTO and the UNDP highlight that, although being explicitly mentioned in the targets of only three out of the 17 SDGs – i.e., SDG 8, SDG 12 and SDG 14, tourism 'can and must contribute – directly and indirectly – to the achievement of all 17 SDGs, from generating inclusive growth and eradicating extreme poverty to combatting climate change, from fostering gender equality to conserving marine and terrestrial ecosystems, and from promoting dialogue among diverse cultures to enhancing mutual understanding and peace'. [1, p. 18]. The same UNWTO and UNDP point out the challenges that the tourism sector must face in order to effectively contribute to the implementation of the SDGs and the UN Agenda 2030: among the others, the development of integrated and co-created policies that fully reflect the cross-cutting nature of sustainable tourism and the variety of its stakeholders, the creation of an enabling environment for private sector investments and the launch of innovative financing mechanism that go beyond development cooperation [1].

The academic literature as well underlines that tourism is related and has the potential to contribute to most, if not all, of the SDGs [9]–[14]. Some in-depth studies have also been carried out on the potential contribution, sometimes not fully acknowledged, of tourism to specific SDGs, like SDG 12 on responsible consumption and production [15] or SDG16 on peace and justice [9]. While recognising tourism' potential in the context of the SDGs, scholars and researchers highlight that, in order to be able to effectively contribute to the ambitious objectives of UN Agenda 2030, the tourism sector has to address a number of challenges. From a more conceptual point of view, there is the need to integrate sustainable tourism within the broader framework of global development and sustainability goals, which also implies the exchange and cross fertilisation of knowledge between the tourism sector and the other sectors of the global economy [11]. In this context, it is key to mobilise and engage tourism and hospitality companies and make sure that their business strategies are aligned with the global priorities outlined in the SDGs [10]. The call for an active involvement of tourism businesses is linked to another challenge, which is an SDG in itself (i.e., SDG 17): the establishment of effective tourism partnerships that in their composition structure and functioning make it possible for institutions, communities, organisations and, more broadly, stakeholders to cooperate and deliver on the SDGs [16]. To assess the impact of these partnerships and, more in general, to ensure that tourism policies and initiatives are indeed sustainable and meet both the needs of stakeholders and the objectives and targets of UN Agenda 2030, an additional challenge for the tourism sector is the identification and development of appropriate indicators and monitoring strategies. In this context as well, it is important to bear in mind that all the 17 SDGs are closely interconnected, which implies that that a siloed approach has to be avoided when drafting reports on the implementation of the SDGs [13], [17].

2.3 Reporting on the implementation of the SDGs at national level

Since the adoption of UN Agenda 2030, the United Nations have been emphasising the importance of monitoring and reporting on the implementation of the SDGs at national level. This is why the UN Member States have been encouraged to perform VNRs of the implementation of the SDGs within their borders and to present their progress in this area at the annual meetings of the High-Level Political Forum on Sustainable Development (HLPF) held under the auspices of the United Nations Economic and Social Council (ECOSOC) [18]–[20]. Countries from different regions of the world have acknowledged the challenge of both incorporating global objectives in their national policy and providing comprehensive reports on their achievements in this direction; to this purpose, international entities like, among others, the Organisation for Economic Cooperation and Development (OECD), the Sustainable Development Solutions Network (SDSN) or the World Bank Group have provided guidelines and tools on how to monitor progress with a focus on the adaptation of global targets to the domestic sphere as well as on systems thinking [17], [21].

Concerning the VNRs, there are two important elements that need to be pointed out. First, as mentioned above, the UN Member States have only been encouraged to perform and submit VNRs, which means that there it is not compulsory for them to carry out and share their reviews, nor is there an obligation to report on an annual basis. Second, there is no binding structure and format for the UN Member States to follow; therefore, there might be significant differences in the content and information provided in each individual VNR, and reviewing and comparing all the VNRs submitted in a given year and across a number of years might prove to be challenging [22]–[24].

Bearing in mind the limitations which have just been illustrated, the VNRs may represent a valid source of information to see how the UN Member States are considering and addressing the different policy areas that are connected with the implementation of the UN Agenda 2030, tourism being one of them.

3 METHODOLOGY

VNRs have been reviewed by scholars and researchers with the purpose of examining how UN Member States have been addressing different thematic areas, including tourism, as part of the implementation at national level of the SDGs [1], [17], [18], [22]–[26].

In order to understand the place currently dedicated to tourism in the implementation of the SDGs at domestic level, the present study has reviewed the most recent VNRs submitted by the UN Member States and compared them with the VNRs that the same group of countries had submitted in the previous years.

At the time of carrying out the study, 2023 was the most recent year for which all the VNRs submitted by the UN Member States in that particular year could be downloaded from the dedicated online VNR database available in the HLPF's website [20]. As mentioned above, the submission of VNRs is not compulsory. This explains why in 2023 only the following 38 UN Member States submitted their VNR: Bahrain, Barbados, Belgium, Bosnia and Herzegovina, Brunei Darussalam, Burkina Faso, Cambodia, Canada, Central African Republic, Chile, Comoros, Croatia, Democratic Republic of the Congo, Fiji, France, Guyana, Iceland, Ireland, Kuwait, Liechtenstein, Lithuania, Maldives, Mongolia, Poland, Portugal, Romania, Rwanda, Saint Kitts and Nevis, Saudi Arabia, Singapore, Slovakia, Tajikistan, Timor Leste, Turkmenistan, the United Republic of Tanzania, Uzbekistan, Vietnam, and Zambia. Apart from Saint Kitts and Nevis, all the other 37 UN Member States from this group had already submitted a previous version of their VNR in the years going from 2016 to 2020, depending on the country. In the case of Chile, two VNRs had been submitted before 2023, the first one in 2017 and the second one in 2019, and both versions have been taken into account in the context of this study. For the sake of completeness, it must be mentioned here that in 2023 the European Union as well submitted its first VNR. Aiming the present study to examine the relevance of tourism in the implementation of the SDGs at national level, it was deliberately decided not to examine the European Union's VNR and to focus exclusively on the reports submitted by the UN Member States.

A two-step analysis was applied to both the VNRs submitted in 2023 and the VNRs submitted before 2023 by the same group of UN Member States. As first step, a search by the keyword 'tourism' – 'tourisme' in those VNRs available only in French and 'turismo' in the VNR available only in Spanish – was performed to examine whether tourism is covered in each individual VNR downloaded from the HLPF's website [20]. For those VNRs in which the keyword search had led to zero matches, an in-depth analysis of the VNRs was carried out to check whether tourism had still been addressed in the document but in a more indirect way, for instance by mentioning hospitality or leisure. As second step, the VNRs in which tourism had been covered were further reviewed to identify the SDGs which had been most frequently associated to tourism. For the purpose of this study, a link between an individual SDG and tourism was recorded every time tourism was mentioned in the section of a VNR related to a particular SDG, with no need to have tourism-related targets explicitly developed for that particular SDG. For the purpose of facilitating the reporting of results, every time tourism was put in relation to an individual SDG, a *connection* was logged.

4 FINDINGS

The results of the analysis are presented in two separate sections: the first one reports on the inclusion of tourism in the VNRs submitted in 2023 (first batch of VNRs) as well as in those submitted before 2023 (second batch of VNRs); the second one focuses on the SDGs associated to tourism in both batches of VNRs.

4.1 VNRs and tourism

All the 38 VNRs submitted by the UN Member States in 2023 include tourism among the areas covered by the implementation of UN Agenda 2030. All VNRs explicitly mention the word 'tourism', with the exception of France's VNR, where the word 'tourism' – more correctly, 'tourisme', as the document is available only in French – cannot be found; nevertheless, the document still addresses the sector of leisure ('loisirs', in French), which is related to tourism. In addition to covering tourism, the VNRs from the following ten UN Member States also include a generally short section specifically dedicated to tourism, and tourism-related initiatives: Bahrain, Barbados, Brunei Darussalam, Burkina Faso, Croatia, Fiji, Maldives, Saint Kitts and Nevis, the United Republic of Tanzania and Zambia.

Tourism is also covered by the majority (35 out of 38) of the VNRs submitted before 2023 by the same group of UN Member States (with the exception, as mentioned above, of Saint Kitts and Nevis). As for the three pre-2023 VNRs (i.e., the VNRs from Liechtenstein, Slovakia, Uzbekistan) that did not explicitly address tourism, a check was performed to verify if any related aspect, such as hospitality or leisure, was still considered; the result of the check confirmed that tourism was not covered in any of the three VNRs, except for a very marginal mention of tourism in the context of Slovakia's international development cooperation. As for the VNRs submitted before 2023 that explicitly address tourism, in comparison to 2023, fewer – 7 versus 10 – are the UN Member States that opted to include a short section specifically focusing on tourism in their VNR: Brunei Darussalam, Burkina Faso, Croatia, Iceland, Saudi Arabia, Singapore and the United Republic of Tanzania. As one may observe in the case of the VNRs submitted in 2023 as well, the choice to include a short session dedicated tourism appears to be more common for those UN Member States where tourism ranks among the most important sectors in terms of contribution to national GDP.

4.2 VNRs and tourism-related SDGs

If the VNRs submitted in 2023 are considered all together, the 17 SDGs have been associated to tourism 168 times, with each individual SDG having been put in relation to tourism at least twice. As it was indicated in the methodology session, each time tourism was linked to any of the 17 SDGs, a *connection* was logged. Therefore, 168 connections were logged in the case of the 38 VNRs submitted in 2023. SDG 8 (decent work and economic growth) is the SDG to which tourism is most frequently associated to, with 28 connections (i.e., 16.7% of the total number of connections), followed by SDG 12 (promoting responsible consumption and production) with 19 connections (i.e., 11.3% of the total); SDG 9 (building resilient infrastructure and promoting a sustainable industrialisation through innovation) and SDG 14 (protecting marine resources) are the third-highest ranked ones, each of them being associated to tourism 16 times (i.e., 9.5% of the total number of connections). The SDGs which have been least frequently put in relation to tourism are SDG 2 (ending hunger) with four connections (i.e., 2.4% of the total), SDG 7 (clean energy) with 3 connections (i.e., 1.8% of the total) and SDG 16 (promoting peace and justice) with two connections (i.e., 1.2% of the total).

Differently from what has just been observed in the case of the VNRs submitted in 2023, not all the 17 SDGs are associated to tourism if one considers all the 38 VNRs submitted by the same UN Member States in the years going from 2016 to 2020. Individual SDGs have been linked to tourism 100 times in total, corresponding to a total of 100 connections. SDG 8 ranks first with 23 connections (i.e., 23% of the total number of connections), followed by SDG 12 with 18 connections (i.e., 18% of the total) and SDG 14 with 13 connections (i.e., 13% of the total). At the oppositive side of the ranking, SDG 1 (ending poverty) and SDG 3 (ensuring healthy lives) have been linked to tourism only once each (i.e., 1% of the total number of connections), while SDG 5 (gender equality) and SDG 16 have never been put in relation to tourism.

Looking at the SDGs which have been linked to tourism by the 37 UN Member States that submitted their VNRs both in 2023 and before 2023, it is worth pointing out that for the majority of these UN Member States (20 out of 37, i.e., 54.1%) the number of SDGs associated to tourism in the most recent VNRs has increased, which an average increase of 3.6 percentage points; nine out of 37 UN Member States (i.e., 24.3%) have decreased the number of SDGs linked to tourism in their most recent VNRs by an average 1.4 percentage points; the remaining eight UN Member States (i.e., 21.6%) have associated tourism to the same number of SDGs in both their most recent and least recent VNRs.

5 DISCUSSION

The two-step analysis of the VNRs has shown that tourism has been gaining relevance in the implementation of the SDGs at national level. All the most recent VNRs reviewed in the context of this study do cover tourism; this was not the case for the previous batch of VNRs from the same UN Member States, with tourism not being addressed in three of the VNRs submitted before 2023. Another sign of the growing relevance of tourism in the context of the implementation of UN Agenda 2030 is the fact that, if the VNRs submitted in 2023 are considered all together, all the SDGs appear as linked to tourism, with, of course, tourism being more frequently associated to some SDGs (i.e., SDG 8, SDG 12, SDG 9, and SDG 14) than others. As it was highlighted, this was not the case of the VNRs submitted by the same group of UN Member States before 2023, where some SDGs (notably, SDG 5 and SDG 16) had not been associated to tourism.

The results of this two-step analysis appear to confirm what was highlighted in the literature review section. In line with what the UNWTO and the UNDP [1] as well as the tourism literature [9]–[14] have pointed out, tourism has a major role to play in the implementation of the UN Agenda 2023, as it can contribute to most, if not – based on the most recent VNRs – all, of the SDGs. The results also reaffirm the validity in 2023 of the conclusions of two previous studies that analysed the VNRs submitted in 2016 and 2017 [1], [25]: SDG 8 and SDG 12 are the SDGs which are most frequently associated to tourism. This appears to suggest that promoting decent work and economic growth (SDG 8) as well as responsible consumption and production (SDG 12) are the policy areas and actions which UN Member States regard as most crucial in boosting the development of sustainable tourism in their territory. Other areas and actions like the development of a resilient infrastructure and the promotion, through innovation, of a sustainable industrialisation (SDG 9) as well as the protection of natural resources such as the marine ones (SDG 14) also emerge as very relevant in this context. As the UNWTO and the UNDP strongly highlighted [1], the development of co-created policies integrating inputs and knowledge from all these different areas is one of the challenges that the tourism sector has to face in order to be able to effectively contribute to the implementation of UN Agenda 2030 and its ambitious objectives. To overcome this challenge, as it was pointed out [10], [16], it is important to mobilise and involve all the relevant stakeholders and establish effective partnerships. This seems to be clear to the UN Member States as well: although not being among the SDGs which were most frequently associated to tourism, SDG 17 was put in relation with tourism 11 times in the VNRs submitted in 2023 (i.e., 6.5% of the total number of connections), with an increase of 3.5 percentage points in comparison to the VNRs submitted before 2023, where SDG 17 was linked to tourism three times in total (i.e., 3% of the total number of connections).

6 CONCLUSION

The results of this study show that the relevance of tourism in the implementation of the SDGs at national level is growing: tourism has been mentioned in all the most recent VNRs, and some of these VNRs also have a short session specifically dedicated to tourism. The results also confirm that UN Member States perceive tourism as a sector with the potential to contribute to most or even all the SDGs, in line with what both the UNTWO and the UNDP as well as the tourism literature have been highlighting. Furthermore, promoting decent work and economic growth as well responsible consumption and production have emerged as the policy areas and actions which UN Member States regard as most crucial in boosting the development of sustainable tourism.

This study focused on the VNRs submitted in the year going from 2016 to 2023 by a limited number of UN Member States. The possibility for UN Member States to submit their VNRs is always open: at the time of writing, for instance, 37 new VNRs have already been submitted since 1 January 2024 in the dedicated online VNR database available in the HLPF's website [20]. To ensure an effective monitoring of the place of tourism in the implementation of the SDGs at national level, it is therefore important to keep an eye on the VNR database and continue comparing the content of the most and the least recent VNRs. Future studies could also consider a more in-depth and country-specific analysis of the individual VNRs, with the aim, for instance, to identify any potential evolution over time of the priority given by a specific UN Member State to the individual tourism-related SDGs. Further research is also needed to assess the implementation of what is stated in the VNRs: including tourism in their VNRs and identifying the most crucial policy actions to support the sustainable development of tourism does not per se imply that UN Member States are actually taking concrete and effective measures to support the transition towards sustainable tourism at national level.

DISCLAIMER

All views expressed herein are entirely of the author, do not reflect the position of the European Institutions or bodies and do not, in any way, engage any of them.

REFERENCES

[1] United Nations World Tourism Organization (UNWTO) & United Nations Development Programme (UNDP), *Tourism and the Sustainable Development Goals: Journey to 2030*, UNWTO: Madrid, 2018.
[2] United Nations (UN), Department of Economic and Social Affairs, Division for Sustainable Development Goals, Sustainable Development. https://sdgs.un.org/. Accessed on: 18 May 2024.
[3] Fukuda-Parr, S., From the Millennium Development Goals to the Sustainable Development Goals: Shifts in purpose, concept, and politics of global goal setting for development. *Gender and Development*, **24**(1), pp. 43–52, 2016.
[4] Lomazzi, M., Borisch, B. & Laaser, U., The Millennium Development Goals: Experiences, achievements and what's next. *Global Health Action*, 7(1), 23695, 2014. https://doi.org/10.3402/gha.v7.23695.
[5] World Health Organization (WHO), www.who.int. Accessed on: 18 May 2024.
[6] United Nations (UN), *Rio+20 Outcome Document: 'The Future We Want'*, 2012. https://www.unep.org/resources/report/rio20-outcome-document-future-we-want. Accessed on: 17 May 2024.
[7] Díaz-López, C., Martín-Blanco, C., De la Torre Bayo, J.J., Rubio-Rivera, B. & Zamorano, M., Analyzing the scientific evolution of the sustainable development goals. *Applied Sciences*, **11**(18), 8286, 2021. https://doi.org/10.3390/app11188286.
[8] Le Blanc, D., Towards integration at last? The Sustainable Development Goals as a network of targets. *Sustainable Development*, **23**(3), pp. 176–187, 2015.
[9] Anouti, A., Chaperon, S. & Kennell, J., Tourism policy and United Nations Sustainable Development Goal 16: Peace and stability in the Middle East and North Africa. *Worldwide Hospitality and Tourism Themes*, **15**(2), pp. 108–116, 2023.
[10] Jones, P., Hillier, D. & Comfort, D., The Sustainable Development Goals and the tourism and hospitality industry. *Athens Journal of Tourism*, **4**(1), pp. 7–18, 2017.
[11] Nunkoo, R., Sharma, A., Rana, N.P., Dwivedi, Y.K. & Sunnassee, V.A., Advancing sustainable development goals through interdisciplinarity in sustainable tourism research. *Journal of Sustainable Tourism*, **31**(3), pp. 735–759, 2023.
[12] Rajani, F. & Boluk, K.A., A critical commentary on the SDGs and the role of tourism. *Tourism and Hospitality*, **3**(4), pp. 855–860, 2022.
[13] Rasoolimanesh, S.M., Ramakrishna, S., Hall, C.M., Esfandiar, K. & Seyfi, S., A systematic scoping review of sustainable tourism indicators in relation to the sustainable development goals. *Journal of Sustainable Tourism*, **31**(7), pp. 1497–1517, 2023.
[14] Seraphin, H. & Gowreesunkar, V.G., Tourism: How to achieve the sustainable development goals? *Worldwide Hospitality and Tourism Themes*, **13**(1), pp. 3–8, 2021.
[15] Dolnicar, S., Tourist behaviour change for sustainable consumption (SDG Goal 12): Tourism Agenda 2030 perspective article. *Tourism Review*, **78**(2), pp. 326–331, 2023.
[16] Scheyvens, R. & Cheer, J.M., Tourism, the SDGs and partnerships. *Journal of Sustainable Tourism*, **30**(10), pp. 2271–2281, 2022.
[17] Allen, C., Metternicht, G. & Wiedmann, T., Initial progress in implementing the Sustainable Development Goals (SDGs): A review of evidence from countries. *Sustainability Science*, **13**, pp. 1453–1467, 2018.
[18] Okitasari, M. et al., Governance and national implementation of the 2030 Agenda: Lessons from voluntary national reviews. *UNU-IAS: Policy Brief*, **18**, pp. 1–4, 2019.

[19] United Nations (UN), Department of Economic and Social Affairs, Office of Intergovernmental Support and Coordination for Sustainable Development, 2021 Voluntary national reviews synthesis report, 2021. https://desapublications.un.org/publications/2021-voluntary-national-reviews-synthesis-report. Accessed on: 24 Apr. 2024.
[20] United Nations (UN), Economic and Social Council, High-Level Political Forum on Sustainable Development. https://hlpf.un.org/2024. Accessed on: 22 Apr. 2024.
[21] Okitasari, M. & Katramiz, T., The national development plans after the SDGs: Steering implications of the global goals towards national development planning. *Earth System Governance*, **12**, 100136, 2022. https://doi.org/10.1016/j.esg.2022.100136.
[22] Elder, M. & Bartalini, A., *Assessment of the G20 Countries' Concrete SDG Implementation Efforts: Policies and Budgets Reported in Their 2016–2018 Voluntary National Reviews*, Institute for Global Environmental Strategies (IGES): Kamiyamaguchi Hayama Kanagawa, 2019.
[23] Lillehagen, I., Heggen, K.M., Tomson, G. & Engebretsen, E., Implementing the UN Sustainable Development Goals: How is health framed in the Norwegian and Swedish Voluntary National Review reports? *International Journal of Health Policy and Management*, **11**(6), pp. 810–819, 2022.
[24] Sebestyén, V., Domokos, E. & Abonyi, J., Focal points for sustainable development strategies: Text mining-based comparative analysis of voluntary national reviews. *Journal of Environmental Management*, **263**, 110414, 2020. https://doi.org/10.1016/j.jenvman.2020.110414.
[25] Dube, K., Tourism and Sustainable Development Goals in the African context. *International Journal of Economics and Finance Studies*, **12**(1), pp. 88–102, 2020.
[26] El Bilali, H., Cardone, G., Ottomano Palmisano, G., Bottalico, F. & Capone, R., Mainstreaming of the Sustainable Development Goals in the Mediterranean: Integration into policies and strategies. *AGROFOR International Journal*, **5**(2), pp. 15–26, 2020.

MANAGEMENT OF SUSTAINABLE TOURISM IN TOURIST DESTINATION PORTS: THE USE OF SUSTAINABLE INDICATORS IN THE CASE STUDY OF PIRAEUS PORT, GREECE

IOANNIS ANASTASOPOULOS[1], NIKOLAOS GEORGOPOULOS[2], IOANNIS KATSANAKIS[1], NIKOLETTA KLADA[2], CHRYSSOULA KONSTANTOPOULOU[1], EVANGELIA KOPANAKI[2], ASTERIOS STROUMPOULIS[2], GEORGIOS TSOUPROS[1] & SOTIRIOS VARELAS[1]
[1]Department of Tourism Studies, University of Piraeus, Greece
[2]Department of Business Administration, University of Piraeus, Greece

ABSTRACT
The main study of this research is a combined framework for effective management of tourist flows in the Port of Piraeus, Greece. The purpose is to highlight the necessity of introducing a holistic management of the tourism product of Piraeus and the development of a dynamic tourism knowledge base that will show any social, economic and environmental impacts caused by cruise and ship passengers to Piraeus. Achieving sustainability is challenging without practical policy options that can translate ideas into action. The strategic location of the Port of Piraeus makes it a crucial hub for transport, trade, logistics, tourism and communication, linking the Greek islands with the mainland and serving as an international centre for maritime tourism and cargo transport. The Port of Piraeus is essential to the Greek economy and significantly impacts the quality of life and economic performance of the islands it serves. Nevertheless, the services provided to maritime passengers and the overall quality of the maritime travel experience have been somewhat neglected or undervalued for many years. Indicators play a key role in the development of both quantitative and qualitative research, providing researchers with key tools for investigating, measuring and analysing complex phenomena. Sustainability indicators are of significant importance to the cruise industry due to the multifaceted nature of their impacts on environmental, social and economic dimensions. This case study underscores the importance of using sustainable indicators as tools for assessing and guiding the sustainable development of tourism in Piraeus Port. By adopting comprehensive management strategies, Piraeus Port can serve as a model for other ports aiming to achieve sustainable tourism.
Keywords: sustainable tourism, sustainability, strategic management.

1 INTRODUCTION
Understanding how people choose to enjoy cruise tourism and the use of passenger ships is necessary for inspiring port planners and managers of these destinations. Cruise tourism is an important source of economic activity and passenger ships are the means of transport connecting travellers to their desired destinations.

Data generated from the experience of cruise passengers and passenger ship traffic is a very good source for developing data-based knowledge that can be useful for strategic management. Although previous studies have looked at cruise tourism and passenger ship use, there is still a need to develop new methods – especially for recording passenger traffic flows and details of passenger behaviour.

The aim of this research is to highlight the necessity of introducing a holistic management of the tourism product of Piraeus and the development of a dynamic tourism knowledge base that will show any social, economic and environmental impacts caused by cruise and ship passengers of Piraeus.

2 THE 'CRUISE TOURISM' PHENOMENON IN THE MODERN PORT DESTINATION

For decades, many European port cities have invested in the 'transformation' of their beaches and the revitalisation of their historic centres, thus creating highly attractive cities that compete with other tourist destinations worldwide [1], [2]. Some of these cities, such as Barcelona and Venice, act as ports used by many shipping companies. Other port destinations, such as Lisbon, Malaga and Naples, have focused their efforts on increasing the cultural offer and are trying to become ports of the main cruise routes, aspiring to become 'home ports', a quality that significantly and incrementally benefits the local economy [3]–[6]. Rosa-Jiménez et al. [5] report in their research on the territorial imbalance of cruise activity in the main Mediterranean port destinations, the construction of cruise terminals (CT) has improved the value of nearby historic centres [7] with the subsequent upgrade of the cultural resources of the destination [8]. At the same time, these cities are implementing strategies aimed at attracting more cruise passengers. However, the increase in the docking of large cruise ships and low-cost tourism have led to more mass tourism in these European port cities, which threatens their identity and worsens their tourism [9]–[11].

The World Tourism Organization et al. [12] characterises the phenomenon of overtourism, and by extension overcrowding, as the negative impact of tourism on a tourist destination or parts of it, which excessively affects the perceived quality of life of residents and/or the quality of visitor experiences. According to Picard [13], hypertourism can be understood as the reaction of the society that welcomes tourists to external agents of change, turning it into an inert object that passively undergoes the influences. As described by Andrade et al. [2], this phenomenon blurs the boundaries between the internal and external worlds of society, as well as between elements belonging to culture and those related to tourism.

The adverse effects of tourism development have been linked to concepts such as 'touristophobia' [14], 'hypertourism' [15] and 'overpopulation' [16]. The historic centre of a port city often finds itself confined within a 'tourism bubble', a term first introduced by Cohen in 1972 [17], later described by Judd [18] as a theme park, and more recently refined by Jaakson [19]. These bubbles are typically small in scale, lacking local activity and character [18], and are generally inadequate for accommodating all visitors, making it challenging for residents to maintain their daily lives.

It is no surprise that Phi [20] highlights Barcelona, Venice, and Dubrovnik as the most frequently cited cities in hypertourism studies, serving as prime examples of 'tourist ports'. In response, some of these port cities, including Venice, Barcelona, Lisbon, and Amsterdam, have introduced measures to manage tourist traffic, such as regulating digital rental platforms, raising tourist taxes, and controlling housing prices [16]. Beyond these challenges, port cities must also address the unique issues associated with cruise tourism, which is increasingly scrutinised for its impact on destinations [21]. This often leads to overcrowding at cultural heritage sites, transportation complexities [22], strained tourism infrastructure, limited spending by cruise passengers onshore [23]–[25], and disruptions to local life. The recent surge in anti-cruise sentiment among local communities in cities like Venice, Dubrovnik, and Santorini is understandable in this context [21]. Numerous studies have questioned the economic benefits [26] of cruise tourism, also highlighting its social and environmental costs [27], [28]. Consequently, local governments in cities such as Barcelona, Amsterdam, Venice and Dubrovnik are beginning to implement municipal policies that take these short-term visitors into account while balancing the interests and needs of local residents. The ongoing debate revolves around finding a balance between societal concerns and local economic priorities, with the COVID-19 crisis offering a moment to explore best practices [29], [30] and an opportunity to align economic recovery with social, environmental, and cultural sustainability. As Dodds and Butler [16] observe, the forces driving the continuous growth of tourism in cities generally outweigh those attempting to limit or reduce travel to these impacted communities.

Effective management of responsible cruise tourism is crucial, given that it is the fastest-growing segment of the leisure-wellness industry. Recognising the port as a vital aspect of the city's identity, many port cities have recently encouraged tourism-related activities that align with the city's other port functions [31].

The cruise industry is integral to both tourism and port activities [2], [32]. These port cities have undertaken major initiatives within both the port and the city, equipping them with the essential infrastructure and cultural attractions needed to be featured on cruise itineraries. As a result, these cities have taken on the role of 'tourist ports' [31]. With the significant growth of cruise tourism in these areas, its impact on local development requires careful consideration. This has led to a substantial increase in recent literature examining the positive and negative effects of cruise tourism on port cities [33]–[38].

Many researchers have explored the negative aspects of cruise tourism [38]–[40], focusing primarily on its true economic impact on cities, pollution from ships, congestion, and the risks it poses to architectural heritage. Cruising is a highly complex tourism product, and its management is equally challenging [7], often leading to conflicts between the city and its residents. It tends to generate fewer economic benefits for the local economy compared to other forms of tourism or local residents themselves, as passengers typically spend most of their time (and money) on the cruise ship [2]. In recent years, it has become common to see up to 20,000 cruise passengers disembark at once. This, coupled with the rise of low-cost tourism, has led to a significant shift from local to global dynamics in historic centres. Here, services, amenities, and shops are increasingly tailored exclusively to tourists rather than residents, resulting in what is known as 'tourist gentrification' [9] or 'touristisation' [11].

On one hand, the threat that tourism poses to built heritage has been recognised for nearly two decades [40]. However, on the other hand, tourism also facilitates the restoration of abandoned buildings (even if they are repurposed as tourist accommodations) that might otherwise have been lost, and it contributes to cultural preservation [41]. Foroudi et al. [42] highlighted tourism's role in enhancing a city's image and fostering a stronger sense of identity. It is important to recognise that a city's appeal to tourists lies not only in its built heritage but also in its citizens, their customs, cuisine, local culture, and the everyday activities of its residents [2].

According to Brito [43] and Barrera Fernández [44], cultural tourism encompasses activities that involve experiencing historical and cultural heritage and appreciating and promoting both tangible and intangible cultural assets. However, mass tourism undermines this essence by transforming the city into a stage for tourism, with the genuine urban experience relegated to distant, non-tourist areas. In essence, the real risk is not to the city itself but to the vibrant life and daily existence of the city.

Cruise operators select itineraries and specific ports based on the positive experiences they can offer their customers [45]. However, this concentration of destinations and the resulting resident dissatisfaction can lead to negative experiences for visitors, potentially causing business decline or even closures [46]. Additionally, satisfied cruise passengers are more likely to return as tourists to further explore the highlights of their previous visit [46], [47]. Given that cruise tourism is a persistent trend, it is crucial to develop policies that enhance the benefits of cruise tourism while addressing its negative effects. Such policies should aim to harmonise the interests of both visitors and residents, ultimately supporting the long-term sustainability of both tourism and local community activities.

3 MANAGEMENT OF SUSTAINABLE TOURISM IN TOURIST DESTINATION PORTS

Achieving sustainability is challenging without practical policy solutions that can transform ideas into actionable steps [48], [49]. The effort to advance sustainable tourism in destinations requires a collective commitment from national and provincial governments, international agencies, tourism operators, stakeholders, and travellers. Effective governance entails a framework of rules, norms, and procedures designed to regulate behaviour [50].

The characteristics of effective tourism governance and known barriers to the implementation of sustainable practices are listed in Table 1.

Table 1: Characteristics of effective tourism governance in contrast with known barriers to the implementation of sustainable practices [49].

Characteristics of effective tourism governance [51]–[53]	Known barriers to implementing sustainable practices [54], [55]
• Coordination and monitoring of activities; • Involvement of multiple sectors and stakeholders collective action; • Public participation; • Use a consensus-based approach; • Shared strategy and vision; • Responding to stakeholders; • Effectiveness, efficiency and accountability; • Transparency; and • Law and justice.	• Preference for short-term financial benefits versus of long-term social and environmental concerns; • Absence of planning process; • Lack of stakeholder involvement.; • No shared understanding of sustainability goals; • Lack of integration and coordination of government agencies; • Lack of accountability; and • The absence of capacity or political will to implement the policy.

New approaches are needed to integrate the interests of site managers, stakeholders, industry and government institutions at multiple levels and across multiple sites, particularly approaches that integrate inputs from multiple spatial scales [56].

Cerveny et al. [49] conducted research indicating that environmental strategies for cruise ships aimed at upgrading technology to minimise waste, emissions, and fuel consumption. These strategies included establishing spatial or temporal guidelines for cruise ship operations in 'sensitive' tourism spots like port destinations. Additionally, there were suggestions for using big data to monitor visitor activities and implementing educational programs for tourists. Economic strategies were geared towards creating local jobs and developing revenue programs to reinvest in the community. Socio-cultural approaches highlighted the importance of local guides and interpreters in providing cultural insights and managing visitor numbers in crowded areas. Lastly, site administrators discussed the need for mechanisms to engage stakeholders, improve communication with cruise lines, and enhance dialogue between public and private sectors. At the UNESCO conference, site managers sought specific guidelines or standards to foster sustainable cruise ship practices in sensitive tourism areas, emphasising the need for adaptable standards tailored to local conditions.

4 CASE STUDY: THE PIRAEUS PORT

Greece boasts one of the world's densest maritime transport networks and holds the second-largest share of total passenger traffic at EU ports (Italy: 85.4 million passengers, accounted for 20.8% of the total in 2018; Greece: 72.5 million passengers, represented 17.7% of the total in 2018) [57]. The Port of Piraeus was selected for this study due to its prominence. As one of Europe's five largest ports and among the largest globally, Piraeus handles over 20 million passengers and more than 24,000 passenger ships annually. It serves as the principal passenger hub connecting mainland Greece with the Aegean Islands and Crete, as well as the main maritime gateway to southeastern Europe.

Athens News Agency [58] reports that, according to the data of the Piraeus Port Authority, during the 9 months and third quarter of 2023, compared to the same period of 2022, there was a spectacular increase in the cruise sector. This happened due to the increase in the number of cruise ships using the Port of Piraeus as a starting point (homeport/ship arrival and departure from the same port) from 340 to 455 (+33.8%), while the increase in homeport cruise passengers was approximately 129.3% (from 378,899 to 627,017 passengers). In particular, in the first 9 months of 2023, 588 cruise ships with 1,148,017 passengers had sailed in the Port of Piraeus, compared to 511 cruise ships in the same period of 2022 and 632,642 passengers. The coastal shipping sector also showed an increase where in the 9 months of 2023 a total of 13,137,700 million passengers were handled compared to 12,244,288, in the same period of 2022 (7.3% increase).

As for the usual range of air pollution, this was between 3,000 and 5,000 parts per cubic centimetre (ppc) [59], while the environmental damage from cruise ships arriving at the Piraeus terminal is reported to be over 100,000 ppc. This number does not include damages caused by municipal solid waste, public nuisance, noise pollution, etc. It has been observed that despite the numerous arrivals, only a few of the visitors (40%) spend the night in Piraeus (compared to the average overnight stay in the country). Most of them choose to spend the night in other areas of Attica, leaving Piraeus with only environmental damage caused by visitors. Therefore, Piraeus seems to be preferred as a place of transit, rather than a place of overnight stays. A priority for any modern destination, such as Piraeus, is the attraction of quality and sustainable tourism, not only with the protection, but also with the measurable support of the local residents from the tourist activity [60], [61].

Of the eight port organisations of Greece, the largest passenger traffic took place in the Port of Piraeus, which served 1,098,091 passengers, occupying first place in the country as a whole. Compared to 2018, Piraeus showed an increase of 14.2%. In second place was Corfu and in third was Heraklion. A total of five organisations showed an increase in traffic compared to 2018 and three organisations closed 2019 with a negative sign. In total traffic of the 13 port organisations, Piraeus holds 50% while in second place is Corfu with 35% and third is Heraklion with 14%.

The Port of Piraeus is the largest port in Greece, which extends along a coastline of more than 24 km and a total area of more than 5,000,000 square metres. The geographical position of the Port of Piraeus makes it a vital transport, trade and logistics, tourism and communication hub connecting the Greek islands with the mainland, as well as an international centre for maritime tourism and goods transport. As part of the core network of the Trans-European Transport Networks (TEN-T), the port hosts a complex variety of port activities, among which are: cruises, coastal shipping, cargo handling (mainly containers and vehicles), ship repairs, as well as the type I free customs control zone. The Port of Piraeus has quays with a total length of 2.8 km to serve passenger traffic (coastal shipping and cruises).

The Port of Piraeus is crucial to the Greek economy and significantly impacts the quality of life and economic performance of the islands it serves [57]. However, for many years, the provision of services for maritime passengers and the overall travel experience have been somewhat neglected or undervalued [62].

A key factor in assessing the health impacts of air pollution at ports is the population density of nearby residential areas [63]. Piraeus, with a population of 163,688 spread over 11.2 km², is one of Greece's most densely populated areas, with a density of 14,615 people per km² [64]. Similarly, the Port of Barcelona presents an interesting case. It has two main cruise ship areas: one very close to the city centre (854 m away) and another, which houses the primary terminals for daily cruise ships, located further out (approximately 2–2.5 km from the centre). Air pollution from cruise and ferry activities is likely to affect the broader urban area of Barcelona and its residents [65].

It has been observed that despite the numerous arrivals, only a few of the visitors (40%) spend the night in Piraeus (compared to the average overnight stay in the country). Most of them choose to spend the night in other areas of Attica, leaving Piraeus with only environmental damage caused by visitors. Therefore, Piraeus seems to be preferred as a place of transit, rather than a place of overnight stays. A priority for any modern port and tourist destination, such as Piraeus, is the attraction of quality and sustainable tourism, not only with the protection, but also with the measurable support of the local residents from the tourist activity [66]. A thorough and specific analysis of research findings from other regions is essential for developing an effective plan. Coastal tourism areas that see cruise ship tourism as a critical component for local development should regularly study the purchasing behaviour of cruise travellers using established indicators and research methods [67]. This approach enables comparisons with other competitive coastal regions.

Smart technology represents an integrated intelligent system designed to manage all aspects, controls, and systems to optimise ship operations and management, while delivering value efficiently to guests and crew [68]. The main challenge is to provide a comprehensive view of the smart cruise tourism sector, focusing on innovations, interfaces, dependencies, and the associated constraints and challenges related to the port-tourism destination of Piraeus.

5 DEFINITION OF INDICATORS

Indicators play a key role in the development of both quantitative and qualitative research, providing researchers with key tools for investigating, measuring and analysing complex phenomena [69]. In the realm of quantitative research, indicators serve as building blocks for operationalising variables into measurable entities. These numerical representations not only allow researchers to quantify the characteristics under investigation, but also facilitate the application of statistical methods for robust analysis. The precision that indicators provide in quantifying variables ensures a systematic and standardised approach to data collection, reducing the potential for bias and enhancing the reliability of study results.

In addition, indicators contribute significantly to the comparability of findings between different studies in quantitative research [70]. Standardised indicators create a common ground for researchers, promoting consistency in measurement and allowing meaningful comparisons between different data sets. This comparability enhances the generalisability of research findings, making them applicable beyond the specific context of a single study. Consequently, indicators not only shape the very structure of quantitative research studies, but also play a key role in the broader scientific discourse, enabling the synthesis and meta-analysis of accumulated knowledge [71].

In the field of qualitative research, indicators serve a different but equally critical purpose [72]. In qualitative research, where the focus is on understanding the depth and complexity of human experiences, indicators guide researchers in delving deeper into specific aspects of the phenomena under investigation. Rather than numerical values, qualitative indicators often manifest as themes, patterns, or recurring concepts. These indicators help in the systematic analysis of qualitative data by providing a framework for coding and categorising information. They help to create rich and nuanced descriptions, allowing researchers to draw important insights from the intricacies of qualitative data.

In addition, indicators in qualitative research enhance the validity and reliability of the study [73]. Clear and well-defined indicators help to establish the credibility of the research process and findings. They provide a transparent roadmap for interpreting the data, allowing other researchers to follow the analytic path and assess the rigor of the study. This transparency is essential to establishing the credibility of qualitative research in academic and scientific communities.

Sustainability indicators are of significant importance to the cruise industry due to the multifaceted nature of their impacts on environmental, social and economic dimensions [73]. These indicators serve as key tools to assess and guide industry practices, ensuring that cruise activities are aligned with the principles of sustainability and responsible tourism.

5.1 Environmental impact [74]

Sustainability indicators play a key role in monitoring and mitigating the environmental footprint of the cruise industry. By monitoring indicators related to energy consumption, waste management and emissions, cruise operators can assess their impact on the ecosystems they cross. These indicators may be air quality, water quality, waste management, energy consumption, noise pollution. These indicators are vital for promoting environmentally conscious practices such as the adoption of cleaner technologies, fuel efficiency measures and waste reduction strategies. At a time when environmental sustainability is a global imperative, these indicators are guiding the cruise industry towards minimising its ecological impact.

5.2 Social responsibility [37]

In the social dimension, sustainable indicators relate to the industry's responsibilities towards local communities and cultural heritage. These indicators may be community well-being, cultural preservation, community engagement, visitor satisfaction. Cruise tourism often involves interactions with different communities and indicators measuring economic benefits, employment opportunities and cultural preservation efforts become imperative. By prioritising community engagement, respecting local cultures and promoting social inclusion, the cruise industry can make a positive contribution to the societies it encounters. Sustainable indicators serve as benchmarks for assessing and reinforcing social responsibility, promoting a harmonious relationship between cruise operators and local communities.

5.3 Economic sustainability [75]

Economic sustainability is a key aspect of the long-term success of the cruise industry and sustainable indicators help to assess and enhance economic sustainability. Indicators that measure the industry's contribution to local economies, job creation and economic diversification provide information on its overall economic impact. These indicators may be tourism revenue, employment generation, local business development. Cruise lines can use these indicators to make informed decisions that not only benefit their bottom line, but also support the economic resilience and growth of their host communities. It is also very important to measure the purchasing power of travellers and whether this contributes to the growth of the local economy. Economic sustainability indicators therefore contribute to the industry's ability to thrive, while promoting prosperity at the local level.

5.4 Regulatory compliance and international standards [76]

Sustainability indicators are an integral part of demonstrating regulatory compliance and industry accountability. As environmental regulations become more stringent and consumers increasingly prioritise sustainable practices, the cruise industry must comply with and exceed these standards. Certification programs using sustainable indicators allow cruise companies to demonstrate their commitment to responsible practices. This not only enhances their reputation, but also ensures alignment with global sustainability goals and regulatory expectations, strengthening the credibility and confidence of the industry.

5.5 Stakeholder trust and transparency [77]

Stakeholder trust is of paramount importance for the cruise industry, including passengers, local communities, regulators and investors. Sustainable indicators contribute to transparency by allowing stakeholders to assess and understand the industry's impact and commitment to sustainable practices. Transparent reporting on sustainability performance builds trust and confidence, demonstrating that cruise operators are actively addressing environmental and social concerns. This confidence is vital to maintaining a positive image of the industry, attracting environmentally conscious travellers and ensuring continued support from regulators.

In conclusion, sustainability indicators are essential in shaping the cruise industry's path towards responsible and sustainable practices. They provide a comprehensive framework for assessing and improving the industry's impact on the environment, society and the economy, ensuring that cruise tourism evolves in a way that is sustainable.

6 CONCLUSIONS

The publication presents a combined framework for effective management of tourist flows in the Port of Piraeus, services and products. Emphasis is placed on sustainable, responsible and viable tourism, by all groups of visitors, local and regional stakeholders, who are invited to make appropriate decisions based on information, data and analysis derived from the indicators that have been described. This is a very demanding study which has to approach the project from the perspective of sustainable tourism data as described in this publication. Methodologically, a multi-methodological research technique at the level of indicators has been presented in order to achieve a cross-sectoral approach, as all businesses included in the value chain of tourism and the Port of Piraeus and the destination of Piraeus more broadly are part of the analysis. The utilisation of the indicators in a holistic way will bring important information and data for destination managers, cruise companies as well as for the professionals and citizens of Piraeus.

ACKNOWLEDGEMENTS

This work has been partly supported by the University of Piraeus Research Center.

REFERENCES

[1] Giovinazzi, O. & Moretti, M., Port cities and urban waterfront: Transformations and opportunities. *TeMA-Journal of Land Use, Mobility and Environment*, **2**, 2009.

[2] Andrade, M.J., Costa, J.P. & Jiménez-Morales, E., Challenges for European tourist-city-ports: Strategies for a sustainable coexistence in the cruise post-COVID context. *Land*, **10**(11), 1269, 2021. https://doi.org/10.3390/land10111269.

[3] Cruise Lines International Association (CLIA), Contributions of cruise tourism of the economies of Europe 2017, pp. 3–28, 2018. https://cruising.org/-/media/research-updates/research/economic-impact-studies/contribution-of-cruise-tourism-to-the-economies-of-europe-2017.pdf. Accessed on: 10 Aug. 2024.

[4] Lekakou, M.B., Pallis, A.A. & Vaggelas, G.K., Is this a home-port? An analysis of the cruise industry's selection criteria. *Proceedings of the International Association of Maritime Economists Conference*, Copenhagen, Denmark, pp. 24–26, 2009.

[5] Rosa-Jiménez, C., Perea-Medina, B., Andrade, M.J. & Nebot, N., An examination of the territorial imbalance of the cruising activity in the main Mediterranean port destinations: Effects on sustainable transport. *Journal of Transport Geography*, **68**, pp. 94–101, 2018.

[6] Gastaldi, F. & Camerin, F., El proceso de remodelación del waterfront de Génova y los proyectos de Renzo Piano desde los años 80 hasta el Blue Print [The redevelopment process of genoa's waterfront and the projects by renzo piano since the '80 to the Blue Print]. *ACE: Architecture, City and Environment Open Access*, **11**(33), pp. 33–64, 2017.

[7] Castillo-Manzano, J.I., Fageda, X. & Gonzalez-Laxe, F., An analysis of the determinants of cruise traffic: An empirical application to the Spanish port system. *Transportation Research Part E: Logistics and Transportation Review*, **66**, pp. 115–125, 2014. https://doi.org/10.1016/j.tre.2014.03.008.

[8] Brida, J.G., Pulina, M., Riaño, E. & Aguirre, S.Z., Cruise passengers in a homeport: A market analysis. *Understanding Tropical Coastal and Island Tourism Development*, Routledge, pp. 68–86, 2016.

[9] Jover, J. & Díaz-Parra, I., Gentrification, transnational gentrification and touristification in Seville, Spain. *Urban Studies*, **57**(15), pp. 3044–3059, 2020.

[10] Sequera, J. & Nofre, J., Shaken, not stirred: New debates on touristification and the limits of gentrification. *City*, **22**(5–6), pp. 843–855, 2018.

[11] Sequera, J. & Nofre, J., Touristification, transnational gentrification and urban change in Lisbon: The neighbourhood of Alfama. *Urban Studies*, **57**(15), pp. 3169–3189, 2020.

[12] World Tourism Organization (UNWTO), Centre of Expertise Leisure, Tourism and Hospitality, NHTV Breda University of Applied Sciences and NHL Stenden University of Applied Sciences, 'Overtourism'? Understanding and managing urban tourism growth beyond perceptions. UNWTO: Madrid, 2018.

[13] Picard, M., Touristification and balinization in a time of reformasi. *Indonesia and the Malay World*, **31**(89), pp. 108–118, 2003.

[14] Milano, C., Novelli, M. & Cheer, J.M. Overtourism and tourismphobia: A journey through four decades of tourism development, planning and local concerns. *Tourism Planning and Development*, **16**(4), pp. 353–357, 2019.

[15] Richardson, D., Suffering the strain of tourism. *Travel Trade Gazette* (special issue Word Travel Market 2017), 2017.

[16] Dodds, R. & Butler, R., The phenomena of overtourism: A review. *International Journal of Tourism Cities*, **5**(4), pp. 519–528, 2019.

[17] Cohen, E., The sociology of tourism: Theoretical and empirical investigations. *The Sociology of Tourism*, Routledge, pp. 51–71, 1996.

[18] Judd, D.R., Constructing the tourist bubble. *The Tourist City*, pp. 35–53, 1999.

[19] Jaakson, R., Beyond the tourist bubble? Cruise ship passengers in port. *Annals of Tourism Research*, **31**(1), pp. 44–60, 2004.

[20] Phi, G.T., Framing overtourism: A critical news media analysis. *Current Issues in Tourism*, **23**(17), pp. 2093–2097, 2020.

[21] Papathanassis, A., Cruise tourism management: State of the art. *Tourism Review*, **72**(1), pp. 104–119, 2017. https://doi.org/10.1108/TR-01-2017-0003.

[22] Cavallaro, F., Galati, O.I. & Nocera, S., Policy strategies for the mitigation of GHG emissions caused by the mass-tourism mobility in coastal areas. *Transportation Research Procedia*, **27**, pp. 317–324, 2017.

[23] Papathanassis, A. & Bundă, N.R., Action research for sustainable cruise tourism development: The Black Sea region case study. *Tourism in Marine Environments*, **11**(2–3), pp. 159–177, 2016. https://doi.org/10.3727/154427315X14513374773562.

[24] Larsen, S. & Wolff, K., Exploring assumptions about cruise tourists' visits to ports. *Tourism Management Perspectives*, **17**, pp. 44–49. 2016.

[25] Klein, R.A., Keeping the cruise tourism responsible: The challenge for ports to maintain high self-esteem. *Proceedings of the International Conference for Responsible Tourism*, pp. 1–17, 2009.

[26] Johnson, J.L., Adkins, D. & Chauvin, S., A review of the quality indicators of rigor in qualitative research. *American Journal of Pharmaceutical Education*, **84**(1), 7120, 2020. https://doi.org/10.5688/ajpe7120.

[27] Carić, H. & Mackelworth, P., Cruise tourism environmental impacts: The perspective from the Adriatic Sea. *Ocean and Coastal Management*, **102**, pp. 350–363, 2014.

[28] Cavallaro, F., Irranca Galati, O. & Nocera, S., Climate change impacts and tourism mobility: A destination-based approach for coastal areas. *International Journal of Sustainable Transportation*, **15**(6), pp. 456–473, 2021.

[29] Fabris, L.M.F., Camerin, F., Semprebon, G. & Balzarotti, R.M., New healthy settlements responding to pandemic outbreaks: Approaches from (and for) the global city. *The Plan Journal*, **5**(2), pp. 385–406, 2020.

[30] Sharifi, A. & Khavarian-Garmsir, A.R., The COVID-19 pandemic: Impacts on cities and major lessons for urban planning, design, and management. *Science of the Total Environment*, **749**, 142391, 2020.

[31] McCarthy, J., The cruise industry and port city regeneration: The case of Valletta. *European Planning Studies*, **11**(3), pp. 341–350, 2003.

[32] Capocaccia, F., Cruising in the Mediterranean. *Portus*, **1**(2), pp. 14–19, 2001.

[33] Brida, J.G. & Zapata, S., Cruise tourism: Economic, socio-cultural and environmental impacts. *International Journal of Leisure and Tourism Marketing*, **1**(3), pp. 205–226, 2010. https://doi.org/10.1504/IJLTM.2010.029585.

[34] Hritz, N. & Cecil, A.K., Investigating the sustainability of cruise tourism: A case study of Key West. *Journal of Sustainable Tourism*, **16**(2), pp. 168–181, 2008.

[35] Klein, R.A., Responsible cruise tourism: Issues of cruise tourism and sustainability. *Journal of Hospitality and Tourism Management*, **18**, pp. 107–116, 2011.

[36] Papathanassis, A. & Beckmann, I., Assessing the 'poverty of cruise theory' hypothesis. *Annals of Tourism Research*, **38**(1), pp. 153–174, 2011.

[37] Bonilla-Priego, M.J., Font, X. & del Rosario Pacheco-Olivares, M., Corporate sustainability reporting index and baseline data for the cruise industry. *Tourism Management*, **44**, pp. 149–160, 2014. https://doi.org/10.1016/j.tourman.2014.03.004.

[38] MacNeill, T. & Wozniak, D., The economic, social, and environmental impacts of cruise tourism. *Tourism Management*, **66**, pp. 387–404, 2018.

[39] Figueira de Sousa, J., The tourist cruise industry. *Portus*, **2**, pp. 6–12, 2001.

[40] Marshall, C.A., Morris, E. & Unwin, N., An epidemiological study of rates of illness in passengers and crew at a busy Caribbean cruise port. *BMC Public Health*, **16**, pp. 1–6, 2016.

[41] Wismayer, M., Tourism and the commoditisation of culture. *The Malta Financial and Business Times*, 7, 2002.

[42] Foroudi, P., Gupta, S., Kitchen, P., Foroudi, M.M. & Nguyen, B., A framework of place branding, place image, and place reputation: Antecedents and moderators. *Qualitative Market Research: An International Journal*, **19**(2), pp. 241–264, 2016.

[43] Brito, M., Ciudades históricas como destinos patrimoniales: una mirada comparada: España y Brasil, 2009.

[44] Barrera Fernández, D., Corrientes de pensamiento en la gestión patrimonial y turística de la ciudad histórica. Doctoral thesis, Universidad de Málaga, Servicio de Publicaciones y Divulgación Científica, 2014.

[45] Henthorne, T.L., An analysis of expenditure by cruise passengers in Jamaica. *Journal of Travel Research*, **38**(3), 246e250, 2000.

[46] Parola, F., Satta, G., Penco, L. & Persico, L., Destination satisfaction and cruiser behaviour: The moderating effect of excursion package. *Research in Transportation Business and Management*, **13**, pp. 53–64, 2014.

[47] Brida, J.G. & Risso, W.A., Cruise passengers expenditure analysis and probability of repeat visits to Costa Rica: A cross section data analysis. *Tourism Analysis*, **15**(4), pp. 425–434, 2010.

[48] Pigram, J.J., Sustainable tourism-policy considerations. *Journal of Tourism Studies*, **1**(2), pp. 2–9, 1990.

[49] Cerveny, L.K., Miller, A. & Gende, S., Sustainable cruise tourism in marine world heritage sites. *Sustainability*, **12**(2), p. 611, 2020. https://doi.org/10.3390/su12020611.

[50] Ostrom, E., *Governing the Commons: The Evolution of Institutions for Collective Action*, Cambridge University Press, 1990.

[51] Bingham, L.B., Nabatchi, T. & O'Leary, R., The new governance: Practices and processes for stakeholder and citizen participation in the work of government. *Public Administration Review*, **65**(5), pp. 547–558, 2005.

[52] Eagles, P.F., Research priorities in park tourism. *Journal of Sustainable Tourism*, **22**(4), pp. 528–549, 2014.

[53] Bushell, R. & Bricker, K., Tourism in protected areas: Developing meaningful standards. *Tourism and Hospitality Research*, **17**(1), pp. 106–120, 2017.

[54] Dodds, R., Sustainable tourism and policy implementation: Lessons from the case of Calvia, Spain. *Current Issues in Tourism*, **10**(4), pp. 296–322, 2007.

[55] Howes, M. et al., Environmental sustainability: A case of policy implementation failure? *Sustainability*, **9**(2), p. 165, 2017.

[56] Nkhata, B.A. & McCool, S.F., Coupling protected area governance and management through planning. *Journal of Environmental Policy and Planning*, **14**(4), pp. 394–410, 2012.

[57] Papantonopoulos, S., Famelitis, O. & Karasavova, M., A Study of port passenger journey. *Proceedings of the 2021 Zooming Innovation in Consumer Technologies Conference (ZINC)*, IEEE, pp. 123–128, 2021.

[58] Athens News Agency, ΟΛΠ: Αύξηση εσόδων και κερδών στο εννεάμηνο, 25 Oct. 2023. https://www.amna.gr/business/article/770725/OLP-Auxisi-esodon-kai-kerdon-sto-enneamino-2023. Accessed on: 20 Nov. 2023.

[59] Integrated Spatial Investments (ISI), Integrated urban development plan: Evaluation of the integrated spatial investment tool. Municipality of Piraeus, 2017.

[60] Belias, D. et al., The differences on consumer behavior between mass tourism and sustainable tourism in Greece. *Proceedings of the 5th International Conference on Contemporary Marketing Issues ICCMI*, p. 176, 2017.

[61] Klada, N., Stroumpoulis, A., Varelas, S. & Georgopoulos, N., Information systems in sustainable hospitality and the creation of business value. *ENTRENOVA: ENTerprise REsearch InNOVAtion*, **9**(1), pp. 290–295, 2023.

[62] Pantouvakis, A., Port-service quality dimensions and passenger profiles: An exploratory examination and analysis. *Maritime Economics and Logistics*, **8**, pp. 402–418, 2006.

[63] Doundoulakis, E., Papaefthimiou, S. & Sitzimis, I., Environmental impact assessment of passenger ferries and cruise vessels: The case study of Crete. *European Transport*, **87**(15), pp. 1–15, 2020.

[64] Hellenic Statistical Authority, 2014.

[65] Perdiguero, J. & Sanz, A., Cruise activity and pollution: The case of Barcelona. *Transportation Research Part D: Transport and Environment*, **78**, 102181, 2020.

[66] Belias, D. et al., The use of digital CRM in the operation of Greek hotels. *Proceedings of the 5th International Conference on Contemporary Marketing Issues ICCMI*, p. 384, 2017.

[67] Kizielewicz, J., Measuring the economic and social contribution of cruise tourism development to coastal tourist destinations. *European Research Studies Journal*, **23**(3), pp. 147–171, 2020.

[68] Buhalis, D., Papathanassis, A. & Vafeidou, M., Smart cruising: Smart technology applications and their diffusion in cruise tourism. *Journal of Hospitality and Tourism Technology*, **13**(4), pp. 626–649, 2022. https://doi.org/10.1108/JHTT-05-2021-0155.

[69] Alsarmi, A.M. & Al-Hemyari, Z.A., Quantitative and qualitative statistical indicators to assess the quality of teaching and learning in higher education institutions. *International Journal of Information and Decision Sciences*, **6**(4), pp. 369–392, 2014.

[70] Cloquell-Ballester, V.A., Cloquell-Ballester, V.A., Monterde-Diaz, R. & Santamarina-Siurana, M.C., Indicators validation for the improvement of environmental and social impact quantitative assessment. *Environmental Impact Assessment Review*, **26**(1), pp. 79–105, 2006. https://doi.org/10.1016/j.eiar.2005.06.002.

[71] Tonmoy, F.N., El-Zein, A. & Hinkel, J., Assessment of vulnerability to climate change using indicators: A meta-analysis of the literature. *Wiley Interdisciplinary Reviews: Climate Change*, **5**(6), pp. 775–792, 2014.

[72] Johnson, P.C., Cultural literacy, cosmopolitanism and tourism research. *Annals of Tourism Research*, **44**, pp. 255–269, 2014.

[73] Wu, X., Chen, H. & Min, J., Sustainability assessment of cruise-industry development: A case study of Xiamen, China. *Maritime Policy and Management*, **48**(2), pp. 213–224, 2021.

[74] Ramoa, C.E.D.A., Flores, L.C.D.S. & Herle, F.B., Environmental sustainability: A strategic value in guiding cruise industry management. *Journal of Hospitality and Tourism Insights*, **3**(2), pp. 229–251, 2020.

[75] Chase, G. & Alon, I., Evaluating the economic impact of cruise tourism: A case study of Barbados. *Anatolia*, **13**(1), pp. 5–18, 2002.

[76] Könnölä, K., Kangas, K., Seppälä, K., Mäkelä, M. & Lehtonen, T., Considering sustainability in cruise vessel design and construction based on existing sustainability certification systems. *Journal of Cleaner Production*, **259**, 120763, 2020.

[77] Wang, G., Li, K.X. & Xiao, Y., Measuring marine environmental efficiency of a cruise shipping company considering corporate social responsibility. *Marine Policy*, **99**, pp. 140–147, 2019.

SECTION 2
STRATEGIES AND SUSTAINABLE BUSINESS MODELS

THE FUTURE OF COMPETITIVE ADVANTAGE IN THE HOTEL INDUSTRY: ESG INITIATIVES AS A KEY DIFFERENTIATOR

KONSTANTINA K. AGORAKI, ALEXANDRA ALEXANDROPOULOU,
ELENI DIDASKALOU & DIMITRIOS A. GEORGAKELLOS
Department of Business Administration, University of Piraeus, Greece

ABSTRACT

In the highly competitive hotel industry, the integration of environmental, social, and governance (ESG) principles is rapidly evolving from a niche trend to a core element of strategic positioning. ESG initiatives are becoming pivotal in shaping the future of the hospitality sector, enabling businesses not only to contribute positively to the environment and society but also to secure and enhance their market position in a rapidly changing world. ESG initiatives have increasingly become a cornerstone for businesses seeking to secure a long-term competitive advantage in the ever-evolving global market. As consumer preferences shift towards more eco-friendly and socially responsible products and services, companies are recognising the importance of integrating sustainable practices into their operations. Gaining a competitive advantage in the hotel industry through ESG strategies involves a multifaceted approach focusing on sustainability, ethical practices and responsible governance. To this end, several dimensions and initiatives of ESG provide the framework towards this direction. The environmental sustainability pillar incorporates several initiatives, such as energy efficiency, waste reduction, and water conservation. Social responsibility highlights the significant positive externalities that could be achieved, such as community engagement, employee well-being and inclusion. The third pillar of ESG calls for decision-making that considers not only the firm's profit-maximisation principle but also the interests of various stakeholders. Adopting ESG practices offers the hotel industry a pathway to operate more sustainably and ethically while differentiating themselves in a competitive market. This forward-thinking approach is essential for hotels aiming to thrive in the future travel and tourism landscape, marking a significant step towards a more sustainable future. The present research aims to provide a critical review of the emerging concept of ESG principles as a main mechanism that the hotel industry uses to achieve sustainable competitive advantage and superior managerial performance.

Keywords: competitive advantage, ESG, ESG practices, sustainability, performance, hotel industry.

1 INTRODUCTION

Sustainability is a crucial aspect of the hotel industry, given that hotels consume substantial amounts of important resources. Such consumer and industry behaviour is linked to the broader human consumption of large amounts of natural resources to survive and maintain a good standard of living. These human activities have already led to substantial damage to the planet's ecosystems. The environmental impact of the hotel industry globally stems from the excessive consumption of non-durable resources, including water, food, energy, and paper, along with their emissions of pollutants and eco-unfriendly materials [1]–[3]. Therefore, the hotel industry today faces enormous environmental and economic pressure from domestic and international stakeholders [2], [4]. Considering the significant environmental concerns and challenges that the global hotel industry faces, the driving forces in the industry are stringent environmental regulations and increased consumer awareness around environmental protection and sustainability. Within this framework, the adoption of ESG principles is at the centre of hotel strategies to gain a green competitive advantage and green core competence. It is well documented that sustainability is the outcome of several factors, including: (a) economic practices; (b) environmental practices; and (c) social practices.

Empirical evidence on the relationship between sustainability and hotel performance provides substantial support for a positive impact of ESG practices on hotel performance [5]–[8]. However, there are also studies that show a negative relationship between sustainability and hotel performance.

A study by Thomson Reuters [9] shows that 71% of C-suite and functional leaders strongly believe that ESG considerations will be a key feature in the hotel industry in the years to come. ESG factors appear to be in the front-and-centre for today's hotel customers. These customers carefully investigate not just the amenities that a hotel offers, but also its carbon footprint, community engagement, and other ethical practices. Therefore, hotel customers significantly value the ESG practices that a hotel adopts when choosing their hotel accommodation. Many hospitality groups have adopted policies to address environmental concerns and meet investors' attitudes toward investing in environmentally friendly hotels, making ESG a major part of their businesses. This approach will influence how they invest moving forward and give them a green advantage over their competitors in the hotel industry. A study published by JLL Research [10] reported that in 2009, Hilton developed their in-house award-winning system named LightStay to report on ESG. Within this initiative, the Hilton group announced its commitment to reducing emissions by 61% by 2030 in accordance with the 2015 Paris Agreement. Furthermore, in 2020, most hotels managed by the Hilton Group in the United Kingdom started using 100% renewable electricity.

In the same vein, in 2021, IHG Hotels and Resorts launched a programme to adopt ESG goals. The initiative, named 'Journey to Tomorrow', aimed to develop a framework of ESG principles and commitments to make a positive impact on customers, communities, and the earth up to 2030. Moreover, the group launched the 'IHG Green Engage' programme, which provides the hotel brand with tools to develop and track specific goals for dramatically reducing carbon, energy, water, and waste. Similarly, recognising the green competitive advantage that adopting ESG principles could offer green competitive advantages to its hotel chain. The Radisson Group Hotel Group has set a target to reduce the carbon footprint and water consumption of all its hospitality units by 10% in 2022 and 30% by 2025. Additionally, organisations such as the Sustainability Hospitality Alliance and the Energy and Environment have launched several ESG programmes to assist the hospitality industry in achieving their sustainability goals, with an immediate priority on achieving faster carbon reduction in the hotel industry [10].

The urgent need for sustainability in the hotel industry is greatly linked to the significant shift in consumer behaviour and values. Increased awareness of the negative effects of climate change, along with behavioural changes such as recycling, consuming locally produced goods and reducing plastic usage, has become the norm. For the hotel sector to maximise the value that can be achieved from sustainable operations and buildings, it is crucial to understand the complexity of owning and operating hotels as well as the operational and development challenges the industry faces [10]. The growing importance of ESG practices in the hotel industry is highlighted in a study by Vuram [11], which argues that a commitment to ESG principles can provide a competitive advantage for the hospitality sector. Hotels that promote sustainability will be able to attract eco-friendly and environmentally concerned customers and travellers, leading to the creation of new brand loyalty and a competitive advantage in a crowded industry. Thus, ESG can operate as a crucial differentiator. Within this framework a hotel chain which has designed a clear sustainability project will attract eco-conscious travellers leading to greater brand loyalty and the potential to implement premium pricing. Conversely, hotels that have not developed a clear sustainability strategy, risk losing environmentally aware customers. Hotels that prioritise ESG practices can enhance their brand reputation. As consumers become more eco-conscious, they are likely to prefer hotels with strong ESG commitments. This preference can translate into increased customer loyalty and higher occupancy rates.

The focus of hotels in their strategy for sustainability is on different pillars: investment in renewable energy systems to reduce carbon emissions, alternative techniques of minimising food waste like composting and vital recycling programs, and community engagement. The targeted sustainability mission and application of ESG principles by hotels will give unprecedented benefits in gaining an improved brand reputation, cost-saving, talent attraction, risk mitigation, and fostering innovation. In particular, Vuram [11] stated that hotels that have actively developed and adopted ESG principles gain immense visibility as sustainability leaders with goodwill in the media while fostering a loyal customer base. Cost savings arise from energy saving and waste reduction, coupled with streamlined operations that reduce operating costs, increase competitive advantage, and boost financial performance. This further turns into the motivation for young and talented potential employees to work for sustainably responsible firms. Furthermore, it assists hotels in reducing business risk with the investment in water-efficient machines and ethical suppliers while also reducing the risk of facing supply chain disruptions related to labour exploitation and environmental damage in its network of suppliers. Finally, from using ESG strategies, hotels could also realise innovative solutions, enhancements to processes, and revenue generation. In a nutshell, the cost-saving potential of implementing ESG principles allows hotels that invest in energy-saving technologies, waste-reduction programs, and water conservation measures to save on their operational costs.

In a nutshell, a set of important ESG strategies in hospitality could lead to substantial competitive advantage, as proposed by Raub [12]. First, cost leadership strategies which focus on reducing the cost of production of goods and services, giving a hotel a competitive advantage over competitors that do not consider sustainable development a critical element in promoting their business. Second, differentiation strategies, focus on adding quality attitudes to the product or service that competitors cannot offer. Therefore, hoteliers face an important question: Do you consider sustainability as the main channel to gain a competitive advantage over your competitors? A study that included 200 hotels from France and the French-speaking parts of Switzerland provided a list of 30 sustainability actions, and hotel management was asked to evaluate them in terms of their potential to contribute to a cost leadership and/or differentiation strategy [12]. Based on the responses of the hotel managers, the most important sustainability actions leading to potential cost leadership are energy-related issues, as well as water saving and waste reduction. By contrast, the assessment from a differentiation strategy perspective concludes that the highest priorities are waste-related topics, actions related to economic sustainability, and social and labour market issues.

The aim of this paper is to provide a critical review of the recent literature on the relationship between sustainability, competitive advantage and performance in the hotel industry. We complement our analysis with suggestions for future research.

2 LITERATURE REVIEW

The relationship between sustainability, competitive advantage, and performance has become a critical issue for the global hotel industry over the last decade. According to Attila [13], Jurigová and Lencsésová [14] and Jurigová et al. [15], sustainability is a crucial element for improving the competitiveness of the hotel industry. As previously discussed, investing in sustainability and adopting ESG practices can enhance hotel performance. Three alternative theoretical approaches have been proposed to explain the potential relationship between sustainability activities, competitive advantage, and hotel performance: instrumental theory, political theory, and normative theory. Each of these theoretical approaches explains different elements of this relationship, indicating that no unified theory exists.

The first theoretical framework, instrumental theory, is a resource-based approach. It argues that firms implementing ESG practices can obtain cost and differentiation competitive advantages through the acquisition and development of resources and capabilities, providing the basis for developing a product and/or service that is difficult for competitors to replicate [8]. Peloza and Papania [16] suggest that hotel chains or individual hotels can choose sustainability activities that lead to competitive advantage through cost reductions, such as energy efficiency practices. Additionally, to satisfy stakeholders' demands, hotel top management can adopt sustainability practices that result in differentiation competitive advantage. Fernández-Gámez et al. [17] highlights cause-related marketing, which can generate reputational benefits by linking the socially responsible values shared by guests and supply chain intermediaries with a hotel brand.

Political theories provide the second theoretical approach to the examined relationship. The political approach considers sustainability as an organisation's response to stakeholder expectations (self-fulfilling expectation theory). There are alternative competing theories within this framework. Farha et al. [18] follow the institutional approach, which views sustainability as a source of legitimacy and reputation among stakeholders. Alternatively, the stakeholder theory emphasises the positive link between sustainability and hotel financial performance [5], [6]. Streimikiene and Ahmed [19] and Holotová et al. [20] argue that a hotel's performance can improve legitimacy and reputation with customers. Farooq et al. [21] suggest that hotel performance through the adoption of green human resource management and self-efficacy facilitates green creativity. Ahmed et al. [22] and Pham et al. [23] also note that employee loyalty and a commitment to achieving objectives can improve organisational performance.

Normative theories provide the third theoretical approach to the issue under investigation. This value-based theory considers sustainability as a moral issue and duty for both producers and consumers. For the hotel industry, it is argued that hotels implementing ESG strategies have a broader responsibility to the hotel company itself, its stakeholders, and the earth as a whole [24]. Within this normative approach, the slack theory has been developed, arguing that hotel management deliberately allocates resources toward sustainability rather than other activities that do not promote Sustainable Development Goals (SDGs) [25]. Another normative theory, the synergy theory, highlights the existence of a circular feedback loop of ESG practices impacting hotel performance. Coupled with the provisions of the slack resources theory, hotel managers might be inclined to develop and adopt sustainability practices [26]. However, Moneva et al. [27] found that higher financial performance leads to lower sustainability commitment, arguing against the slack resources theory. Moneva et al. [27] suggest there is no evidence of a positive relationship between sustainability and financial performance, indicating that a hotel's decision to adopt sustainability practices is independent of its corporate financial performance. Finally, Singal [28] found that small, family-owned hotels with limited financial access do not invest in sustainability, which could harm their long-term survival.

In the context of hotel operations, sustainability is focused on increasing operating efficiency and lowering costs while boosting attraction and retention among customers. Hotels undertake numerous activities to fulfil these objectives, such as energy efficiency programs, water conservation measures, and waste reduction strategies. Moreover, sustainability practices play a crucial role in attracting a segment of environmentally conscious travellers and building a brand reputation and competitiveness.

There is ample empirical evidence on the impact of sustainability on competitive advantage and performance in the hotel industry. From the slack resources theory perspective, Waddock and Graves [25] argue that hotels attaining high organisational performance levels will invest more resources in ESG practices. The synergy theory posits that hotel companies investing in sustainability are often more profitable due to the positive relationship between sustainability and financial performance [26]. However, Theodoulidis et al. [6], Moneva et al. [27], González-Rodríguez et al. [29], Haldorai et al. [30] and Umrani et al. [31] argue that the positive relationship between sustainability and performance depends on the attained level of company performance. Environmentally and socially responsible hotels can, therefore, stand out in this crowded market space, make premium pricing possible, and ensure greater customer loyalty. Moreover, it results in better engagement of employees and the attraction of more talent because people are more motivated and attached to organisations whose purposes coincide with their values in striving for a positive change in society and the environment.

Recently, Pereira-Moliner et al. [32] further investigated the relationship between sustainability, competitive advantage, and performance in the hotel industry. They analysed the influence of sustainability on cost and differentiation competitive advantages and investigated the potential synergy between sustainability and performance. Using data from 3-, 4-, and 5-star hotels in Spain, they employed perceptual and hotel-specific objective performance measurements such as occupancy rate, average daily rate, and revenue per available room. The empirical analysis was conducted by estimating structural equation models with Partial Least Squares (PLS-SEM). Their findings indicate a positive and statistically significant impact of sustainability practices on cost and differentiation advantages, perceptual performance, average daily rate, and revenue per available room. Furthermore, the analysis documented that hotels with these three performance variables above the median experienced a positive and significant relationship between sustainability and performance. Pereira-Moliner et al. [32] argue that their results support the existence of a synergistic sustainability–performance relationship in the hotel industry. An important aspect of this analysis is that contrary to previous research focusing solely on environmental sustainability, Pereira-Moliner et al. [32] also consider the effects of economic and social sustainability.

Kuo et al. [1] focus on a related issue: how the adoption of sustainability practices through various environmental regulations leads to the implementation of proactive environmental strategies in the hotel industry. They analyse the channels through which ESG strategies foster eco-innovation, green competitive advantage, and green core competence. Using a sample of 366 hotel manager responses, their findings show that proactive environmental strategies positively influence eco-innovation, which in turn directly affects green competitive advantage. However, there was no significant statistical evidence of any effect from eco-innovation on green core competence. The managerial implications of Kuo et al. [1] suggest that hotel companies must adopt new technologies to become more innovative and meet increasing environmental demands and green competitive strategies. Furthermore, the results provide an understanding of eco-innovation's impact on guest satisfaction and hotel image, building brand loyalty.

Asante [33] developed conceptual models to clarify hotels' green leadership and its non-homogeneous effect on employee pro-environmental behaviour in the hospitality industry. The study employed data from managers and employees in Ghana's hotel industry, based on person–organisation fit and norm activation theory. Two psychosocial antecedents, value congruence and moral consciousness, mediated the unexplained variations between green leadership and employee pro-environmental behaviour. Using PLS-SEM methodology, the empirical analysis found strong evidence of the interactive role that moral consciousness plays in employee behavioural outcomes, highlighting its significance in stimulating pro-environmental behaviour among employees in the hospitality sector. Bodhanwala and Bodhanwala [34] explore the relationship between sustainability and firm performance in the travel and tourism industry. Specifically, the authors investigate the relationship between aggregate and individual dimensions of sustainability and financial and stock market performances of firms in the travel and tourism industry (TTI) across different geographies. The analysis is conducted by estimating a multivariate panel data model using data on 146 travel and tourism industry firms that have consistently obtained ESG ratings over the period 2011–2017. Moreover, Bodhanwala and Bodhanwala [34] find that among the transportation, hotel and leisure industries, the hotel industry has the highest ESG compliance. Furthermore, the analysis shows that although agency and stakeholder theories predict that all ESG components should have significant positive effect on financial and stock market performance, each dimension has a different impact on financial performance and market value in the tourism industry. From an investment perspective, sustainability significantly enhances the attractiveness, long-term value, and resilience of hotels. Investors are increasingly prioritising properties that adopt ESG principles, viewing them as less risky and more likely to deliver stable returns in the face of environmental and regulatory challenges. Sustainable hotels are perceived to have a better long-term value due to their ability to comply with stringent environmental regulations, attract eco-conscious consumers, and avoid penalties associated with non-compliance.

Finally, Trabandt et al. [35] introduce hedonic appeals to encourage guests to reduce their room cleaning requests. This strategy is linked to the hotel industry's search for methods to reduce its adverse environmental impact and gain a green competitive advantage. Combining a field experiment at a European hotel and a laboratory experiment, Trabandt et al. [35] provide evidence supporting the proposed effects and explanatory mechanisms. They also demonstrate that the newly designed strategy using hedonic appeals is the most profitable by implementing a profitability index that includes room cleaning requests, monetary investments, and side effects. Therefore, Trabandt et al. [35] argue that hotels should adopt this cost-effective strategy to reduce room cleaning requests without affecting overall guest satisfaction, thereby providing a competitive advantage.

To summarise, ESG practices help mitigate various risks, including those related to supply chain disruptions, labour exploitation, and environmental damage, thereby ensuring financial stability and attractiveness to investors. As a result, hotels that invest in sustainable technologies and ethical practices are better positioned to achieve long-term success and resilience in the competitive hospitality market.

3 CONCLUSIONS AND FUTURE RESEARCH

The present paper discusses the recent literature on the relationship between sustainability, competitive advantage and performance in the hotel industry. This relationship has only recently been studied in the context of the hotel industry; therefore, we provide a review of the emerging analysis of this relationship. Based on the literature discussed, it is clear that there is a positive and statistically significant link between sustainability and cost and differentiation competitive advantages. Furthermore, we presented alternative theoretical approaches that offer explanations for the existence of this important link, namely instrumental theories, political theories, and normative theories.

Given that the study of the relationship between sustainability, competitive advantage, and performance in the hotel industry is still in its early stages, future research could consider short- and long-term performance measurements specifically developed for the hotel sector.

This will help analyse whether sustainability practices have a positive impact on performance and competitive advantage. Additionally, the inclusion of mediating or moderating variables could provide further insights into this baseline relationship.

In addition to the theoretical and empirical insights provided, it is crucial for future studies to explore the practical implications of these findings for hotel managers and policymakers. Understanding the sustainability practices that drive competitive advantage may help hotel managers as well as policymakers to allocate resources more effectively and devise strategies that align with overall business goals, while provide incentives that would further encourage sustainability adoption in the hospitality industry. Nevertheless, the role of technological advancement in enhancing this sustainability–performance link needs to be studied. The technologies of energy-efficient systems, along with waste management solutions, would be one of the most impacting solutions toward the effectiveness of sustainability initiatives.

A future research area deals with regional differences in the relationship between sustainability and performance. Factors such as cultural attitudes toward sustainability, local regulation, and market demand tend to be significantly different across various geographical regions. Comparative studies, further analysing these regional variations, can hopefully bring more of the context in which sustainability practices affect competitive advantage and performance. Finally, it is necessary to conduct longitudinal studies to track the long-term effects of sustainability practices on hotel performance. Therefore, such studies can provide insights into the strategies for sustainability that tend to realise more benefits across time and recognise possible trade-offs or challenges that could be linked to maintaining sustainable operations across time.

In conclusion, the relationship between sustainability, competitive advantage, and performance in the hotel industry is complex and an evolving area of research. Such areas of gaps may be addressed, with subsequent studies contributing to more conclusive results on how sustainability practices lead toward long-term success in the hospitality sector.

REFERENCES

[1] Kuo, F.-I., Fang, W.-T. & LePage, B.A., Proactive environmental strategies in the hotel innovation, green competitive advantage, and green core competence. *Journal of Sustainable Tourism,* **30**, pp. 1240–1261, 2022.

[2] Aboelmaged, M., Direct and indirect effects of eco-innovation, environmental orientation and supplier collaboration on hotel performance: An empirical study. *Journal of Cleaner Production,* **184**, pp. 537–549, 2018.

[3] Fang, S., Zhang, C. & Li, Y., Physical attractiveness of service employees and customer engagement in tourism industry. *Annals of Tourism Research*, **80**, 102756, 2020.

[4] Wang, Y., Font, X. & Liu, J., Antecedents, mediation effects and outcomes of hotel eco-innovation practice. *International Journal of Hospitality Management*, **85**, 102345, 2020.

[5] Ghaderi, Z., Mirzapour, M., Henderson, J.C. & Richardson, S., Corporate social responsibility and hotel performance: A view from Tehran, Iran. *Tourism Management Perspectives*, **29**, pp. 41–47, 2019.

[6] Theodoulidis, B., Diaz, D., Crotto, F. & Rancati, E., Exploring corporate social responsibility and financial performance through stakeholder theory in the tourism industries. *Tourism Management*, **62**, pp. 173–188, 2017.

[7] Garay, L. & Font, X., Doing good to do well? Corporate social responsibility reasons, practices and impacts in small and medium accommodation enterprises. *International Journal of Hospitality Management*, **31**, pp. 329–337, 2012.

[8] Garay, L. & Font, X., Corporate social responsibility in tourism small and medium enterprises evidence from Europe and Latin America. *Tourism Management Perspectives*, **7**, pp. 38–46, 2013.

[9] Thomson Reuters, The 2023 State of Corporate ESG: How companies are embracing ESG for resilience and growth. https://www.thomsonreuters.com/en-us/posts/esg/state-of-corporate-esg-report-2023/. Accessed on: 20 Apr. 2024.

[10] JLL Research, ESG at the heart of hotel strategies. Report, Sep. 2021.

[11] Vuram, WNS Vuram, 2024. The growing importance of ESG practices in the hotel industry. https://www.vuram.com/blog/esg-in-hotel-industry/. Accessed on: 20 Apr. 2024.

[12] Raub, S., *Sustainable Actions in Hospitality: A Driver for Competitive Advantage*, 2022.

[13] Attila, A.T., The impact of the hotel industry on the competitiveness of tourism destinations in Hungary. *Journal of Competitiveness*, **8**(4), pp. 85–104, 2016.

[14] Jurigová, Z. & Lencsésová, Z., Monitoring system of sustainable development in cultural and mountain tourism destinations. *Journal of Competitiveness*, 2015.

[15] Jurigová, Z., Tucková, Z. & Kuncová, M., Economic sustainability as a future phenomenon: Moving towards a sustainable hotel industry. *Journal of Security and Sustainability*, **6**(1), pp. 103–112, 2016.

[16] Peloza, J. & Papania, L., The missing link between corporate social responsibility and financial performance: Stakeholder salience and identification. *Corporate Reputation Review*, **11**, pp. 169–181, 2008.

[17] Fernández-Gámez, M.Á., Gutiérrez-Ruiz, A.M., Becerra-Vicario, R. & Ruiz-Palomo, D., The impact of creating shared value on hotels online reputation. *Corporate Social Responsibility and Environmental Management*, **27**(5), pp. 2201–2211, 2020.

[18] Farha, A.K.A., Al-Kwifi, O.S. & Ahmed, Z.U., Deploying partial least squares to investigate the influence of managerial assumptions on corporate social responsibility in the hotel industry. *Journal of Hospitality and Tourism Technology*, **9**(3), pp. 471–486, 2018.

[19] Streimikiene, D. & Ahmed, R.R., The integration of corporate social responsibility and marketing concepts as a business strategy: Evidence from SEM-based multivariate and Toda-Yamamoto causality models. *Oeconomia Copernicana*, **12**(1), pp. 125–157, 2021.

[20] Holotová, M., Nagyová, Ľ. & Holota, T., The impact of environmental responsibility on changing consumer behaviour-sustainable market in Slovakia. *Economics and Sociology*, **13**(3), pp. 84–96, 2020.

[21] Farooq, R., Zhang, Z., Talwar, S. & Dhir, A., Do green human resource management and self-efficacy facilitate green creativity? A study of luxury hotels and resorts. *Journal of Sustainable Tourism*, pp. 1–22, 2021.

[22] Ahmed, U., AlZgool, M.D.H. & Shah, S.M.M., The impact of green human resource practices on environmental sustainability. *Polish Journal of Management Studies*, **20**(1), pp. 9–18, 2019.

[23] Pham, N.T., Chiappetta Jabbour, C.J., Vo-Thanh, T., Huynh, T.L.D. & Santos, C., Greening hotels: Does motivating hotel employees promote in-role green performance? The role of culture. *Journal of Sustainable Tourism*, pp. 1–20, 2020.

[24] Font, X., Garay, L. & Jones, S., A social cognitive theory of sustainability empathy. *Annals of Tourism Research*, **58**, pp. 65–80, 2016.

[25] Waddock, S.A. & Graves, S.B., The corporate social performance–financial performance link. *Strategic Management Journal*, **18**(4), pp. 303–319, 1997.

[26] Calveras, A., Corporate social responsibility strategy in the hotel industry: Evidence from the Balearic Islands. *International Journal of Tourism Research*, **17**, pp. 399–408, 2015.

[27] Moneva, J.M., Bonilla-Priego, M.J. & Ortas, E., Corporate social responsibility and organisational performance in the tourism sector. *Journal of Sustainable Tourism*, **28**(6), pp. 853–872, 2020.

[28] Singal, M., The link between firm financial performance and investment in sustainability initiatives. *Cornell Hospitality Quarterly*, **55**(1), pp. 19–30, 2014.

[29] González-Rodríguez, M.R., Martín-Samper, R.C., Köseoglu, M.A. & Okumus, F., Hotels' corporate social responsibility practices, organizational culture, firm reputation, and performance. *Journal of Sustainable Tourism*, **27**(3), pp. 398–419, 2019.

[30] Haldorai, K., Kim, W.G. & Garcia, R.F., Top management green commitment and green intellectual capital as enablers of hotel environmental performance: The mediating role of green human resource management. *Tourism Management*, **88**, 104431, 2022.

[31] Umrani, W.A., Channa, N.A., Yousaf, A., Ahmed, U., Pahi, M.H. & Ramayah, T., Greening the workforce to achieve environmental performance in hotel industry: A serial mediation model. *Journal of Hospitality and Tourism Management*, **44**, pp. 50–60, 2020.

[32] Pereira-Moliner, J., López-Gamero, M.D., Font, X., Molina-Azorín, J.F., Tarí, J.J. & Pertusa-Ortega, E.M., Sustainability, competitive advantages and performance in the hotel industry: A synergistic relationship. *Journal of Tourism and Services*, **12**(23), pp. 132–149, 2021.

[33] Asante, K.W., Hotels' green leadership and employee pro-environmental behaviour, the role of value congruence and moral consciousness: evidence from symmetrical and asymmetrical approaches. *Journal of Tourism Management*, pp. 1–22, 2023.

[34] Bodhanwala, S. & Bodhanwala, R., Exploring relationship between sustainability and firm performance in travel and tourism industry: A global evidence. *Social Responsibility Journal*, **18**, pp. 1251–1269, 2022.

[35] Trabandt, M., Lasarov, W. & Viglia, G., It's a pleasure to stay sustainably: Leveraging hedonic appeals in tourism and hospitality. *Tourism Management*, **103**, 104907, 2024.

USING AGRICULTURE TO IMPROVE AND INCREASE THE SUSTAINABLE TOURISM INDUSTRY IN IDAHO, USA

ROBERT L. MAHLER[1], NAV GHIMIRE[2], BRAD STOKES[3] & IRIS MAYES[3]
[1]Department of Soil and Water Systems, University of Idaho, USA
[2]Cooperative Extension Service, University of Nebraska, USA
[3]Cooperative Extension Service, University of Idaho, USA

ABSTRACT

Tourism is the third largest industry in Idaho, surpassed by only agriculture and technology, as it accounts for more than $4.8 billion in annual income. Over 84% of this income is generated by out-of-state visitors. The tourism industry is healthy and growing at an annual rate of 6%–8%. Idaho is known for its outdoor beauty, as eight of its 14 top tourist attractions are water-related. Even though agriculture is Idaho's largest industry, it currently has little positive impact on tourism. The purpose of this paper is to determine the potential value of agriculture to Idaho's sustainable tourism industry and to recommend a list of sustainable programmes that need to be developed or improved upon to ensure that agriculture is much more important to Idaho's sustainable tourism future. Conversely, agriculture currently contributes little to tourism; however, its potential for the future is outstanding. A public survey developed for this study indicated that there is widespread support to develop sustainable agritourism in Idaho and that the public is receptive to the inclusion of wine/wineries, dairy products, farmers markets, potatoes/potato products and small farms in a sustainable tourism programme. Programmes are in the development phase to capitalise on unique Idaho commodities including farmer's markets, sustainable small farms, the growing wine industry, specialty crops, agricultural diversity and the development of a historical agricultural heritage trail. Many of these resources are within 1 hour's driving distance of over half of Idaho's population and the state capital, Boise. The potential to use unique and sustainable agricultural commodities should be the basis for the expansion of sustainable agritourism in Idaho over the next 20 years.

Keywords: agricultural tourism, wine industry, water canals, farmers markets, agricultural diversity.

1 INTRODUCTION

The current popular definition of sustainable tourism is the use of sustainable practices in and by the tourist industry. Sustainable tourism strives to acknowledge both positive and negative impacts of tourism, ideally by minimising the negative impacts and maximising the positive impacts on people, cultures and the environment. Going further, the United Nation's World Tourism Organization (UNWTO) and United Nations Environmental Program (UNEP) defines sustainable tourism as tourism that accounts for its current and future social, economic and environmental impacts, while addressing the needs of visitors, the environment, industry and the local community [1]. Typical positive impacts of sustainable tourism include wildlife preservation, landscape conservation, local job creation and cultural heritage preservation and interpretation. Negative impacts that should be minimised or eliminated with sustainable tourism include damage to the natural environment, loss of biodiversity, economic damage and economic leakage.

Over 1.4 billion people travel each year. Data shows that more and more people travel across planet Earth every year and much of this travel can be linked to tourism. This increase in tourism has an increasing impact on the environment, biodiversity, culture and economics. Tourism travel not only brings about positive economic benefits but can result in excess energy consumption and increasing negative environmental impacts on local, regional and global environments including climate change [2]. There are many complex aspects of increasing tourism especially when trying to make international tourism more sustainable [3]. One of the major problems with tourism is that it is growing at a fast pace. This fast growth has shown to result in unsustainable consequences at some of the most popular tourist locations [4]. Scholars agree that current and future research about sustainable tourism should address the following four thematic areas: (1) community stakeholder perspectives; (2) business approaches to sustainability in tourism; (3) cultural responses; and (4) methodological challenges related to sustainability [5]. Another important challenge to sustainable tourism is the development and testing of sustainable tourism indicators that can be used to identify successes and failures under field conditions in this increasingly complex industry [6]. Sustainability-related initiatives have a 30-year tradition of being embedded in many aspects of tourism [7]. Also, there is increasing merit in considering connections between tourism and the sustainability of planet Earth [8].

Agritourism and sustainable agritourism have an extensive history in western Europe and this momentum has also recently developed in the USA and Canada [9]. Agritourism can not only offer sustainable recreational activities to tourists but can also relate to and display important parts of a region's agricultural heritage [10]. Agritourism can not only provide educational opportunities to the 80% of non-farm residents of developed countries but can also help diversify the income of local farmers and thus make agriculture more economically viable [11].

Tourism is the third largest industry in Idaho, surpassed by only agriculture and technology, as it accounts for more than $4.8 billion in annual income [12]. Over 84% of this income is generated by out-of-state visitors. A significant portion of this draw to tourists is the availability of many different types of outdoor water-related activities. Idaho is known for its: (1) 18 ski resorts; (2) 140 natural usable hot springs (#1 in USA); (3) 1.9 million ha of mountainous wilderness (#3 in USA); and (4) 8.2 million ha of National Forests (#3 in USA). Most famously, Idaho is known as the white-water state with more than 4,960 km of rough and challenging river water (#1 in USA). There are 11 international famous white-water rivers in the state that are used for rafting, kayaking, floating and fishing. Conversely, agriculture currently contributes little to tourism; however, its potential for the future is outstanding. Recent surveys in 2016 and 2021 have shown that the public is interested in the agriculture industry becoming an important part of Idaho's sustainable tourism industry [13]. Based on these surveys and recent interest by agricultural groups in the state a plan is in the development and implementation phase to incorporate several agriculture components into Idaho's sustainable tourism industry. The purpose of this study is to measure the enthusiasm of Idahoans to develop a sustainable agritourism programme.

2 MATERIALS AND METHODS

2.1 Public surveys about the importance of agriculture to tourism in Idaho

This survey instrument was developed as a follow-up to tourism surveys conducted in Idaho in 2016 and 2021. The four survey questions were:

Question 1 – Which of the following labels describes you best? (1) Resident of Idaho; (2) resident of Idaho involved in the agriculture industry; (3) resident of Idaho not directly involved in agriculture – but with some knowledge of the importance of agriculture; or (4) other.

Question 2 – Please select THREE of the following items associated with agriculture that would be good tourist destinations in Idaho: (1) cheese/cheese related products; (2) ethnic restaurants; (3) local farmers markets; (4) local produce stands; (5) locally grown honey; (6) microbreweries; (7) potatoes; or (8) wine/wineries.

Question 3 – If you had friends visiting you from out of state, which of the following TWO agricultural activities would you encourage your friends to visit or take part in? (1) The manufacture of cheese/cheese related products; (2) dine at ethnic restaurants; (3) shop at local farmers markets; (4) shop at local produce stands; (5) buy locally grown honey; (6) visit microbreweries; (7) visit potato processing plants; or (8) buy wine/visit local wineries.

Question 4 – After reading through this survey do you believe that the agriculture industry can have a significant impact on tourism? (1) Yes; (2) no; (3) unsure; or (4) no opinion.

The survey target audience was a representative sample of the 1,430,000 adult residents of Idaho. The target audience was divided into three groups of residents; (1) general adult residents of Idaho; (2) adult residents involved in the agricultural industry; and (3) adult residents not involved in the agricultural industry but with some knowledge of the importance of agriculture to the state. In addition, demographic information including gender, age, education level, community size, length of residency in Idaho and geographic location in the state were also collected.

The survey conducted in 2023 was developed using the Dillman methodology [14], [15]. The survey was delivered to clientele via the United States Postal Service [14], [15]. A sufficient number of completed surveys was the goal to result in a sampling error of less than 6% [16]. The survey process was also designed to receive a completed survey return rate in excess of 50%. For the general public, addresses were obtained from a professional social sciences survey company (SSI, Norwich, CT). To increase the response level from the general public with an agricultural background, addresses were also obtained from agricultural commodity commissions and county Extension offices. The goal was to raise the response rate from those with an agricultural background or agricultural knowledge to at least 20% of the residents surveyed.

In 2023 the four survey questions shown above were embedded into a 50-question survey that was sent to more than 1,600 adult residents in Idaho. The actual survey process and analysis including demographic questions was identical to surveys conducted in the region over the last 20 years [17]–[19].

Survey answers were coded and entered into Microsoft Excel. Missing data were excluded from the analysis. The data were analysed at two levels using SAS [16]. The first level of analysis generated frequencies. The second level evaluated how the respondents' demography influenced their responses. Significance ($P < 0.05$) to demographic factors was tested using a chi-squared distribution [14]–[16].

2.2 Wineries and wine production

To collect historical and recent data, members of the Idaho Wine Commission were interviewed to ascertain Idaho wine industry trends, challenges, and successes. The Commission also provided data on grape hectares, tasting rooms, and tourist visits to wineries. To collect the secondary data, literature was reviewed. The Idaho Wine Commission allowed us to review their literature to collect secondary information and Google Scholar was also used. The key concepts identified in the interview and secondary data were grouped to develop categories for this report. The categories were assembled to identify the causal relationship among themes and understand the areas of interest as guided by the study objectives.

2.3 Farmers markets and small farms

The section relies on fact sheets and attendance data collected at farmers markets. First-hand knowledge of Airbnb's and Mary Jane's farm were used as examples.

2.4 Agricultural diversity in southwestern Idaho

The agricultural industry in southwestern Idaho is the largest and most diverse in the state and it is located within one hour's drive of over half the state's population. Data about the types of crops grown in the region, types of farms, size of farms and urban population were collected. Potential tourism attractions were identified.

2.5 Development of a historical agricultural heritage trail

Surface water irrigation data was collected for two rapidly urbanising counties in southwestern Idaho. The size of these surface water irrigation systems was determined as was the transition from agricultural service to urban service. The potential to establish signage about the history of irrigated agriculture in the state and the development of a historical trail to understand Idaho's agricultural heritage was evaluated.

3 RESULTS AND DISCUSSION

Most Americans know that Idaho is an agricultural state. In fact, most people know Idaho as the 'potato state'. One of the most famous license plates on motor vehicles has the moniker 'Famous Potatoes' that provides visibility for the state's most important crop. Not all the publicity about potatoes has been positive in the past. A famous American singer and writer famous for his parodies, Weird Al Yankovic, wrote a song called 'Addicted to Spuds'. Spuds is slang for potatoes. In this song he lampooned people with a boring life stating 'You planned a trip to Idaho just to watch potatoes grow…'.

The Dillman Tailored Design Method (TDM) was conceived in the early 1970s as an approach to conduct valid surveys of the general public. This survey method has evolved over time and is one of the most widely used methods associated with agriculture. Four books have been published about this methodology.

The survey conducted in 2023 was designed to assess the level of public interest in the development and expansion of tourism related to agriculture in Idaho. The mail-based Dillman survey methodology received a response rate of 50.9%. The goal of a greater than 50% response rate was achieved, resulting in a sampling error of less than 6% for this study.

3.1 Tourism surveys

76% of the surveyed residents had no tie to agriculture, while 10% were actively involved in the agricultural industry. Another 12% of survey respondents were not involved in the agricultural industry but had some knowledge of the importance of agriculture to Idaho's economy. Based on the first survey question approximately 22% of the survey respondents considered agriculture important, while the other 78% had little or no knowledge of Idaho agriculture.

When asked to select three potential agriculture tourism items in Idaho from a list of nine, three items rose to the top of suggestions provided by survey respondents (Table 1). Wine and wineries were listed as potential Idaho tourism destinations by 56% of survey respondents. Cheese and cheese-related manufacturing and products were ranked as potential tourism destinations by 47% of Idahoans. Local farmers markets were also selected by 38% of those surveyed as being potential tourist destinations. Conversely, less than 20% of the public thought that locally produced honey (16%) and ethnic restaurants (14%) were a higher priority for tourist development.

Table 1: Public views of three items associated with agriculture that would be good tourist destinations in Idaho based on 2023 survey.

Agriculture tourism items	Answering yes, %[a]
Wine/wineries	56
Cheese/cheese-related products	47
Local farmers markets	38
Potatoes	31
Microbreweries	26
Sustainable agriculture farms	25
Local produce stands	24
Locally produced honey	16
Ethnic restaurants	14

[a]This column should add to 300% if all respondents selected three items; however not all respondents selected three items.

It is one thing for Idahoans to select agriculture items/commodities for targeted tourism, but much different to take advantage of these tourism opportunities. Consequently, a question asked what the top two tourism activities are that surveyed respondents would do with out-of-state visitors. Respondents selected wine tasting/wineries (50%) and local farmers markets (46%) as things that they would do with out-of-state visitors (Table 2). There was also significant interest in visiting microbreweries (27%) and in visiting cheese/yogurt manufacturing facilities (22%).

Table 2: Public views of the top two items associated with agriculture that would be good things to do with visitors from out of state based on 2023 survey.

Water resources tourism items	Top two items, %[a]
Wine tasting/wineries	50
Local farmers markets	46
Microbreweries	27
Cheese/yogurt/cheese related items	22
Local produce stands	16
Locally produced honey	12
Potatoes	10
Ethnic restaurants	7
Sustainable agriculture farms	4

[a]This column should add to 200% if all respondents selected three items; however, not all respondents selected three items.

The majority of survey respondents (57%) felt that the agricultural industry would not have a significant impact on Idaho tourism (Table 3). However, the 21% of the public with a positive attitude about the future sustainable agricultural tourism, may be a large enough base to make agricultural tourism positively impact on the tourism industry.

Table 3: Do you believe that the agricultural industry can make a significant impact on tourism in Idaho based on survey conducted in 2023?

Can agriculture have a significant impact on tourism?	%
Yes	21
No	57
Unsure	12
No opinion	10

Table 4: The impact of demographic factors on the choice of wine/wineries, cheese products, local farmers markets and potatoes as potentially important to tourism in Idaho based on the 2023 survey.

Tourism issue	Demographic factor	Best	Worst	Significance[a]
Wine/wineries	Gender	Female	Male	**
	Age	> 60 years	< 30 years	***
	Education	College degree	No college	***
	Com. size	> 100,000	< 1,000	NS
	Time in Idaho	< 5 years	Native	****
	Part of state	North	Southeast	**
Cheese products	Gender	Female	Male	**
	Age	30–40 years	> 60 years	***
	Education	College degree	No HS diploma	****
	Com. size	> 100,000	1,000–10,000	NS
	Time in Idaho	< 5 years	5–15 years	**
	Part of state	Southcentral	North	***
Local farmers markets	Gender	Female	Male	***
	Age	40–60 years	< 30 years	***
	Education	Some college	No college	***
	Com. size	1,000–10,000	> 100,000	NS
	Time in Idaho	Native	5–15 years	****
	Part of state	Southwest	Southeast	***
Potatoes	Gender	Male	Female	***
	Age	> 60 years	< 30 years	***
	Education	No college	College degree	**
	Com. size	1,000–10,000	> 100,000	NS
	Time in Idaho	Native	5–15 years	**
	Part of state	Southeast	North	***

[a]NS = not significant; **, *** and **** = significant at the 95%, 99% and 99.9% levels of probability.

The demographic factors of gender, age, education level, length of time living in Idaho and state geography impacted respondent answers about wine/wineries, cheese manufacturing/products, local farmers markets and potatoes (Table 4). However, the demographic factor of community size did not impact respondent answers to tourism questions.

Survey respondents thought that wines/wineries would be an important component of sustainable agricultural tourism in Idaho. From a demographic standpoint, respondents that were (1) female; (2) greater than 60 years old; (3) had a college degree; (4) had lived in Idaho less than 5 years; and (5) were from the northern part of the state were most likely to support wines and wineries as part of a sustainable tourism effort.

Females with college degrees were most likely to support the development of a tourism industry around cheese/cheese products. In addition, residents between 30 and 40 years of age and Idaho newcomers were more likely to support cheese-related tourism. As expected, support for cheese tourism is greatest in southcentral Idaho where most of the dairy cows and cheese manufacturing plants are located.

There was widespread support to promote local farmers markets as part of sustainable agriculture in Idaho. In particular, females between the ages of 40 and 60 with some college were most likely to support the development of this industry for tourism. Idaho natives and residents of southwestern Idaho were more likely to support local farmers market as agricultural tourism.

As expected, the greatest support for developing the potato industry as sustainable agricultural tourism came from Idaho natives and residents of south-eastern Idaho. Older males (> 60 years old) were most likely to support the development of sustainable tourism based on potatoes – Idaho's biggest crop. In general, residents that had not been exposed to college were most likely to support tourism that takes advantage of potatoes.

3.2 Wine and wineries

Idaho is a growing wine region with the natural resources to sustain world-class vineyards and wineries statewide. The state's rich, volcanic soils, desert climate, and direct access to water make it an ideal location for fruit-forward wines with good structure. Planted elevations range from roughly 200 to 1,000 m above sea level. Historically, wines produced from grapes grown at high elevations attract people because of their unique taste and rich texture. This distinct flavour, coupled with better exposure, better drainage, and higher daily temperature swings, creates a conducive environment for grape cultivation that rivals, and in some cases surpasses, California, Oregon, and Washington. Idaho's warm days, cool nights, limited rainfall, and geographical location make it an ideal place for growing grapes.

In 1975, Idaho had a single winery. However, the latest USDA Fruit Tree Census for Idaho revealed a remarkable growth spurt between 1999 and 2006, with Idaho's wine grapes increasing from 265 to 500 ha [20]. Currently, 520 ha of planted vineyards are in Idaho, with 75 wineries and eight cideries [21]. This growth is a testament to the region's potential for wine production, making it an attractive prospect for wine enthusiasts and investors alike. In 2018, Idaho harvested 2,800 tons of grapes. Not all harvested grapes become wine; only 132,000 gallons were produced into wine, or 54,875 cases. That's roughly 658,500 bottles of wine in 2018 alone.

Idaho's wine industry is not just about wine. It's a powerhouse, significantly contributing to the state's economy and attracting both in-state and out-of-state tourists. The Agritourism industry, of which Idaho wineries are a vital part, not only brings in revenue but also fosters a sense of pride and community among local residents and businesses. It requires a united voice from the wineries, local residents, businesses, universities, and state government agencies to continue its growth and achieve success. Hotels and restaurants usually serve as amplifiers of the wine industry, by including Idaho wine on their wine lists and raising awareness of Idaho wine among tourists, many of whom seek to sample local food and beverage products. According to the Idaho Wine Commission, Idaho's wine industry had direct revenues of $46 million in 2017, including $31.4 million in winery revenue [22].

Idaho's wine industry has excellent potential for sustainable agritourism. It offers unique experiences that connect visitors with the land, local culture, and wine making. The wineries engage the tourists by offering guided tours showcasing the vineyards, explaining grape varietals, and providing insights into the winemaking process. This concludes with tastings featuring a variety of wines paired with local cheeses, charcuterie, or other snacks. The harvest festivals host events during the harvest season, allowing visitors to participate in grape picking, learn about traditional techniques, and enjoy the festive atmosphere. Wine blending workshops provide interactive experiences where visitors can blend their wine, creating a personalised souvenir and gaining a deeper understanding of the art of winemaking. The Culinary experiences programme partners with local chefs to offer farm-to-table dinners featuring seasonal ingredients paired with the winery's wines. This creates a memorable connection between the land, food, and wine. The winery tourism activities include educational programmes that organise workshops or seminars on grape varietals, wine styles, food pairings, or the history of Idaho's wine industry. In addition, the wine industry promotes tours on the established wine trails, encouraging visitors to explore multiple wineries in a region, maximising their experience and supporting the entire industry.

Idaho's various wine growing regions offer something different for every taste. Outside of the urban corridor, there's Sunnyslope Wine Trail, which is a subregion of the Snake River Valley AVA, which features several vineyards and wineries. Tour packages are made available to visit various vineyards, said Moya Dolsby, executive director of the Idaho wine Commission. There are also the Lewiston and Moscow region, Coeur d'Alene and Sandpoint region and the South-Central region, all with various climates and vineyards suited to those environments. 'Idaho is great to visit for wine throughout the year', Dolsby said. 'It depends on the experience the visitor wants to have while here. Late spring through fall, and summer in particular, offer great weather that is perfect for picnicking at the wineries or enjoying a leisurely afternoon on a patio with great scenery and a glass of local wine, or witnessing the fall harvest'.

3.3 Farmers markets

Farmers markets offer the opportunity for customers to purchase fresh fruits and vegetables directly from the farmer. Markets also offer other products such as fresh flowers, baked goods, local cheese, local meat, prepared food, entertainment and booths hosted by non-profit organisations. Markets reduce economic leakage as dollars spent stay longer in the local economy. Given these various assets and opportunities for creating economic and social connections, farmers markets help strengthen economic and social capital overall in their neighbourhoods and communities [23].

According to the Idaho Department of Agriculture there are 52 farmers markets throughout the state. They range in size and are located in cities and small towns. The Capital City Public (CCP) Market in Boise attracts up to 15,000 people each Saturday [24], [25]. The Moscow Farmers Market hosts up to 10,000 visitors per Saturday [26]. Both markets have spun off additional farmers markets indicating the potential for expansion as the number of vendors and the customer base grows. Consequently, several vendors from the CCP Market created a more 'food-centric' market called the 'Boise Farmers Market'. Moscow is also home to a smaller mid-week 'Tuesday Market' that provides beginning farmers with an opportunity to learn various facets of selling at a farmers market such as how much product to bring, sales skills, product display, etc. Many visitors to any municipality find attending a farmers market a pleasurable activity. Attendance surges at farmers markets in college towns on weekends where families attend sporting events, or other college-based events such as Mom's Weekends. Tourism is a factor that improves economic impact at farmers markets [23]. Simple brochures and websites offer the opportunity to expand and increase attendance at these local markets.

Other forms of direct sales besides farmers markets mainly include roadside stands and farm stores. Sales at these on-farm locations can be greatly increased with tours, and other on-farm events. The USDA Agricultural Census has documented 1,908 farms in Idaho that offer direct sales and other forms of agritourism [27]. Most of these operators are full owners (over 80%) indicating improved economic impact for the farmers when compared with other forms of grocery purchasing. Of these farms, 1,732 offer only direct sales with no agritourism indicating that there is a potential for growth for some farms to expand into additional agritourism activities. One way some small farm owners have expanded into agritourism is through the use of online platforms such as Airbnb and Vrbo that make it easy to arrange overnight on-farm visits. Even prior to these platforms, an example of agritourism was pioneered by a North Idaho farmer Mary Jane Butters who initiated 'glamping' on her farm (a combination of 'glamorous' and 'camping') where guests are provided a camping experience furnished with antiques and where they are fed a fresh farm breakfast. Butters has created a nationally distributed magazine called 'Mary Jane's Farm' and product lines such as linens sold at Target indicating the potential for savvy farmers to create off-shoot brands and businesses from agritourism-based businesses.

Fifty-two farmers markets already exist in the state. The markets in Boise and Moscow show that some markets are capable of handling in excess of 10,000 people per day. A good marketing plan will allow these other 50 markets to greatly increase crowds, expand the number and types of commodities offered for sale, and increase resulting sales of sustainable products

3.4 Agricultural diversity

Southwest Idaho is comprised of a multitude of diverse landscapes and ecosystems prime for tourism opportunities. Landscapes include: desert shrubland, sagebrush steppe, rivers, reservoirs, mountains, livestock, agricultural operations and small to large rapidly expanding municipalities. Agriculture is the largest economic driver in southwest Idaho, compromising an estimated economic impact of more than $1.3 billion dollars per year to the economy of Idaho, with 6,623 farms and compromising more than 0.93 million ha. Of the 6,623 farms, 4,818 (73%) of them are smaller farming operations, being less than 20.2 ha (small agricultural operations. Farming operations ranging from small acreage to very large multi-million-dollar industries lie very close in proximity to rapidly expanding and growing urban municipalities. Larger cities in southwestern include: Boise (population 235,000), Meridian (population 119,000), Nampa (population 100,000) and Caldwell (population 60,000). These cities abut the agricultural production areas.

In southwest Idaho agricultural operations are varied, with a multitude of commodities available grown and managed for the market. As an example, Canyon County alone compromises 156,000 total ha, with 111,000 ha being owned/operated by agricultural and livestock operations (71.1% of the total area). Over 140 different major and minor agricultural commodities are produced in Canyon County, including crops such as alfalfa, pasture/hay, corn, grass, dry beans, herbs, sugar beets, onions, potatoes and various other specialty crops such as: grapes (wine), seeds (multiple crops), and orchards (apples, peaches, plums, nectarines, cherries, apricots, pears). Small to large livestock operations (cattle, lamb, sheep) also exist.

Agritourism is beginning to attract visitors to agricultural operations in this geographic area. This tourism educates, entertains, and generates additional income for the operation without degrading the environment. Given the growing population of southwest Idaho, travel routes, and proximity to urban metropolises both the large and small agricultural operations in southwest Idaho have an innovative opportunity to engage in this growing social and economic trend of agritourism more actively in the future. Innovative ideas, targeted marketing strategies and immersive agricultural tours could be a start in capturing this growing economic market, especially for smaller agricultural or livestock operations. Immersive and varied in-depth, hands-on, sensory-rich and memory-lasting tours have been initiated in this region on a few farms with success. These types of sustainable tours are poised for expansion to highlight this innovative and sustainable agritourism specialty market.

3.5 Agriculture heritage trail

Compared to other states, Idaho has the fifth largest agriculture economy as a percent of its gross domestic product. Idaho has over 4,800,000 ha of farmland. Only three states – California, Texas and Nebraska – have more irrigated farmland than Idaho. It's the irrigated farmland that accounts for a large majority of agricultural production in the state. More than 75% of Idaho's 1,525,000 ha of irrigated agricultural land is watered by surface water flowing from the Rocky Mountains into rivers that is delivered to fields via surface canals. Over 75,000 ha of this land is serviced by the Boise and Meridian and Nampa irrigation districts in Southwestern Idaho. One hundred years ago all 75,000 ha were used for growing food; however, by 2023 over 65% of this land was urban. The canals still deliver water to this land; however, a majority of water is now delivered to urban and suburban lots within these irrigation districts. In the next 30 years almost 100% of this land will be urban. Consequently, these two irrigation districts which helped establish agriculture in Idaho and develop the state's economy will no longer play an important role in Idaho's agricultural economy. Unlike other western states, Idaho has plenty of irrigation water for agriculture, the urban public, wildlife and recreation.

The existing canal network is completely working, delivers irrigation water to neighbourhoods, and is visible to urban residents of the region. Many of the canals deliver water near existing main highways. Sites along these canals could be used to tell the story of landscape transformation over the last 75 years. Scientists have proposed to develop a History of Agriculture Heritage Trail along a portion of these canals highlighting water sources (mountain snowpack), water storage reservoirs, the Boise River and the canal delivery system over time. In addition, famous Idaho crops produced in the region can be highlighted for locals and tourists in the area. Signage, kiosks, pamphlets and a website will be developed to provide relevant information about this heritage trail to the public. This would be an educational and historic trail for school children, the general public and tourists. The trail would provide people with information about their agricultural heritage and be sustainable because these important cultural sites will be preserved without degrading the existing environment. This agricultural heritage trail could impact upwards of 15,000 locals and 10,000 visitors on an annual basis. The canals can be used to tell a visual history of agriculture and the development of the state using signage, kiosks and websites (Fig. 1). Over three quarters of the state's population lives within driving distance of this historic farmland. This would help educate local school children and out-of-state visitors about the uniqueness of this agriculture.

Figure 1: An example of a canal belonging to the Boise Irrigation District flowing through a newer neighbourhood near the Boise/Meridian city border.

4 CONCLUSIONS AND RECOMMENDATIONS

This study was important because, through the survey process, it identified public support for developing a sustainable agritourism industry in Idaho. The survey also identified the types of agricultural products/activities that could be developed as foundational tourist destinations within the state. The answers to survey questions were used to develop priority areas for agritourism expansion. After these priorities were set, discussion for the expansion of each priority area was strategised. The key findings of this study were:

- 76% of survey respondents had no ties to agriculture, while 22% were either involved in the agricultural industry or considered agriculture very important to Idaho.
- Wine and wineries were listed as potential agricultural tourism destinations by more than half of surveyed Idaho residents. Cheese and cheese-related manufacturing, local farmers markets, and potato production and processing were considered potential tourism destinations by 47, 38 and 31% of Idahoans, respectively.
- Surveyed Idahoans overwhelmingly selected wine tasting/wineries (50%) and local farmers markets (46%) as places where they would take out-of-state visitors.
- Demographic factors of gender, age, education level, length of time living in Idaho and state geography often impacted the agritourism topics chosen by survey respondents.
- Idaho's wine industry has grown from one winery in 1975 to over 75 wineries and eight cideries in 2024. Grapes, wine production and wine tasting rooms continue to expand, resulting in an excellent growth potential for agritourism in Idaho.
- There are currently 52 farmers markets in Idaho. The weekly markets in Boise and Moscow each attract over 10,000 visitors. Idahoans find that visiting these local markets is a pleasant experience and tourists buy many of the commodities offered at these events. In addition to farmers markets, roadside stands and farm stores also attract many tourists. The addition of brochures and websites hold the potential to further increase this form of agritourism.

- Over 140 different major agricultural commodities are grown/produced in southwestern Idaho. Agritourism is beginning to attract visitors to agricultural operations here. Immersive and varied in-depth, hands-on, sensory-rich and memory-lasting agricultural tours have been initiated on a few farms and are poised for expansion to highlight this innovative and sustainable agritourism specialty market.
- A historic agriculture heritage trail is proposed with sites located along canals in the Boise and Meridian and Nampa irrigation districts. Landscape transformation and the canals can be used to tell a visual history of agriculture and the development of the state using signage, kiosks and websites. Over three quarters of the state's population lives within driving distance of this historic farmland. This would help educate local school children, local adults and out-of-state visitors about the uniqueness of this agriculture.

The agricultural commodities currently exist to make sustainable agritourism a much bigger factor in sustainable tourism in Idaho. Both large and small farms, commodity commissions and people with a stake in agriculture are enthusiastic about expanding this promising form of tourism in Idaho.

REFERENCES

[1] United Nations Environment Program & United Nations World Tourism Organization, *Making Tourism More Sustainable: A Guide for Policy Makers*, New York, pp. 11–12, 2005.
[2] Streimikiene, D., Svagzdiene, B., Jasinskas, E. & Simanavicius, A., Sustainable tourism development and competitiveness: The systematic literature review. *Sustainable Development,* **29**(1), pp. 259–271, 2021.
[3] Lu, J. & Nepal, S.K., Sustainable tourism research: An analysis of papers published in the *Journal of Sustainable Tourism. Journal of Sustainable Tourism,* **17**(1), pp. 5–16, 2009.
[4] Higgins-Desbiolles, F., Sustainable tourism: Sustaining tourism or something more? *Tourism Management Perspectives,* **25**(1), pp. 157–160, 2018.
[5] Budeanu, A., Miller, G., Mascardo, G. & Ool, C.-S., Sustainable tourism, progress, challenges and opportunities: An introduction. *Journal of Cleaner Production,* **111**(8), pp. 285–294, 2016.
[6] Miller, G. & Torres-Delgado, A., Measuring sustainable tourism: A state of the art review of sustainable tourism indicators. *Journal of Sustainable Tourism,* **31**(7), pp. 1483–1496, 2023.
[7] World Travel and Tourism Council, Agenda 21 for the Travel and Tourism Industry Towards Environmentally Sustainable Development. 1998. http:www.unep.fr/shared/publications/pdf/3207-TourismAgenda.pdf.
[8] Editorial: Sustainable tourism, progress, challenges, and opportunities: An introduction. *Journal of Cleaner Production,* **111**, pp. 285–294, 2016.
[9] Veeck, G., Che, D. & Veeck, A., America's changing farmscape: A study of agricultural tourism in Michigan. *The Professional Geographer,* **58**(3), pp. 235–248, 2006. https://doi.org/10/1111/j.1467-9272.2006.00565.x.
[10] Farsani, N.T., Ghotbabadi, S.S. & Altafi, M., Agricultural heritage as a creative tourism attraction. *Asia Pacific Journal of Tourism Research,* **24**(6), pp. 541–549, 2019. https://doi.org/10.1080/10941665.2019.1593205.
[11] Lee, M., Tourism and sustainable livelihoods: The case of Taiwan. *Third World Quarterly,* **29**(5), pp. 961–978, 2008. https://doi.org/10.1080/01436590802106148.

[12] Idaho Department of Labour, Idaho's resilient tourism sector and the increasing cost of travel. 2023. Idahoatwork.com.
[13] Mahler, R.L., Ghimire, N. & Agenbroad, A., Adding an agricultural component to sustainable tourism in Idaho, USA. *International Journal of Environmental Impacts*, **5**(2), pp. 116–127, 2022.
[14] Salent, P. & Dillman, D., *How to Conduct Your Own Survey*, John Wiley and Sons: New York, 1994.
[15] Dillman, D., *Mail and Internet Surveys: The Tailored Design Method*, John Wiley and Sons: New York, 2000.
[16] SAS Institute Inc., SAS Online Document 9.1.3. SAS Institute Inc.: Cary, NC, 2004.
[17] Mahler, R.L., Gamroth, M., Pearson, P., Sorenson, F., Barber, M.E. & Simmons, R., Information sources, learning opportunities and priority water issues in the Pacific Northwest. *Journal of Extension*, **48**(2), 2RIB2, 2010. http://www.joe.org/joe/2010april/rb2.php.
[18] Mahler, R. L., Simmons, R. & Sorensen, F., Drinking water issues in the Pacific Northwest. *Journal of Extension*, **43**(6), 6RIB6, 2005. http://www.joe.org/joe/2005december/rb6.php.
[19] Mahler, R.L. & Barber, M.E., Rivers and river basin management issues and concerns in the Pacific Northwest, USA. *WIT Transactions on Ecology and the Environment*, vol. 197, 2015. https://doi.org/10.2495/RM150011.
[20] United States Department of Agriculture, Idaho fruit tree census. 2006. https://www.agriculture.gov.au/sites/default/files/sitecollectiondocuments/ba/plant/submissions/paprika/idaho-fruit-tree-census-2006.pdf.
[21] Idaho Wine Commission, Who we are? 2024. https://idahowines.org/who-we-are/.
[22] Idaho Wine Commission, Economic Impact Report. 2019. https://idahowines.org/content/uploads/2023/06/CAI.ID-Wine-Commission.Econ-Impacts.Final-Report.-2019-0916.pdf.
[23] Warsaw, P., Archambault, S., He, A. & Miller, S., The economic, social and environmental impacts of farmers markets: Recent evidence from the US. *Sustainability*, **13**(6), 3423, 2021. https://www.mdpi.com/2071-1050/13/6/3423.
[24] Mayes, I., Tuesday market: An integrated management approach for a small farmers market for synergistic community benefits. *Journal of National Association of County Agricultural Agents*, **16**, 1, 2023.
[25] Ellis, S., Idaho's biggest foodie market thriving in Boise. Idaho Farm Bureau Federation. 2022. https://www.idahofb/org/news-room/posts/idaho-s-biggest-foodie-market-thriving-in-boise/.
[26] DePhelps, C. & Peterson, S., Estimating the economic contributions of the Moscow's farmers market. Western Economics Forum. 2020. https://ageconsearch.umn.edu.record/308127/?v=pdf.
[27] Pennsylvania State University College of Agricultural Sciences, Department of Agricultural Economics, Sociology and Education, Agritourism in Idaho. 2023. https://aese.psu.edu/outreach/agritourism/projects/nifa-agritourism/state-factsheets/west.

CHARACTERISATION OF SHORT-TERM RENTALS IN GRANADA, SPAIN: SPATIAL ANALYSIS

SOFÍA MENDOZA DE MIGUEL[1], RUBÉN VILLAR NAVASCUÉS[1], MANUEL DE LA CALLE[1], PATRICIA VALENZUELA[2], BEGOÑA GUIRAO[2], ARMANDO ORTUÑO[3], DANIEL GÁLVEZ-PÉREZ[2], FERNANDO DE MINGO[2] & JAIRO CASARES[4]
[1]Department of Geography, Universidad Complutense de Madrid, Spain
[2]Department of Transport Engineering, Regional and Urban Planning, Universidad Politécnica de Madrid, Spain
[3]Department of Civil Engineering, Universidad de Alicante, Spain
[4]Technical Civil Engineer, Spain

ABSTRACT

The popularisation of short-term rentals (STRs) as an alternative to traditional accommodation has changed the supply of accommodation in cities, as well as how tourists make use of the city. This type of accommodation is delocalised, which implies a greater use of the entire urban area, as well as its services and transport infrastructures. However, most of the supply follows the patterns of traditional accommodation and is concentrated in city centres, where most of the tourist resources are located, increasing the pressure on these spaces. This research aims to characterise the STRs in Granada to determine the mode and intensity of use of these accommodations in the urban area. The methodology is based on a detailed analysis by census sections of the supply of STRs, considering the number of accommodations and beds offered, their level of occupancy, the average rate per night, the average length of stay and indicators of tourist intensity. For this purpose, the database of the Andalusia Tourism Registry for the year 2023 and the database provided by the AirDNA platform for the period from January 2022 to June 2023 have been analysed and spatially represented at the census tract scale. The results indicate that Granada shows spatial distribution patterns where STR align closely with traditional accommodations, leading to increased tourist pressure in densely populated neighbourhoods. The highest concentrations are found around the historic centre and adjacent to the Alhambra-Generalife complex, specifically in the Albaicín and San Matías-Realejo neighbourhoods. These areas demonstrate higher occupancy rates that are on the rise, underscoring the need for measures to regulate the STR in Granada.

Keywords: short-term rentals, touristification, Airbnb, collaborative economy.

1 INTRODUCTION

In the years before the COVID-19 pandemic and again after the end of mobility restrictions, many European cities with cultural and monumental attractions, such as Granada, have experienced a rapid growth in the arrival of tourists and excursionists [1]. This tourist growth has been linked to processes of touristification with effects on space of a formal, functional, social and symbolic nature [2] in certain spaces, especially urban centres, where the leisure and tourism offer, and heritage and tourist resources are concentrated.

According to de la Calle Vaquero [3], touristification is manifested, in general terms, in: (a) the increase in the presence of visitors in the central areas of the city (to which can be added other areas of high tourist interest in the first urban periphery, as in the case of Granada); (b) the increase and expansion of consumer activities aimed at tourists: there is a proliferation of different forms of tourist accommodation (large hotel chains, boutique hotels, tourist apartments, short-term rentals (STRs), hostels, etc.), an increase in the number of souvenir shops, the opening of currency exchange businesses and the emergence of new forms of urban mobility linked to the development of digital businesses such as chauffeur-driven shuttle services, electric bike rentals and motorbike rentals; (c) a transformation of the commercial landscape, which is tending to become more Disneyfied and franchised: fast food and take-away businesses increase, there are changes in opening hours, prices and even customer service languages; (d) the tertiarisation of housing linked to new digital business models such as Airbnb and Vrbo (formerly HomeAway); and (e) the modification of the urban landscape, which is transformed into a recognisable tourist landscape in many European urban centres.

All these changes have several effects on city life, such as the displacement of residents away from tourist areas due to the proliferation of STRs and other types of tourist accommodation. As a result of increasing concern about the effects of STRs on residents' lives [4]–[7], some administrations have sought to regulate this activity [8], [9].

At the local (city) level, the regulation of tourist accommodation is mainly carried out from an urban planning approach, through instruments that refer to the physical planning of the city and that regulate the implementation of land uses. Accommodation, in its different types, is treated as a tertiary land use, with different levels of compatibility with residential use. The urban planning regulations, which are part of the urban development plans, regulate the procedure for the implementation of this land use. This procedure involves the processing of a municipal licence and may even involve the drawing up of a specific plan, as is the case in Barcelona and Madrid. In general terms, the regulations adopted make use of the practice of zoning. All the studies carried out recognise that tourist pressure is not homogeneous but tends to be concentrated in certain areas of urban centres. Thus, the territorial strategy is to contain the growth of accommodation in central areas by implementing the most restrictive measures such as higher licensing requirements or even the establishment of a moratorium. In contrast, in other parts of the city less affected by touristification, measures are much lenient, and accommodation is allowed to continue to grow. Indirectly, these zone-related differences in regulation may favour the expansion of tourism activities in peripheral areas, without jeopardising the tourism success of the destination as a whole [8]. As we will see in Section 2, since Granada intends to adopt a regulation and to apply zoning, it is appropriate to study the concentration of STR activity in the city.

Therefore, the aim of this research is to characterise the STRs in Granada in order to determine the mode and intensity of use of these accommodations in the urban area. The paper is structured as follows: the study area – the city of Granada – and the methodology are presented. The results section provides data and indicators that can help policy makers to make decisions on the application of the Junta de Andalucía's STR decree for the regulation of STRs. Finally, the conclusions of the paper are presented.

2 STUDY AREA

Granada is one of the main Andalusian cities, both in terms of population and economic activity and in terms of attracting tourists. In fact, the tourism sector is one of the main pillars of the economy and employment in this city [10], which has an important historical and cultural heritage, as well as international recognition. Granada has experienced a remarkable growth in the number of visitors to become the city with the highest number of tourists per resident (243,059 inhabitants in 2022 [11]) and one of the main urban destinations in Spain. According to the National Statistics Institute (NSI) [12], the city receives more than 4.5 million travellers per year between those who stay overnight and those who only visit for a day [1], [13]–[15].

The tourist area of Granada coincides with the places where the most emblematic monuments are located, some of which are declared World Heritage Sites by UNESCO. Above all, the 'Alhambra and Generalife' complex stands out, the most visited monument in the country with more than 2.5 million visitors in 2023 (a number very close to the maximum capacity of 2,763,500 visitors per year regulated by its public and marketing regulations) [14]–[16].

The city of Granada has shown signs of touristification for decades. Smith in his 1996 work [17] highlighted the phenomenon of tourist gentrification in the city, and de la Calle-Vaquero in his 2002 work [18] already pointed to the specialisation of tourism in the historic districts. However, it is only in recent years that critical voices have arisen in the face of the increase in tourist arrivals and the proliferation of STRs associated with this tourist growth, which is why Granada City Council has opted to regulate them. In February 2024, the Junta de Andalucía (regional government) approved Decree 31/2024, of 29 January, which modifies various regulations on tourist accommodation, tourist apartment establishments and hotels in the Autonomous Community of Andalusia. This decree gives local councils the power to put a stop to STRs. One of the cities that contemplates the application of this decree at municipal level is Granada, through the modification of the General Urban Development Plan (PGOU) that has been in force in the city since 2001. Until the final approval of the plan, the Granada City Council has suspended the granting of new licences for STRs. The modification of the PGOU contemplates a series of mandatory requirements such as having independent supply installations (electricity, water or telephone), as well as independent access from the street, a measure that has already been approved in the regulation of STRs in Madrid [19]. Despite the intention to approve a specific regulation for STRs, the Granada City Council denies that the city is under stress, except in specific situations [20].

This study is based on the fundamental idea that not all the municipality of Granada is affected in the same way by the growth of STRs and that the rest of the accommodation and its concentration, although to a lesser extent, also favours the touristification of certain areas. This study aims to analyse the spatial distribution of the supply of all types of accommodation in the city, as well as, in a more detailed way, of the STRs (Section 3), also offering indicators of tourist density and intensity at the census section level.

3 DATA AND METHODS

Recently, some studies have already analysed the spatial distribution of tourism supply using data from the Andalusian Tourism Registry (ATR) [21] or data mapped from Airbnb [14], at the neighbourhood scale. This study combines the use of different sources and performs an analysis at the census section level, to obtain an updated and more detailed picture of the phenomenon and improve its characterisation. To meet the proposed objectives, a descriptive spatial analysis has been carried out at the census section and district level of the following variables: the number of accommodations and beds offered, their spatial distribution, their occupancy level, the average rate per night, indicators of tourist intensity (beds in tourist accommodations per 1,000 registered inhabitants and percentage of STR concerning the total number of dwellings).

Three sources of information were used to extract the data. Firstly, for the analysis of both the hotel and STRs offer, the database of the ATR for the year 2023 has been consulted, a database that the regional government of Andalusia makes available for consultation of the accommodation offer in the region (hotels, hostels, STRs, etc.). Secondly, to evaluate some of the characteristics of the STRs, the database provided by the AirDNA platform (a company that uses web scraping techniques to provide data from P2P tourist rental platforms) has been consulted for the period between January 2022 and June 2023. The analysis has focused on the high season, which in Granada coincides with October 2022, as since 2017 it has always registered the highest occupancy peak. This database, which mainly includes the STRs offered on the Airbnb platform, allows for a more in-depth analysis of this type of accommodation by analysing occupancy (calculated as the percentage of days of the month booked), the type of accommodation (full or room), the average stay (days booked divided by total bookings), the maximum number of guests per accommodation or the average daily rate (ADR). The ADR according to AirDNA is a metric that represents the average revenue earned per occupied room paid per day. It is calculated by dividing the total revenue generated by nights booked by the number of nights booked, and cleaning fees are included in the calculation. To identify those accommodations that were active, only those that had a day available or booked in the month analysed were considered. Thirdly, for the calculation of the tourism density and intensity indicators, population and housing data at the census section level from the NSI's 2021 Population and Housing Census have been used.

4 RESULTS

4.1 Data from the Andalusian Tourism Registry

According to data from the ATR for 2023, the city of Granada has 3,309 accommodation units, with a total of 35,517 bed places. Hotel establishments and STRs provide a similar number of bed places, although the latter are much more numerous than the former (Table 1).

Table 1: Tourist accommodation in the city of Granada. *(Source: ATR, 2023.)*

Type	Establishments		Beds	
	Number	Percentage	Number	Percentage
Hotel establishments (hotels, guesthouses, hostels, etc.)	205	6.20	16,054	46.50
Tourist apartments	109	3.29	3,354	9.71
Tourist dwelling for rural accommodation	18	0.54	121	0.35
STR	2,977	89.97	14,998	43.44
Total	3,309	100	34,527	100

Hotel establishments make up the most traditional and consolidated offer of accommodation in urban destinations. Granada's offer is made up of 205 establishments with 16,054 beds. Most of the capacity corresponds to hotels in the strict sense of the term (102 establishments and 12,870 beds), mainly three-, and four-star hotels. Another traditional component is guesthouses (66 with 1,525 beds), with similar dynamics to hostels (21 and 714), especially those of the lowest category (Table 2). At another level, hostels, establishments with collective rooms that represent a relatively recent component of the accommodation offer in Spanish cities, stand out.

Tourist apartments also provide a significant accommodation capacity, with a total of 109 establishments (3.29% of the total) and 3,354 bed places (9.71). In contrast, there are only 18 rural tourist accommodation establishments, in all cases rural tourist accommodation dwellings: 18 units (0.54%) with 121 bed places (0.35%).

As far as STRs are concerned, they account for most of the registered accommodation establishments (2,977, 89.97%). On the other hand, their contribution in terms of accommodation capacity is slightly lower than that of hotel establishments, with 6,583 rooms (41.78%) and 14,998 bed places (43.44%). Thus, the average number of rooms per dwelling is 2.21 and the average number of bed places is 5.04. Regarding typologies, most of them are

Table 2: Hotel establishments in the city of Granada. *(Source: ATR, 2023.)*

Type and category		Establishments		Bed places	
		Number	Percentage	Number	Percentage
Youth hostels		16	7.80	945	5.89
Guesthouses		66	32.20	1,525	9.50
Hostel	1*	10	4.88	259	1.61
	2*	11	5.37	455	2.83
	Total hostels	21	10.24	714	4.45
Hotels	1*	5	2.44	167	1.04
	2*	13	6.34	546	3.40
	3*	40	19.51	2,348	14.63
	4*	37	18.05	8,607	53.61
	5*	6	2.93	1,160	7.23
	Grand luxury	1	0.49	42	0.26
	Total hotels	102	49.76	12,870	80.17
Total		205	100	16,054	100

complete dwellings (2,795), with the presence of dwellings offered by rooms being much more exceptional (182). It should be noted that this is a quantitatively very important supply, now almost equivalent in magnitude to the hotel component, and above all that it has grown vertiginously over the last few years. Among other factors, this growth has been encouraged by the ease of converting a property into a holiday home, which contrasts with the lengthy periods associated with the creation of a hotel establishment.

According to the 2022 Municipal Register, Granada has a population of 228,682 inhabitants. This means that there are 150.98 officially registered accommodation places per 1,000 inhabitants. If we limit ourselves to STRs, the figure is 65.58. These are very high figures, reflecting the high tourist pressure on the city. As a comparative example, in Donostia-San Sebastián, the figures are 92.99 accommodation places per 1,000 inhabitants and 32.99 for STRs. Moreover, this accommodation pressure is not homogeneously distributed, as tourists and tourist activities have very selective spatial consumption patterns. In this sense, the spatial distribution of accommodation supply also reflects a strong concentration. If we take as a reference the administrative districts of the municipality, we observe a strong concentration of supply in five districts which are above two thousand accommodation places between STR and traditional accommodation, which are the five districts which occupy the city centre, in order of places: Centro-Sagrario (8,495), San Matías-Realejo (8,302), Figares (4,534), Albaicín (3,038) and Ronda (2,263) (cf. Fig. 1). The distribution of accommodation types within each neighbourhood also reflects a very contrasting reality. As noted above, 46.5% of the tourist accommodation in Granada corresponds to hotel establishments and another 43.44% to STRs. This distribution is like the distribution registered in the neighbourhoods with the most accommodation places: Centro-Sagrario (57.69% and 42.31%), which also provides the largest accommodation capacity for the city, San Matías-Realejo (57.58% and 42.42%), Figares (66.08% and 33.92%) and Ronda (65.98% and 34.02%). On the other hand, Albaicín stands out for its strong specialisation in tourist accommodation, whose STR vacancies represent 74.79% of the total number of vacancies.

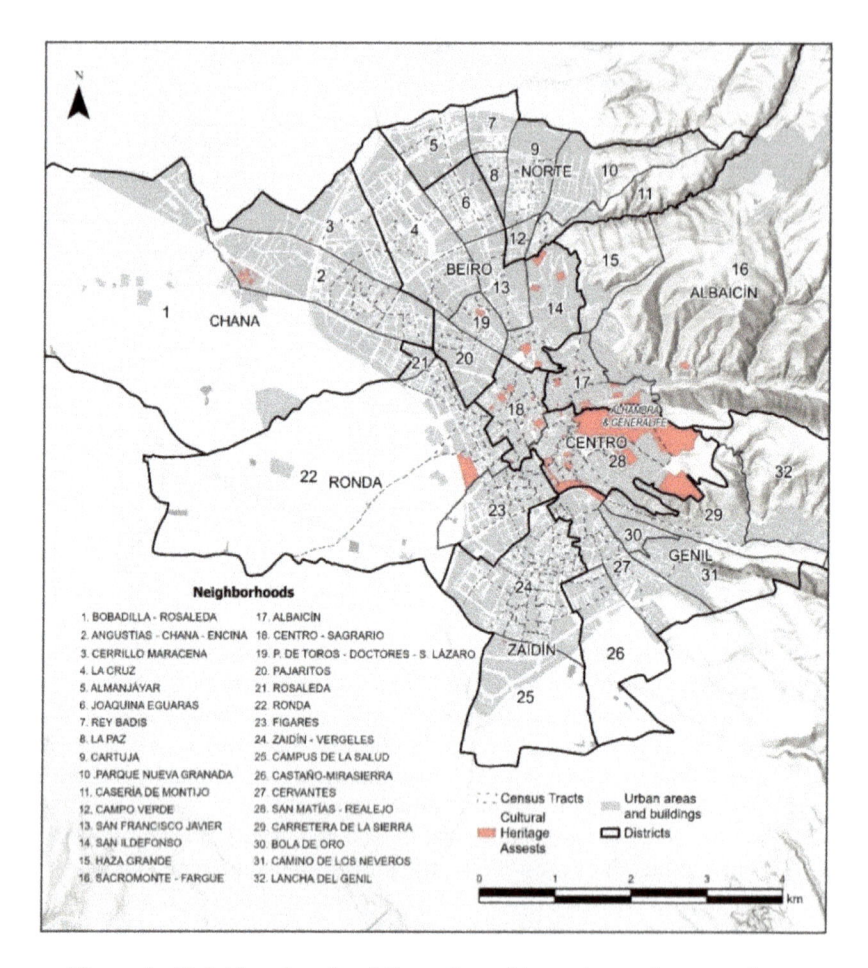

Figure 1: Neighbourhoods of Granada and its main tourist attractions.

Historically, this distribution pattern corresponds to a concentration of conventional accommodation in the city centre, where several large, high-class hotels were in the main streets and squares. At the same time, there was a wide range of hostels and guesthouses in shared-use buildings. Subsequently, there was a significant growth in the conventional offer in more peripheral areas, with the establishment of three and four-star hotels that took advantage of lower land prices with greater availability of surface area and accessibility by private vehicle. The recent wave of touristification, whose distinctive feature is the expansion of tourist housing, has led to the widespread introduction of this type of accommodation throughout the urban area. In the case of Granada, the penetration in the Albaicín neighbourhood stands out, a neighbourhood of undeniable tourist attraction, but with urban conditions that made it difficult to establish large hotels.

As noted above, at city level there are 150.98 officially registered accommodation places per 1,000 inhabitants. This average is much higher in the neighbourhoods close to the Alhambra and Generalife heritage complex: Centro-Sagrario (667.7), Albaicín (745.9) and San Matías-Realejo (878.2), where the installed accommodation capacity tends to be closer to the registered population (Table 3).

Table 3: Supply and indicators of tourist pressure in Granada's most overcrowded neighbourhoods. (*Source: ATR, 2023.*)

District	Neighbourhood	Population	STR beds	Remaining beds	Total beds	STR beds per 1,000 inhab.	Total beds per 1,000 inhab.	STR/total dwellings
Centro	San Matías-Realejo	9,453	3,522	4,780	8,302	372.6	878,2	20.9%
Albaicín	Albaicín	4,073	2,272	766	3,038	557.8	745.9	35.1%
Centro	Centro-Sagrario	12,723	3,594	4,901	8,495	282.5	667.7	14%
Beiro	San Ildefonso	4,209	631	528	1159	149.9	275.4	8.4%
Ronda	Figares	19,316	1,538	2,996	4,534	79.6	234.7	5.6%
Chana	Bobadilla-Rosaleda	1,567	10	217	227	6.4	144.9	0.6%
Albaicín	Sacromonte-Fargue	2,525	234	84	318	92.7	125.9	7.7%
Genil	Carretera de la sierra	4,979	199	424	623	40	125.1	3.3%
Genil	Castaño-Mirasierra	5,403	30	535	565	5.6	104.6	0.7%
Beiro	Pajaritos	5,074	173	414	587	34.1	115.7	2.1%
Ronda	Ronda	20,243	770	1,493	2,263	38	111.8	2.3%

In terms of STRs, these three neighbourhoods also have the highest values, but the values for the Albaicín (557.8) are higher than those for Centro-Sagrario (282.5) and San Matías-Realejo (372.6), and in any case much higher than those recorded for the city (65.58). The percentage of STRs concerning residential dwellings is quite high in the most touristy neighbourhoods close to the heritage complex of the Alhambra and the Generalife. In Albaicín, 35.1% of dwellings are destined for STRs, 14% in Centro-Sagrario and 20.9% in San Matías-Realejo, very high percentages which testify to the tension in the area and explain the displacement of residents away from the most touristy areas of the city. Furthermore, if we focus the analysis on the census units, it can be seen in Fig. 2 that the centre shows the highest indicators of tourist pressure, a phenomenon which extends not to the whole of the Albaicín, but only to the lower part, which is more touristy and closer to the Alhambra and Generalife complex.

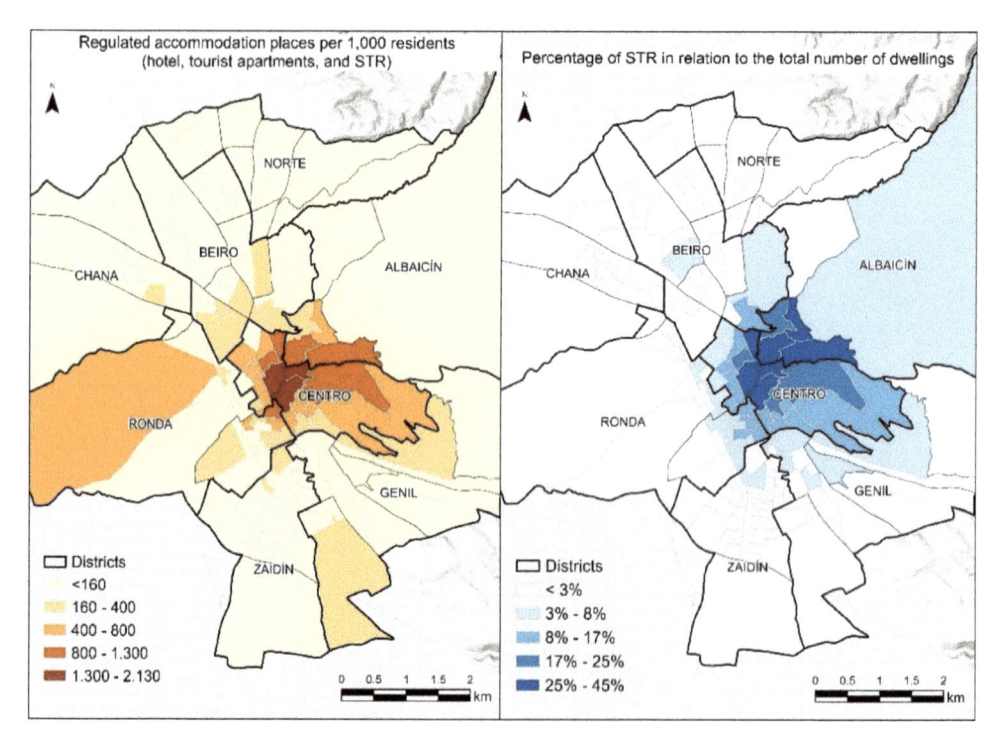

Figure 2: Indicators of tourism pressure and intensity by census tract (2023). *(Source: Own elaboration with data from ATR, 2023.)*

4.2 Data from AirDNA

According to the AirDNA data for the year 2023, the municipality of Granada has 3,203 STRs, totalling 16,015 bed places, which is 226 dwellings and 1,017 bed places more than those provided by the ATR database. These data mean that, according to the AirDNA database, there are 70.03 parking spaces per thousand inhabitants in Granada, a very high number which, moreover, as we saw in the previous section, is not evenly distributed throughout the urban area. However, considering the occupancy data, during the last high season (October 2022), the total number of STRs with a day available or booked was limited to 3,125 and 13,370 beds.

As can be seen in Table 4, the vast majority of STRs are concentrated in the Centro district with 1,636 units representing almost half of the supply (52.3%), followed by Albaicín with 20% of the units. The average length of stay for the whole city is 2.9 days per booking made in a STR, with average values between 2 and 3 days for the most touristic census sections in the Centro and Albaicín districts.

Table 4: Distribution and characteristics of STRs by districts in October 2022. *(Source: Own elaboration with data from AirDNA, 2022.)*

District	Typology	Number of STR	Beds	Average beds per STR	ADR	Occupancy rate	Average length of stay
Centro	Entire home	1,368	6,270	4.58	126	57.52	2.46
Centro	Room	268	703	2.62	69.16	43.51	1.89
Albaicín	Entire home	521	2,293	4.40	128	58	2.62
Albaicín	Room	102	230	2.25	69.46	48.23	2.65
Ronda	Entire home	290	1,609	5.55	119.32	50.57	2.70
Ronda	Room	57	133	2.33	72.44	40.41	2.20
Beiro	Entire home	146	686	4.70	95.39	45.85	2.26
Beiro	Room	71	118	1.66	40.04	33.21	2.82
Zaidín	Entire home	81	407	5.02	99.52	42.05	2.80
Zaidín	Room	50	89	1.78	37.19	38.77	3.50
Genil	Entire home	100	621	6.21	180.38	42.13	2.31
Genil	Room	16	33	2.06	38.22	22.98	1.43
Chana	Entire home	16	76	4.75	110.43	33.06	3.16
Chana	Room	15	24	1.60	45.71	27.74	2.38
Norte	Entire home	9	49	5.44	69.24	37.63	1.29
Norte	Room	15	29	1.93	52.68	29.25	2.59
TOTAL		3,125	13,370	4.28	112.98	52.18	2.90

On the other hand, the AirDNA database allows us to know the type of renting of STRs depending on whether the whole house is rented or individual or shared rooms. In Granada, 80% of the ads represent complete dwellings, compared to 20% that are private or shared rooms, data that draw attention to the specialisation of this activity as a business, far removed from the initial spirit of the collaborative economy. In terms of occupancy, the trend is increasing in the period from January 2022 to June 2023. For example, in April 2022, occupancy was 54%, compared to 66% in the same month in 2023. The lowest occupancy months are January (37% in 2022 and 41% in 2023) and July (41% in 2022), while the highest occupancy months are April (54% in 2022 and 66% in 2023) and October (58% in 2022). Spatially, the highest occupancy values, located in the range of 50%–66%, are in the most touristic neighbourhoods of the Centro and Albaicín districts. It is also worth noting the high occupancy values of census tracts in neighbourhoods close to the aforementioned districts, such as Figares, Ronda, San Ildefonso or Carretera de la Sierra (Fig. 3).

Likewise, the AirDNA database allows us to know the ADR in the city of Granada. For October 2022, traditionally the busiest month in the city, the highest rates per night are found

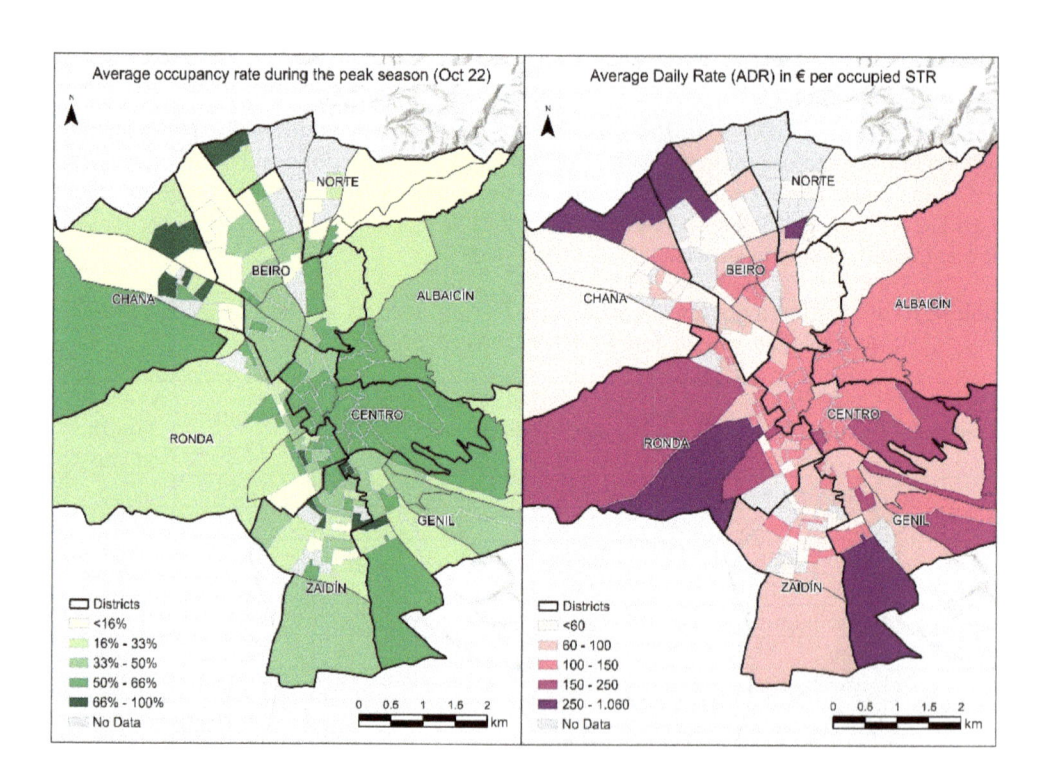

Figure 3: STR characteristics: Average daily rate and occupancy per census track. *(Source: Own elaboration with data from AirDNA, October 2022.)*

in the Genil district for full accommodation (€180.38/night), one of the districts where there is less supply of STR but with the highest capacity (on average 6.21 beds per STR). The next districts with the highest rates are, in order, Albaicín (€128/night), Centro (€126/night), and Ronda (€119.32/night). The spatial distribution of the ADRs allows us to identify different areas, with the lowest prices in the northern and southern districts, values of around €100–€150/night in the census sections of the Centro and Albaicín districts, and the highest values in peripheral areas of the city, possibly linked to single-family housing typologies.

5 CONCLUSIONS

Granada has experienced a remarkable growth in the supply of accommodation in recent years in which the growth in the supply of STRs stands out. The results obtained from the spatial analysis of STRs are very similar to those described in the literature [14], [15], [21], which suggest that the radius of action of tourist activity is concentrated in the historic city centres and adjacent neighbourhoods. On the other hand, the use of two database sources (ATR and AirDNA) and their relationship with the NSI's 2021 Population and Housing Census, has allowed us to carry out a detailed analysis of the characteristics of the STRs and to contrast whether there is a pronounced shadow economy linked to this activity. As already exposed by Cerezo-Medina et al. [21], the similarity of the number of STRs in the ATR and AirDNA databases suggests that in the city of Granada the volume of STRs in the shadow economy is dynamic and very sensitive to economic, social and regulatory changes, which makes STRs vary over time.

The spatial analysis carried out in Granada indicates a recent upward trend in the occupancy levels of STRs that could continue to increase in the coming years if their activity is not regulated. This type of accommodation represents almost half of the tourist bed spaces and is located, like the rest of the tourist accommodation on offer, mainly in the districts of the Centro and Albaicín districts, where the main tourist resources of the city and the best transport connections are located. The average length of stay is less than 3 days on average, and the average nightly rate in the more central accommodation is not excessively higher than in the more peripheral locations.

The calculated indicators of tourist intensity (beds in any type of accommodation per 1,000 residents) show significantly high values in the neighbourhoods closest to the Alhambra, such as San Matías-Realejo (878 beds per 1,000 inhabitants), Albaicín (745), and Centro-Sagrario (667). Likewise, in these neighbourhoods, a high percentage of STRs concerning total dwellings has been identified, especially in Albaicín, with 35.1%, and San Matías-Realejo, with 20.9%. In both cases, the concentration of STRs is directly linked to the distance to the Alhambra and Generalife heritage complex, but there are also economic factors that explain the concentration of STRs in city centres, for example, the profits from STRs, which in Granada can reach values of around €100-€150/night, are higher than the returns from residential rentals [21].

This data could be used to establish a zoning system for the regulation of STRs in Granada. If we look at the models approved in other Spanish cities such as Barcelona, Madrid or San Sebastian, which have developed explicit zoning in the regulation of STRs, the city could be divided into at least three zones: a first 'saturated' zone including the city centre and the areas of Albaicín and San Matías-Realejo closer to the heritage complex of Alhambra and Generalife, with greater restrictions; a second 'high demand' zone including the rest of Albaicín and San Matías-Realejo, and the areas adjacent to the neighbourhoods bordering Centro, Albaicín and San Matías-Realejo, where supply can be increased with restrictions; and a third ring with the rest of the city with no restrictions on increasing supply.

The central argument for establishing zoning in the regulation of the STRs is to contain the touristification of urban centres and, in this case, also of the Albaicín area, whose functionality is changing with the increase in tourists. This tourist development puts pressure on the housing market, as it means a reduction in the supply of housing for the resident population. It also implies problems of coexistence and nuisance to neighbours. It also favours the commercial transformation of the neighbourhoods affected, as the supply tends to be oriented towards tourist demand. As a final result, displacement processes are accentuated, affecting above all the groups with the least purchasing power. In short, the regulation of STRs is seen as a necessary instrument for the containment of touristification.

Finally, although the regulation of STRs is a priority, it is also considered necessary to balance the tourist offer, in the sense of advocating an equivalent framework for all types of accommodation, the proliferation of which affects the transformation of historic centres in the same way.

ACKNOWLEDGEMENTS

The publication is part of the project PID2021-124428OB-I00, funded by 'MCIN/AEI/10.13039/501100011033/ERDF, EU', where PID2021-124428OB-I00 is the reference that appears in the award resolution; MCIN is the acronym of the Ministry of Science and Innovation; AEI is the acronym of the State Research Agency; 10.13039/501100011033 is the DOI (Digital Object Identifier) of the Agency; and ERDF is the acronym of the European Regional Development Fund

REFERENCES

[1] Navarro Valverde, F.A. & Capote Lama, A., ¿Overtourism en la ciudad de Granada?: una aproximación a la percepción de turistas, residentes y partidos políticos locales. *Cuadernos Geográficos*, **60**(1), pp. 35–53, 2020. https://doi.org/10.30827/cuadgeo.v60i1.13717.

[2] García-Hernández, M., de la Calle-Vaquero, M. & Yubero, C., Cultural heritage and urban tourism: Historic city centres under pressure. *Sustainability (Switzerland)*, **9**(8), 2017. https://doi.org/10.3390/su9081346.

[3] de la Calle Vaquero, M., Turistificación de centros urbanos: clarificando el debate. *Boletin de La Asociacion de Geografos Espanoles*, **83**, pp. 1–40, 2019.

[4] Chamusca, P., Rio Fernandes, J., Carvalho, L. & Mendes, T., The role of Airbnb creating a 'new'-old city centre: Facts, problems and controversies in Porto. *Boletín de la Asociación de Geógrafos Españoles*, **83**, 2820, 2019. http://doi.org/10.21138/bage.2820.

[5] Garay, L., Morales, S. & Wilson, J., Tweeting the right to the city: Digital protest and resistance surrounding the Airbnb effect. *Scandinavian Journal of Hospitality and Tourism*, pp. 1–22, 2020. https://doi.org/10.1080/15022250.2020.1772867.

[6] Milano, C., Overtourism, malestar social y turismofobia. Un debate controvertido. *PASOS. Revista de Turismo y Patrimonio Cultural*, **18**(3), pp. 551–564, 2018. https://doi.org/10.25145/j.pasos.2018.16.041.

[7] Novy, J. & Colomb, C., Urban tourism as a source of contention and social mobilisations: A critical review urban tourism as a source of contention and social. *Tourism Planning and Development*, pp. 1–18, 2019. https://doi.org/10.1080/21568316.2019.1577293.

[8] de la Calle-Vaquero M., García-Hernández, M. & Mendoza de Miguel, S., Urban planning regulations for tourism in the context of overtourism: Applications in historic centres. *Sustainability*, **13**(1), p. 70, 2021. https://doi.org/10.3390/su13010070.

[9] Cassell, M.K. & Deutsch, A.M., Urban challenges and the gig economy: How German cities cope with the rise of Airbnb. *German Politics*, pp. 1–22, 2020. https://doi.org/10.1080/09644008.2020.1719072.

[10] Consejo Social de la Ciudad de Granada, EG2020: Haciendo humano lo urbano. Documento marco: Plan Estratégico de Granada. https://www.granada.org/ob2.nsf/in/EG2020/$file/EG2020_Estrategia_Granada_2020_Haciendo_humano_lo_urbano.pdf. Accessed on: 7 Jul. 2024.

[11] Estadísticas de población y empadronados: Municipio Granada a 1 de enero de 2022. https://www.granada.org/intranet/idegeogr.nsf/v/estadisticas-pob-2022#:~:text=CIFRAS%20PADR%C3%93N%20MUNICIPAL%20DE%20HABITANTES,de%20los%20registros%20administrativamente%20activos. Accessed on: 7 Jul. 2024.

[12] National Statistics Institute, Encuesta de Ocupación Hotelera, 2023. https://www.ine.es/jaxiT3/Tabla.htm?t=2078. Accessed on: 2 Jul. 2024.

[13] Guaita Martínez, J.M., Martín Martín, J.M., Salinas Fernández, J.A. & Ribeiro Soriano, D.E., Tourist accommodation, consumption and platforms. *International Journal of Consumer Studies*, **47**(3), pp. 1011–1022, 2023.

[14] Navarro-Valverde, F.A., Capote-Lama, A., Barrero-Rescalvo, M. & Díaz-Parra, I., The pain of being a resident in Granada: Analysis of the accommodation offer and residents' perception. *Urban Dynamics in the Post-Pandemic Period*, eds E. Navarro-Jurado, R. Larrubia Vargas, F. Almeida-García & J.J. Natera Rivas, Springer: Cham, 2023. https://doi.org/10.1007/978-3-031-36017-6_2.

[15] García Álvarez, D., Análisis espacial del alojamiento ofertado a través de nuevas plataformas de economía colaborativa en la ciudad de Granada. *XXVI Congreso de la Asociación Española de Geografía. Crisis y espacios de oportunidad. Retos para la geografía*, October, 2019.

[16] Patronato de la Alhambra y Generalife. https://www.alhambra-patronato.es/notas-prensa/la-alhambra-recibe-y-homenajea-a-su-visitante-numero-un-millon. Accessed on: 7 Jul. 2024.

[17] Smith, N., La nueva frontera urbana. Ciudad revanchista y gentrificación. Traficantes de sueños, Madrid, 2012.

[18] de la Calle-Vaquero, M., La ciudad histórica como destino turístico, Ariel: Barcelona, 2002

[19] Vallejo, S., Las medidas de Granada para limitar los pisos turísticos: congela temporalmente las licencias y endurece los requisitos. Granada Hoy. https://www.granadahoy.com/granada/Granada-medidas-limite-pisos-turisticos-congelar-licencias-PGOU-requisitos_0_1911409555.html.

[20] Vallejo, S., Límite a los pisos turísticos: Granada asumirá el decreto de la Junta y niega que la ciudad esté tensionada. Granada Hoy. https://www.granadahoy.com/granada/Limite-pisos-turisticos-Granada-decreto-Junta_0_1870013762.html.

[21] Cerezo-Medina, A., Romero-Padilla, Y., García-López, A., Navarro-Jurado, E., Sortino-Barrionuevo, J.F. & Guevara-Plaza, A., Comparative analysis of short-term rental homes and traditional accommodation in Andalusian tourist cities: Intensity, density, and potential expansion areas. *Current Issues in Tourism*, **25**(11), pp. 1782–1797, 2021. https://doi.org/10.1080/13683500.2021.1983522.

PUBLIC TRANSPORT AS AN OPPORTUNITY TO PROMOTE TOURIST HOMES IN URBAN PERIPHERIES: THE CASE OF MADRID, SPAIN

DANIEL GÁLVEZ-PÉREZ[1], BEGOÑA GUIRAO[1], PATRICIA VALENZUELA[1], ARMANDO ORTUÑO[2], INMACULADA MOHÍNO[1], FERNANDO DE MINGO[1] & MANUEL DE LA CALLE[3]
[1]Department of Transport Engineering, Regional and Urban Planning, Universidad Politécnica de Madrid, Spain
[2]Department of Civil Engineering, Universidad de Alicante, Spain
[3]Universidad Complutense de Madrid, Spain

ABSTRACT

The implementation of the collaborative economy in the tourist sector has led to a partial relocation of the accommodation (traditionally concentrated on hotels and resorts) through tourist homes scattered all over the city. Although some aspects of this new phenomenon (such as its impact on hotel occupation, the housing and long-time rental price) have been already analysed, socioeconomic and urban factors influencing tourists' accommodation choice need to be explored. This research aims to analyse and quantify the role of the urban public transport network on the occupation and promotion of tourist homes in contrast to other urban factors. The research is based in Madrid, a first-class urban tourist destination with a dense and efficient public transport system which may be an opportunity for peripheral accommodation locations compared to homes located in the city centre (usually at higher fares). Based on information of tourist homes in the city of Madrid provided by AirDNA for the period 2022–2023 (number of housings, fares, occupation rates, type of home, etc.), this research develops a methodology that relates the role of the urban public transport network and the occupation of tourist homes. To achieve this, linear regression models have been applied to two groups of accommodations separately: those located in the city centre and those located in the periphery. Results show that, for all accommodations, occupancy is strongly dependent on the average daily rate and the rating. However, for the group of accommodations located in the periphery, the distance to the nearest bus station also exhibits significant importance, highlighting the role of public transportation in decentralising the concentration of tourist accommodations and promoting greater sustainability in tourism within our cities.
Keywords: tourist homes, collaborative economy, urban mobility, social cohesion, public transport.

1 INTRODUCTION

City tourism, or urban tourism [1], [2], is a growing sector, and one of the fundamental causes of this expansion, especially in European capitals, is attributed to the emergence of new types of accommodation compared to the traditional hotel and catering industry. The rise of the collaborative economy, called the 'platform economy', has brought with it a relocation of traditional hotel accommodation, previously concentrated in fixed points of the city, and thus, tourist apartments, tourist homes and even shared rooms have emerged scattered around the city, most of them managed by large digital platforms 'of minimums' (lean platforms), with minimal costs, as they only manage the matching of hosts and guests, without owning any real estate assets. One of the main attractions [1] of this type of accommodation, apart from the cost and the ease of digital booking, lies in the tourist's desire to break away from traditional tourist circuits (off the beaten track) and identify with the local residents (live like a local). In the context of the growing urban tourism due to the proliferation of tourist accommodations, the leading international platform managing a significant portion of real estate assets is Airbnb, founded in 2018. It stands as the largest operator of tourist accommodations, with its success attributed to the seamless digital connection between hosts and guests. Any study analysing the supply and demand of tourist accommodations relies on the Airbnb database.

The rental of tourist housing scattered throughout the urban fabric places a 'floating tourist' in the city who moves, generating impacts on the centres of activity (restaurants, shops, museums, etc.), on public space and on mobility. To date, some aspects of this new tourism model have been analysed, such as the competitive advantages offered by this type of accommodation compared to pre-existing hotels for certain tourist profiles [3], its impact on hotel occupancy [4], sustainability [5] and house prices [6]. However, there are still unexplored lines of research around these new tourism models that examine the nature of the relationships between the mobility of this guest profile and the territory. The new tourist will trace new routes around the city, access public transport in a more delocalised way and likely visit activity centres different from those they would have explored if accommodated in a traditional hotel establishment.

While most major European tourist capitals boast dense and efficient public transportation systems, the concentration of tourist accommodations in the urban centre, often coinciding with the historic district, is a reality. This concentration is, in many cases, exerting pressure on the local population, leading to civic resistance from the inhabitants of these urban centres [7], phenomena associated with the concepts of 'gentrification' and 'touristification' [8]. Additionally, the clustering of tourist accommodations in the city centre implies a concentration of income (for hosts and local businesses) in this area, so a decentralisation of accommodations would bring about a redistribution of tourism-derived income to other areas, fostering greater social and territorial cohesion in the pursuit of a more sustainable form of tourism.

The study of the current spatial distribution of tourist housing in a city, characterising the supply, is key to identifying the neighbourhoods with the highest concentration of tourist housing. On the other hand, the analysis of access to the public transport system of accommodation located in non-central geographical locations (usually with lower fares) is essential to promote a decentralisation of tourist housing in cities; even laying the foundations for a possible zoning regulation (as has already been done in Barcelona).

In this context, the aim of this paper is to analyse the conditioning factors of the choice of a tourist home using a weighted occupancy indicator and paying special attention to the accessibility of the homes to the public transport system. Madrid is a good case study, as it is representative of urban tourism in large cities in a country that is a world power in the tourism sector (more than 10% of GDP in 2019 came from this economic sector). In addition, the city offers a consolidated market for tourist housing (according to AirDNA data, 19,000 units in 2023), and has a dense and efficient public transport system. The methodology is based on an analysis of occupancy, with data provided by AirDNA of tourist homes in Madrid in the period 2022–2023, together with a study of the accessibility of tourist homes to the transport network.

This article is structured as follows: Section 1 includes the introduction; Section 2, the case study; Section 3, the methodology used; Section 4, the results of the analysis; and, finally, Section 5 includes the conclusions and future research lines.

2 MADRID CASE STUDY

Madrid is the capital of Spain, a country where tourism plays a crucial role in the economy. In 2019, tourism accounted for 12.4% of the total GDP and 13.5% of employment. However, the COVID-19 pandemic that began in 2020 led to a significant decline in the tourism GDP, reducing it to 5.5% of the total GDP, although it continued to represent 12% of Spanish employments [9]. Additionally, in recent years, tourism has been gaining importance in the

Community of Madrid, increasing from representing 6.0% of the GDP in 2015 to 7.1% in 2019 [10].

The selection of Madrid as a case study is, therefore, representative of urban tourism in major European capitals and additionally provides a dataset comprising nearly 20,000 tourist accommodations. With a population exceeding three million inhabitants, Madrid is part of one of the most segregated metropolitan areas in Europe [11]. Consequently, various distinct realities coexist within the city of Madrid, spatially configured into three major areas: the central core, or Central Almond, the north periphery, and the south periphery (Fig. 1). These zones exhibit differentiated characteristics in factors related to the existing residential stock, the resident population, prices, the real estate market, or the influence of new phenomena, such as the so-called 'collaborative economy', manifested in the emergence of tourist-use residences [12], which are analysed in this article.

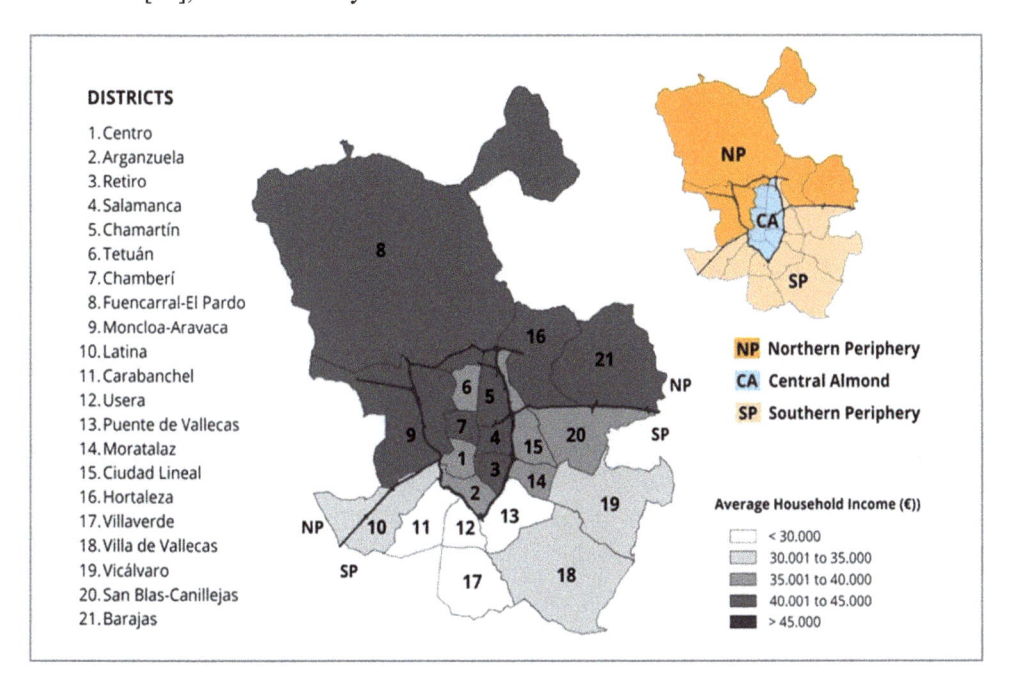

Figure 1: Distribution of the average annual income of households in each district of Madrid.

The Central Almond comprises primarily the districts of Centro, Arganzuela, Retiro, Salamanca, Chamartín, Tetuán, and Chamberí, although the City Council of Madrid also occasionally includes part of an eighth district, Moncloa-Aravaca (Fig. 1). This area is privileged, where individuals with medium and low incomes face diminishing prospects for housing access. It is subject to real estate dynamics, with recent years witnessing processes such as gentrification, touristification [13], and the channelling of international financial flows into real estate investments.

The north periphery encompasses the northern arc of the city limited by the A-2 and A-5 motorways and comprises the districts of Moncloa-Aravaca, Fuencarral-El Pardo, Hortaleza, Ciudad Lineal, and Barajas (Fig. 1). This area is characterised by a concentration of middle and high incomes. Lastly, the south periphery covers the southern arc of the city limited by the A-2 and A-5 access roads, including the districts of Latina, Carabanchel, Usera, Puente de Vallecas, Moratalaz, Villaverde, Villa de Vallecas, Vicálvaro, and San Blas Canillejas (Fig. 1). The latter area is home to almost half of the city's population (44.2%), households (42.5%) and homes (42.1%). Most of the popular classes are concentrated in it, with the lowest incomes and the lowest cost housing stock, and with the fewest contrasts between maximum and minimum, both in rent and prices [12].

Madrid's public transport network is characterised by its extension and the diversity of transport modes available, including the Madrid Metro, the city bus operated by the Municipal Transport Company (EMT), the intercity buses, the commuter rail service (*Cercanías*) and the light rail. In 2022, a total of 1,362.7 million journeys were recorded. Of the modes present in the city, the Madrid Metro and urban buses stand out, representing 42.0% and 27.4% of total trips, respectively [14]. In addition, the Metro network and urban buses are the main means of intra-municipal travel [14], so the accessibility of tourist homes to the transport system will be analysed in terms of the proximity of tourist homes to stations of these two modes of transport.

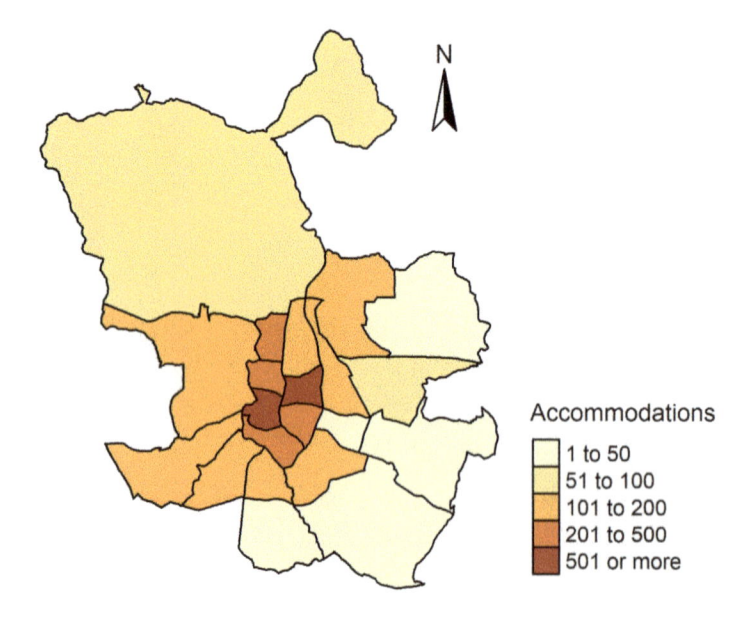

Figure 2: Spatial distribution of Madrid tourism homes (number of tourism accommodations per district).

In terms of mobility between the areas of the city, there is a great use of the public transport network, especially in the area known as Central Almond. In particular, 69% of mechanised journeys within this area are made by public transport. In addition, transport between the central area and the urban peripheries takes place 64% of the time using public transport. In contrast, private vehicles prevail in the peripheries, representing 54% of journeys, while public transportation accounts for 42% [15]. Regarding non-motorised journeys, they are more common for trips with both origin and destination within the same zone and much less common in journeys between the two zones, possibly due to the considerable distance separating them. Lastly, concerning mechanised modes, public transport constitutes more than half of the journeys with origin and/or destination in the central core. However, its usage decreases for journeys within the urban periphery, as the transportation network is heavily focused on centre-periphery movements and virtually neglects movements within the periphery [16].

3 METHODOLOGY

This study seeks which factors affect tourism homes occupation rates, or indirectly which factors make a tourist choose housing depending on the city zone, based on the reservation process. The reservation process for tourist accommodations typically involves three steps. Initially, a tourist chooses a city and a date range, and the reservation platform (e.g., Airbnb) displays available accommodations for the chosen city and timeframe. Note that, in this stage, tourists cannot view accommodations that are fully booked. Subsequently, the tourist narrows their search to a specific area within the city. In the final stage, the tourist selects an accommodation from those available in the chosen area that best meets their needs. If no suitable options are found, the tourist can either restart the entire process or return to the second stage to select a different city area.

The proposed methodology analyses housings of different zones of the city (centre and periphery) separately. First, dependent (tourist housing occupation) and independent variables for each tourist housing were collected, processed, and examined, leading to the creation of an ad hoc database. Secondly, this database was divided in two samples: centre and periphery housings. Finally, these samples were used in the modelling process, which included the application of the multiple linear regression.

3.1 Dependent variable

The dependent variable should reflect the answers to the question 'Why do tourists prefer certain city areas for their stay?'. The proposed output variable is the occupation rate of each housing, calculated as total number of reservation days over total number of offered days (eqn (1)). Where OR_i is the occupation rate of the housing i, and R_i and O_i are the number of reserved and offered, respectively, for the tourist housing i.

$$OR_i = R_i/O_i \qquad (1)$$

3.2 Independent variables

Once the possible housings are showed to the tourists, they should decide which one to choose. This election depends on a wide range of factors that could be grouped in house variables, house surrounding variables, and proximity to tourism attractions variables.

House variables included in the AirDNA database are average daily rate (ADR), number of bedrooms, number of bathrooms, maximum guests, number of amenities, and overall rating. In this study, the tourists are expected to seek for different housings depending on the number of guests in their group. Hence, some house factors were normalised considering that the maximum number of guests of a housing is equal to the number of people in the tourists' groups. With this consideration, house factors are ADR per person, bedrooms per person, bathrooms per person and overall rating.

House surrounding variables include the economic status and the amenities of the area of the housings. The economic status is shown in the average income per person of the census tract where the house is located, being Madrid divided in more than 2,000 census zones. In addition, the amenities are the number of local commerce points of interest (POIs) within a 5-minute walk from the house (400 m). The number of tourist housings within 200 m from the house was also recorded, as a customer could perceive an area with many housings as more attractive or safer.

Proximity to tourism attractions variables reflects the proximity of tourism POIs from the housings. The proximity is calculated as the mean of the distances between the housing and 15 selected most-visited tourism POIs (Fig. 3).

Regarding **public transport network**, tourists are expected to find how near the housing is to access the network. In this sense, the number of transfers is not expected to matter to them. Instead, the Euclidean distances to the nearest bus stop and metro entrance were obtained for each housing.

Table 1: Definition of independent variables.

Group	Variable	Definition
House features	ADR per person	ADR per person (€)
	Bedrooms per person	Number of bedrooms per person
	Bathrooms per person	Number of bathrooms per persons
	Rating	Overall rating of the housing
House surrounding	Average income per person	The average income per person (€) of the census tract where the house is located
	Local commerce	The number of shopping and catering POIs within a 5 minute walk from the house (400 m)
	Competence	Number of tourist housings in 200 m
Proximity to tourism attractions	Proximity to tourist POIs	Mean distance to the top 15 tourist destinations from the housing
Public transport network	Bus	Distance to the nearest bus stop from the housing
	Metro	Distance to the nearest metro station from the housing

3.3 Data sources

The database was built with data obtained from different sources. Tourist housing data was extracted from the AirDNA database. AirDNA collects the most comprehensive database of tourist accommodations, as it includes information on tourist-use properties offered through the Airbnb and Vrbo platforms. Property owners often list their homes on more than one platform, but according to verified data, AirDNA accounts for 90% of the total supply [17], thus making AirDNA's supply and demand data for the city of Madrid considered representative. For each vacation rental and for every month, the data includes its location, property features (number of bedrooms, bathrooms, type of property, etc.), offer (ADR, number of available days) and demand (number of reserved days, occupation rate).

Regarding house surroundings, the average income per person was extracted for the last year available, 2021, from the Spanish National Statistics Institute (INE). The local commerce POIs were extracted from OpenStreetMap [18], considering only the catering and shopping points, through Geofabrik (download.geofabrik.de). Additionally, the list of the top-visited tourist attraction was extracted from TripAdvisor [19], which is based on the quality, quantity, recency, consistency of reviews, and the number of page views over time. These locations were geolocated in an ad hoc GIS file. Fig. 3 shows the names and locations of the chosen tourist attraction. Finally, bus stops and metro entrances were gathered from the Open Data Portal of the Consortium of Transportation for Madrid [20].

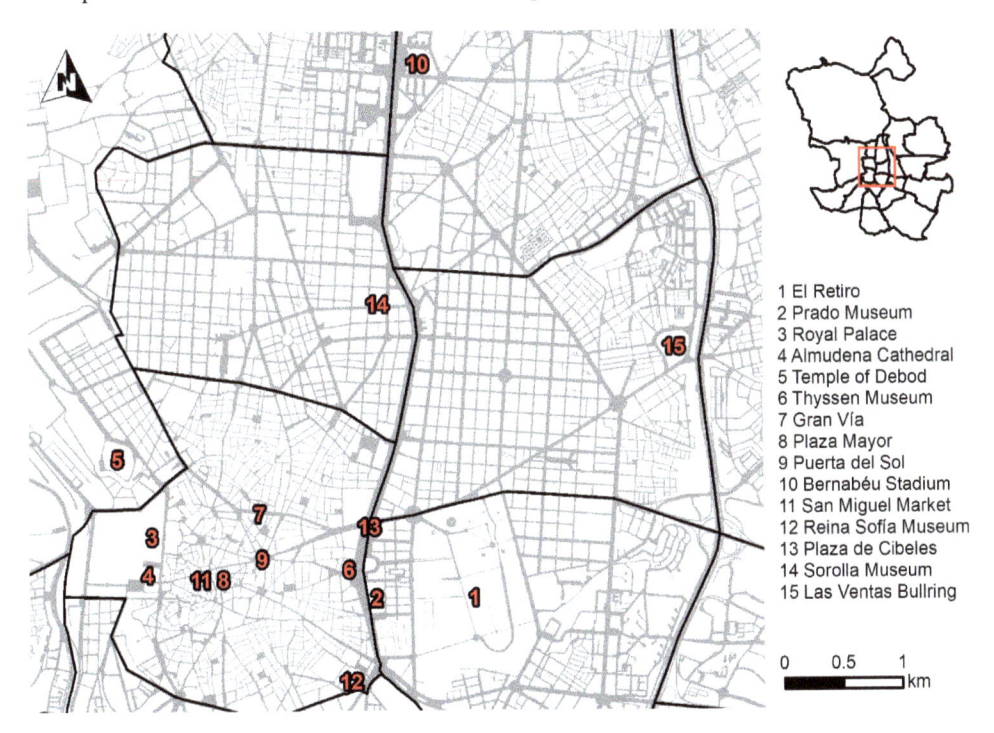

Figure 3: Madrid main 15 tourist POIs, provided by TripAdvisor [19].

3.4 Housing selection

Some housings were excluded from this study based on the following criteria. The month of the AirDNA data was October 2022, because it was the month with the highest occupation. Housings included in the analysis were those being entire homes or apartments, thus excluding rooms, those that were offered to the tourist at least one day of that month, and those with at least one bedroom. Also, only records with no missing data were studied. Finally, data from 7,888 tourist housings were suitable for this study.

3.5 City zones

The relationships between dependent and independent variables are expected to differ across the geographical extension of the data. In addition, this study aims to analyse these differences. Madrid city was divided in two zones: Central Almond which correspond to district inside of the M-30 highway, and periphery, which are the rest of districts. Considering the location of each tourist housing inside of these two zones, the created dataset was divided in two samples. Central Almond includes most housings (6,629), and the periphery includes about 15% of them (1,259). The spatial distribution of these housings is shown in Fig. 2. Data modelling was applied to these two separate data samples separately. Table 2 shows the descriptive statistics of the collected variables considering the city zone.

Table 2: Descriptive statistics of the collected variables considering the city zone.

Variable	Central Almond n = 6,629 Mean (SD)	Periphery n = 1,259 Mean (SD)	Total n = 7,888 Mean (SD)
Occupation	0.841 (0.221)	0.786 (0.255)	0.832 (0.228)
ADR per person	46.3 (26.8)	32.6 (19.0)	44.1 (26.2)
Bedrooms per person	0.412 (0.155)	0.417 (0.143)	0.412 (0.153)
Bathrooms per person	0.358 (0.149)	0.334 (0.149)	0.354 (0.150)
Rating	91.9 (8.29)	91.8 (8.67)	91.9 (8.35)
Average income per person	20,100 (4,680)	15,700 (5,960)	19,400 (5,170)
Local commerce	304 (193)	39.1 (51.6)	262 (203)
Tourist distance	2,020 (804)	5,440 (2370)	2,570 (1730)
Competence	120 (85.1)	8.09 (12.0)	102 (88.3)
Distance to nearest bus stop	98.1 (55.3)	123 (94.6)	102 (63.9)
Distance to nearest metro station	192 (119)	486 (631)	239 (295)

3.6 Multiple linear regression

The multiple linear regression (eqn (2)) was applied to central and peripherical tourist housings separately. This model provides parameters and p-values, which can be interpreted to analyse how variables affect the dependent variable and if these effects are statistically significant. The linear regression relation is given by

$$y_i = \beta_0 + \sum_k^p \beta_k x_{ik} + \varepsilon_i \qquad (2)$$

where y_i is the dependent variable at location i, β_0 and β_k are the intercept and parameters of the regression for the location i, respectively, x_{ik} are the independent variables in location i, p is the number of covariates, and ε_i is the error at location i.

3.7 Variable importance

The sign and significance level of the parameters of the covariates in the linear regression models give valuable insight in how independent variables affect the occupation of the housings of the two zones of the city. However, this approach is sensible to the variables included in the modelling process, as some could change the sign or significance level when the set of variables is modified. Furthermore, as independent variables present different units of measure, their effect should not be compared in terms of what variables are more important for occupation.

To solve these issues, an exhaustive model selection process was performed. This included computing all possible regression models with the list of independent variables (presented in Table 1) for the two samples. For each city zone, the number of models is 1,024 (2^{10}, being 10 the number of covariates). The intercept of the model was included all possible variable combinations. For each combination, parameters, p-values and, as a measures of the goodness-of-fit, the Akaike information criterion (AIC) were recorded. Later, for each possible combination of variables, the Akaike weight (w_i) was calculated as exposed in eqn (3). This Akaike weight is a normalised measure of each model being the best model, in terms of the AIC, inside a set of models. For a set of models, the sum of the weights is equal to 1 [21].

$$w_i = \frac{exp\left(-\frac{1}{2}\Delta(AIC)_i\right)}{\sum_{k=1}^{K} exp\left(-\frac{1}{2}\Delta(AIC)_k\right)} = \frac{exp\left(-\frac{1}{2}(AIC_i - min(AIC))\right)}{\sum_{k=1}^{K} exp\left(-\frac{1}{2}(AIC_k - min(AIC))\right)} \quad (3)$$

where w_i and AIC_i are the Akaike weight and the AIC of the model formed with the ith combination of independent variables, respectively, and K is the total number of combinations of independent variables.

This value can be used to evaluate the models, as better adjusted models present higher weights. More interestingly, the Akaike weight can be used to detect which covariates are more important for the model adjustment, thus for defining the occupation of each housing. The idea is that more important variables appear in better adjusted models, so this importance is calculated as the sum of weights of the models where the variable appears. Note that each variable should appear in the same number of models for a fair comparison of the variable importance [21], [22]. In our case, each variable is used in half (512) of the regressions in each set of models. This process was carried out separately for both data samples. With this approach, we should inspect and compare the model with all variables, the best fitted model and the variables' importance for each sample. These are presented in the next section.

4 RESULTS

The results of this study are based on the parameters and *p*-values of the covariates in the multiple linear regression for both samples, and on the relative importance of these covariates in the accurate calculation of the dependent variable.

Regarding the regression models with all the independent variables, parameters and *p*-values are shown in Table 3. The same effects of the statistically significant variables on occupation are shown in both models. More bathrooms per person and more rating imply more occupation, while higher ADR per person and more distance to tourist destinations are related to lower occupation. The effect of ADR per person is higher in the periphery, and the

Table 3: Main statistics for the models (central almond and periphery) with all covariates.

Variable	Central Almond Estimate	Central Almond *p*-value	Periphery Estimate	Periphery *p*-value
Intercept	3.70E-01	0.000***	4.53E-01	0.000***
ADR per person	−2.18E-03	0.000***	−3.25E-03	0.000***
Bedrooms per person	1.81E-02	0.355	−7.33E-02	0.192
Bathrooms per person	1.62E-01	0.000***	1.43E-01	0.012**
Rating	5.51E-03	0.000***	5.36E-03	0.000***
Average income per person	1.33E-06	0.055*	−1.44E-07	0.914
Local commerce	1.37E-05	0.581	8.09E-05	0.731
Tourist distance	−1.64E-05	0.001***	−9.22E-06	0.011**
Competence	4.67E-06	0.942	−9.34E-05	0.924
Distance to nearest bus stop	−3.83E-05	0.419	−1.14E-04	0.133
Distance to nearest metro station	2.98E-05	0.205	−1.08E-05	0.390
n	6,629		1,259	
AIC	−1855.85		45.06	

*** for 1%, ** for 5%, and * for 10%.

rest of variables affect more the occupation on central almond housings. The average income per person is statistically significant in the central almond model only, and higher values improve the occupation.

Turning to the regression models with the best goodness-of-fit considering the AIC (Table 4), these present a smaller and different set of independent variables for each sample. Note that AIC values are lower than those showed in Table 3. We find that some factors affect the occupation of all the housings regardless of the city zone, which are ADR per person, bathrooms per person, rating, and tourist distance. As in the models with all the variables, the effect of the ADR per person is higher in the periphery, while the rest of variables affect housings located inside the central almond more. Also, the effect of these variables is equal as in those models. Other variables are present in one of the models only. On the one hand, average income per person affects occupation only in central almond, and higher values are related with higher occupation. On the other hand, shorter distances to nearest bus stop are related with more occupation in the periphery, bus this effect is not significant at alpha 10%.

Table 4: Main statistics for the best-fitted models (central almond and periphery housings).

Variable	Central Almond Estimate	Central Almond p-value	Periphery Estimate	Periphery p-value
Intercept	3.82E-01	0.000***	4.40E-01	0.000***
ADR per person	−2.17E-03	0.000***	−3.26E-03	0.000***
Bathrooms per person	1.70E-01	0.000***	1.04E-01	0.040**
Rating	5.54E-03	0.000***	5.36E-03	0.000***
Tourist distance	−1.75E-05	0.000***	−1.09E-05	0.000***
Average income per person	1.24E−06	0.029**	–	–
Distance to nearest bus stop	–	–	−1.20E-04	0.109
n	6,629		1,259	
AIC	−1862.741		37.92	

*** for 1%, ** for 5%, and * for 10%.

About the variable importance, Fig. 4 shows the Akaike weight for the independent variables in the two studied samples. ADR per person and rating are the most important variables in both zones, presenting the maximum possible value of the Akaike weights. Distance to tourist destinations and bathrooms per persons are also important variables, having both higher Akaike weights in the central almond. Less important variables with similar Akaike weights for both city zones are distance to nearest metro station (0.42 and 0.39), local commerce (0.30 and 0.29) and competence (0.30 and 0.28). Average income per person is remarkably more important in the central almond (0.78) than in the periphery (0.27). Finally, more important variables in the peripherical housings are bedrooms per person (0.42 versus 0.35) and distance to nearest bus stop (0.55 versus 0.33).

5 CONCLUSIONS AND FUTURE RESEARCH LINES

This research highlights that in the selection of tourist accommodation within a city, two factors are particularly significant regardless of the location of the accommodation (city centre or periphery): the average price daily rate and the rating given by previously accommodated tourists. The third most important factor, the average distance to tourist points of interest, depends on the location of the accommodation and its connectivity with the transportation system. For the group of accommodations located in the periphery of the city,

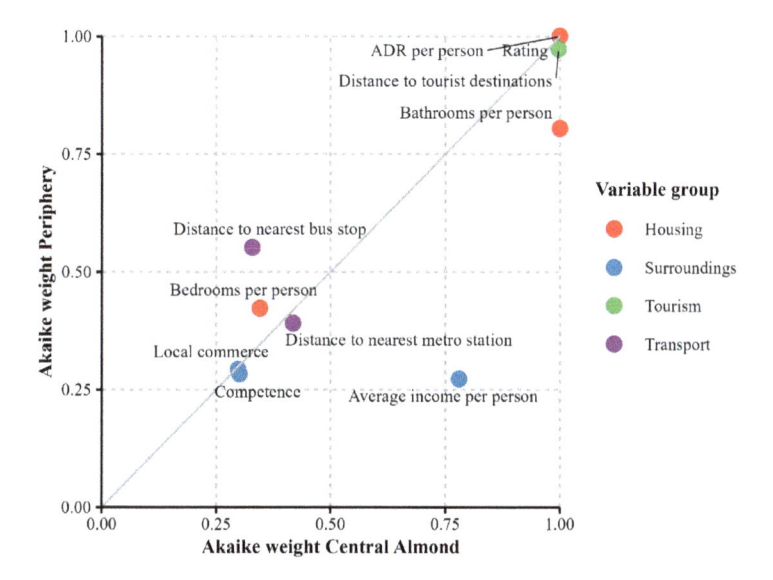

Figure 4: Akaike weight of the variables in the Central Almond and periphery housings samples.

occupancy levels are significantly more dependent on the distance from the accommodation to the nearest bus station than on the distance from the accommodation to the nearest metro station. In the selection of accommodations located in the city centre, the proximity of the accommodation to public transportation stations (neither metro nor bus) does not seem to have influenced the decision. This fact appears to be justified by the density of the public transportation network, which is higher in the city centre than in the periphery, and the proximity to touristic POIs. Accommodations in the city centre always have both bus and metro stops nearby. However, in accommodations in the periphery, metro stations are usually farther away, and the bus network serves as the first stage of the journey towards tourist points of interest.

In this context, if public administrations wish to promote tourist accommodations in the periphery, they should provide the bus public transportation network with greater reach and density of stations in these areas of the city. This would be a tool that could help to relocate the presence of tourist accommodations from the city centre, contributing to a greater sustainability of this new type of lodging. This result has a clear practical application in the regulation of tourist homes in city centres redistributing them throughout the city. In this sense, in some big cities, peripheral locations can let to the redistribution of the wealth generated by tourism around the city, favouring territorial and social cohesion.

With regard to future lines of research that may stem from this publication, concerning methodology, a new indicator of average accessibility to tourist points of interest could be studied. This time, it would not be based on the average Euclidean distance, but rather on travel times via public transportation from tourist accommodations to the 15 most significant points of interest. This indicator could weigh these access times based on the importance (tourist influx) of each tourist point of interest. This methodological improvement would serve to reassess the true role of public transportation in the choice of tourist accommodations located in the periphery.

ACKNOWLEDGEMENTS

The paper is part of the project PID2021-124428OB-I00, funded by 'MCIN/AEI/10.13039/501100011033/ERDF, EU', where PID2021-124428OB-I00 is the reference that appears in the award resolution.

REFERENCES

[1] Maitland, R., Everyday life as a creative experience in cities. *International Journal of Culture, Tourism and Hospitality Research*, **4**(3), pp. 176–185, 2010. https://doi.org/10.1108/17506181011067574.

[2] Füller, H. & Michel, B., 'Stop being a tourist!' New dynamics of urban tourism in Berlin-Kreuzberg. *International Journal of Urban and Regional Research*, **38**(4), pp. 1304–1318, 2014. https://doi.org/10.1111/1468-2427.12124.

[3] Guttentag, D., Smith, S., Potwarka, L. & Havitz, M., Why tourists choose Airbnb: A motivation-based segmentation study. *Journal of Travel Research*, **57**(3), pp. 342–359, 2018. https://doi.org/10.1177/0047287517696980.

[4] Zervas, G., Proserpio, D. & Byers, J.W., The rise of the sharing economy: Estimating the impact of Airbnb on the hotel industry. *Journal of Marketing Research*, **54**(5), pp. 687–705, 2017. https://doi.org/10.1509/jmr.15.0204.

[5] Midgett, C., Bendickson, J.S., Muldoon, J. & Solomon, S.J., The sharing economy and sustainability: A case for AirBnB. *Small Business Institute Journal*, **13**(2), pp. 51–71, 2017.

[6] Sheppard, S. & Udell, A., Do Airbnb properties affect house prices? *Williams College Department of Economics Working Papers*, **3**(1), p. 43, 2016.

[7] Colomb, C. & Novy, J. (eds), *Protest and Resistance in the Tourist City*, Routledge, 2016. https://doi.org/10.4324/9781315719306.

[8] Aalbers, M.B., Introduction to the Forum: From third to fifth-wave gentrification. *Tijdschrift voor Economische en Sociale Geografie*, **110**(1), pp. 1–11, 2019. https://doi.org/10.1111/tesg.12332.

[9] OECD, *OECD Tourism Trends and Policies 2022*, OECD, 2022. https://doi.org/10.1787/a8dd3019-en.

[10] Instituto de Estadística, Cuenta Satélite del Turismo de la Comunidad de Madrid, 2015–2021, 2024.

[11] Tammaru, T., Marcińczak, S., Van Ham, M. & Musterd, S., *Socio-Economic Segregation in European Capital Cities: East Meets West*, Taylor and Francis, 2015. https://doi.org/10.4324/9781315758879.

[12] Rodríguez-Suárez, I., Álvarez-del-Valle, L., Fernández-Ramírez, C. & Hernández-Aja, A., The impossible access to housing in Madrid: when prices exceed income. *Ciudad y Territorio Estudios Territoriales*, **55**(215), pp. 61–76, 2023. https://doi.org/10.37230/cytet.2023.215.4.

[13] Crespi-Vallbona, M. & Domínguez-Pérez, M., Las consecuencias de la turistificación en el centro de las grandes ciudades: el caso de Madrid y Barcelona. *Ciudad y Territorio Estudios Territoriales*, **53**(M), pp. 61–82, 2021.

[14] CRTM, Informe Anual 2022, Madrid, 2023.

[15] CRTM, Encuesta domiciliaria de movilidad en día laborable de 2018 en la Comunidad de Madrid. Análisis espacial y temporal de la movilidad, Madrid, 2019.

[16] Flor, M., Ortuño, A. & Guirao, B., Ride-hailing services: Competition or complement to public transport to reduce accident rates: The case of Madrid. *Front Psychol.*, **13**, 2022. https://doi.org/10.3389/fpsyg.2022.951258.

[17] Ayuntamiento de Denia and Universidad de Alicante, Diagnóstico relativo a las viviendas de uso turístico ofertadas por plataformas on-line en Denia, 2023.
[18] OpenStreetMap contributors, OpenStreetMap. https://www.openstreetmap.org/.
[19] TripAdvisor, Things to do in Madrid. https://www.tripadvisor.com/Attractions-g187514-Activities-oa0-Madrid.html. Accessed on: 15 Feb. 2024.
[20] CRTM, Portal de Datos Abiertos del Consorcio Regional de Transportes de Madrid. https://data-crtm.opendata.arcgis.com/. Accessed on: 15 Feb. 2024.
[21] Burnham, K.P. & Anderson, D.R., *Model Selection and Multimodel Inference*, 2nd ed., Springer-Verlag: New York, p. 10, 2004.
[22] Murray, K. & Conner, M.M., Methods to quantify variable importance: Implications for the analysis of noisy ecological data. *Ecology*, **90**,(2), pp. 348–355, 2009.

SECTION 3
DESTINATION MANAGEMENT

SWOT ANALYSIS FOR THE DEVELOPMENT OF STRATEGIES TO DESIGN SUSTAINABLE TOURISM INDICATORS IN GALAPAGOS, ECUADOR

LADY SOTO-NAVARRETE[1], ÓSCAR SALADIÉ[2], MARÍA JAYA-MONTALVO[3,4],
MARIBEL AGUILAR-AGUILAR[3,4] & PAÚL CARRIÓN-MERO[3,4]
[1]Facultad de Ciencias Sociales y Humanísticas, ESPOL Polytechnic University, Ecuador
[2]Faculty of Tourism and Geography, Universitat Rovira i Virgili, Spain
[3]Centro de Investigaciones y Proyectos Aplicados a las Ciencias de la Tierra,
ESPOL Polytechnic University, Ecuador
[4]Facultad de Ingeniería en Ciencias de la Tierra, ESPOL Polytechnic University, Ecuador

ABSTRACT

Sustainable tourism provides social, environmental and economic benefits and is vital in natural areas. The Galapagos Islands represent a natural environment that integrates unique species of flora and fauna. The tourist growth of the islands, in addition to their fragility and vulnerability to anthropic activities, requires sustainable tourism approaches that promote ecological and social balance. This study aims to propose strategies for the development of sustainable tourism indicators by integrating a strengths, weaknesses, opportunities, and threats (SWOT) analysis based on the perception of key actors, such as municipal authorities, the community, academia and tourists in general, related to tourism and the environment. The methodological process addressed three main phases: (i) integration and analysis of tourism data; (ii) definition of questionnaires and key actors; and (iii) design of strategies to formulate sustainable tourism indicators. In general, SWOT analysis allowed us to define strategies aligned with three main aspects: (i) strengthening public policies and territorial planning; (ii) sustainable management of natural and geological heritage; and (iii) integration of academia to design environmentally and economically sustainable tourism strategies. This research provides tools for the use of strategies based on ecological, economic, and sociocultural criteria for decision-makers and short- and long-term tourism planning.

Keywords: environmental conservation, tourism management, sustainable development, management strategies, innovation in destinations.

1 INTRODUCTION

Tourism is considered a socioeconomic activity that contributes to reducing community poverty and promoting national socioeconomic development [1]. However, owing to its possible impact on the environment, experts in the field have focused on sustainable tourism as an inclusive notion that involves the environmental, social, economic, cultural, ethical, and political axes [2]. This type of socioeconomic activity reflects its importance in fulfilling the Sustainable Development Goals (SDGs) for 2030, thereby increasing the relevance of research in sustainable tourism [3].

In recent decades, the effects of overtourism have become evident with the increase in the number of tourists, mobility, and high demand for novel experiences, registering consequences for human and environmental well-being [4]. Additionally, alternative livelihoods, such as agriculture and fishing, are displaced in local communities, increasing their vulnerability to market volatility [5]. In protected areas, the sustainability of tourism is complex, and many researchers contemplate and promote forms of nature-based tourism with administrative and governmental support to preserve ecosystems and address the economic and social needs of local communities [6].

In this context, there is a clear need to strengthen tourism planning and development by adopting responsible and sustainable models and practices [7]. Sustainability indicators are tools that allow for analysing and evaluating the sustainability of tourism in its environmental, economic, social, and political dimensions, as well as the interconnectivity between them [8]. The design of sustainable tourism indicators stimulates learning processes, improves understanding of social and environmental problems and needs, strengthens community capacities, and allows for the formulation of sustainable management and development strategies [9].

At the global level, there are a wide variety of studies on the design and evaluation of sustainable tourism indicators [10]–[12]. For example, in Taiwan, Lee and Hsieh [13] identified indicators for sustainable tourism in wetlands as valuable tools to strengthen the planning, management, and monitoring of sustainable tourism in this ecosystem. In Spain, Lozano-Oyola et al. [14] considered the proposal of indicators for cultural destinations as a critical aspect for formulating action plans and defining strategies.

The Galapagos Islands, located in the Pacific Ocean approximately 1000 km from the continental coast of Ecuador, are unique flora and fauna conservation sites on a global level, declared by UNESCO as a World Natural Heritage Site in 1978 and a Biosphere Reserve in 1987 [15]. 97% of the land area includes the Galapagos National Park [16], whereas the marine area is protected by the Galapagos Marine Reserve and the Hermandad Marine Reserve, where the land and marine areas are managed by the Galapagos Management Plan [17]. This area of global geological importance is a well-known tourist destination, where strategies to promote environmental conservation and community interests are constantly sought.

In the Galapagos Islands, tourism has been characterised by cruise tourism since its beginning, which, over time, has been transformed into an inclusive tourism model that integrates land tourism [18]. Under this management, the number of visitors has increased steadily, reaching 329,475 tourists in 2023, experiencing a 23% increase in total arrivals compared with 2022 [19]. The increase in the influx of tourists represents an environmental threat that, from 2007 to 2010, led the Ecuadorian government to declare the islands as in a state of emergency [20] and UNESCO to add them to the List of Natural Heritage in Danger [21]. This situation has generated the need to strengthen tourism management models towards a framework of a socio-ecological and sustainable system [22].

Since 2011, ecotourism models have been proposed for islands to integrate stakeholders and promote the implementation of plans and strategies that promote environmental conservation [20], [23]. However, with the COVID-19 pandemic, the collapse of tourism was evident, affecting the population that depended directly or indirectly on this industry, reflecting the need for more sustainable, inclusive, and resilient tourism planning and management [24]. 60% of the annual budget of the Galapagos National Park Directorate (DPNG, acronym in Spanish) is financed with income from entry fees from visitors arriving on the islands, intended to cover the needs of conservation and heritage protection [25].

Studies have been conducted based on indicators that serve as tools for decision makers in Galapagos in the implementation of policies towards adequate conservation management, such as Benítez-Capistros et al. [26], who identified the key environmental impacts of Galapagos and developed 37 comprehensive sustainability indicators using the Delphi method with the Drivers-Pressures-State-Impact-Response (DPSIR) framework. Martínez-Fernández et al. [27] created the Galapagos Water Indicators System (SIAG) and showed the interactions between water and other social and environmental components of the dynamics of the Galapagos, highlighting how tourism influences these factors. Espin et al. [28] mentioned some crucial social (employment rate, tourism income per capita) and ecological (introduction of invasive species, saturation of carrying capacity, land use) indicators to monitor and manage the balance between tourism and environmental conservation.

As tourism destinations seek to recover and adapt to internal and external factors in island ecosystems, there is a need to develop sustainable tourism indicator strategies post COVID-19, including the perspective of stakeholders related to the tourism sector in a protected island environment. In this context, the research question arises: How can strategies for sustainable tourism indicators be developed post COVID-19 based on the perception of key actors in protected island ecosystems? The present study aims to propose strategies for the development of sustainable tourism indicators in Galapagos by applying the strengths, weaknesses, opportunities, and threats (SWOT) method and semi-structured interviews based on the perception of key actors, such as representatives of municipal authorities, national park management, government agencies, community, academia, and tourists for the identification of the subsystems and their relationship with the tourism sector in the human–nature interaction in the post-pandemic scenario.

2 MATERIALS AND METHODS

The methodology is based on the construction of a case study [29] of sustainable tourism developed in the island ecosystem (Galapagos Island) combining qualitative tools such as SWOT analysis and in-depth semi-structured interviews that allowed the establishment of a conceptual system of environmental–social–economic–institutional coupling in tourism in the post COVID-19 scenario of the Galapagos Islands. The study phases are summarised in Fig. 1.

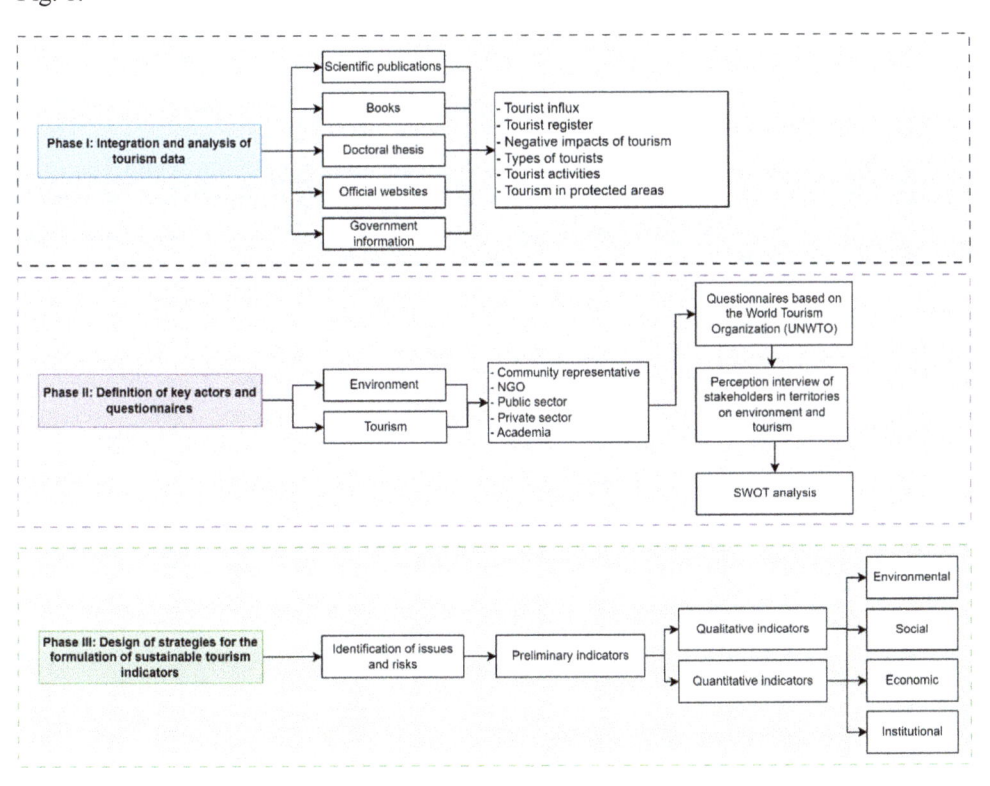

Figure 1: Study phases applied to case study.

2.1 Phase I: Integration and analysis of tourism data

The first phase includes the documentary analysis method [30], which is an iterative process of superficial reading, exhaustive reading and interpretation of the main primary and secondary sources available related to the tourism sector of the Galapagos. These include annual report on visitor influx to protected areas, load capacity and ecological sustainability, information on employment and working conditions, Galápagos 2030 Plan, Sustainable Development Plan and Territorial Planning of the Special Regime of Galapagos, active programmes developed by the Charles Darwin Foundation (CDF) (https://www.darwinfoundation.org/en/), demographic and socioeconomic information were provided by the National Institute of Statistics and Census of Ecuador (INEC) (https://www.ecuadorencifras.gob.ec/censo-de-poblacion-y-vivienda-galapagos/), Organic Law of the Special Regime in the Province of Galapagos and academic articles and theses on sustainable tourism and conservation in Galapagos.

The analysis of the information during this phase was verified and contrasted, determining the baseline in the tourism context of the case study, identifying the characteristics of the tourist destinations, roles of the interested parties, historical risks in the industry, initial contacts, and establishing potential key actors within the study. This qualitative analysis supports the design of indicators and establishes a conceptual model of the environmental–social–economic–institutional coupling in the tourism system.

2.2 Phase II: Definition of key actors and questionnaires

In this phase, the key actors were defined using the stakeholder strategy matrix model that determines the level of interest and power/influence of each potential stakeholder [29]. Additionally, a questionnaire was designed following the guidelines of the World Tourism Organization [30] using open questions categorised into (a) current state of tourism, (b) trends and risks, (c) tourist attractions and resources, (d) human resources and skills, (e) management and financing capacity, (f) tourism vision and community cohesion, (g) contribution of tourism to heritage development and (h) main environmental impacts. Fifteen in-depth semi-structured interviews were conducted in March 2022 in Spanish. To contact the actors, email was used, and in other cases, by phone, to confirm date and time availability in their agendas. The interviews had an average duration of 44 minutes. Each interviewee was informed of the purpose of the study and provided informed consent. Table 1 presents the details of each stakeholder (interviews) along with their role and interest/potentiality.

The SWOT analysis [33] of the current situation of the tourism sector was conducted using the information from the 15 interviews to identify the efforts made by tourism, tourism assets, and potential risks. The SWOT analysis assessed tourism potential and allowed us to define the types of indicators that will be useful to monitor the trends and progress of tourism objectives.

2.3 Phase III: Design of strategies for the formulation of sustainable tourism indicators

In this phase were evaluated the results of the previous qualitative analysis of the internal and external context of the tourism sector, and the most critical problems were determined, as well as those that may potentially require indicators. Thirteen qualitative and semi-quantitative indicators were established, focusing on the environmental, social, economic and institutional axes. Additionally, guidelines were provided for developing strategies in the four axes of the study.

Table 1: Participant for the Galapagos SWOT study.

Stakeholders	Number	Role	Interest/potentiality
Public administration: Tourism sector	3	Tourism sector actors	Development and management of tourism policies
Parish representative	1	Local community representative	Representation of local community interests
Galápagos National Park Directorate: Environmental	2	Environmental sector	Conservation and environmental management
Galápagos National Park Directorate: Tourism	1	Tourism sector	Sustainable tourism management
Private sector: Hotel industry	2	Hotel sector representatives	Accommodation services and tourism growth
Private sector: Travel services	3	Travel service providers	Tourist services and customer satisfaction
Private sector: Environmental NGO	1	Environmental NGO representative	Conservation and sustainable tourism advocacy
Academia: Research	2	Academic representative	Research and development in tourism and environment

3 RESULTS

3.1 Environmental–social–economic–institutional coupling in Galapagos tourism

Fig. 2 illustrates how tourism is positively or negatively related to various environmental, social, economic, and institutional components, including governance, population growth, immigration, employment generation, the introduction of invasive species, energy–water use, food production, waste, and employment. Each arrow indicates a specific relationship or impact between two components.

Following the pandemic, the tourism sector of the Galapagos Islands was forced to return to primary sector activities, such as fishing, agriculture, and livestock. According to the interviews, there was a phenomenon of migration to the mainland in search of economic sources, especially among tourist guides whose income is based on land and water tourism [31]. With the reactivation of tourism in June 2021, Fig. 2 identifies immigration in Galapagos as having a positive relationship with several factors (e.g., labour demand and population growth) driven by economic recovery, labour demand, and population dynamics. The negative relationships (black dashed lines) highlight the cycles considered in 'equilibrium' that stabilise the system by counteracting growth cycles. However, in the case of the 'carrying capacity' factor, it represents the need for continuous monitoring of the number of visitors to tourist destinations, the pressure of which has affected other island destinations around the world (e.g., Balearic Islands, Spain [32] and Jeju Island, South Korea [33]). Owing to their size and scale, island socio-ecological systems are more susceptible to external and internal pressures [34]. Tourist labour immigration is a relevant factor that

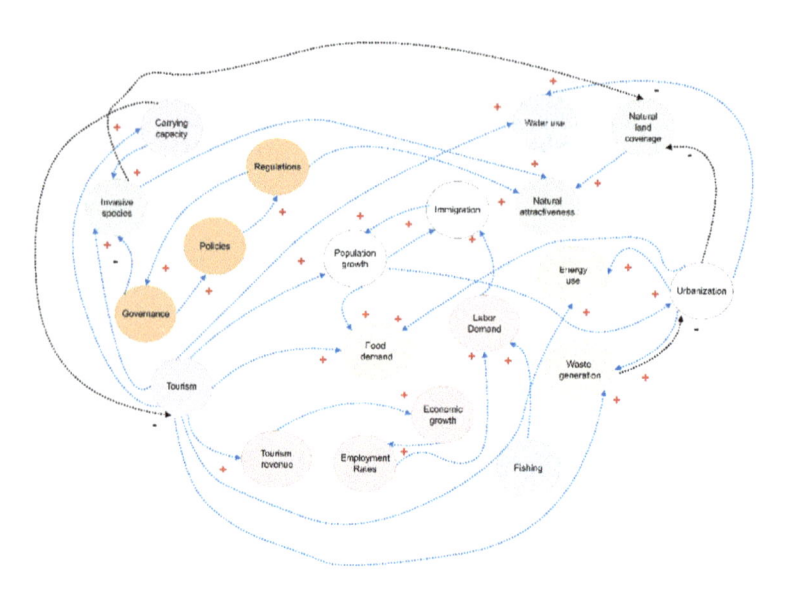

Figure 2: Conceptual model of the environmental–social–economic–institutional coupling system in Galapagos tourism.

activates population growth and negatively affects attractiveness and scenic value, especially in coastal areas. It is necessary to evaluate long-term pressures and create early ecological alerts for sustainable tourism development in island environments, such as case study.

3.2 SWOT analysis

The results of the questionnaires applied to the key actors in this study reflect, as internal aspects (Fig. 3), the tourism potential of the islands integrated with the actions of stakeholders based on adaptability and resilience to adverse economic, organisational, and climatic factors. However, the low level of community knowledge about sustainable tourism (e.g., [35]) and its dependence on tourism demand compromise alternative sources of socioeconomic development.

Strengths

Municipal authorities
o Capacity to implement public policies
o Influence on territorial planning

Local Community
o Resilience and adaptability to changes
o Inherited sustainable traditions and practices

Academy
o Research capacity and knowledge generation
o International collaboration network

Private sector
o Flexibility and adaptability to the market
o Innovation in tourism products and services

Non-governmental organization (NGO)
o Access to international financing
o Capacity for political and social influence

Weakness

Municipal authorities
o Limited resources for the implementation of all projects
o Bureaucracy and slow administrative processes

Local Community
o Poor diversification of income sources
o Lack of formal education in sustainable tourism

Academy
o Dependence on external funding for research
o Low participation in the implementation of policies

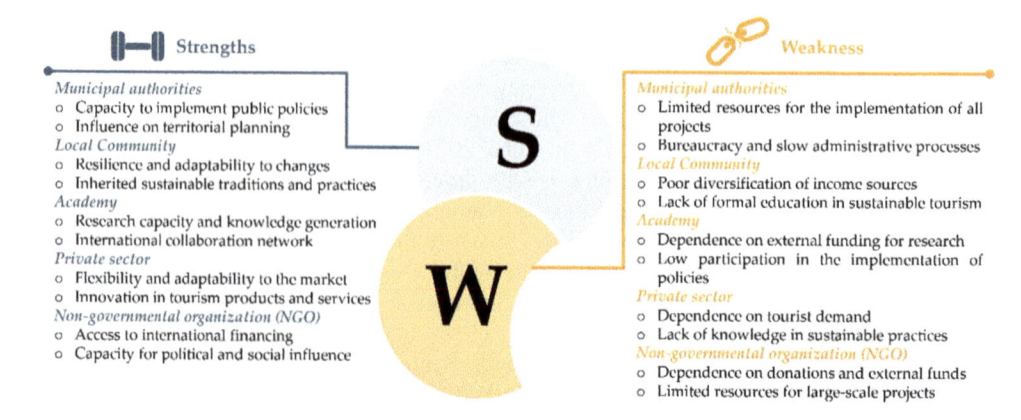

Private sector
o Dependence on tourist demand
o Lack of knowledge in sustainable practices

Non-governmental organization (NGO)
o Dependence on donations and external funds
o Limited resources for large-scale projects

Figure 3: Main internal aspects of tourism development in Galapagos.

In contrast, the external aspects of tourism (Fig. 4) point to the foremost future opportunity to integrate key actors in reformulating public policies that consider the sustainable use of resources, land use, and tourism development plans to protect community interests and ecosystem conservation. However, the sustainable development of this activity is seriously threatened by the effects of climate change and the anthropogenic degradation of natural sites due to overtourism.

Opportunities

Municipal authorities
- Possibility of establishing strategic alliances with international organizations
- Tax incentives for green initiatives

Local Community
- Participation in decision-making
- Training and education in sustainable tourism practices

Academy
- Collaboration with other key stakeholders for innovative solutions
- Publication of studies that influence public policies

Private sector
- Tax benefits for sustainable practices
- Growing demand for sustainable tourism

Non-governmental organization (NGO)
- Using innovative technologies for conservation
- Environmental education and awareness projects

Threats

Municipal authorities
- Environmental degradation due to unregulated tourism
- Change in government policies

Local Community
- Increase in living costs due to tourism
- Displacement of local communities

Academy
- Little or no government support
- Health crises that may disrupt academic and research activities

Private sector
- Degradation of the natural environment affecting tourist attraction
- Conflicts with local communities over resource use

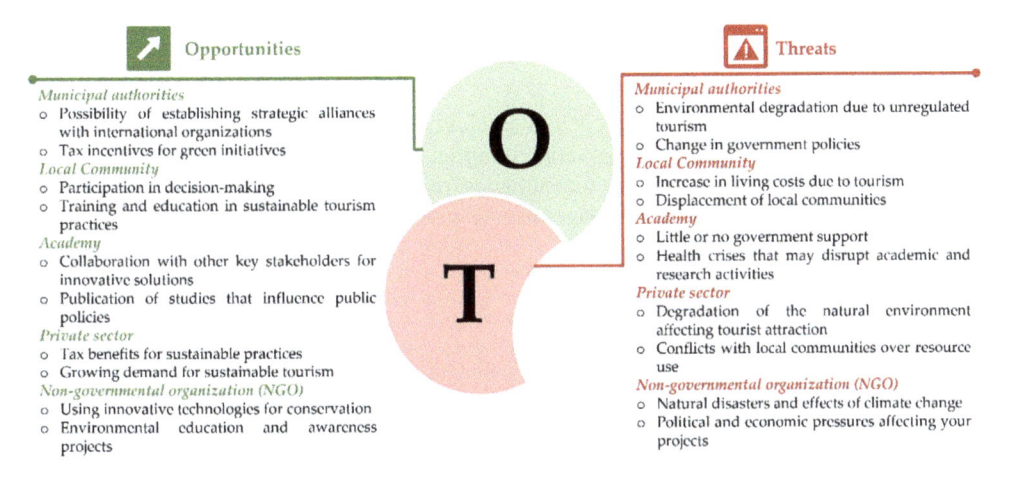

Non-governmental organization (NGO)
- Natural disasters and effects of climate change
- Political and economic pressures affecting your projects

Figure 4: Main external aspects of tourism development in Galapagos.

Based on the SWOT analysis, this study proposes strategies to promote sustainable tourism development according to the type of key actor:

- Municipal authorities:

  o Reformulation of policies that promote sustainable tourism practices, including tax incentives for businesses or communities that adopt innovative and environmentally friendly tourism approaches.
  o Creation of inter-institutional committees/organisations that integrate key actors to strengthen cooperation and planning of tourism development, prioritising human well-being, and environmental conservation.
  o Implement effective solid and liquid waste management systems in tourist areas as well as sustainable water resource management (e.g., [36]).
  o Promote policies that encourage shorter tourist stays and reduce the environmental impact of different components of natural heritage.
  o Implement stricter immigration regulation policies.

- Local community:

  o Education and awareness programs for conservation strategies in island environments for tourists, agencies, and the community.
  o Design socioeconomic development plans that promote the diversification of complementary or adaptable sources of income to tourism, such as agrotourism and geotourism [37], and increase community economic resilience.

- Academy:
  - Periodic studies on (i) the visitor management system of tourist destinations; (ii) tourist carrying capacity in sites of natural, geological, and cultural interest; and (iii) the environmental impact of tourist development works.
  - Promote the strengthening of strategic alliances for research projects on islands related to tourism and sustainable use of natural resources.

- Private sector:
  - Innovation in tourism products and services encourages the consumption of local products and supports the marketing of agricultural products in the tourism market.
  - The implementation of green technologies, resource conservation practices, and the creation of tourism experiences educate visitors about the importance of island sustainability.

- Non-governmental organisation (NGO):
  - Strengthening conservation and environmental monitoring projects that integrate community participation and tourists to mitigate the negative impacts of overtourism on the environment.
  - Microfinance initiatives and support for local entrepreneurs provide financial and training resources to strengthen the economy.

3.3 Proposal for sustainable tourism indicators in Galapagos

Table 2 shows the 13 proposed indicators that evaluate sustainable tourism development from different perspectives, including the environmental, social, economic and institutional dimensions. They are categorised into the well-being of host communities (E04, E05, S01, S02, S03), tourist satisfaction (E01, S04), health and safety (E01), environmental sustainability (E02, E03), carrying capacity management (S05), economic benefits of tourism (S01, EC01, EC02) and planning (I01).

4 DISCUSSION AND CONCLUSIONS

The methodological approach proposed in this study through in-depth semi-structured interviews and SWOT analysis allowed for the establishment of strategies for the development of 13 sustainable tourism indicators that address the environmental, economic, social, and institutional axes. The findings represent a key element that can help decision makers on the islands find solutions to the problems and conflicts, both real and potential, faced by tourism.

According to the SWOT analysis, in the context of the Galapagos Islands, implementing sustainable tourism strategies is essential for promoting the balance between socioeconomic development and environmental conservation. In this sense, local policies represent an axis that articulates correct tourism management from social, environmental, economic, and academic perspectives. The active participation of the community and private sector makes it possible to understand the importance of caring for nature and include sustainable tourism models such as agrotourism [5], [38] and geotourism [37] as resilient and replicable economic diversification models. The application of sustainable tourism indicators would contribute to the different efforts to improve the sustainability of the destination. The Canary Islands [39],

Table 2: Proposal for sustainable tourism indicators for the case study.

Axes	No.	Indicators	Time	Description	Verification method
Environmental	E01	Perception of sea water quality according to tourists	Quarterly	Measures tourists' satisfaction with the quality of sea water in the tourist destination	Satisfaction surveys
	E02	Percentage of visitors who receive information about sustainable tourism practices before and during their visit to the destination	Quarterly	Evaluate the effectiveness of information and educational campaigns on sustainable tourism.	Surveys or records of information activities
	E03	Fossil fuel consumption in the tourism sector	Annual	Quantify the consumption of fuels used for electricity generation.	ARCERNNR reports*
	E04	Total volume of water consumed and litres per tourist per day	Monthly	Measures the total volume of water consumed by the tourism sector in a specific destination, divided by the number of tourists and the average number of days of their stay. It is expressed in litres per tourist per day.	Water consumption reports from hotels and other tourist facilities.
	E05	Volume of waste produced at the destination (tonnes) per year/person per year (per month)	Monthly and Annual	Measures the total amount of solid waste generated in a tourist destination for one year, as well as the amount of waste generated per person (inhabitant and tourist) in one month.	Environmental audit reports

Table 2: Continued.

Axes	No.	Indicators	Time	Description	Verification method
Social	S01	Percentage of people who believe that tourism has helped create new services or infrastructure.	Annual	Evaluates the perception of the local population on the benefits of tourism in terms of development of services and infrastructure.	Surveys of local residents
	S02	Percentage of sites with free public access to the local population	Annual	Evaluates the accessibility of tourist sites for the local population.	Surveys of local residents
	S03	Frequency of visits by the local population to the main sites.	Annual	Measures the frequency with which residents visit major tourist sites.	Check-in and surveys
	S04	Level of satisfaction of visitors upon leaving.	Monthly	Evaluates the overall satisfaction of tourists' experience at the end of the visit to the tourist destination	Tourist exit surveys
	S05	Percentage of tourists and residents who believe the destination is overcrowded.	Annual	Measures the perception of tourist overload among both tourists and residents of the islands.	Surveys for tourists and residents
Economic	EC01	Number of domestic and foreign tourist arrivals	Monthly	Total number of tourists arriving at the destination, broken down by national and foreign tourists.	Entry records and tourism statistics
	EC02	Locals working in the tourism sector.	Annual	Quantifies the number of local people employed in the tourism sector.	Employment records and labour surveys
Institutional	I01	Frequency of updating tourist plans.	Annual	Evaluates how frequently tourism development plans are reviewed and updated.	Workshop records

* Agencia de Regulación y Control de Energía y Recursos Naturales.

the Balearic Islands [40] and the Kangaroo Islands [41] have applied indicators with tangible results to help decision-making and curb the impact on the islands' resources.

The indicators proposed in this study are designed for islands but can be applied to any destination, making sustainable use of their resources through tourism. Future research should consider the perspective of the local community on the impacts generated by tourism activity on its environment, considering its fragility as a protected area.

ACKNOWLEDGEMENTS

The authors sincerely thank the projects 'Registro de sitios de interés geológicos del Ecuador para estrategias de desarrollo sostenible' (Register of geological sites of interest in Ecuador for sustainable development strategies), with code No. CIPAT-004–2024 and 'Turismo sostenible en las Islas Galápagos: de la teoría a la práctica, mediante indicadores de sostenibilidad' (Sustainable tourism in the Galapagos Islands: from theory to practice, using sustainability indicators), with code No. FCSH-2-2018.

REFERENCES

[1] Fauzi, M.A., Sustainable tourism and sustainable development goals (SDGs): A state-of-the-art review of past, present, and future trends. *Environ. Dev. Sustain.*, 2023. https://doi.org/10.1007/s10668-023-04077-0.

[2] Moyle, B., Moyle, C., Ruhanen, L., Weaver, D. & Hadinejad, A., Are we really progressing sustainable tourism research? A bibliometric analysis. *J. Sustain. Tour.*, **29**(1), pp. 106–122, 2021. https://doi.org/10.1080/09669582.2020.1817048.

[3] Nguyen, T.Q.T., Young, T., Johnson, P. & Wearing, S., Conceptualising networks in sustainable tourism development. *Tour. Manag. Perspect.*, **32**, 100575, 2019. https://doi.org/10.1016/j.tmp.2019.100575.

[4] Milano, C., Novelli, M. & Cheer, J.M., Overtourism and tourismphobia: A journey through four decades of tourism development, planning and local concerns. *Tour. Plan. Dev.*, **16**(4), pp. 353–357, 2019.

[5] Burbano, D.V. & Meredith, T.C., Effects of tourism growth in a UNESCO World Heritage site: Resource-based livelihood diversification in the Galapagos Islands, Ecuador. *J. Sustain. Tour.*, **29**(8), pp. 1270–1289, 2021. https://doi.org/10.1080/09669582.2020.1832101.

[6] Boley, B.B. & Green, G.T., Ecotourism and natural resource conservation: the 'potential' for a sustainable symbiotic relationship. *J. Ecotourism*, **15**(1), pp. 36–50, 2016. https://doi.org/10.1080/14724049.2015.1094080.

[7] Mostafanezhad, M. & Norum, R., The anthropocenic imaginary: Political ecologies of tourism in a geological epoch. *J. Sustain. Tour.*, **27**(4), pp. 421–435, 2019. https://doi.org/10.1080/09669582.2018.1544252.

[8] Mendola, D. & Volo, S., Building composite indicators in tourism studies: Measurements and applications in tourism destination competitiveness. *Tour. Manag.*, **59**, pp. 541–553, 2017. https://doi.org/10.1016/j.tourman.2016.08.011.

[9] Diéguez-Castrillón, M.I., Gueimonde-Canto, A. & Rodríguez-López, N., Sustainability indicators for tourism destinations: Bibliometric analysis and proposed research agenda. *Environ. Dev. Sustain.*, **24**(10), pp. 11548–11575, 2022. https://doi.org/10.1007/s10668-021-01951-7.

[10] Font, X., Torres-Delgado, A., Crabolu, G., Palomo Martinez, J., Kantenbacher, J. & Miller, G., The impact of sustainable tourism indicators on destination competitiveness: The European Tourism Indicator System. *J. Sustain. Tour.*, **31**(7), pp. 1608–1630, 2023. https://doi.org/10.1080/09669582.2021.1910281.

[11] Ivars-Baidal, J.A., Vera-Rebollo, J.F., Perles-Ribes, J., Femenia-Serra, F. & Celdrán-Bernabeu, M.A., Sustainable tourism indicators: What's new within the smart city/destination approach? *J. Sustain. Tour.*, **31**(7), pp. 1556–1582, 2023. https://doi.org/10.1080/09669582.2021.1876075.

[12] Bošković, N., Vujičić, M. & Ristić, L., Sustainable tourism development indicators for mountain destinations in the Republic of Serbia. *Curr. Issues Tour.*, **23**(22), pp. 2766–2778, 2020. https://doi.org/10.1080/13683500.2019.1666807.

[13] Lee, T.H. & Hsieh, H.-P., Indicators of sustainable tourism: A case study from a Taiwan's wetland. *Ecol. Indic.*, **67**, pp. 779–787, 2016. https://doi.org/10.1016/j.ecolind.2016.03.023.

[14] Lozano-Oyola, M., Blancas, F.J., González, M. & Caballero, R., Sustainable tourism indicators as planning tools in cultural destinations. *Ecol. Indic.*, **18**, pp. 659–675, 2012. https://doi.org/10.1016/j.ecolind.2012.01.014.

[15] Mateus, C. et al., Anthropogenic emission inventory and spatial analysis of greenhouse gases and primary pollutants for the Galapagos Islands. *Environ. Sci. Pollut. Res.*, **30**(26), pp. 68900–68918, 2023. https://doi.org/10.1007/s11356-023-26816-6.

[16] Colloredo-Mansfeld, M., Laso, F.J. & Arce-Nazario, J., Drone-based participatory mapping: Examining local agricultural knowledge in the Galapagos. *Drones*, **4**(4), p. 62, 2020. https://doi.org/10.3390/drones4040062.

[17] Ministerio del Medio Ambiente y Dirección de Parques Nacionales, Plan de Manejo de las Áreas Protegidas de Galápagos para el Buen Vivir. Puerto Ayora, Galápagos. Quito, Ecuador, 2014. https://www.galapagos.gob.ec/wp-content/uploads/downloads/2016/08/35_PLAN_DE_MANEJO_DE_AREAS_PROTEGIDAS_DE_GALAPAGOS_PARA_EL_BUEN_VIVIR_22_jul_2014.pdf.

[18] Epler, B., Tourism, the economy, population growth, and conservation in Galapagos. Galapagos Islands, Ecuador, 2007. https://www.geog.psu.edu/sites/www.geog.psu.edu/files/event/coffee-hour/tourismreport1epler2007.pdf.

[19] Dirección del Parque Nacional Galápagos, Informe anual ingreso de visitantes a las áreas protegidas de Galápagos del año 2023. https://galapagos.gob.ec/wp-content/uploads/2024/03/INFORME_ANUAL_VISITANTES-2023_WEB-LQ.pdf.

[20] García, J., Orellana, D. & Araujo, E., The new model of tourism: Definition and implementation of the principles of ecotourism in Galapagos. Galapagos Report 2011–2012, pp. 95–99, 2013.

[21] UNESCO, State of conservation of properties inscribed on the list of world heritage in danger: Reactive monitoring mission. Report Galapagos Islands. 2007. https://whc.unesco.org/en/soc/994. Accessed on: 25 May 2024.

[22] González, J.A., Montes, C., Rodríguez, J. & Tapia, W., Rethinking the Galapagos Islands as a complex social-ecological system: Implications for conservation and management. *Ecol. Soc.*, **13**(2), 2008. http://www.jstor.org/stable/26267990.

[23] Pizzitutti, F. et al., Scenario planning for tourism management: A participatory and system dynamics model applied to the Galapagos Islands of Ecuador. *J. Sustain. Tour.*, **25**(8), pp. 1117–1137, 2017. https://doi.org/10.1080/09669582.2016.1257011.

[24] Figueroa B.E., Rotarou, E.S., Island tourism-based sustainable development at a crossroads: Facing the challenges of the COVID-19 pandemic. *Sustainability*, **13**(18), 10081, 2021. https://doi.org/10.3390/su131810081.

[25] Viteri Mejía, C. et al., Fishing during the 'new normality': Social and economic changes in Galapagos small-scale fisheries due to the COVID-19 pandemic. *Marit. Stud.*, **21**(2), pp. 193–208, 2022. https://doi.org/10.1007/s40152-022-00268-z.

[26] Benítez-Capistros, F., Hugé, J. & Koedam, N., Environmental impacts on the Galapagos Islands: Identification of interactions, perceptions and steps ahead. *Ecol. Indic.*, **38**, pp. 113–123, 2014. https://doi.org/10.1016/j.ecolind.2013.10.019.

[27] Martínez-Fernández, J., Esteve-Selma, M.Á., Banos-Gonzalez, I., Sampedro, C., Mena, C. & Carrión-Tacuri, J., Managing the Galapagos National Park: A systemic approach based on socio-ecological modeling and sustainability indicators. *Socio-Ecological Studies in Natural Protected Areas*, Springer: Cham, pp. 187–214, 2020. https://doi.org/10.1007/978-3-030-47264-1_11.

[28] Espin, P.A., Mena, C.F. & Pizzitutti, F., A model-based approach to study the tourism sustainability in an island environment: The case of Galapagos Islands, pp. 97–113, 2019. https://doi.org/10.1007/978-3-319-99534-2_7.

[29] Polonsky, M.J. & Scott, D., An empirical examination of the stakeholder strategy matrix. *Eur. J. Mark.*, **39**(9/10), pp. 1199–1215, 2005. https://doi.org/10.1108/03090560510610806.

[30] World Tourism Organization, *Indicators of Sustainable Development for Tourism Destinations: A Guidebook (English version)*. World Tourism Organization (UNWTO): Madrid, 2004. https://doi.org/10.18111/9789284407262.

[31] Burbano, D.V., Valdivieso, J.C., Izurieta, J.C., Meredith, T.C. & Ferri, D.Q., 'Rethink and reset' tourism in the Galapagos Islands: Stakeholders' views on the sustainability of tourism development. *Ann. Tour. Res. Empir. Insights*, **3**(2), 100057, 2022. https://doi.org/10.1016/j.annale.2022.100057.

[32] Amrhein, S., Hospers, G.-J. & Reiser, D., Transformative effects of overtourism and COVID-19-caused reduction of tourism on residents: An investigation of the anti-overtourism movement on the island of Mallorca. *Urban Sci.*, **6**(1), p. 25, 2022. https://doi.org/10.3390/urbansci6010025.

[33] Kim, M., Choi, K.-W., Chang, M. & Lee, C.-H., Overtourism in Jeju Island: The influencing factors and mediating role of quality of life. *J. Asian Financ. Econ. Bus.*, **7**(5), pp. 145–154, 2020. https://doi.org/10.13106/jafeb.2020.vol7.no5.145.

[34] Peterson, R. & DiPietro, R.B., Is Caribbean tourism in overdrive? Investigating the antecedents and effects of overtourism in sovereign and nonsovereign small island tourism economies (SITEs). *Int. Hosp. Rev.*, **35**(1), pp. 19–40, 2021. https://doi.org/10.1108/IHR-07-2020-0022.

[35] Mestanza-Ramón, C., Chica-Ruiz, J.A., Anfuso, G., Mooser, A., Botero, C.M. & Pranzini, E., Tourism in continental Ecuador and the Galapagos Islands: An integrated coastal zone management (ICZM) perspective. *Water*, **12**(6), p. 1647, 2020. https://doi.org/10.3390/w12061647.

[36] Carrión-Mero, P. et al., Water quality from natural sources for sustainable agricultural development strategies: Galapagos, Ecuador. *Water*, **16**(11), p. 1516, 2024. https://doi.org/10.3390/w16111516.

[37] Carrión-Mero, P. et al., Geosites assessment in a volcanic hotspot environment and its impact on geotourism, Santa Cruz-Galapagos Islands, Ecuador. *Int. J. Geoheritage Park.*, **12**(1), pp. 147–167, Mar. 2024. https://doi.org/10.1016/j.ijgeop.2024.01.006.

[38] Burke, A., The crossroads of ecotourism dependency, food security and a global pandemic in Galápagos, Ecuador. *Sustainability*, **13**(23), 13094, 2021. https://doi.org/3390/su132313094.

[39] Schiemann, J.M., Towards a system of tourism indicators of sustainability for the Canary Islands. Lessons from INSTO-UNWTO [Hacia un sistema de indicadores de sostenibilidad turística en Canarias. Lecciones desde la Red INSTO-UNWTO], 2022. http://riull.ull.es/xmlui/handle/915/31868. Accessed on: 9 Sep. 2024.

[40] Serra-Cantallops, A., Ramón-Cardona, J. & Vachiano, M., Increasing sustainability through wine tourism in mass tourism destinations: The case of the Balearic Islands. *Sustainability*, **13**(5), p. 2481, 2021. https://doi.org/10.3390/su13052481.

[41] Higgins-Desbiolles, F., Death by a thousand cuts: Governance and environmental trade-offs in ecotourism development at Kangaroo Island, South Australia. *J. Sustain. Tour.*, **19**(4–5), pp. 553–570, 2011. https://doi.org/10.1080/09669582.2011.560942.

EFFECTS OF LOCAL PLANTING ON THE URBAN MICROCLIMATE: A CASE STUDY IN A TOURISTIC CITY IN ITALY

ALESSANDRA CHIAPPINI[1], UMBERTO RIZZA[2], DILETTA BEVILACQUA[1] & GIORGIO PASSERINI[1]
[1]Department of Industrial Engineering and Mathematical Sciences, Marche Polytechnic University, Italy
[2]Institute of Atmospheric Sciences and Climate, National Research Council of Italy, Italy

ABSTRACT

Urban heat island effects are increasingly impacting on the outdoor thermal comfort and human health in urban areas, showing the need for a wiser planning of the urban environment with specific attention to the presence of green areas. Nonetheless, in the past years, several Italian municipalities have removed many trees within urban areas mainly due to the fear of their possible collapse. This paper describes a case study in the coastal city of Senigallia, Italy, aimed at quantitatively assessing the effects of local planting removal on the urban microclimate, in terms of air temperature, predicted mean vote (PMV) and predicted percentage of dissatisfied (PPD) comfort indexes. The scenarios were modelled using ENVI-met, a holistic three-dimensional modelling software. Simulations were run for the summer period for which a comparison between the domain with and without greenery was carried out. Results show that during summer, the removal of trees significantly modifies the outdoor local microclimate. An average increase in ambient air temperature of approximately 2°C at a height of 1.5 m and in the central hours of a representative summer day was calculated. The comparison between the PMVs and PPDs also shows a substantial worsening of outdoor comfort conditions with an increase of 2 points in PMV values with respect to the case with urban green.
Keywords: ENVI-met, outdoor comfort, urban greenery, temperature.

1 INTRODUCTION

The problem of outdoor comfort is linked to multidisciplinary aspects involving microclimatic and architectural analyses. Comfort is achieved when the usability of a comfortable environment is ensured not only inside confined spaces but also outside buildings, also managing to reduce energy consumption and improving air quality. Besides, the factors involved in reaching a good outdoor and indoor comfort concern both physiological and psychological aspects [1].

The urbanisation and the related change in land use have led to the reduction of urban green spaces increasing the effects of the urban heat island (UHI) phenomenon, i.e., the increase of ambient temperature in urbanised areas compared to neighbouring rural areas. Considering that in Italy coastal municipalities count a population of about 17 million inhabitants, 30% of the Italian population, concentrated on a surface that is about 13% of the national territory, it is essential to study coastal climate and its impact on human well-being [2].

The UHI phenomenon significantly influences global energy consumption and the quality of urban life. Several studies [3]–[5], show that careful urban planning and the choice of the building materials play an important role in determining outdoor comfort.

In the light of the number of elements to consider, the impact that the lack of greenery has on the temperature and on the perception that the population has of the air temperature is often overlooked [6]. In urban environments, several studies [7]–[9], have shown that trees and vegetation in general, help mitigate UHI by increasing the latent heat flux due to evapotranspiration and decreasing the sensible heat flux through shading, all of which leads to a reduction in ambient temperature. On the contrary, it has been demonstrated that the absence of vegetation implies a sharp deterioration in the quality of life causing an evident increase in temperature [10]. An interesting aspect is that the amount of urban green appears to be the parameter that most influences the temperature variation and the perceived comfort. Therefore, the layout of the green areas is important but secondary in urban planning [11] and Pastore et al. [5] demonstrated that the effects of shading, radiation interactions and evapotranspiration during very hot days have an even greater impact inside buildings with a decrease in temperature up to 3.4°C. This result confirms the significant consequences also in terms of energy consumption due to increases in cooling demand.

Numerical modelling can represent a powerful tool to support urban planning aimed at developing outdoor climate optimisation strategies. For this study, ENVI-met software was used to simulate the ambient air conditions within a domain including the presence of urban greenery and its absence. ENVI-met® [12] is a multidisciplinary modelling software that allows to model the physical and microclimatic behaviour of buildings, urban greenery, and landscape, including applications for urban planning, climate adaptation, comfort, and human health [13].

This model is a valid tool in the simulation and modelling of outdoor comfort and has been widely used and validated. There is evidence in literature about the ability of the software to obtain excellent performance. Several studies [14], [15], reported that there is a good correlation between simulated and measured ambient air temperatures and, among the others, for the temperature parameters the results obtained were the most accurate.

The purpose of this work is to investigate the impact that the presence of vegetation has on the urban outdoor environment with particular interest in verifying its influence in terms of air temperature variation and alteration of comfort indexes.

In the past, the authors have already carried out simulations based on the evaluation of present scenarios in several locations within the Ancona province to optimise the adoption of UHI mitigation strategies. This paper shows results of a somewhat reverse case study: the renovation of an urban area that included the removal of greenery and, thus, a possible worsening of local UHI effects. The domain is a portion of an urban driveway located in Senigallia, a coastal town in the Marche region of Italy. The area analysed was subject to a conservative and static restoration intervention. The first phase of this intervention included the felling of the tall maritime pines that distinguish the neighbourhood to completely replace them with other species. Even if an accurate assessment had evaluated that they were mostly in good health, this decision was taken due to difficulties in the management of their radical apparatus which had almost shattered the surface of the road and some of the infrastructures located underground.

The temperature and humidity profiles relating to the day chosen for the simulation were collected for a typical summer day and were used to create the boundary conditions using the 'simple forcing' method for which, in previous studies, satisfactory results were obtained in the comparison between simulated and measured data [16].

The 'forced boundary condition' is the most stable condition because a one-dimensional model is used to stabilise the 3D model. The 'simple forcing' method is expressed by applying a forcing to the temperature and humidity variables, attributing to these variables the values of the profiles provided for the chosen period. For this reason, the one-dimensional model shall be well representative of the average conditions of the domain [12].

Finally, chromatic tables were created to analyse the results.

2 URBAN HEAT ISLAND EFFECT

The term 'urban heat island' was created to mark a set of phenomena that trigger an increase in ambient air temperature in urbanised areas compared to neighbouring rural areas. It is recorded at all latitudes but at medium and low latitudes, where the climate is warmer, an increase in temperature causes more perceptible and non-negligible effects [17].

UHI presents itself with multiple space–time variations and can be divided into surface UHI and atmospheric UHI. To better approach the study of the phenomena, it is preferable to use different scales both horizontally and vertically. Air UHI involves urban canopy layer, which includes the urban cover layer but below the average height of the buildings, and urban boundary layer which includes the layer above the average height of the buildings. To perform analyses at local level to evaluate the relationship between the development of the urban heat island, the use of certain building materials and the presence of green areas, it is preferable to refer to a model that considers the microscale [18].

The main causes that can lead to the exacerbation of the analysed phenomena are the properties of the materials, the increase in anthropogenic heat, the variation of the wind, the effect of urban canyons, the scarcity of vegetation. The related consequences are many as well, on a general level, the loss of proper thermo-hygrometric conditions has consequences in form of discomfort within population. The increasingly frequent heat waves also have repercussions on the health of the population. Other consequences on the environment of the affected area have been highlighted such as the deterioration of air quality, alterations of the microclimate, variation of the local wind trend [19]. Moreover, the temperature increase in summer causes an increased demand of air conditioning in urban centres, which in turn leads to extra air pollution and an increased anthropogenic heat production: as reported in several studies, every 0.6°C increase in temperature is followed by a 5%–10% increase in energy demand [20].

Finally, there is evidence in literature that, under certain weather patterns, the concentrations of some airborne pollutants increase significantly with the UHI intensity. For example, a study conducted by Lai and Cheng [21] showed that the convergence usually associated with nocturnal UHI causes accumulation of O^3 precursors and other pollutants in significant amounts, worsening the air quality at night and during the following day.

3 MITIGATING EFFECTS OF VEGETATION

The term 'mitigation techniques' refers to solutions and strategies aimed at minimising the UHI phenomena and/or the related effects. In such framework, a correct urban planning plays an important role. Throughout such planning, particular attention should be paid to the design and redistribution of green areas, which are indicators of excellent urban-environment quality as well as sustainable urban development, simultaneously fostering economic efficiency, social equity, and environmental integrity [22].

Regarding UHI mitigation, the advantages offered by urban greenery can be traced back to its ability to favour the processes of evapotranspiration which leads to a lowering of the air temperature as the water is vaporised. In few words, evapotranspiration turns a large quantity of sensible heat into latent heat so to lower local ambient air temperature. Trees also provide shading with a consequent reduction in the amount of incident solar radiation absorbed and a consequent reduction in energy consumption for cooling in the summer.

Years ago, the different cooling rate recorded between parks and urban areas was brought to light by the study conducted by Ca et al. [23] in Tama New Town, a city located in the western part of the Tokyo metropolitan area, Japan. The observations have indicated that the vegetation, other than causing a surface temperature of the grass cover 19°C lower than that of an asphalted surface and 15°C lower than that of a concrete surface, also implies air temperature at 1.2 m above the ground more than 2°C lower in the park than in the surrounding commercial and parking areas. Furthermore, the fact that immediately after sunset the temperature of the surface of the ground in the park drops faster than that of the asphalt or concrete surfaces of the city leads to the creation of a 'cool island' also called 'cool oasis' which allows the reduction of the air temperature in a busy commercial area 1 km downwind by up to 1.5°C. This can bring various advantages, including above all a significant reduction in the energy used for air conditioning (about 4,000 kWh from 1.00 pm to 2.00 pm).

Shashua-Bar et al. [24] investigated the predominant role of trees in attenuating the urban heat island and its dependence on the level of coverage offered by the canopy as well as on the density and geometry of the buildings.

4 SIMULATION DETAILS

The study domain covers a stretch of the avenue Anita Garibaldi in Senigallia, Italy, a municipality of around 44,000 inhabitants (October 2023) that during the summer period tends to triple due to the high seaside tourism, in the province of Ancona in the Marche region located by the Adriatic Sea (Fig. 1).

Figure 1: The case study location with a detail of the section of the avenue analysed.

The analysed area goes from the roundabout in Via Marche to Via La Marca for a total of about 90 m in length and about 84 m in the orthogonal direction (highlighted in yellow in Fig. 1). This section appears to be well representative of the characteristics of the entire avenue.

Numerical simulations were performed with ENVI-met software, a model for the simulation of complex urban environments used in interdisciplinary studies for investigating the influences of urbanisation on urban microclimate and on human health, and to allow climate-appropriate urban planning. The potential of the software and its calculations have been validated and verified in more than 3,000 scientific publications and independent studies [12].

This article reports and discusses simulations carried out to evaluate the trend and evolution of the temperature gradient and the predicted mean vote (PMV) and predicted percentage of dissatisfied (PPD) comfort indices considering the presence or absence of urban greenery.

The PMV index represents the average judgment of a group of people and gives an idea of how much the real thermal situation perceived by an individual differs from that of well-being. The PMV index can vary from +3 to −3 but ENVI-met considers −4 and +4 as extremes for its calculation. The PPD index indicates the predictable percentage of people dissatisfied with the thermal condition and is mathematically derived from the PMV value.

A comparison has been performed between the air temperature and the comfort indexes, relating to the state-of-the-art situation, i.e., the situation prior to the works with the pine trees still on site, and the situation following the removal intervention, so the same domain but no trees. This comparison was conducted for a representative summer day which was framed, through statistical analysis, on 25 August 2022.

4.1 Simulation characteristics

The domain was initially investigated using Google Earth software (https://www.google.com/intl/it/earth/about/) (Fig. 2(a)), which also allows spatial measurements of areas. Subsequently, detailed site inspections, including precise measurements, were carried out. Following inspections, information related to the 'ante-operam' scenario were collected such as materials and heights of buildings, flooring types and materials, and type and size of vegetation.

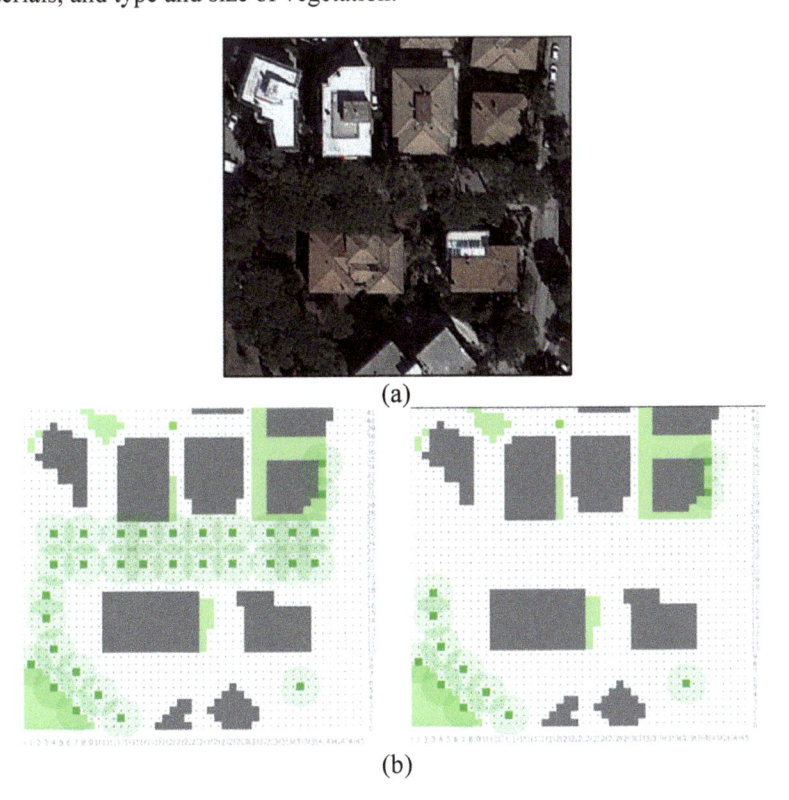

Figure 2: (a) Domain from Google Earth; (b, left) Domain in ENVI-met avenue with trees; and (b, right) Domain in ENVI-met rehabilitation scenario without trees.

The domain has been generated within the software with the tools to create input areas in the 'Spaces' section. It has been rotated 45° clockwise in accordance with the actual bearing of the roads, thus the model assumes the main geometries perfectly horizontal and vertical, making it easier to represent them using grids. The area was rendered with a grid of 46 × 42 × 30 cells (x–y–z), keeping the cell size 2 m (dx = dy = dx).

The grid nesting feature was used to reduce the chance of numerical problems due to the interference of the borders with the internal model dynamics. Given the limited extension of the domain, the value used for the nesting grid was 2.

Regarding the ante-operam scenario, the input information and data can be split into two categories: determined values and assumed values. The spatial extent of the domain, the heights of the buildings, the positioning and typology of the plants present on the avenue and the weather data are among the actual values entered. The materials chosen for the creation of the built elements of the domain such as walls and roofs of the buildings and the pavements are among the assumed data. These building materials were selected from the set of materials available in the ENVI-met database according to the results of site inspections.

The buildings were represented with default walls and roofs (albedo = 0.5), with an elevation that varies between 11 and 19 m. For the modelling of the vegetation, three different types of plants were introduced:

- Palm tree, small trunk, dense foliage, small (5 m tall).
- Palm tree, large trunk, dense foliage, medium (15 m tall).
- Pinus Pinea, medium (15 m tall).

The paving material of the sidewalk is granite, characterised by an emissivity value of 90% and an albedo of 0.40, the roughness is 0.01 m according to ENVI-met database. The original road was built in asphalt, whose properties in the ENVI-met software are an emissivity of 90%, an albedo value of 0.20, and roughness 0.01 m (Fig. 2(b left)).

The same features were used to create the post-operam scenario where the Pinus Pinea trees on the boulevard have been removed, as shown in Fig. 2(b right).

Weather data for both simulations were obtained from the Marche Region Civil Protection historical database. The reference meteorological station is in Senigallia at the coordinates 13°12' longitude and 43°42' latitude and at an elevation of 6 m [25].

Hourly values of temperature, relative humidity, and wind speed and direction were entered. The start time was 6 am of the two chosen days, the default value suggested by the ENVI-met guide [12]. Both simulations were run over the next 24 hours. The minimum simulation duration, as suggested by the software guidelines, is 6 hours. Several authors considered 1-hour simulation [26]–[28], whereas other authors up to 72 hours [29].

5 RESULTS AND DISCUSSION

The results of the simulations will be displayed showing the behaviour of parameters chosen as representative for the present study, namely the air temperature and the outdoor comfort indexes PMV and PPD.

The results are related to early afternoon (2.00 pm) on the simulated day thus a time when an elevated air temperature is usually perceived and happens to be an interval far enough from simulation start-time.

5.1 Air temperature variations with changes in tree presence

The following images show maps representing the air temperature of the domain analysed for the 'ante-operam' case and for the simulated 'post-operam' scenario, without trees.

All output images are characterised by a horizontal view from above and refer to 2.00 pm. Output data is related to an elevation that represents the average bust-height of a generic pedestrian (namely $z = 1.40$ m), thus representing the value mostly perceived by pedestrians.

5.1.1 Scenario with trees

In full summer (Fig. 3), the central zone of the avenue with trees is characterised by rather low temperatures, which go from less than 25°C to 26°C while other areas, near the other roads within the domain analysed reach about 28°C (pink areas). It is therefore clear that the tree-lined area maintains a temperature at least 2°C lower than the areas on the map characterised by the presence of asphalt and little or no presence of trees.

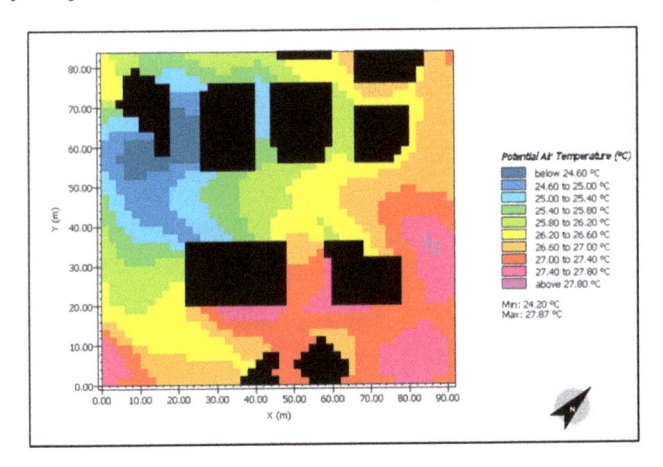

Figure 3: ENVI-met output with trees summer.

5.1.2 Scenario without trees

In Fig. 4 the central area of the domain, devoid of trees, presents colours from red to purple, indicating significantly higher temperatures above 27°C, at least 2°C higher than the situation of the 'ante-operam' scenario (Fig. 3), which showed temperatures around 25°C. The temperatures remain approximately unchanged in the areas with no alteration in tree canopy but also these zones show a small increase. In particular, 'pink' areas expand all over the entire domain.

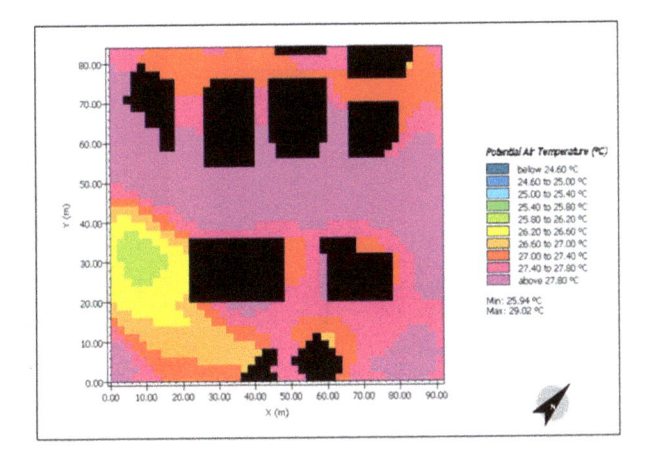

Figure 4: ENVI-met output avenue without trees summer.

5.2 Outdoor comfort indexes variations with changes in tree presence

ENVI-met can determine, based on meteorological data, PMV and PPD outdoor comfort indices, i.e., indices that attest the thermo-hygrometric human's well-being, given the set of conditions perceived in the investigated area. Figs 5–8 show the behaviour of PMV and PPD in the various scenarios.

5.2.1 Scenario with trees

Regarding the PMV-index (Fig. 5), the areas affected by the presence of trees show blue colours with PMV values below 1.5, so slightly warm. On the contrary, the areas without trees show colours between orange and red, with PMV values around 3, so perceived as very hot.

Considering the PPD index (Fig. 6), the areas affected by the presence of trees have a percentage of dissatisfied approximately around 16.50% these are the lowest values on the scale.

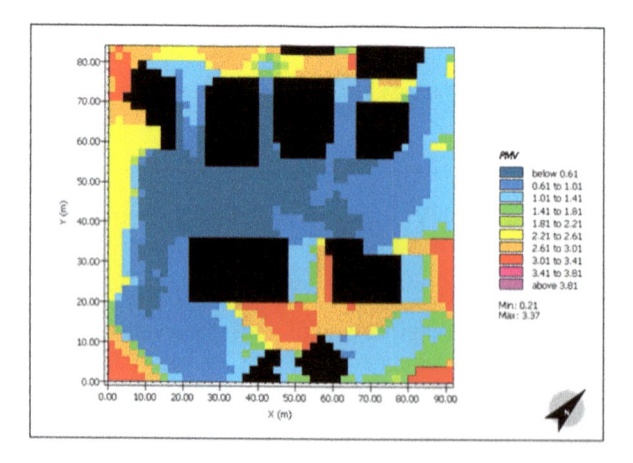

Figure 5: ENVI-met output relating to the scenario with trees for the PMV in summer.

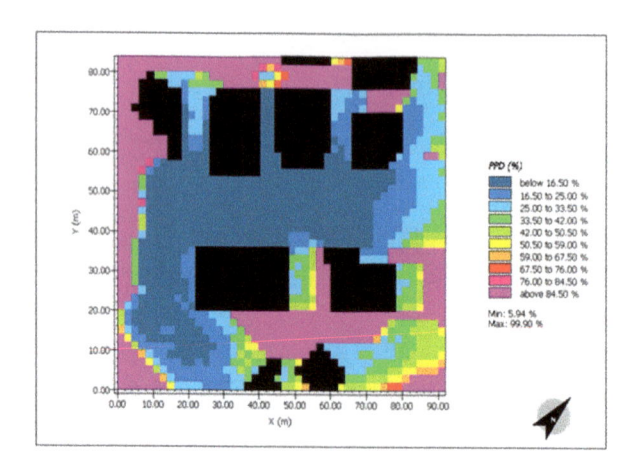

Figure 6: ENVI-met output relating to the scenario with trees for the PPD in summer.

5.2.2 Scenario without trees

In Fig. 7, regarding the PMV index, the portions of the avenue, now without trees, present in this case a colour scale from pink to red (values of PMV from 3 to almost 4). Therefore, the maximum values recorded are approximately 2 points higher than the state of the art with worse performances.

However, as regards the PPD index (Fig. 8), it is clear from the legend that the portions of the avenue, now without trees, have a percentage of dissatisfied people between 85% and 100%.

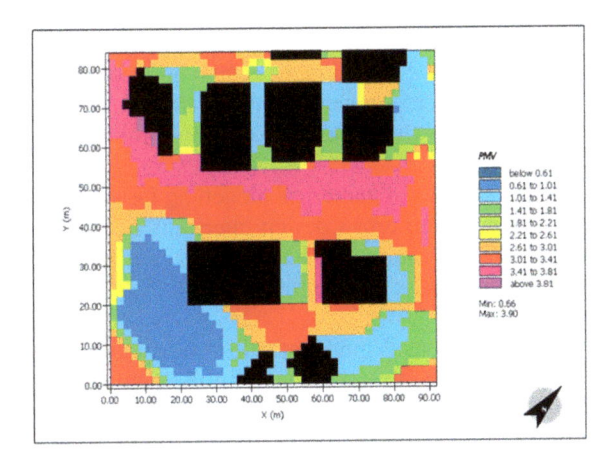

Figure 7: ENVI-met outputs relating to the avenue without trees for the PMV in summer.

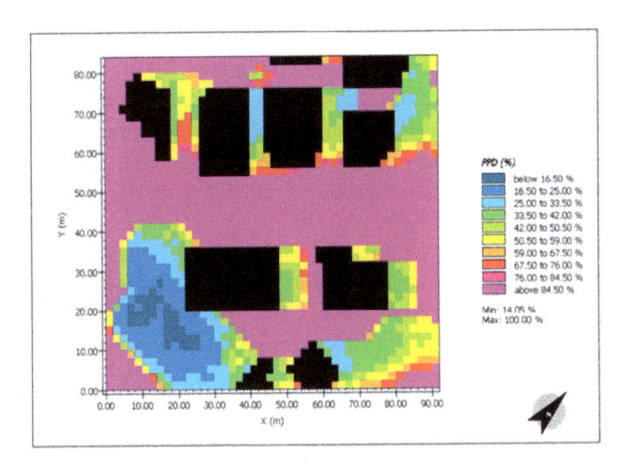

Figure 8: ENVI-met outputs relating to the avenue without trees for the PPD in summer.

6 CONCLUSIONS

The present study described an investigation on the impact that the presence or absence of vegetation in an urban context has on the ambient air temperature and, consequently, on the well-being perceived by the resident population.

ENVI-met software was used and comparisons between tree presence and absence were presented for summer period.

Although the study domain was of limited extension and this software shows some limits such as some approximations in calculations, for meso-research as thermal environment of residential areas, this model performs well.

The results highlighted substantial differences between the two situations examined, mainly in the summer scenarios.

It can be stated that as regards the distribution of the ambient air temperature in the avenue analysed, during summer the removal of trees leads to a significantly increase the local air temperature. The average increase in ambient air temperature is approximately 2°C compared to the state of the art, at a height of 1.5 m and in the central hours of a representative summer day. In the summer case, the comparison between the PMV and PPD indices also shows a substantial worsening of outdoor well-being conditions following the rehabilitation intervention and the tree removal.

This work showed the importance of numerical modelling for assessing potential impacts on outdoor well-being deriving from urban design interventions and, more specifically, it highlighted that maintenance interventions can have a significant and negative impact on the usability of outdoor spaces, confirming the idea that these studies should become mandatory to verify such impacts.

As expected, the present study has demonstrated that the removal of urban greenery has significant negative effects on air temperatures and on the outdoor comfort and that it is important to consider that these affects can be mitigated only in many years through the instalment and the growth of new greenery.

REFERENCES

[1] Gherri, B., Il comfort outdoor per gli spazi urbani, 258. 2012. https://www.researchgate.net/publication/323006526.

[2] ISPRA, Urbanizzazione costiera nei 300 m dalla riva. 2019. https://indicatoriambientali.isprambiente.it/ada/downreport/html/4940]#C4940.

[3] Lee, K.J., Han, B.H., Hong, S.H. & Choi, J.W., A study on the characteristics of urban ecosystems and plans for the environment and ecosystem in Gangnam-gu, Seoul, Korea. *Landscape and Ecological Engineering*, **1**, pp. 207–219, 2005. https://doi.org/10.1007/s11355-005-0025-x.

[4] Simson, A., The place of trees in the city of the future. *Arboricultural Journal*, **31**(2), pp. 97–108, 2008. https://doi.org/10.1080/03071375.2008.9747525.

[5] Pastore, L., Corrao, R. & Heiselberg, P.K., The effects of vegetation on indoor thermal comfort: The application of a multi-scale simulation methodology on a residential neighborhood renovation case study. *Energy and Buildings*, **146**, pp. 1–11, 2017. https://doi.org/10.1016/j.enbuild.2017.04.022.

[6] Al-hagla, K.S. & El-sayad, Z.T., Using simulation methods to investigate the impact of urban form on human comfort. Case study: Coast of Baltim, North Coast, Egypt. *Alexandria Engineering Journal*, **58**(1), pp. 273–282, 2019. https://doi.org/10.1016/j.aej.2019.02.002.

[7] Anyanwu, E.C. & Kanu, I., The role of urban forest in the protection of human environmental health in geographically-prone unpredictable hostile weather conditions, 2006.

[8] Yu, C. & Hien, W.N., Thermal benefits of city parks. *Energy and Buildings*, **38**(2), pp. 105–120, 2006. https://doi.org/10.1016/j.enbuild.2005.04.003.

[9] Simon, H., Lindén, J., Hoffmann, D., Braun, P., Bruse, M. & Esper, J., Modeling transpiration and leaf temperature of urban trees: A case study evaluating the microclimate model ENVI-met against measurement data. *Landscape and Urban Planning*, **174**, pp. 33–40, 2018. https://doi.org/10.1016/j.landurbplan.2018.03.003.

[10] Boukhabl, M. & Alkam, D., Impact of vegetation on thermal conditions outside. Thermal modeling of urban microclimate, Case study: The street of the republic, Biskra. *Energy Procedia*, **18**, pp. 73–84, 2012. https://doi.org/10.1016/j.egypro.2012.05.019.

[11] Rui, L., Buccolieri, R., Gao, Z., Gatto, E. & Ding, W., Study of the effect of green quantity and structure on thermal comfort and air quality in an urban-like residential district by ENVI-met modelling. *Building Simulation*, **12**, pp. 183–194, 2019. https://doi.org/10.1007/s12273-018-0498-9.

[12] ENVI-met®! http://www.envi-met.com. Accessed on: Jan. 2024.

[13] Fabbri, K. & Roberti, G., Guida all'utilizzo di ENVI-met. 2018. https://territorio.regione.emilia-romagna.it/paesaggio/formazione-lab-app-1/REBUS_12Envimet.pdf.

[14] Ouyang, W., Sinsel, T., Simon, H., Morakinyo, T.E., Liu, H. & Ng, E., Evaluating the thermal-radiative performance of ENVI-met model for green infrastructure typologies: Experience from a subtropical climate. *Building and Environment*, **207**, 108427, 2022. https://doi.org/10.1016/j.buildenv.2021.108427.

[15] Ayyad, Y.N. & Sharples, S., Envi-met validation and sensitivity analysis using field measurements in a hot arid climate. *IOP Conference Series: Earth and Environmental Science*, **329**(1), 012040, 2019. https://doi.org/10.1088/1755-1315/329/1/012040.

[16] Gusson, C.S. & Duarte, D.H., Effects of built density and urban morphology on urban microclimate-calibration of the model ENVI-met V4 for the subtropical Sao Paulo, Brazil. *Procedia Engineering*, **169**, pp. 2–10, 2016. https://doi.org/10.1016/j.proeng.2016.10.001.

[17] Taha, H., Urban climates and heat islands: Albedo, evapotranspiration, and anthropogenic heat. *Energy and Buildings*, **25**(2), pp. 99–103, 1997. https://doi.org/10.1016/S0378-7788(96)00999-1.

[18] Musco, F., Fregolent, L., Magni, F., Maragno, D. & Ferro, D., Calmierare gli impatti del fenomeno delle isole di calore urbano con la pianificazione urbanistica: esiti e applicazioni del progetto uhi (Central Europe) in Veneto. *Focus su Le città e le sfida dei cambiamenti climatici: Qualità dell'ambiente Urbano X Rapporto*, eds D. Gaudioso, F. Giordano & E. Taurino, ISPRA – Istituto Superiore per la Protezione e la Ricerca Ambientale: Rome, pp. 265–274, 2014.

[19] Aflaki, A. et al., Urban heat island mitigation strategies: A state-of-the-art review on Kuala Lumpur, Singapore and Hong Kong. *Cities*, **62**, pp. 131–145, 2017. https://doi.org/10.1016/j.cities.2016.09.003.

[20] Khodakarami, J. & Ghobadi, P., Urban pollution and solar radiation impacts. *Renewable and Sustainable Energy Reviews*, **57**, pp. 965–976, 2016. https://doi.org/10.1016/j.rser.2015.12.166.

[21] Lai, L.W. & Cheng, W.L., Air quality influenced by urban heat island coupled with synoptic weather patterns. *Science of the Total Environment*, **407**(8), pp. 2724–2733, 2009. https://doi.org/10.1016/j.scitotenv.2008.12.002.

[22] Camagni, R., Capello, R. & Nijkamp, P., Towards sustainable city policy: an economy-environment technology nexus. *Ecological Economics*, **24**(1), pp. 103–118, 1998. https://doi.org/10.1016/S0921-8009(97)00032-3.

[23] Ca, V.T., Asaeda, T. & Abu, E.M., Reductions in air conditioning energy caused by a nearby park. *Energy and Buildings*, **29**(1), pp. 83–92, 1998. https://doi.org/10.1016/S0378-7788(98)00032-2.
[24] Shashua-Bar, L., Potchter, O., Bitan, A., Boltansky, D. & Yaakov, Y., Microclimate modelling of street tree species effects within the varied urban morphology in the Mediterranean city of Tel Aviv, Israel. *International Journal of Climatology: A Journal of the Royal Meteorological Society*, **30**(1), pp. 44–57, 2010.
[25] SIRMIP, Dipartimento per le politiche integrate di sicurezza e per la protezione civile. https://www.regione.marche.it/Regione-Utile/Protezione-Civile/Console-Servizi-Protezione-Civile/SIRMIP-online.
[26] Taleb, D. & Abu-Hijleh, B., Urban heat islands: Potential effect of organic and structured urban configurations on temperature variations in Dubai, UAE. *Renewable Energy*, **50**, pp. 747–762, 2013. https://doi.org/10.1016/j.renene.2012.07.030.
[27] Huttner, S., Bruse, M. & Dostal, P., Using ENVI-met to simulate the impact of global warming on the microclimate in central European cities. *5th Japanese-German Meeting on Urban Climatology*, **18**(18), pp. 307–312, 2008.
[28] Ng, E., Chen, L., Wang, Y. & Yuan, C., A study on the cooling effects of greening in a high-density city: An experience from Hong Kong. *Building and Environment*, **47**, pp. 256–271, 2012. https://doi.org/10.1016/j.buildenv.2011.07.014.
[29] Ambrosini, D., Galli, G., Mancini, B., Nardi, I. & Sfarra, S., Evaluating mitigation effects of urban heat islands in a historical small center with the ENVI-Met® climate model. *Sustainability*, **6**(10), pp. 7013–7029, 2014. https://doi.org/10.3390/su6107013.

TOURISM AND SUSTAINABLE DESTINATIONS: A BIBLIOMETRIC EXAMINATION

MEHMET BAHADIR KALIPÇI
Manavgat Vocational School, Akdeniz University, Antalya, Turkey

ABSTRACT

This study aims to understand the dynamics and relationship between tourism and sustainable destinations via bibliometric analysis as these terms are among the 2030 goals of WTO. For this reason, the Web of Science (WoS) database was used to be able to obtain the dataset. Author keywords were used for the search. 406 studies were found; 384 of them were included. An R package, Bibliometrix, was used for the analysis as Bibliometrix performs the entire process. Main information, annual scientific production, most relevant sources and authors, most global cited documents, wordcloud and collaboration worldmap analysis were used. Findings show that between 2002 and 2023 the annual growth rate was 25.73%. *Sustainability* is the most relevant source while Mazilu, M. is the most relevant author. The Stylidis et al. (2014) article titled as 'Residents' support for tourism development: The role of residents' place image and perceived tourism impacts' is the most globally cited document. Wordcloud indicated that tourism, sustainable, and destination are the most frequent terms in the titles of the studies. China, UK and Spain are the lead countries which have the collaboration about the topic. Finally, future research directions were proposed.

Keywords: tourism, sustainable destinations, bibliometric analysis.

1 INTRODUCTION

Global attempts to lessen the negative effects of rising travel and tourism on the environment, society, and economy must now prioritise sustainable tourism [1]. The idea of sustainable destinations – places that give sustainability top priority in their development plans and tourism operations – is essential to this topic [2]. In order to maintain long-term viability and advantages for all stakeholders, these destinations strive to strike a balance between the requirements of tourists, local residents, and the environment [3]. The goal of this study's bibliometric analysis of sustainable destinations is to pinpoint key ideas, ground-breaking publications, and collaborative networks in this area of inquiry. This study uses quantitative approaches to analyse academic literature to understand how sustainable destinations are conceptualised, researched, and implemented in various situations.

2 LITERATURE REVIEW

Since its inception, worldwide policy frameworks and global environmental movements have significantly evolved the concept of sustainable tourism [4]. In the 1980s and 1990s, discussions of sustainable development centred on the need for tourism to be commercially, environmentally, and socially sustainable [5]. These ideas were informed by the Brundtland Report's definition of sustainable development. To accomplish these objectives, researchers like Bramwell and Lane [6] emphasised the need of integrated planning and management. Destinations that incorporate sustainable development principles into their tourism operations and policies are considered sustainable [7]. This entails controlling the expansion of tourism in a way that protects the destination's social, cultural, and natural fabric [8]. The fundamental tenets of sustainable tourism encompass cultural conservation, economic feasibility, social justice, and environmental responsibility [9]. A number of frameworks and standards have been created to help places become more environmentally friendly. Among the most frequently accepted standards are the Global Sustainable Tourism Council's

(GSTC) criteria, which offer a thorough set of recommendations covering sustainable management, socioeconomic advantages, cultural heritage protection, and environmental conservation. The United Nations World Tourism Organization (UNWTO) standards, Green Destinations, and the European Tourism Indicator System (ETIS) are a few more noteworthy frameworks.

3 METHODOLOGY

This study aims to understand the dynamics and relation between tourism and sustainable destinations. So, bibliometric analysis was used. Bibliometric analysis is used for performance analysis and science mapping. Performance analysis shows the evaluation of research and publications of individuals and institutions. Science mapping aims to reveal the structure and dynamics of the scientific field. Here, it is used to analyse the institutions, authors, publications and their relationships [10]–[12].

For this reason, main information, annual scientific production, most relevant sources and authors, most global cited documents, wordcloud and collaboration worldmap analysis were used respectively by using Bibliometrix. This is because Bibliometrix can perform the entire process unlike the other software programs [13].

Web of Science (WoS) database was used to be able to obtain the dataset, as it is advised by many authors who have published SSCI and SCI-E indexed bibliometric articles [14]–[16]. Author keywords were used for the search as this is the best parameter for this search [17]. 406 studies were found; 384 of them were included by excluding the year 2024 as it has not finished.

3.1 Findings

Table 1, which contains the main information about the data, is displayed below. The table shows that the first study was published in 2002. 384 different studies were published in 184 different sources such as journals, books, etc. Average citations per documents was found to be 5.89 whereas average citations per documents was found 2.85. 17,605 references were used in 384 studies. Most of the documents are articles in this category ($n = 287$). While it was found that 625 keywords plus (ID) were used, 1,193 author's keywords (DE) were used in these studies. Only 53 of 958 authors have single-authored documents. Most of the authors have multi-authored documents ($n = 905$). Collaboration index was found equal to 2.76. The table is presented below for the other details.

The annual growth rate was found to be 25.73%. Although there are micro fluctuations in the figure since 2002, there is an increasing tendency which shows that this topic has a potential, and researchers will pay more attention to it (Fig. 1).

In Fig. 2, the most relevant sources were displayed. According to the figure, *Sustainability* is the most relevant source with the number of documents it has published ($n = 69$) till 2024. The second one is *Journal of Sustainable Tourism* ($n = 20$) whereas *Worldwide Hospitality and Tourism Themes* ($n = 10$) is the third one. The others with the number of documents can be seen below.

According to the Bibliometrix, the top three most relevant authors who have published documents about these topics are Mazilu, M. ($n = 5$), Birkic, D. ($n = 4$), and Dwyer, L. ($n = 4$). Other authors and the number of documents they have published are given in Fig. 3.

In Fig. 4, the most global cited documents were given. The figure displays that the article by Stylidis et al. [18] 'Residents' support for tourism development: The role of residents' place image and perceived tourism impacts' is the most global cited document according to

Table 1: Main information. *(Source: Own elaboration done by Bibliometrix.)*

Description		Results
Main information about data	Timespan	2002–2023
	Sources (journals, books, etc.)	183
	Documents	384
	Average years from publication	5.89
	Average citations per documents	18.06
	Average citations per year per document	2.85
	References	17,605
Document types	Article	287
	Article; book chapter	4
	Article; early access	9
	Article; proceedings paper	2
	Editorial material	4
	Proceedings paper	62
	Review	16
Document contents	Keywords plus (ID)	625
	Author's keywords (DE)	1,193
Authors	Authors	958
	Author appearances	1,090
	Authors of single-authored documents	53
	Authors of multi-authored documents	905
Authors collaboration	Single-authored documents	56
	Documents per author	0.401
	Authors per document	2.49
	Co-authors per documents	2.84
	Collaboration index	2.76

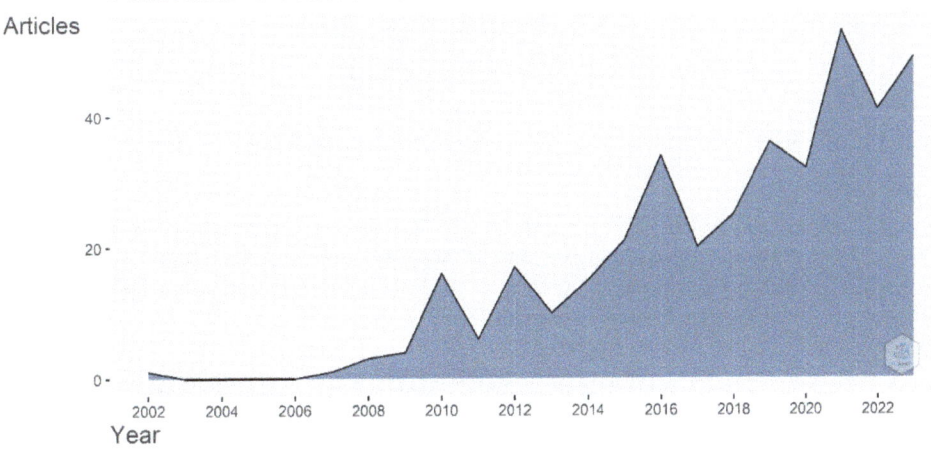

Figure 1: Annual scientific production. *(Source: Own elaboration done by Bibliometrix.)*

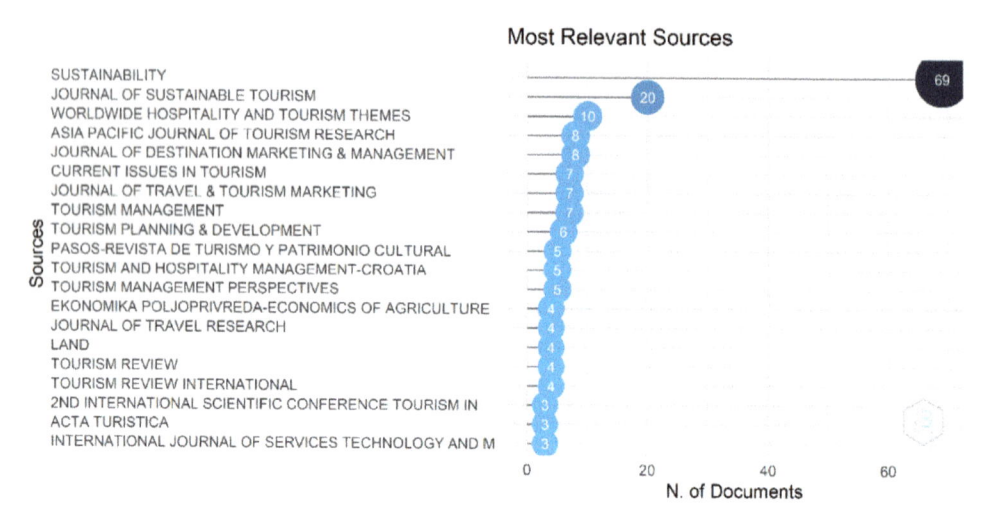

Figure 2: Most relevant sources. *(Source: Own elaboration done by Bibliometrix.)*

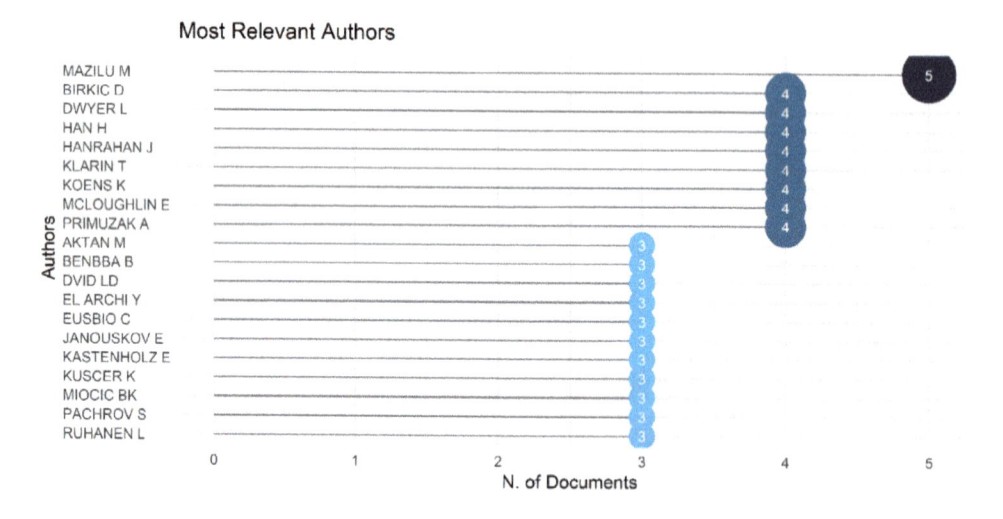

Figure 3: Most relevant authors. *(Source: Own elaboration done by Bibliometrix.)*

the total citations (TC) (TC = 363). The article by Koens et al. [19] entitled 'Is overtourism overused? Understanding the impact of tourism in a city context' is the second document on the list (TC = 328). The article by Dwyer et al. [20] entitled 'Destination and enterprise management for a tourism future' is the third one on the list (TC = 283). The details about other documents can be seen in Fig. 4.

By selecting titles as a parameter, wordcloud gives the researchers clues about the tendency of the studies about these topics. As a result, tourism (frequency (f) = 281), sustainable (f = 203), destination (f = 122), development (f = 111), destinations (f = 94), tourist (f = 67), sustainability (f = 42), management (f = 40), analysis (f = 26), and rural (f = 25) are the most dominant top 10 words in the titles. This can be seen in Fig. 5.

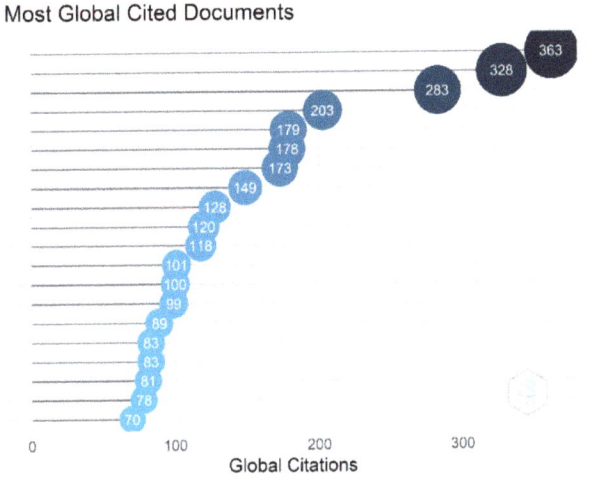

Figure 4: Most global cited documents. *(Source: Own elaboration done by Bibliometrix.)*

Figure 5: Wordcloud parameter: Titles. *(Source: Own elaboration done by Bibliometrix.)*

The country collaboration map shows us the network of the countries which work on these topics together. Bold lines show us that there is a strong network between the countries. According to that, China–UK (f = 4), China–USA (f = 4), Netherlands–South Africa (f = 4), Spain–Ecuador (f = 4), Spain–Italy (f = 4), and UK–Germany (f = 4) are the countries which collaborate most together about tourism and sustainable destinations (Fig. 6).

4 CONCLUSION

This study provides an extensive overview of the research trends, main contributors, and collaboration networks in the field of tourism and sustainable destinations from 2002 to 2023 by bibliometric analysis. The results shed important light on how research on sustainable

Country Collaboration Map

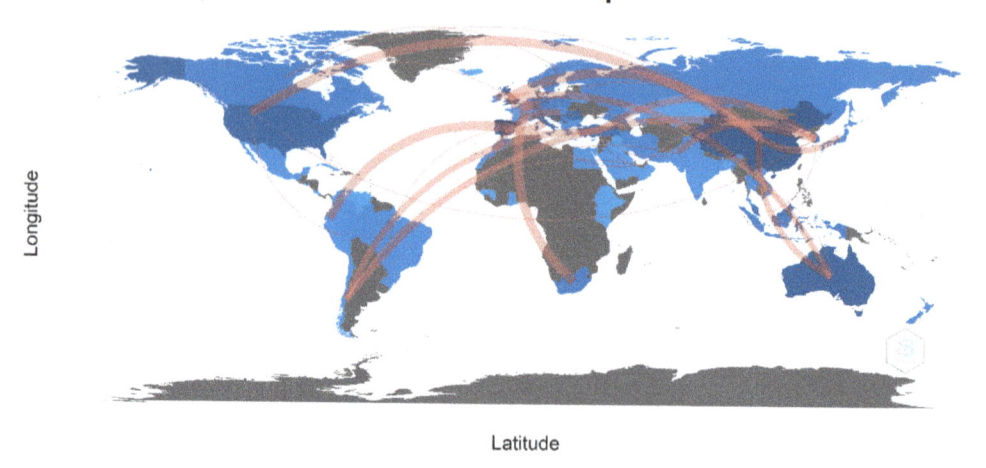

Figure 6: Country collaboration map. *(Source: Own elaboration done by Bibliometrix.)*

tourism and destinations has developed over time. A total of 384 studies – published in 184 different publications and books – have been published since the initial research was released in 2002. 5.89 citations on average per publication indicates a moderate level of recognition and impact within the academic world. The total number of references cited in these publications is 17,605, which illustrates the depth and scope of the field's study. According to these parameters, research on sustainable tourism is being conducted in a way that is both impactful and prolific, greatly advancing both academic and practical knowledge in the field.

Journal papers represent the bulk of the documents ($n = 287$), demonstrating the importance of peer-reviewed literature in distributing knowledge about sustainable destinations. Journal publications are preferred because of their thorough review procedures and wider distribution, which enhance the legitimacy and visibility of the research. Significant keyword usage was also found by the investigation, with 1,193 author's keywords (DE) and 625 keywords plus (ID) being used. A broad range of research interests and emphasis points, from particular sustainability practices to more general conceptual frameworks, are indicated by the diversity of keywords. This suggests that the literature has a rich and varied theme landscape. This study field is dominated by collaborative efforts, as seen by authorship patterns. With 905 authors contributing to multi-authored works, out of 958 contributors, only 53 have single-authored publications; this results in a collaboration index of 2.76. This high degree of cooperation indicates the multidisciplinary character of research on sustainable tourism, which calls for contributions from various disciplines including economics, sociology, environmental science, and urban planning. It also implies that scholars understand how complicated sustainability issues are and how different skills are required to solve them successfully. This emphasises how crucial collaborative research is to the advancement of sustainable tourism research. Despite variations over time, the annual growth rate of 25.73% indicates a robust and growing interest in sustainable destinations for travel. This implies that the subject has a lot of potential and will probably keep getting scholarly attention in the future.

With 69 studies published on the topic, the journal *Sustainability* comes out on top, followed by the *Journal of Sustainable Tourism* ($n = 20$) and *Worldwide Hospitality and Tourism Themes* ($n = 10$). The fact that these journals are at the forefront of publishing research on sustainable tourism suggests how important a role they play in influencing the conversation and determining the direction of future research. This demonstrates how important these journals are in influencing the conversation about environmentally friendly travel.

Mazilu, M. ($n = 5$), Birkic, D. ($n = 4$), and Dwyer, L. ($n = 4$) are the top authors who have contributed to the scholarship on sustainable destinations. Their efforts have played a crucial role in expanding knowledge and understanding in this area. The word cloud analysis sheds light on the recurring topics and areas of interest in the literature based on study titles. The most common keywords, which highlight the main areas of interest and research, are tourism, sustainable, destination, development, tourism, sustainable, management, analysis, and rural. The frequency of keywords like 'rural' indicates an elevated interest in the relationship between sustainability and rural tourism, emphasising the necessity of sustainable practices in less developed and frequently environmentally sensitive destinations.

Significant international cooperation is revealed by the country collaboration map, with notable collaborations between China, the UK and the USA. They also demonstrate the understanding that to effectively address the global character of sustainability concerns in tourism, coordinated international actions are necessary. This demonstrates how international research on sustainable destinations is and how crucial international collaborations are to the field's advancement. This bibliometric research concludes by highlighting the active and expanding interest in eco-friendly travel destinations and tourism. The results emphasise significant figures, overarching themes, and cooperative networks that influence this field's scholarly environment. Research on sustainable destinations is expected to increase as interest in sustainability grows, offering important insights and answers to the problems associated with the development of sustainable tourism.

This bibliometric analysis highlights a vibrant and expanding area of study devoted to environmentally friendly travel and travel destinations. The significance and applicability of this research are demonstrated by the growing scholarly interest, high levels of collaboration, and noteworthy contributions from important authors and journals. Research on sustainable destinations is expected to grow as sustainability continues to gain traction in international conversations, offering vital insights and answers to the urgent problems confronting the travel and tourism sector. In addition to mapping the existing status of the sector, this analysis lays the groundwork for future studies that may promote more environmentally friendly travel patterns across the entire world.

REFERENCES

[1] Aall, C., Sustainable tourism in practice: Promoting or perverting the quest for a sustainable development? *Sustainability*, **6**(5), pp. 2562–2583, 2014.

[2] Roxas, F.M.Y., Rivera, J.P.R. & Gutierrez, E.L.M., Mapping stakeholders' roles in governing sustainable tourism destinations. *Journal of Hospitality and Tourism Management*, **45**, pp. 387–398, 2020.

[3] Kastenholz, E., 'Management of demand' as a tool in sustainable tourist destination development. *Journal of Sustainable Tourism*, **12**(5), pp. 388–408, 2004.

[4] Stoddart, M.C. & Nezhadhossein, E., Is nature-oriented tourism a pro-environmental practice? Examining tourism–environmentalism alignments through discourse networks and intersectoral relationships. *The Sociological Quarterly*, **57**(3), pp. 544–568, 2016.

[5]   Ruhanen, L. et al., Trends and patterns in sustainable tourism research: A 25-year bibliometric analysis. *Journal of Sustainable Tourism*, **23**(4), pp. 517–535, 2015.
[6]   Bramwell, B. & Lane, B., Interpretation and sustainable tourism: The potential and the pitfalls. *Journal of Sustainable Tourism*, **1**(2), pp. 71–80, 1993.
[7]   Simão, J.N. & Partidario, M.d.R., How does tourism planning contribute to sustainable development? *Sustainable Development*, **20**(6), pp. 372–385, 2012.
[8]   Higgins-Desbiolles, F. et al., Degrowing tourism: Rethinking tourism. *Journal of Sustainable Tourism*, 2019.
[9]   Sharpley, R., Tourism and sustainable development: Exploring the theoretical divide. *Journal of Sustainable Tourism*, **8**(1), pp. 1–19, 2000.
[10] Durieux, V. & Gevenois, P.A., Bibliometric indicators: Quality measurements of scientific publication. *Radiology*, **255**(2), pp. 342–351, 2010.
[11] Krauskopf, E., A bibiliometric analysis of the *Journal of Infection and Public Health*: 2008–2016. *Journal of Infection and Public Health*, **11**(2), pp. 224–229, 2018.
[12] Zupic, I. & Čater, T., Bibliometric methods in management and organization. *Organizational Research Methods*, **18**(3), pp. 429–472, 2015.
[13] Aria, M. & Cuccurullo, C., Bibliometrix: An R-tool for comprehensive science mapping analysis. *Journal of Informetrics*, **11**(4), pp. 959–975, 2017.
[14] Şimşek, E.K. & Kalıpçı, M.B., A bibliometric study on higher tourism education and curriculum. *Journal of Hospitality, Leisure, Sport and Tourism Education*, **33**, 100442, 2023.
[15] Kalipçi, M.B., Şimşek, E.K. & Ramazan, E., Decoding the trends and the emerging research directions of e-commerce and tourism in the light of resource dependence theory: A bibliometric analysis. 2024.
[16] Şimşek, E.K. et al., Sustainability and the food industry: A bibliometric analysis. *Sustainability*, **16**(7), p. 3070, 2024.
[17] Lu, W. et al., How do authors select keywords? A preliminary study of author keyword selection behavior. *Journal of Informetrics*, **14**(4), 101066, 2020.
[18] Stylidis, D., Biran, A., Sit, J. & Szivas, E.M., Residents' support for tourism development: The role of residents' place image and perceived tourism impacts. *Tourism Management*, **45**, pp. 260–274, 2014.
[19] Koens, K., Postma, A. & Papp, B., Is overtourism overused? Understanding the impact of tourism in a city context. *Sustainability*, **10**(12), 4384, 2018.
[20] Dwyer, L., Edwards, D., Mistilis, N., Roman, C. & Scott, N., Destination and enterprise management for a tourism future. *Tourism Management*, **30**(1), pp. 63–74, 2009.

TOURISM CARRYING CAPACITY OF GEOSITES ON SANTA CRUZ ISLAND, GALAPAGOS, FOR ITS SUSTAINABILITY

MARÍA JAYA-MONTALVO[1,2], JOSUÉ BRIONES-BITAR[1,2,3], LADY SOTO-NAVARRETE[4], RAMÓN ESPINEL[5] & PAÚL CARRIÓN-MERO[1,2]
[1]Centro de Investigación y Proyectos Aplicados a la Ciencias de la Tierra, ESPOL Polytechnic University, Ecuador
[2]Facultad de Ingeniería en Ciencias de la Tierra, ESPOL Polytechnic University, Ecuador
[3]E.T.S. de Ingenieros de Caminos, Canales y Puertos, Universidad Politécnica de Madrid, Spain
[4]Facultad de Ciencias Sociales y Humanísticas, ESPOL Polytechnic University, Ecuador
[5]Centro de Investigaciones Rurales, ESPOL Polytechnic University, Ecuador

ABSTRACT
Galapagos was declared a Natural World Heritage Site (1976), UNESCO Biosphere Reserve (1984), and Ramsar Site (2001) because of its unique flora, fauna and landscapes, which inspired Charles Darwin. Due to the variety of tourist sites around the four large inhabited islands, there is an increase in national and foreign tourists (267,688 people in 2022), which may cause deterioration of the tourist facilities if not adequately monitored or regulated. This study aims to evaluate the tourism carrying capacity of 15 geosites on Santa Cruz Island, Galapagos, through qualitative and quantitative information for the sustainable enhancement and optimal use of geotourism. Field visits were made to collect data and information from each of the 15 geosites, and the tourism carrying capacity was calculated and evaluated using a methodology proposed by several authors for the development of sustainable geotourism strategies. In the evaluation of the carrying capacity, the visitor numbers varied between 500 and 2,000 per day, with Tortuga Bay and Playa 'El Garrapatero' standing out for their large size to accommodate tourists and adequate geotourism facilities. This analysis and evaluation allowed us to propose improvement strategies to promote and optimise the use of geosites based on geotourism, geo-education and geoconservation pillars. A fundamental axis is governmental participation through plans that motivate awareness-raising and sustainable tourism, as well as geocommunication of the unique values of each geosite, to argue technically for the sustainability of natural heritage.
Keywords: geotourism, geological sites of interest, sustainability, ecotourism, environmental protection, Galapagos.

1 INTRODUCTION
Geotourism is a type of tourism that highlights and gives importance to the geology and landscape of destinations for the promotion of sustainable tourism development to improve the local economy, well-being of communities, and conservation of the destination [1], [2]. Geotourism, proposed as a valuable tool for promoting natural and cultural heritage, enables sustainable economic and social growth in a region [3], [4]. Geotourism also seeks to minimise the negative impacts of mass tourism on geographically or geologically sensitive tourism ecosystems, while supporting sustainable rural development [5], [6].

Geotourism focuses on showcasing a destination's unique natural and cultural heritage and preserving and protecting its authenticity [7]. The set of unique geological features that are the product of the Earth's history can be seen in various forms (rocks, minerals, fossils, and soil), which bring together a diverse landscape system known as geodiversity [8], [9]. Therefore, quantitative or qualitative geoheritage assessment is an essential topic worldwide, as it allows proper monitoring and sustainable development planning of sites with geological potential [10], [11].

Interest in conserving abiotic landscapes and landforms for tourism, heritage or recognition of natural values has been both dynamic and uneven [12]. The growing interest in geoconservation has been demonstrated by numerous inventories of sites of interest conducted in different countries [4], [13]. Some sites of geological interest (SGIs) are at risk due to their vulnerability to natural and anthropogenic degradation (e.g. mines and construction of civil works) [14].

The tourism development of geological sites of interest can bring considerable economic benefits, but it will also put tremendous pressure on public resources, the cultural atmosphere, and the ecological environment, jeopardising the sustainable promotion of the destination [15], [16]. As a basis for tourism development planning, academics, industry professionals, and governments have proposed a tourism carrying capacity (TCC) [17], [18]. TCC is the maximum tourist presence at a destination that does not disrupt the ordinary activities of residents or prevent tourists from appreciating the destination, causing overtourism [19], [20].

In terms of biodiversity, Ecuador ranks 17th globally. In recent years, Ecuador has maintained increased tourist arrivals because of its natural beauty [21]. According to the Ecuadorian environmental legislation, the conservation of geological heritage is linked to protected natural areas [22]. The term geoheritage was unknown until recently [23]; however, since the creation of the Ecuadorian Geoparks Committee in 2019, the dissemination of the topic has gained greater public attention [24].

Galapagos, known for its volcanic origin ('hotspot'), was declared a UNESCO World Heritage Site in 1978 [25], because of its extraordinary biodiversity and natural surroundings. It is located 972 km off the mainland coast of Ecuador and consists of 13 main volcanic islands and more than 300 islets and rocks [26]. Santa Cruz, San Cristóbal, Isabela and Floreana islands have permanent human settlements [27]. Galapagos is a well-known tourist destination where authorities seek strategies to promote conservation and community interests through tourism [28] (Fig. 1).

Santa Cruz Island is a 990 km^2 elliptical shield volcano that rose 950 m.a.s.l. approximately 2 million years ago [29]. The most notable topographic features are steep volcanic cinder cones, large pit craters (more than 100 m in diameter and 100 m deep), and deeply incised ephemeral or permanent river channels [30], [31]. Soils developed from the in situ weathering of volcanic rocks and pyroclastic materials [32], [33].

Kelley and Salazar [34], Kelley et al. [35], and Carrión-Mero et al. [36] qualitatively explored the geodiversity and geoheritage of the islands, including their origin, geological context and conservation on the islands. Specifically, these authors proposed an inventory covering 15 geosites on Santa Cruz Island, which is essential for the sustainable management of the national park and its surroundings.

The Galapagos National Park Administration (GNP) prepares an annual report on the number of tourists visiting the Galapagos Islands, noting that visits have increased by 23% from 2022 to 2023 (267,688 and 329,475 tourist arrivals, respectively) [37], [38]. Authorised visitor numbers have increased under demand without the necessary studies to justify such increases, and this excess has caused degradation and deterioration of the number of tourist sites visited.

Therefore, how to evaluate the adequate tourism capacity at these SGIs to guarantee a correct monitoring and management system for the GNP? To answer the research question, the objective of this research is to evaluate the TCC of 15 SGIs suggested by Carrión-Mero et al. [36] using a physical, real and practical tourism calculation for the proposal of political, economic, social and environmental solutions that allow the correct management of these sites.

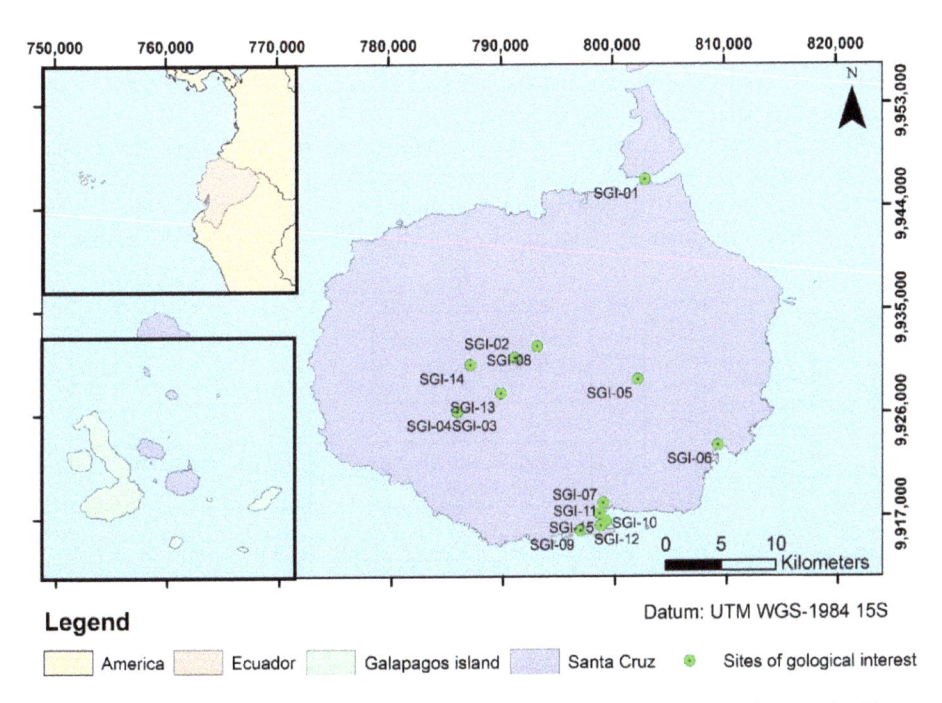

Figure 1: Location map of Santa Cruz Island, Galapagos, and its sites of geological interest (SGIs) (see Table 1).

Table 1: Selection of sites of geological interest (SGIs) on Santa Cruz Island.

Code	Name	Coordinates (UTM WGS-1984 16S)
SGI-01	Itabaca channel	x: 802844; y: 9946335
SGI-02	Los Gemelos	x: 791177; y: 9930863
SGI-03	Primicias tunnel	x: 785994; y: 9926161
SGI-04	Turtle lagoon	x: 785994; y: 9926161
SGI-05	Mesa hill	x: 802151; y: 9928951
SGI-06	'El Garrapatero' beach	x: 809298; y: 9923185
SGI-07	'Misión Franciscana' crack	x: 799020; y: 9918220
SGI-08	Quarry	x: 793167; y: 9931858
SGI-09	Tortoise bay	x: 796975; y: 9915803
SGI-10	'Los Alemanes' beach	x: 799258; y: 9916622
SGI-11	Salt mine	x: 798998; y: 9916439
SGI-12	'Las Grietas'	x: 798795; y: 9916230
SGI-13	Royal Palm tunnels	x: 789896; y: 9927792
SGI-14	'Diego Salazar' lagoon	x: 787163; y: 9930271
SGI-15	'Las Ninfas' lagoon	x: 798709; y: 9917275

2 MATERIALS AND METHODS

Determining the carrying capacity (CC) of visitor sites is essential in taking the first step towards effectively managing these SGIs. This study contributes to strengthening the concept of sustainable tourism with the component of geological sites of interest by using and modifying a TCC assessment methodology. This study also provides a deeper understanding of the geological heritage of the Galapagos Islands and its potential for sustainable tourism development, scientific research, and preservation.

The present research focused on the development of the following three phases: (i) selection of geosites on Santa Cruz Island; (ii) evaluation of the TCC of the selected geosites; and (iii) proposal of geotourism sustainability strategies within the evaluated geosites. Fig. 2 shows a summary diagram of the methodology followed in this research.

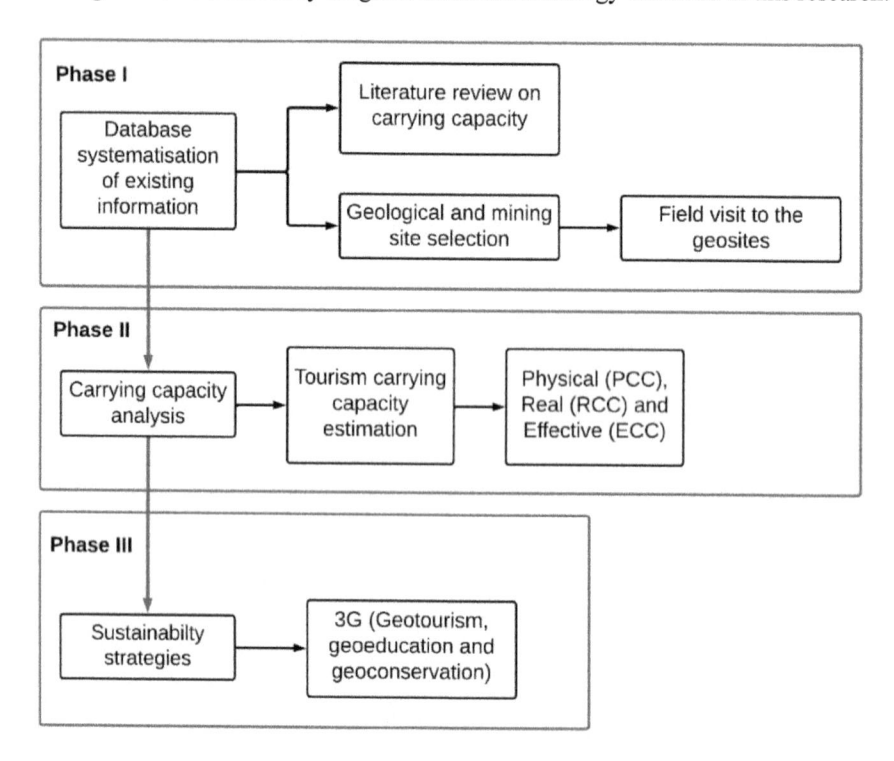

Figure 2: Methodology adopted in this research.

2.1 Geosite selection

This first phase consisted of a literature review of the geosites inventoried and evaluated in the study area for their geological and mining relevance in scientific publications. In this study, the 15 inventoried and evaluated sites of Carrión-Mero et al. [36] were the SGIs chosen.

After selecting the geosites, the authors visited each site to obtain data and information for assessment during this phase.

2.2 TCC assessment

Several authors have proposed a methodology for estimating and assessing the TCC [40]–[42]. The assessment consists of three components: physical carrying capacity (PCC), real carrying capacity (RCC), and effective carrying capacity (ECC). The professionals in charge of these assessments were co-authors of this study (Table 2).

Table 2: Explanation and determination on physical carrying capacity (PCC), real carrying capacity (RCC), and effective carrying capacity (ECC).

	PCC	RCC	ECC
Explanation	Maximum visits can occur at the site during a specific time within a particular space	PCC correction factors that affect the site directly or indirectly	Maximum visits to each SGI can allow for the analysis of certain variables
Determination	PCC = (V/a) × S × t where: V/a: visitors/occupied area; S: area available for visitors' access; t: necessary time for the visit	• Social factor • Solar factor • Precipitation factor • Erodibility factor • Accessibility factor • Temporary closure factor • Waterlogging factor	• Staff (guides) • Infrastructure

2.3 Proposed geotourism sustainability strategies

The results obtained from Phase II provided an analysis of the current state of each geosite, considering the impact of tourism and human activity. With this, it is intended to propose strategies that will help the tourism sustainability of the geosites and allow correct geotourism development on Santa Cruz Island. To this end, applying the modified 3G model enables the development of strategies in three main areas for sustainable tourism at geosites (geotourism, geoeducation, and geoconservation) [43], [44].

3 RESULTS AND DISCUSSION

3.1 TCC assessment

CC is a widely used tool for tourism management. CC refers to the maximum number of visitors a tourism site can support sustainably (without degradation). Table 3 presents the estimated number of people who can visit sites of geological or mining interest.

Table 3: Carrying capacity values (PCC, RCC, ECC) (visits/day) of the evaluated SGIs.

Code	Name	PCC	RCC	ECC	Image
SGI-01	Itabaca channel	28,500	3,996	2,797	

Table 3: Continued.

Code	Name	PCC	RCC	ECC	Image
SGI-02	Los Gemelos	1,600	377	339	
SGI-03	Primicias tunnel	550	130	97	
SGI-04	Turtle lagoon	733	194	156	
SGI-05	Mesa hill	833	132	113	
SGI-06	'El Garrapatero' beach	5,958	1,053	684	
SGI-07	'Misión Franciscana' crack	200	61	44	
SGI-08	Quarry	2,500	282	42	

Table 3: Continued.

Code	Name	PCC	RCC	ECC	Image
SGI-09	Tortoise bay	6,500	1,149	747	
SGI-10	'Los Alemanes' beach	1,200	316	205	
SGI-11	Salt mine	1,200	337	269	
SGI-12	'Las Grietas'	1,200	337	269	
SGI-13	Royal Palm tunnels	550	144	101	
SGI-14	'Diego Salazar' lagoon	667	56	47	
SGI-15	'Las Ninfas' lagoon	500	265	172	

The Itabaca channel was the geosite with the highest PCC (28,500 visitors per day), but it decreased to an ECC of 2,797 visitors per day. This decrease was mainly due to correction factors such as social (because they must be visited in groups and on boats), accessibility (as they must be on boats, people with reduced mobility are a challenge), precipitation, and solar (as it is an outdoor geosite, on days with a lot of precipitation or solar radiation, it can cause people not to make tourist visits).

Geosites such as Royal Palm tunnels, Quarry, 'Misión Franciscana' crack, Primicias tunnel and Mesa hill have a large surface area available for tourist visits; however, there are sections with slopes of between 10%–20%, or sections with gullies, making accessibility difficult for vulnerable groups (reduced mobility and elderly people).

The 'Misión Franciscana' crack, Quarry and 'Diego Salazar' lagoon are privately managed geosites, for the moment, which does not allow tourists to get to know them in their entirety. This means that they do not have infrastructure, or personnel hired for tourism or geotourism activities. These can help the GNP have more tourist sites in its catalogue.

3.2 Proposed geotourism sustainability strategies

Based on information on CC, this study proposes designing a 3G model (focused on geotourism, geoconservation, and geoeducation) to establish proposals for managing and conserving geosites. It shows an approach with strategic proposals that consider the unfavourable (negative) and unexploited aspects of each geosite.

- Geotourism: (i) Promote the development of geoproducts with community participation; (ii) Improve security in each geosite; (iii) Increase the diversity of tourism services in each geosite.
- Geoconservation: (i) Support the preservation of geosites with inclusive operational programmes; (ii) Seek public and private financial support for flora and fauna conservation, (iii) Foster knowledge of geotourism at all educational levels.
- Geoeducation: (i) Enhancing the community–academia–government nexus; (ii) Promote environmental education as a driver of sustainable development; (iii) Provide training for tourism service providers in geotourism issues.

Strengthening geotourism within these geosites allows progress in the development of the Galapagos Geopark proposal. Galapagos has two UNESCO designations for flora and fauna (World Heritage Site and Biosphere Reserve) but can eventually obtain the highest designation for geotourism (Global Geopark). In presenting the idea of these geosites, the authorities (decision-makers) must come together to provide security and diversify their tourism services.

Within the geoeducation axis, the political sector should include geotourism in academic curricula and strengthen the links between the actors of the three subsystems (community, government, and academia). The education industry can contribute to developing a geotourism management model by conducting research and scientific dissemination activities related to geoheritage and sustainable tourism.

4 CONCLUSION

This study comprehensively assesses the TCC of 15 geosites within Santa Cruz Island, Galapagos. These results provide valuable guidance for the sustainable management of geosites, thereby strengthening conservation for the optimal use of geotourism attractions.

The Itabaca Channel has the highest ECC, with 28,500 visitors per day. 'El Garrapatero' beach (5,958), Tortoise Bay (6,500), 'Los Alemanes' beach (1,200) and 'Las Grietas' (1,200) can attract many visitors, but their ECC decreases due to factors such as climate, accessibility and tourist operations related to lack of tour guides. Whereas, Royal Palm tunnels, Quarry, 'Misión Franciscana' crack, Primicias tunnel and Mesa Hill have a larger surface area available for tourist visits; however, the slope or uneven terrain may make accessibility difficult for certain groups of visitors, which reduces the ECC.

This study proposed an integrated 3G model (geotourism, geoconservation, and geoeducation) for the development and management of geosites. The importance of this model lies in its holistic approach, which addresses the attractiveness of tourism and environmental sustainability of geosites. The geotourism axis highlights the need to diversify and improve tourism services, increase the attractiveness of geosites, and generate employment and economic benefits for local communities. The geo-conservation axis stresses the importance of protecting biodiversity and geoheritage, which is crucial for ensuring that geosites can maintain ecosystem balance and can be enjoyed by future generations. The geo-education axis highlights the vital role of education and communication between local and tourist populations, and governments in promoting sustainable geotourism.

Future research should address geo-environmental and social assessments using complementary methodologies to understand how they change in response to management interventions, and environmental and social conditions. These efforts will improve the scientific understanding of these geosites, contribute to effective and sustainable geotourism management, benefit local communities, and promote the prosperity of the Geopark project.

ACKNOWLEDGEMENTS

This work was supported by the research project, 'Registro de sitios de interés geológicos del Ecuador para estrategias de desarrollo sostenible', with Code CIPAT-004-2024 from ESPOL Polytechnic University. Also, thanks to the project entitled 'Generation of base information for irrigation and drainage projects in the Galapagos Islands' of the Consejo de Gobierno del Régimen Especial Galápagos (CGREG) and Centro de Investigaciones Rurales (CIR) of ESPOL for its management support.

REFERENCES

[1] Newsome, D., Ladd, P. & Dowling, R., The scope for geotourism based on Regolith in southwestern Australia: A theoretical and practical perspective. *Geoheritage*, **14**, 5, 2022. https://doi.org/10.1007/s12371-021-00632-1.

[2] Dowling, R. & Newsome, D. (eds), *Handbook of Geotourism*, Edward Elgar, 2018.

[3] Herrera, G., Carrión, P. & Briones, J., Geotourism potential in the context of the geopark project for the development of Santa Elena province, Ecuador. *WIT Transactions on Ecology and the Environment*, Siena, Italy, 4 Sep., pp. 557–568 2018.

[4] Quesada-Valverde, M.E. & Quesada-Román, A., Worldwide trends in methods and resources promoting geoconservation, geotourism, and geoheritage. *Geosciences*, **13**, 39, 2023. https://doi.org/10.3390/geosciences13020039.

[5] Frey, M.-L., Geotourism: Examining tools for sustainable development. *Geosciences*, **11**, 30, 2021. https://doi.org/10.3390/geosciences11010030.

[6] Carrión-Mero, P., Morante-Carballo, F. & Apolo-Masache, B., Evaluation of geosites as an alternative for geotouristic development in Guayaquil, Ecuador. *WIT Transactions on Ecology and the Environment*, Nov. 18, pp. 45–56, 2020.

[7] Selem, K.M., Khalid, R., Tan, C.C., Sinha, R. & Raza, M., Geotourism destination development: Scale development and validation. *J. Outdoor Recreat. Tour.*, **46**, 100763, 2024. https://doi.org/10.1016/j.jort.2024.100763.

[8] Pourfaraj, A., Ghaderi, E., Jomehpour, M. & Ferdowsi, S., Conservation management of geotourism attractions in tourism destinations. *Geoheritage*, **12**, 80, 2020. https://doi.org/10.1007/s12371-020-00500-4.

[9] Gray, M., Geodiversity: Developing the paradigm. *Proc. Geol. Assoc.*, **119**, pp. 287–298, 2008. https://doi.org/10.1016/S0016-7878(08)80307-0.

[10] Xu, K. & Wu, W., Geoparks and geotourism in China: A sustainable approach to geoheritage conservation and local development – A review. *Land*, **11**, 1493, 2022. https://doi.org/10.3390/land11091493.

[11] AbdelMaksoud, K.M., Emam, M., Al Metwaly, W., Sayed, F. & Berry, J., Can innovative tourism benefit the local community: The analysis about establishing a geopark in Abu Roash area, Cairo, Egypt. *Int. J. Geoheritage Park*, **9**, pp. 509–525, 2021. https://doi.org/10.1016/j.ijgeop.2021.11.009.

[12] Williams, M.A., McHenry, M.T. & Boothroyd, A., Geoconservation and geotourism: Challenges and unifying themes. *Geoheritage*, **12**, 63, 2020. https://doi.org/10.1007/s12371-020-00492-1.

[13] Santos, D.S., Reynard, E., Mansur, K.L. & Seoane, J.C.S., The specificities of geomorphosites and their influence on assessment procedures: A methodological comparison. *Geoheritage*, **11**, pp. 2045–2064, 2019. https://doi.org/10.1007/s12371-019-00411-z.

[14] Brilha, J., Geoheritage: Inventories and evaluation. *Geoheritage*, Elsevier, pp. 69–85, 2018.

[15] Wang, J., Huang, X., Gong, Z. & Cao, K., Dynamic assessment of tourism carrying capacity and its impacts on tourism economic growth in urban tourism destinations in China. *J. Destin. Mark. Manag.*, **15**, 100383, 2020. https://doi.org/10.1016/j.jdmm.2019.100383.

[16] Li, J., Weng, G., Pan, Y., Li, C. & Wang, N., A scientometric review of tourism carrying capacity research: Cooperation, hotspots, and prospect. *J. Clean. Prod.*, **325**, 129278, 2021. https://doi.org/10.1016/j.jclepro.2021.129278.

[17] Wang, Y., Xie, T. & Jie, X., A mathematical analysis for the forecast research on tourism carrying capacity to promote the effective and sustainable development of tourism. *Discret. Contin. Dyn. Syst.*, **12**, pp. 837–847, 2019. https://doi.org/10.3934/dcdss.2019056.

[18] Zekan, B., Weismayer, C., Gunter, U., Schuh, B. & Sedlacek, S., Regional sustainability and tourism carrying capacities. *J. Clean. Prod.*, **339**, 130624, 2022. https://doi.org/10.1016/j.jclepro.2022.130624.

[19] Butler, R.W., Tourism carrying capacity research: A perspective article. *Tour. Rev.*, **75**, pp. 207–211, 2020. https://doi.org/10.1108/TR-05-2019-0194.

[20] Tokarchuk, O., Barr, J.C. & Cozzio, C., How much is too much? Estimating tourism carrying capacity in urban context using sentiment analysis. *Tour. Manag.*, 91, 104522, 2022. https://doi.org/10.1016/j.tourman.2022.104522.

[21] Mestanza-Ramón, C., Chica-Ruiz, J.A., Anfuso, G., Mooser, A., Botero, C.M. & Pranzini, E., Tourism in continental Ecuador and the Galapagos Islands: An integrated coastal zone management (ICZM) perspective. *Water*, **12**, 1647, 2020. https://doi.org/10.3390/w12061647.

[22] Sánchez-Cortez, J.L., Conservation of geoheritage in Ecuador: Situation and perspectives. *Int. J. Geoheritage Park*, **7**, pp. 91–101, 2019. https://doi.org/10.1016/j.ijgeop.2019.06.002.

[23] Berrezueta, E., Sánchez-Cortez, J.L. & Aguilar-Aguilar, M., Inventory and characterization of geosites in Ecuador: A review. *Geoheritage*, **13**, 93, 2021. https://doi.org/10.1007/s12371-021-00619-y.

[24] Cayambe, J., Diaz-Ambrona, C.G.H., Torres, B. & Heredia-R, M., Decision support systems for the Imbabura geopark: Ecuadorian Andes. *Advances in Intelligent Systems and Computing*, **2**(1331), pp. 310–320, 2021.

[25] Navarrete, L.S. & Saladié, Ò., Sustainable tourism in Galapagos: The perception of the stakeholders. *Tour. Cases*, 2024. https://doi.org/10.1079/tourism.2024.0054.

[26] Riascos-Flores, L. et al., Polluted paradise: Occurrence of pesticide residues within the urban coastal zones of Santa Cruz and Isabela (Galapagos, Ecuador). *Sci. Total Environ.*, **763**, 142956, 2021. https://doi.org/10.1016/j.scitotenv.2020.142956.

[27] Carrión-Mero, P. et al., Water quality from natural sources for sustainable agricultural development strategies: Galapagos, Ecuador. *Water*, **16**, 1516, 2024. https://doi.org/10.3390/w16111516.

[28] Burbano, D.V., Valdivieso, J.C., Izurieta, J.C., Meredith, T.C. & Ferri, D.Q., 'Rethink and reset' tourism in the Galapagos Islands: Stakeholders' views on the sustainability of tourism development. *Ann. Tour. Res. Empir. Insights*, **3**, 100057, 2022. https://doi.org/10.1016/j.annale.2022.100057.

[29] White, W.M., McBirney, A.R. & Duncan, R.A., Petrology and geochemistry of the Galápagos Islands: Portrait of a pathological mantle plume. *J. Geophys. Res. Solid Earth*, **98**, pp. 19533–19563, 1993. https://doi.org/10.1029/93JB02018.

[30] Schwartz, D., *Volcanic, Structural, and Morphological History of Santa Cruz Island, Galapagos Archipelago*, University of Idaho, 2014.

[31] Alomía Herrera, I., Paque, R., Maertens, M. & Vanacker, V., History of land cover change on Santa Cruz Island, Galapagos. *Land*, **11**, 1017, 2022. https://doi.org/10.3390/land11071017.

[32] Taboada, T., Rodríguez-Lado, L., Ferro-Vázquez, C., Stoops, G. & Martínez Cortizas, A., Chemical weathering in the volcanic soils of Isla Santa Cruz (Galápagos Islands, Ecuador). *Geoderma*, **261**, pp. 160–168, 2016. https://doi.org/10.1016/j.geoderma.2015.07.019.

[33] Stoops, G., Soils and paleosoils of the Galápagos Islands: What we know and what we don't know, a meta-analysis. *Pacific Sci.*, **68**, pp. 1–17, 2014. https://doi.org/10.2984/68.1.1.

[34] Kelley, D. & Salazar, R., Geosites in the Galápagos Islands used for geology education programs. *Geoheritage*, **9**, pp. 351–358, 2017. https://doi.org/10.1007/s12371-016-0190-3.

[35] Kelley, D., Page, K., Quiroga, D. & Salazar, R., In the footsteps of Darwin: Geoheritage, geotourism and conservation in the Galapagos Islands. *Geoheritage, Geoparks and Geotourism*, Springer: Cham, 2019.

[36] Carrión-Mero, P. et al., Geosites assessment in a volcanic hotspot environment and its impact on geotourism, Santa Cruz-Galapagos Islands, Ecuador. *Int. J. Geoheritage Park.*, **12**, pp. 147–167, 2024. https://doi.org/10.1016/j.ijgeop.2024.01.006.

[37] PNG Informe Anual de Visitantes 2023 En Las Islas Galápagos. https://galapagos.gob.ec/wp-content/uploads/2024/03/INFORME_ANUAL_VISITANTES-2023_WEB-LQ.pdf. Accessed on: 21 Jul. 2024.

[38] PNG Informe Anual de Visitantes 2022 En Las Islas Galápagos. https://galapagos.gob.ec/wp-content/uploads/2023/02/INFORME_ANUAL_VISITANTES_2022_DUP.pdf. Accessed on: 21 Jul. 2024.
[39] SNI-Ecuador, Archivos de Información Geográfica. https://sni.gob.ec/coberturas. Accessed on: 31 Jul. 2024.
[40] Carrión-Mero, P., Morante-Carballo, F., Palomeque-Arévalo, P. & Apolo-Masache, B., Environmental assessment and tourist carrying capacity for the development of geosites in the framework of geotourism, Guayaquil, Ecuador. *Proceedings of the Sustainable City 2021*, 14 Dec., pp. 149–160, 2021.
[41] Cifuentes-Arias, M., Determinación de Capacidad de Carga Turística En Áreas Protegidas. https://www.ucm.es/data/cont/media/www/pag-51898/1992_METODOLOGÍACIFUENTES.pdf. Accessed on: 30 Jul. 2024.
[42] Cifuentes Arias, M. et al., Capacidad de Carga Turística de Las Áreas de Uso Público Del Monumento Nacional Guayabo, Costa Rica, 1999.
[43] Aguilar-Aguilar, M., Jaya-Montalvo, M., Loor-Oporto, O., Andrade-Ríos, H., Morante-Carballo, F. & Carrión-Mero, P., Application of geomechanical classification systems in a tourist mine for establishing strategies within 3G's model. *Heritage*, **6**, pp. 4618–4639, 2023. https://doi.org/10.3390/heritage6060245.
[44] Hose, T.A., 3G's for modern geotourism. *Geoheritage*, **4**, pp. 7–24, 2012. https://doi.org/10.1007/s12371-011-0052-y.

TRANSFORMATION DESIGN FOR RESPONSIBLE TOURISM: A PARADIGM SHIFT FOR LOCAL COMMUNITY EMPOWERMENT AND WELL-BEING IN DESTINATION

VALENTINA FACOETTI & LAURA GALLUZZO
Polimi DESIS Laboratory, Department of Design, Politecnico di Milano, Italy

ABSTRACT

This paper addresses the need to reflect on how systems for implementing tourism practices should be redesigned to facilitate sustainable social transformation in destinations. Responsible tourism today is implemented on existing (unsustainable) tourism systems and is visible through the planning of sustainable actions influenced by the political agenda and applied individually by service providers, stakeholders and tourists. If we shift the observation perspective of the system, can there really exist a form of responsible tourism that has a positive impact on the territories and communities that host it? In this scenario, transformation design of tourism fosters the implementation of processes and approaches that involve local communities and stakeholders in the definition of a new systemic social, cultural and economic paradigm. The paper presents a model for co-designing responsible tourism services in destinations, shifting the focus from consumer perception to the actual sustainability implications within host communities. The framework is intended as a cue for critical reflection with a view to resizing the tourism offer by questioning the current model of mass tourism in favour of a tourism structure oriented towards the creation of social and cultural value. The theoretical framework intends to propose a perspective in which destination tourism systems are designed giving greater value to communities, territories and cultural resources. The research aims to reflect on the concept of sustainability as a premise on which to design participatory practices for responsible tourism reaching a systemic sustainable balance moving from an extractive to a generative economy for local communities in destination.
Keywords: transformation design, responsible tourism, community-based practices, local scale systems, tourism degrowth.

1 INTRODUCTION

The tourism sector has undergone multiple evolutions in recent decades due to its dynamic and complex nature. While globalised mass tourism characterised the demand for tourism in the 20th century, in the new millennium this demand is significantly stronger and diversified, induced also by the emergence of new information technologies, greater ease of travel and the increase in the supply of affordable accommodation [1]. As an ever-expanding industry it has become an integral part of the global economy, offering unparalleled opportunities for economic growth and cultural exchange. While the tourism sector has unlocked numerous economic benefits and advantages, it has also given rise to several pressing challenges, many of which are inextricably linked to sustainability issues [2].

The COVID-19 pandemic has made it clear that overdevelopment, environmental degradation, excessive tourism, cultural commodification and economic inequalities within host communities are now unsustainable. Addressing these problems requires systemic changes in production and consumption, driven by high-level policy decisions [3]. The Sustainable Development Goals (SDGs) have put pressure on tourism scholars and practitioners to embrace new ways of understanding, interacting and prioritising sustainable tourism. Several studies have noted that although the SDGs cover a broad spectrum of social, cultural, political and environmental issues, they are primarily articulated in the perspective of economic growth [4]. In the context of tourism, this orientation lays a high priority on marketing development, market-oriented strategies, and policy agendas that fundamentally envision a largely unchanged global system until 2030 [5], [6]. The necessity and consequences of the exponential growth of tourism activity experienced worldwide over the last half-century have been increasingly questioned by a growing number of activists and critical researchers [7]. One of the emerging responses within this debate concerns the call for the reversal of tourism 'degrowth' [8]–[15].

The paper proposes a systemic shift from an extractive to a generative approach to tourism and tries to reflect upon and identify a framework for responsible tourism that could implement processes and approaches involving local communities and stakeholders within socio-cultural and economic paradigms. A collaborative approach emphasises complexity, interdependence, and the essential role of design in fostering sustainable tourism development [16], [17]. Recent literature on the role of design in the tourism sector highlights how experiences of service design and participatory design are confined to the application related to the user experience, while few applications exist to date in the participatory design of tourism services with communities and local administrations. This paper is relevant to this discussion as it aims to highlight the potential of design tools and approaches in reorganising decision-making processes and protocols within tourism service systems. Through this paradigm shift, responsible tourism can achieve long-term sustainability and equitable development, redefining the tourism industry's role within the broader context of global sustainable development.

2 CORRELATION BETWEEN TOURISM PRACTICES AND THE DIMENSION OF SUSTAINABILITY

Over the past few years, discussions on tourism strategies are increasing the consideration and adoption of sustainability-related development drivers [18]. The concept of sustainability originated several decades ago, culminating in the Brundtland report 'Our Common Future', which brought the global environmental debate and the notion of sustainability to the forefront of global and local, social and political agendas and thoughts [19]. Following the 'Our Common Future' legacy, in the early 1990s Edward Inskeep defined five main criteria for sustainable tourism, which addressed the economic, environmental and social responsibility of tourism as well as its responsibility towards tourists (visitor satisfaction), global justice and equity [20]. More specifically, according to the UNWTO, sustainable tourism is a 'tourism that takes full account of its current and future economic, social and environmental impacts, addressing the needs of visitors, the industry, the environment and host communities', while sustainable development refers to three pillars (economic, socio-cultural and environmental) that, when practised by tourism operations, enable long-term sustainability [21].

Theoretically, this concept of sustainable development aims to maintain economic advancement and progress while protecting the long-term value of the environment; it 'provides a framework for the integration of environmental policies and development strategies' [19]. What is immediately apparent is the failure to consider the social aspect of sustainability and the interconnection between the pillars that constitute sustainable development. Indeed, there is no need for a trade-off between environmental sustainability, social sustainability and economic development. The three dimensions are strongly interconnected and work in balance.

The cited definitions, however, are relatively abstract and vague. There is considerable space for interpretation when it comes to identifying concrete sustainable tourist behaviour or sustainable tourism industry practices [22]. The lack of clarity also leads us to fail to consider the topic in its entirety, but always deal with it superficially and discontinuously. It is therefore necessary to manage complexity by defining more clearly the different elements that make up this system. Setting specific systemic objectives to translate the meaning of sustainability into objectives and requirements for the design of tourism products and services would consolidate the environment–society–economy continuity [3]. All these definitions highlight several pluralities. Designing a responsible tourism product-service system (PSS) means considering multiple sustainability issues and creating an experience that reflects all these pluralities.

As a result of these presented considerations, the current discussion around the concept of sustainability in tourism is related to its application. Despite several decades of academic and practical debate on tourism sustainability, its application in practice remains problematic. Wheeller [23] argued that the 'intellectually appealing' concept of sustainable tourism has little practical application because it has been turned into a public relations tool for addressing the criticism of the impact of tourism while allowing essentially the same behaviour as before. Still, tourism authorities continue to promote the growth of tourism through unsustainable models despite the ecological and social constraints we are currently experiencing [4]. These dynamics within host communities are now unsustainable and characterise what could be defined as extractive tourism [24]. A form of tourism that exploits local resources to generate only economic value, subtracting socio-cultural and environmental resources. A tourism that basically takes more than it gives.

As a consequence of this discussion, sustainable tourism research, documents and actions have recently been increasingly accompanied by the notion of responsible tourism, e.g., 'Charter for Sustainable and Responsible Tourism' [25], 'Responsible Tourism' [26] and 'Taking Responsibility for Tourism' [27]. Sustainability, as a concept, encompasses a comprehensive view of long-term viability, addressing economic, environmental, and social dimensions of tourism. Responsible tourism, on the other hand, focuses on action and behaviour, emphasising the imperative to take responsibility for the impacts of mainstream tourism. It involves consumers, suppliers, and governments in a shared commitment to enhance positive aspects and reduce negative impacts. Responsible tourism is grounded in accountability, the capacity to act, and the capacity to respond, promoting a dialogue and action to make tourism more sustainable [27]. While the two concepts are related, they are not synonymous; responsible tourism builds on sustainability-based strategies and policies and emphasises appropriate behaviour and responsibility [28] to ensure tourism practices align with sustainability goals, awareness and ethics.

From a design point of view, a sustainable system that supports a form of responsible tourism is one that maintains or enables a high 'quality of context' without depleting resources, emphasising that a sustainable solution must be combined with a better quality of life, both social and physical. In this direction, a sustainable design solution can be defined as the process through which products, services and know-how compose a system that allows people (who are part of the system) to achieve an outcome according to their needs and expectations, which maintains a high quality of well-being of the destination and its communities. Moreover, it is crucial to acknowledge the challenges faced by communities seeking development as they become increasingly dependent on tourism, often at the cost of their autonomy and well-being, in response to a global trade system that perpetuates their underdevelopment [4]. The complex interplay between sustainability, responsibility, and the consequence for local communities underscores the need for a more holistic and equitable approach to tourism development and management.

3 METHODS

The research was conducted in two main phases. The first phase involved a review of the relevant literature and in particular the synergies between tourism studies (and tourism sector) and design field. From this first phase, the authors outlined the trajectories for the definition of the theoretical framework of reference. Following this, a case study was analysed and discussed in the light of the previously defined theoretical framework.

This study employs a comprehensive theoretical framework centred on the concepts of responsible tourism and sustainable social transformation. By integrating key principles from existing literature on responsible tourism and community empowerment, the framework provides a structured approach to analysing and redesigning tourism systems. We incorporate the criteria defined by prominent scholars and organisations [25]–[27] to outline what constitutes responsible tourism, emphasising accountability, stakeholder engagement, and environmental stewardship. Building on theories of social transformation [29] and community empowerment [4], we explore how tourism practices can be restructured to promote equitable, community-based and authentic PSS and improve local well-being.

To contextualise and validate the theoretical framework, a case study approach is used. This method allows for an in-depth examination of a specific case where responsible tourism initiatives have been implemented, providing empirical evidence on the practical application of responsible tourism principles and their impact on local communities. The chosen case study is Utravel [30], an Italian tour operator company known for its responsible tourism promotion practices. The case was selected for the presence of active community involvement, documented sustainable tourism practices and measurable outcomes related to social sustainability.

Finally, the synthesis and interpretation of theoretical and empirical findings draw conclusions on the transformative potential of responsible tourism. The discussion considers implications for tourism policies, community engagement strategies and future research directions. Combining a sound theoretical framework with detailed case study analysis, this methodology provides a comprehensive approach to examine how tourism systems can be redesigned to promote sustainable social transformation and community empowerment.

4 THEORETICAL FRAMEWORK: A PARADIGM SHIFT MODEL FOR RESPONSIBLE TOURISM IN DESTINATIONS

This contribution intends to bring a critical conceptualisation of how transformation design [31] – through participatory practices – can facilitate the transformation towards responsible tourism models. For this reason, the authors' thesis focuses on responsible tourism as a form of tourism that applies through participatory practices and actions based on principles and theories of sustainability.

The model presented in this paper originates from the analysis of a model for the penetration of environmental awareness in society and its policy for 'responsustable tourism' [29]. Mihalič [29] and Mihalič and Kaspar's responsible tourism model [32], referred to as the 'triple-A model', is a comprehensive framework that aligns the development of environmental responsibility within the tourism sector based on Frey's social stages [33], which underpin the process of sustainable transformation. The model consists of four interconnected stages: Ignorance, Awareness, Agenda, and Action, represented as steps towards the successful implementation of sustainability. At the base of the model lies the Ignorance stage, wherein stakeholders are oblivious to environmental issues, driven primarily by non-environmental values. As awareness grows and stakeholders become informed about tourism's environmental impacts, the destination enters the Awareness stage, recognising the significance of sustainability. The next stage, Agenda, involves the incorporation of sustainability issues into strategic discussions and policy considerations, marking the journey towards sustainable action. Finally, in the Action stage, stakeholders exhibit environmental responsibility by consistently aligning their behaviour with sustainability goals and standards (Fig. 1).

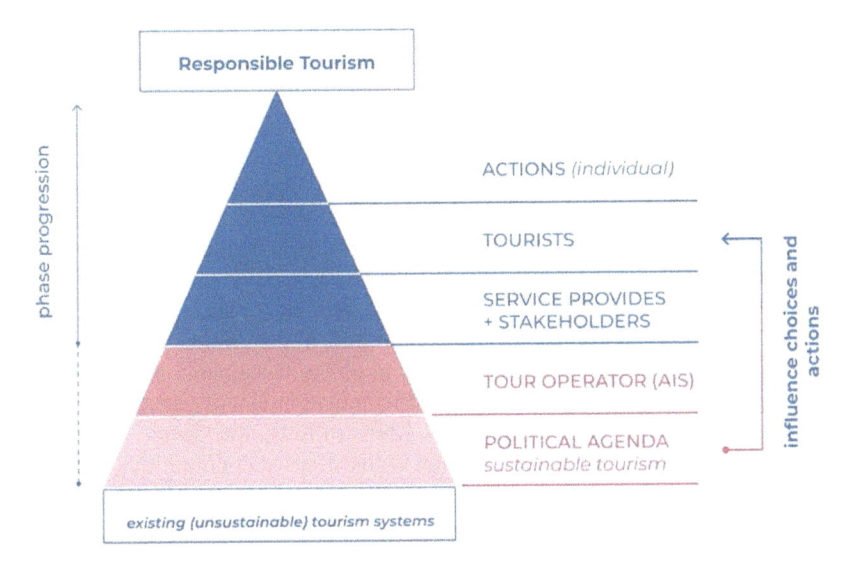

Figure 1: Responsible tourism implementation model. *(Source: Authors' interpretation of Mihalic and Kaspar's model.)*

This model presents a progressive path with stakeholders in the progression of sustainability-responsibility, recognising the potential for asymmetrical development in the economic, environmental and socio-cultural dimensions. The triple-A model emphasises the importance of continuous progress but highlights the difficulty of collaboration between stakeholders in achieving goals. What is clear from this model is that the different stages follow each other by transforming an output of the previous level into an input for the next level, but without interconnections between the different non-adjacent levels. Furthermore, in this model, the destination can reach the highest stage without having fully developed the characteristics of the previous stages, thus losing the possibility of establishing a solid base from which the objectives of responsibility originate. This model assumes that it is based on unsustainable pre-existing systems. Therefore, it is clear that it is not possible to define as sustainable a model of responsible tourism geared on an unsustainable basis.

As mentioned above, sustainability in tourism must be understood as a process of social transformation. In this model, responsible tourism is implemented through the planning of sustainable actions influenced by political agenda and applied individually by service providers, stakeholders and tourists, generating a series of individual actions. Responsible tourism today is mainly visible in the behaviours and action of the actors in the blue belt. In fact, academic research state that the social impact assessment in this system is based mainly on customer satisfaction and perceived destination sustainability [34]. The impact of social sustainability is minimised if territories and local communities are not considered as active participants in the planning of the tourism offer. In this process, communities are seen as passive actors in the system. Research in the tourism sector focused on an outside-in perspective, which means a focus on the customer experience [35]. Adopting an inside-out perspective, through the application of a design approach, it is possible to address tourist experiences and co-design tourism services from host communities favouring sustainable social impact. Design applied to tourism services can support the emergence of a more collaborative, sustainable and creative society and economy. The transformative role of design is combined with the potential transformative role of services.

Therefore, what happens if we try to change the point of view by adopting an inside-out perspective? Is it possible to have a responsible tourism model that positively impacts the sustainability of the regions and communities of destinations? By changing the observational point of view, it is possible to operate at the base of the system. Supporting and encouraging local collaboration, not just partnerships and cooperation, should be a central principle for intentional transformation [36]. This transformation implies a re-imagining of tourism practices from the bottom-up, involving various stakeholders, including local communities, governments and businesses, to bring the tourism system more in line with sustainable development goals, ensuring the harmonisation of economic, social and environmental dimensions. This holistic approach to partnership and collaboration is essential for the evolution of tourism models that truly contribute to global sustainable development. From this perspective, the authors have defined a new theoretical model of participatory design of responsible tourism services in destinations [29], shifting the focus from perceived sustainability to the actual sustainability implicit in place-based communities (Fig. 2).

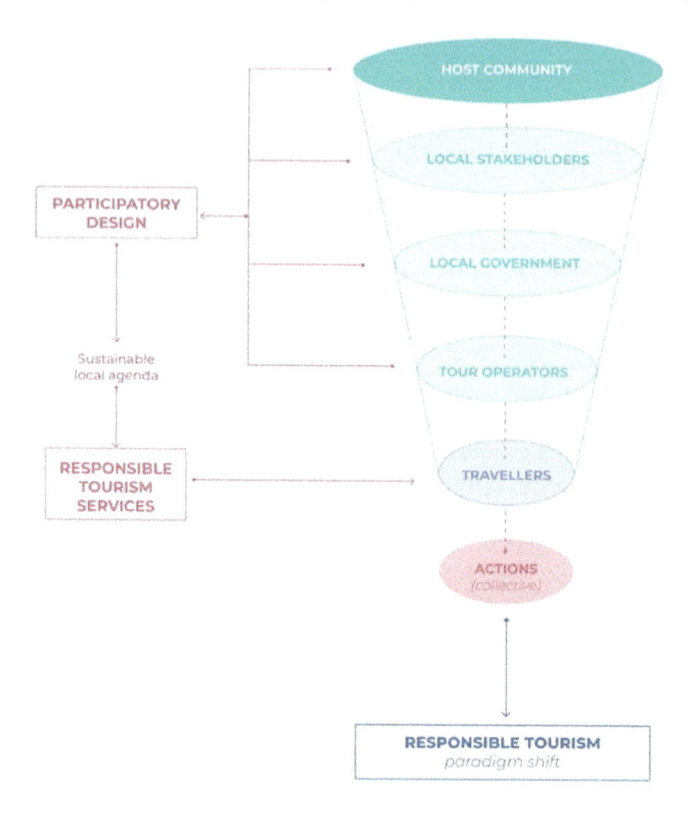

Figure 2: Proposed evolution of the model of Mihalic and Kaspar, (1996, 2016). Hypothesis of a paradigm shift model for responsible tourism in destinations.

The process of transformation integrates the viewpoints of various stakeholders, ranging from businesses and policy makers to tourists and local communities, in order to jointly create services that embody and demonstrate responsible tourism. In their introduction, Burns et al. [37] emphasised the concept of transformation design's emphasis on ongoing innovation and adaptation within organisations that are subject to ongoing change. Transformation Design acts as a catalyst as the tourism industry develops, helping to redefine the destination's role within the larger framework of sustainable development and to rethink the tourism experience itself. Co-production's central tenet highlights the necessity of stakeholder development on a collective level, encompassing service providers as well as the communities they engage with.

Starting with these ideas, the framework for creating a new model for the bottom-up implementation of responsible tourism in destinations presents design as a tool for defining community action and organisational development practises. Our proposal suggests that the co-creation of a responsible tourism service entails a collaborative effort, a radical shift, and the revelation of tourism's role in creating a better world – not just for itself, as in sustainable tourism – in concert with others. Put differently, 'designing with is the essence of an ethical and ongoing involvement of others through respect for their values and ways of being in the world' [16].

5 UTRAVEL: A CASE STUDY OF RESPONSIBLE TOURISM

A case study approach is used to contextualise and validate the theoretical framework. This approach provides empirical evidence on the actual application of responsible tourism principles and their effects on local communities, allowing an in-depth analysis of a particular case where initiatives have been implemented. As a case study was selected the Italian tour operator Utravel, known for its ethical tourism marketing strategies. The case was chosen because it included documented sustainable tourism practices, measurable social sustainability results and active community involvement.

Utravel was founded in 2019 within the Alpitour World Group as travel start-up aimed at under-30s. Its main goal is to generate value in the destinations where it operates, transforming each holiday into an adventure of meeting and personal growth in which young people live in synergy with local community, cultures and territories that welcome them. In just a few years, Utravel has become an important reality dedicated to young people, projected to go beyond the traditional concepts of holidays and spread a new travel philosophy: more than the destination, what counts is the spirit and the approach with which travellers want to explore the world.

Alpitour is one of the most important Italian and European players in the tourism sector specialising in the All-Inclusive offer, which includes all-inclusive travel, transfer and accommodation. Even though Utravel initially based its business model on Alpitour's offer systems, systems that are questionable from the point of view of sustainability and responsibility, over the years it has managed to build its own model of tourism based on local communities and responsible practices. For this reason, we believe that the case is relevant to the reflections proposed in this article.

The offering of Utravel is primarily based on Club trips, group travels where there is no pre-arranged schedule of activities and experiences. Each traveller is given complete autonomy in choosing their experiences. The start-up collaborates with non-profit and local entities, even very small ones, to promote economic development and social growth in communities. This also involves engaging locals as 'Coach' in every destination, Utravel seeks and trains a local Coach and micro-entrepreneurs who can offer authentic experiences. They try to provide locals with collaboration opportunities, helping them with bureaucratic tasks and providing them with our technology. The goal is to create a circular tourism model where the traveller is not just a tourist but has the opportunity to have conscious experiences, respecting the places they visit and generating a positive impact.

Utravel has identified two directions in which it aims to work towards achieving common benefit goals, which have a positive impact both for local communities and travellers. The first pertains to the destinations where Utravel operates and where it can and wants to make a tangible impact. The second pertains to the youth, its primary target, to whom it wants to offer development and sharing opportunities:

First objective: to promote economic development and social growth in the communities where it operates through a tourism model that prioritises collaboration with local suppliers and partners at the destination, and the creation of synergies with companies, non-profit organisations, institutions, and/or foundations whose goals are aligned with those of the company, thereby amplifying the positive impact of its actions.

Second objective: to foster the personal and professional growth of new generations and users through the creation of opportunities for cultural exchange and interaction, the sponsorship of cultural and sports projects for young people, and the promotion of a corporate culture aimed at inclusion, work flexibility, and the appreciation of diversity.

6 DISCUSSION

This paper provides a new conceptual framework for the development of responsible forms of tourism through design practices. The text clearly highlights the urgent need to develop alternative approaches, attitudes and designs capable of promoting more inclusive collaboration processes in the context of responsible tourism. In response to this need, we propose a deliberate link between responsible tourism and the methodology of transformation design. In the last decade, service design has started to consider services less as objects of design and more as means for societal transformation. In this evolution, both organisations and citizens are called upon to evolve and adapt to more collaborative service models, thereby changing their roles and interaction patterns [38]. In light of this, the questions that arise are: How can designers working with communities influence and transform organisations, or vice versa, how can designers working within organisations positively influence and transform user communities? In this multidisciplinary context, it is necessary to adopt key concepts and principles derived from research fields that have focused for decades on themes of transformational change within organisations and communities, such as organisational development and community action research. Participatory action research has been specifically chosen as a possible integrative methodological framework that characterises both the fields of organisational development and community action research, and that could be adapted to the needs of service design practices in tourism [31].

The proposed vision based on the introduction of participatory design is particularly relevant for the understanding and development of responsible tourism. Since practices are forms of activity that are socially recognised and organised around a shared understanding of a problem [39], we suggest that sustainable tourism refers to tourism practices compatible with the concept and norms of sustainability [2].

The ability of designers in this context is to promote approaches and methodologies for the participatory and democratic planning of tourism PSSs. Their ability lies in recognising the best solutions (for the needs and desires of all parties involved) and which, at the same time, can be seen as more sustainable solutions (from a social and environmental point of view). When this happens, designers, and the companies that produce and supply the solutions, enable users/customers to switch from non-sustainable system and non-sustainable behaviour to more sustainable behaviour. What users demand is not a particular system of products or services, but the results that these products and services enable them to achieve.

Given these premises, the case study of Utravel can be analysed as a form of responsible tourism by applying the model proposed by the authors.

Socio-cultural responsibility: (a) Cultural sensitivity. Utravel ensures that its tours are respectful of local cultures and traditions. This involves educating tourists on cultural norms and encouraging respectful interactions with local communities through the figure of the coach; (b) Community engagement. They engage in building relationships with local communities to create tours that benefit them. This includes hiring local guides, supporting local activities and designing tourism services from the existing local offer.

Economic responsibility: (a) Local economic support. Utravel focus on ensuring that the economic benefits of tourism are distributed fairly within the local economy. This involve promoting locally owned businesses, using local suppliers, and ensuring fair wages for all employees involved in their tours; (b) Long-term economic planning. They are engaged in long-term planning to ensure that tourism remains a sustainable and viable industry for the region, without causing economic dependence or resource depletion.

Implementation of policies and management strategies: (a) Comprehensive policies. Utravel implemented a set of policies that guide their operations towards sustainability. This would include clear guidelines on social impact, community relations, and economic practices; (b) Transparency and accountability. The tour operator might maintain transparency in their operations, regularly publishing reports on their sustainability practices and outcomes. This ensures accountability and continuous improvement.

Utravel can be considered a tour operator that proposes a form of responsible tourism, it effectively integrates environmental, socio-cultural, and economic responsibilities into its operations, supported by comprehensive policies and transparent management strategies. This holistic approach ensures that tourism not only thrives but also contributes positively to the destinations and communities involved.

The case study analysed introduces multi-level participatory practices that confirm the paradigm shift model proposed by the authors (Fig. 3). Tourism design in this direction already offers many reflections on new forms of more sustainable tourism. This analysis highlights how the design and co-creation of memorable experiences and transformations is a fundamental design activity in the transition towards a set of more sustainable services and solutions [40]. The interpretation of the theoretical model through the Utravel case study has also highlighted the important role of the communities, as local communities or communities of tourists and peers that operate on the physical world or in online social networks, in tourist practices. Communities provide valuable input in tourist practices that support decision making and the implementation of tourist activities. Especially for sustainable tourism, research can investigate the role of communities in the adoption of sustainable tourism practices and the interconnection between services and the support of tourists' sustainable plans [2].

In this framework, participatory design emerges as an optimal approach for co-designing tourism services to foster the sustainable development of local communities. Participatory design has effectively triggered inclusive projects and dialogues by engaging a complex social dimension comprising diverse actors [41]. Moreover, it aligns with the political role of design in facilitating participatory democracy and advancing themes such as social justice, activism, inclusion, and agonism [43], [44] The reflective nature of participatory design, devoted to the principles of inclusion, ethics, and democracy, makes it a compelling choice [45]. Additionally, its narrative power emerges as a potentially effective method in fostering

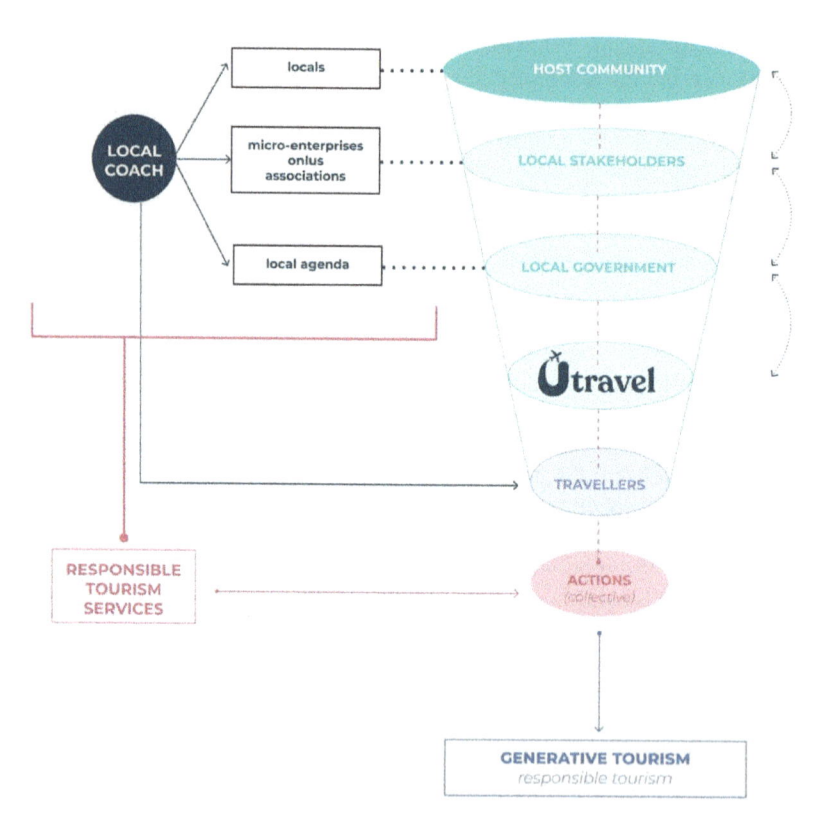

Figure 3: Interpretation of the theoretical framework through the Utravel case study.

empathy and making individuals feel involved in decision-making processes. Moreover, participatory design aligns with the political role of design in facilitating participatory democracy and advancing topics such as social justice, activism, inclusion, ethics, and democracy. A participatory approach involving the social fabric of the tourism system fosters the emergence of generative forms of tourism.

Generative tourism refers to a type of tourism that goes beyond conventional forms of travel and consumption. It emphasises active participation, sustainable practices, and meaningful interactions between tourists and local communities. Generative tourism aims to create positive impacts on both the environment and the socio-cultural fabric of destinations, fostering mutual understanding, respect, and long-term benefits for all stakeholders involved.

7 CONCLUSIONS

In this scenario, transformation design acts as a catalyst in the ongoing evolution of the tourism industry, redefining destinations' roles within the broader context of sustainable development and reimagining the tourism experience. The paper presents a model for co-designing responsible tourism services in destinations, shifting the focus from consumer perception to the actual sustainability implications within host communities.

This approach aims to be a critical reflection on the possibility of downsizing the tourism offering at the destination through a degrowth approach, giving greater value to communities, territories, and cultural resources. From this perspective, design within the sphere of responsible tourism should take on the involvement of local communities and stakeholders not to produce more engaging products, services and experiences for visitors, but to make the tourism experience a balancing act of socio-economic benefits for host communities and tourists. Designing in this direction should provide an opportunity to think about new systems of tourism services that challenge the current model of mass tourism in favour of a tourism set-up oriented towards the creation of social and cultural (not only economic) value.

Secondly, the inclusion of design creates a collaborative space in which administrators and civil society can participate in future world-building. This is something that has not been done before in the literature on collaboration in tourism and sustainability research [46]. Sustainability must be seen more as an opportunity through which design can drive social and cultural transformations in the collective tourism imagination [47]. Recent literature [2] emphasises that sustainability should be a new option for tourists and should be promoted and supported. This is true but the importance of the self-determination of host communities and the need for tourists to adapt to the sustainable practices defined by the communities themselves is crucial. This paper proposes an alternative approach to the analysis and design of sustainable tourism practices, in which the focus is not the consumer's journey, but the well-being and sustainability of host communities. The paper's contribution to the advancement of sustainable tourism focuses on understanding how tourism practices can be designed and controlled by local communities, giving them the power to decide how they want tourism to develop in their territories.

REFERENCES

[1] Gainsforth, S., *Oltre il turismo: Esiste Un Turismo Sostenibile?* Eris, 2020.
[2] Fragidis, G., Riskos, K. & Kotzaivazoglou, I., Designing the tourist journey for the advancement of sustainable tourist practices. *Sustainability*, **14**(15), 2022. https://doi.org/10.3390/su14159778.
[3] Wever, R. & Vogtländer, J., Design for the value of sustainability. *Handbook of Ethics, Values, and Technological Design*, pp. 1–31, 2014. https://doi.org/10.1007/978-94-007-6994-6_20-1.
[4] Higgins-Desbiolles, F., Sustainable tourism: Sustaining tourism or something more? *Tourism Management Perspectives*, **25**, pp. 157–160, 2018. https://doi.org/10.1016/j.tmp.2017.11.017.
[5] Fennell, D.A. & Cooper, C., *Sustainable Tourism: Principles, Context and Practices*, Channel View Publications, 2020.
[6] Higham, J. & Miller, G., Transforming societies and transforming tourism: Sustainable tourism in times of change. *Journal of Sustainable Tourism*, **26**(1), pp. 1–8, 2018. https://doi.org/10.1080/09669582.2018.1407519.
[7] Murray, I., Fletcher, R., Blázquez-Salom, M., Blanco-Romero, A., Cañada, E. & Sekulova, F., Tourism and degrowth. *Tourism Geographies*, pp. 1–11, 2023. https://doi.org/10.1080/14616688.2023.2293956.
[8] Georgescu-Roegen, N., *The Entropy Law and the Economic Process*, Harvard University Press, 1971.
[9] Illich, I., *Tools for Conviviality*, Harper & Row, 1973.
[10] Gorz, A., *Proceedings from a Public Debate Organized by the Club Du Nouvel Observateur*, Nouvel Observateur, p. 397, 1972.
[11] Mies, M., Patriarchy and accumulation on a world scale: Revisited. *International Journal of Green Economics*, *1*(3/4), pp. 268–275, 2007. https://doi.org/10.1504/iJGe.2007.013059.

[12] Waring, M., Counting for something! Recognising women's contribution to the global economy through alternative accounting systems. *Gender and Development*, **11**(1), pp. 35–43, 2003. https://doi.org/10.1080/741954251.
[13] Latouche, S., *Farewell to Growth*, Polity, 2009.
[14] Kallis, G., Kostakis, V., Lange, S., Muraca, B., Paulson, S. & Schmelzer, M., Research on degrowth. *Annual Review of Environment and Resources*, **43**(1), pp. 291–316, 2018. https://doi.org/10.1146/annurev-environ-102017-025941.
[15] Hickel, J., What does degrowth mean? A few points of clarification. *Globalizations*, **18**(7), pp. 1105–1111, 2021. https://doi.org/10.1080/14747731.2020.1812222.
[16] Heape, C. & Liburd, J., Collaborative learning for sustainable tourism development. *Collaboration for Sustainable Tourism Development*, eds J. Liburd & D. Edwards, Goodfellow Publishers, pp. 226–243, 2018.
[17] Liburd, J. & Edwards, D., Introduction. *Collaboration for Sustainable Tourism Development*, eds J. Liburd & D. Edwards, Goodfellow Publishers, pp. 1–7, 2018.
[18] Serrano, L., Sianes, A. & Ariza-Montes, A., Using bibliometric methods to shed light on the concept of sustainable tourism. *Sustainability*, **11**(24), 6964, 2019. https://doi.org/10.3390/su11246964.
[19] WCED, S.W.S., World commission on environment and development. *Our Common Future*, **17**(1), pp. 1–91, 1987.
[20] Inskeep, E., *Tourism Planning: An Integrated and Sustainable Development Approach*, John Wiley, 1991.
[21] UNWTO, Making communities central part of tourism's future. https://www.unwto.org/news/unwto-making-communities-central-part-of-tourisms-future. Accessed on: 1 Sep. 2022.
[22] Bausch, T., Schröder, T. & Tauber, V., What is to be sustained? The polysemy of sustainability and sustainable tourism across languages and cultures. *Journal of Sustainable Tourism*, pp. 1–24, 2022. https://doi.org/10.1080/09669582.2022.2124260.
[23] Wheeller, B., Sustaining the ego. *Journal Of Sustainable Tourism*, **1**(2), pp. 121–129, 1993.
[24] Kolinjivadi, V., Extractive tourism. *The News International*. https://www.thenews.com.pk/print/792130-extractive-tourism.
[25] TSG, Charter for Sustainable and Responsible Tourism, 2012.
[26] Leslie, D. (ed.), *Responsible Tourism: Concepts, Theory and Practice*, CABI, 2012.
[27] Goodwin, H., *Taking Responsibility for Tourism*, Goodfellow Publishers: Woodeaton, pp. 1–256. 2011.
[28] Fennell, D.A., *Tourism Ethics*. 2006. https://doi.org/10.21832/9781845410360.
[29] Mihalič, T., Sustainable-responsible tourism discourse: Towards 'responsustable' tourism. *Journal of Cleaner Production*, **111**, pp. 461–470, 2016. https://doi.org/10.1016/j.jclepro.2014.12.062.
[30] Utravel, Utravel: Discover the world. https://utravel.it/. Accessed on: 9 Jul. 2024.
[31] Sangiorgi, D., Transformative services and transformation design. *International Journal of Design*, **5**(1), pp. 29–40, 2011.
[32] Mihalič, T. & Kaspar, C., *Environmental Economics in Tourism*, Paul Haupt, 1996.
[33] Frey, B.S., *Umweltökonomie*, Vandenhoeck and Ruprecht, 1985.
[34] Mathew, P.V. & Sreejesh, S., Impact of responsible tourism on destination sustainability and quality of life of community in tourism destinations. *Journal of Hospitality and Tourism Management*, **31**, pp. 83–89, 2016. https://doi.org/10.1016/j.jhtm.2016.10.001.

[35] Fesenmaier, D.R. & Xiang, Z., Introduction to tourism design and design science in tourism. *Design Science in Tourism: Foundations of Destination Management*, eds D.R. Fesenmaier & Z. Xiang, Springer, pp. 3–16, 2017.
https://doi.org/10.1007/978-3-319-42773-7_1.

[36] Liburd, J., Duedahl, E. & Heape, C., Co-designing tourism for sustainable development. *Journal of Sustainable Tourism*, **30**(10), pp. 2298–2317, 2020.
https://doi.org/10.1080/09669582.2020.1839473.

[37] Burns, C., Cottam, H., Vanstone, C. & Winhall, J., *RED Paper 02: Transformation Design*, Design Council: London, 2006.

[38] Parker, S. & Parker S., *Unlocking Innovation: Why Citizens Hold the Key to Public Service Reform*, Demos: London, 2007.

[39] Schatzki, T., Introduction to practice theory. *The Practice Turn in Contemporary Theory*, eds T. Schatzki, K. Knorr-Cetina & E. Von Savigny, Routledge: London, 2001.

[40] Nisi, V., Nunes, N., Ayudhya, K. & Forlizzi, J., *Cozinha da Madeira: A Sustainable Service Concept for Madeira Island*, vol. 2, 2012.
https://doi.org/10.4018/978-1-4666-6543-9.ch036.

[41] Manzini, E., *Design, When Everybody Designs: An Introduction to Design for Social Innovation*, MIT Press, 2015.

[42] Botero, A., Karasti, H., Saad-Sulonen, J., Geirbo, C.G., Baker, K.S., Parmiggiani, E. & Marttila, S., *Drawing Together, Infrastructuring and Politics for Participatory Design* (No. 9526222040), University of Oulu, Finland, 2019.

[43] DiSalvo, C., Design, democracy and agonistic pluralism. *Design and Complexity: DRS International Conference 2010*, Montreal, Canada, 7–9 Jul. 2010.
https://dl.designresearchsociety.org/drsconference-papers/drs2010/researchpapers/31.

[44] DiSalvo, C., Lodato, T., Fries, L., Schechter, B. & Barnwell, T., The collective articulation of issues as design practice. *CoDesign*, **7**(3–4), pp. 185–197, 2011.

[45] Binder, T., Brandt, E., Ehn, P. & Halse, J., Democratic design experiments: Between parliament and laboratory. *CoDesign*, **11**(3–4), pp. 152–165, 2015.

[46] Gosh, J., Beyond the Millennium Development Goals: A southern perspective on a global new deal. *Journal of International Development*, **27**(3), pp. 320–329, 2015.
https://doi.org/10.1002/jid.3087.

[47] Sarantou, M., Kugapi, O. & Huhmarniemi, M., Context mapping for creative tourism. *Annals of Tourism Research*, **86**, 103064, 2020.
https://doi.org/10.1016/j.annals.2020.103064.

SERVICE LEARNING: A TECHNIQUE THAT ENHANCES UNIVERSITY STUDENTS' SOCIAL SKILLS

DENISE RODRÍGUEZ-ZURITA[1,2] & HUMBERTO MORÁN-RODRÍGUEZ[1]
[1]Facultad de Ingeniería en Mecánica y Ciencias de la Producción, ESPOL, Ecuador
[2]Centro de Investigaciones y Proyectos Aplicados a las Ciencias de la Tierra, ESPOL, Ecuador

ABSTRACT

In today's highly competitive labour market, employers prioritise social skills over technical skills. Consequently, universities face the challenge of developing not only technical but also social skills among their students. This article presents the application of an experiential learning methodology, specifically service-learning, to strengthen social skills such as communication and teamwork among university students. A total sample of 248 students from engineering, social sciences and tourism programmes were divided into experimental and control groups and surveyed about their social skills, namely communication and teamwork. Non-parametric statistical analysis results indicate a positive influence on effective communication, including the use of appropriate language with different groups and enhanced recognition of the importance of teamwork. This study reveals the importance of the service-learning methodology for developing social skills in engineering, social sciences and tourism students regarding effective communication and teamwork. Therefore, the service-learning methodology should be considered part of the university teaching and learning strategies.
Keywords: communication, service learning, soft skills, teamwork, university.

1 INTRODUCTION

Soft skills, often referred to as interpersonal or social skills, are critical attributes that organisations consider highly valuable during the hiring process [1]. This is particularly true in the tourism industry [2]. In this regard, the research performed by Carlisle et al. [3] highlights the importance of strengthening social skills among university students to achieve sustainable and quality tourism experiences. Leadership, teamwork and effective communication are most required by companies at the Latin American level [4]. Universities play an important role in generating opportunities for the development of students' social skills [5]. University students, as well as higher education institutions, are increasingly aware of the need to strengthen essential skills such as teamwork [6]. Likewise, effective communication is part of the social capabilities combined with the excellent performance of interpersonal work that can be achieved in a diverse human team [7]. This skill is also a prevailing condition that companies consider in selection processes [8].

Universities should provide training spaces in which future professionals develop skills that make them competent for the professional sphere. In this sense, experiential learning serves as a critical support for university students as it allows the theoretical knowledge acquired in the classrooms to be integrated with real-life situations to respond to the market with trained, competent, and confident professionals [9]. Service-learning is a form of experiential learning defined by Bringle and Hatcher [10] as a 'course-based, credit-bearing educational experience in which students (a) participate in an organised service activity that meets identified community needs and (b) reflect on the service activity in such a way as to gain further understanding of course content, a broader appreciation of the discipline, and an enhanced sense of civic responsibility'. Service-learning pedagogy has been integrated into various disciplines, such as health sciences, business, economics, engineering, and others, with reported benefits for students, faculty, and community members [11]. Most of the scientific production on service-learning is concentrated in developed countries, with the

USA leading, followed by Spain and the United Kingdom [23]. In contrast, there is a noticeable gap in studies exploring the impact of service-learning on the development of social skills among university students in Latin America.

Engaging students in service-learning activities can improve their social skills, such as problem-solving and systemic thinking [12]. In this regard, service-learning activities may positively influence students in terms of soft skills, attitudes, and personal attributes, as well as foster growth in their communicative and professional skills [13], [14]. Several authors suggest the positive impact of service-learning on students' social skills, such as teamwork [15]–[17] and communication [15], [18]–[20]. However, it is essential to acknowledge that these skills are affected by the intervention of the students themselves, their teachers, educational institutions, beneficiary communities, non-profit organisations, industry partners, alumni, policymakers, and government bodies [21]. Given this, it is essential to assess the impact of service-learning activities on students' skills. Assessment is a critical stage of service-learning programmes, ensuring that the objectives related to community impact and student skill development are met [22]. The assessment refers to the evaluation of engineering competencies, the effectiveness of the service-learning activities, the participation of students, and the student outcomes and skills developed [24]. In this context, the literature review by Rodríguez-Zurita et al. [23] identifies assessment activities as one of the six thematic clusters derived from a co-occurrence analysis of authors' keywords.

Given that mastering social skills is crucial for the professional careers of university students and, considering the limited research on this topic in Latin America, it is essential to identify effective mechanisms for developing these skills within the Latin American context. This study aims to assess whether participation in service-learning projects influences the development of social skills such as teamwork and effective communication of university students from a Latin American country, specifically Ecuador, through an inferential statistical analysis. The findings contribute to identifying effective learning methodologies that enhance the soft skills of Latin American university students.

2 LITERATURE REVIEW

2.1 Experiential learning

Experiential learning directly involves students in their learning process and generating practical skills, participating in a tangible experience, leading them to reflect and be flexible students [25], [26]. Kolb's proposal [27] is considered one of the most essential theories of experiential learning. The importance of experiential learning lies in facilitating the connections between university education and professional experience [28] and creating new skills, attitudes, and ways of thinking in students [29]. For its application in university education, experiential learning could be given through methodologies such as problem-based learning, project learning, service learning, and cooperative learning, thus different from the strategies and educational spaces that promote experiential learning [30].

2.1.1 Service-learning and its impact on university students

Service learning originated more than 50 years ago and is an experiential learning methodology that seeks to benefit both those who provide the services (i.e., university students) and those who receive (i.e., the community) [13]. Service-learning activities differ from volunteering in that they focus on the learning that students will have in their interaction with the real-time environment. In contrast, volunteer activities are limited to providing the service only [31]. Educational models for participation among students and their communities are natural learning environments that allow future professionals to link academic knowledge with the current needs of society [32], thus facilitating the learning of curricular contents [33] and developing in students a sense of responsibility and commitment to social justice [34].

Through the service-learning methodology, the institutions provide quality training for technically competent professionals while creating the students' capacities to insert, analyse, and understand their professional or social environment and transform it [35]. The development of projects involving service-learning has demonstrated its effect on the development of interpersonal skills and the improvement in the ability to address real problems with critical thinking, solve them, and effectively communicate between cultures [36].

The definition of service-learning on which we base our study is that of Bringle and Hatcher [10], who propose service-learning as an educational experience based on an earn-credit course where students engage in activities that are born of the needs of communities and reflect deeply on service activities in such a way that they internalise knowledge. Salam et al. [22] suggest that the implementation of service-learning in institutions is carried out through a series of steps. The administrative part, in which the service-learning is institutionalised in the universities, is followed by the preparation and planning part, where the service-learning is inserted into the curricula. The relationships with the beneficiary communities are defined, continuing to the implementation part, where projects are executed; the reflection part, where learned is systematised; and finally, the evaluation, where the impact on students and the community is analysed.

3 METHODOLOGY

3.1 Context

ESPOL Polytechnic University, situated in Guayaquil, Ecuador, has institutionalised service-learning according to the service-learning implementation model proposed by Salam et al. [22] by defining outreach programmes, which are composed of a portfolio of multidisciplinary service-learning projects. Service-learning activities are based on a community approach to provide authentic learning environments for students and to solve the real problems of communities, hospitals, educational units, and local governments.

Regarding preparation and planning, the ESPOL intervention protocol applies community approach methodologies that provide information on real problems and needs, such as participatory diagnostics, in-depth interviews, surveys, environmental analysis, stakeholder maps, and involvement matrices. The implementation of service-learning projects is developed by the students under the supervision and guidance of professors. These outreach programmes are multidisciplinary and involve the participation of professors and students from various fields of knowledge. The monitoring of team members' duties and activities is defined during this stage.

Service-learning activities allow students to reflect and internalise the knowledge acquired, interlinking community service and vocational training [37]. It is worth noting that the students together with the professors, measure the learning results and the assimilation of the knowledge gained in practice (reflection step of Salam et al. [22]). Finally, the evaluation consists of measuring the results of the outreach programmes on a 5-year basis. At the end of this methodological process, sustainability is reflected in the adoption of an attitude of empowerment and autonomy on the part of the beneficiaries regarding the results achieved [38].

3.2 Data analysis strategy

This research was conducted under a non-experimental study with a quantitative approach and non-probability sampling technique. The sample includes data from second and third-year students in the fields of engineering, social sciences and tourism. Through the distribution of a digital questionnaire addressed to the total population of 728 students, a 34% response rate was achieved, resulting in 248 valid questionnaires. The students were asked for consent to fill out the questionnaires, and the data was anonymously analysed. Initially, the sample was divided into two groups: (1) an experimental group (EG) consisting of 167 students who performed service-learning activities; and (2) a control group (CG) comprising 81 students who did not perform service-learning activities. Results were also evaluated according to areas of knowledge, comparing whether there is any difference between engineering students (EG1) and social sciences and tourism students (EG2). The data that support the findings of this study are available on request from the corresponding author.

The instrument applied to evaluate effective communication and teamwork was a questionnaire developed by ESPOL professors. The questionnaire consists of two dimensions: (1) effective communication that evaluates the ability to understand instructions, use solid arguments to defend ideas, use appropriate language to communicate with other groups of people, among others; and (2) teamwork that measures recognition of the importance of work within the team, contributing ideas during group discussions, and valuing the skills of group members. Through this questionnaire, students self-assess their actions and choose the frequency of these for each item according to the scale 'rarely', 'never', 'always', and 'almost always'. This questionnaire was submitted for validation by experts in the area.

In addition to expert validation, the reliability of the measuring instrument was assessed through the estimation of the Cronbach Alpha coefficient, obtaining 0.76 for the effective communication dimension and 0.79 for the teamwork dimension. According to the interpretation of Oviedo and Campo-Arias [39], it has an 'acceptable reliability' because it ranges from 0.70 to 0.90. It is therefore concluded that the internal consistency of the instrument used is acceptable and that its implementation is reliable. Finally, the data collected were analysed using inferential statistics.

4 RESULTS

The data distribution for each dimension of the questionnaire was evaluated, and the non-normality in the distribution of observations was identified using the Kolmogorov–Smirnov test statistic of 0.00 significance level. Therefore, non-parametric statistical analysis of the EG and CG groups was carried out to determine whether there is a statistically significant difference in students' self-perception when evaluating their performance in effective social communication and teamwork skills. The Mann–Whitney U test was used to identify significant differences between EG and CG for each questionnaire item. The results show a significant difference between EG and CG medians with a statistical significance ($p = 0.007$) for using appropriate language with different groups of people. Additionally, a statistically significant difference ($p < 0.05$) was observed in the criterion of the level of importance students place on teamwork. No significant differences were found for the other items (refer to Table 1).

Subsequently, the non-parametric Kruskal–Wallis test was used to compare the distribution of the two experimental groups of engineering careers (EG1) and social sciences and tourism (EG2) and the control group (CG) and determine whether there is a statistically

Table 1: Results Mann–Whitney U-test.

Item	EG	CG	Mann–Whitney U	z	Asymptotic significance
Effective communication					
I understand instructions	5	5	6322.500	−1.006	0.315
Others understand me	5	5	6218.000	−1.380	0.168
I defend my ideas	5	5	6365.000	−0.862	0.389
Use of appropriate language	7	5	5521.000	−2.690	0.007*
Interest and listening	7	7	6485.000	−0.608	0.543
I dare to ask questions	5	5	6567.500	−0.400	0.689
Gestures and verbal communication	5	5	6344.500	−0.860	0.39
Teamwork					
Importance of my work	7	5	5210.000	−3.483	0.000**
Give ideas in group discussions	7	7	6692.000	−0.155	0.877
Adaptation to a working team	5	5	6174.000	−1.245	0.213
I value the skills of my team members	7	7	6140.000	−1.482	0.138
Developing my professional skills	7	7	6278.500	−1.054	0.292

* Statistical significance $p < 0.05$; ** Statistical significance $p < 0.001$.

significant difference contrasting by area of knowledge. The results of this test are shown in the following sections.

4.1 Effective communication between engineering, social science and tourism students

The language-related item is the only criterion within the practical communication dimension where compared groups show a significant difference ($p < 0.05$), with a significance of 0.011. The post-hoc tests of Table 2 determined significant differences between students who were not involved in service-learning activities and those who performed service-learning activities from engineering and social sciences and tourism. As shown in Fig. 1, with a significance value of 0.008, the students belonging to the EG1 of engineering present a higher statistic than those in the control group. However, there is no statistically representative difference between engineering and social sciences and tourism career students, nor between social science and tourist students and the control group.

4.2 Teamwork among engineering and social science and tourism students

Items that measured students' teamwork skills were also analysed by identifying significant differences between the group averages for the criterion 'I recognise the importance of my work and the contribution it provides within a working team', with a significance level of 0.002. Through the post-hoc tests of Table 3, it was possible to identify that there are

Table 2: Post-hoc tests for independent samples – Effective communication.

Sample 1 – Sample 2	Contrast statistic	Error	Contrast statistical deviation	Significance
CG vs EG2	14.195	10.704	1.326	0.554
CG vs EG1	27.469	9.192	2.988	0.008*
EG1 vs EG2	−13.274	10.124	−1.311	0.569

* Statistical significance $p < 0.05$.

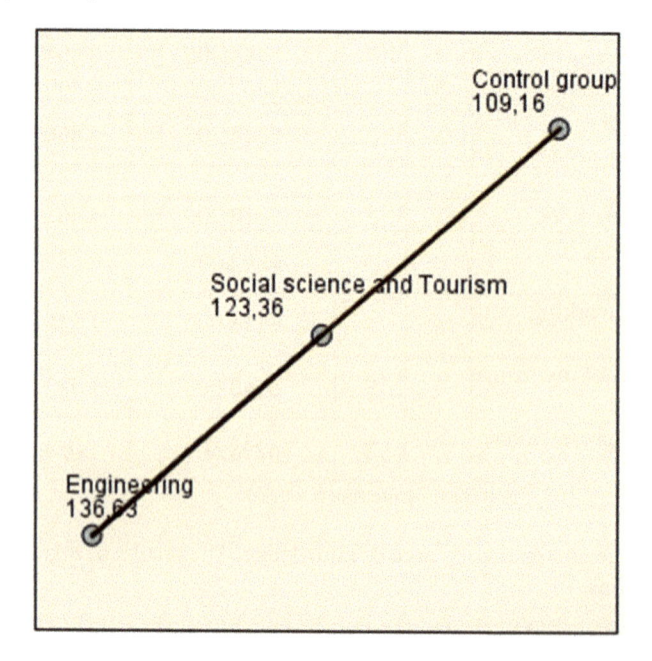

Figure 1: Comparison of means between knowledge areas – Effective communication.

Table 3: Post-hoc tests for independent samples – Teamwork.

Sample 1 – Sample 2	Contrast statistic	Error	Contrast statistical deviation	Significance
CG vs EG1	26.901	8.877	3.030	0.007*
CG vs EG2	31.374	10.337	3.035	0.007*
EG1 vs EG2	4.473	9.777	0.457	1.000

* Statistical significance $p < 0.05$.

significant differences between students who were not involved in service-learning activities and those who performed service-learning activities in engineering and in social sciences and tourism, as shown in Fig. 2. However, there is no statistically representative difference between engineering and social sciences and tourism students.

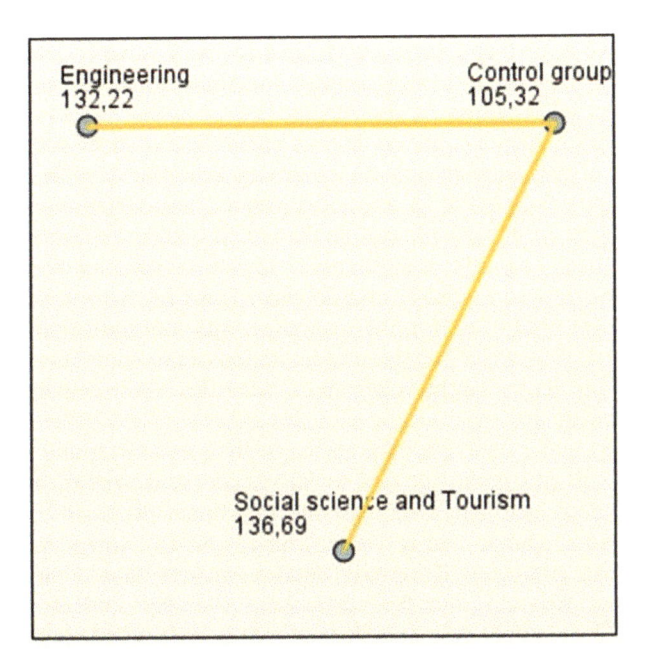

Figure 2: Comparison of means between knowledge areas – Teamwork.

5 DISCUSSION AND CONCLUSIONS

The present study uses non-parametric inferential analysis to determine the influence of service-learning activities on the social skills of university students. The results show a positive influence on effective communication in the form of using appropriate language with different groups of people and teamwork by recognising teamwork's importance. The experience that students acquire when performing service-learning activities is a challenge, considering that they must convey their ideas, thoughts, and knowledge to people of different cultural levels, which encourages the development of their communication skills, coinciding with the proposal by several authors that participation in service-learning activities is conducive to the development in communication skills in students [14], [15], [18]–[20].

Another significant result of this study is the positive impact of service-learning activities on developing teamwork skills. University students of ESPOL perform their service-learning activities within institutional outreach programmes. These activities are carried out by students from different knowledge fields and guided by professors. The principal aim of these service-learning activities is to solve real-life societal problems by applying their knowledge. In this sense, students recognise the importance of teamwork as each group member contributes from his/her perspective to a comprehensive solution to a real problem. The results of our research coincide with the contribution of Schmalenbach et al. [16], who showed positive evidence by experiencing teamwork during a service-learning activity among university students in El Salvador. Also, Kandakatla et al. [15] and Pinfold [17] suggest a positive influence of service-learning on social skills such as teamwork.

Another important finding resulting from the post-hoc tests is that engineering students stand out in using appropriate language over control group students but not over social science and tourism students. Similarly, in teamwork, both engineering students and those in social sciences and tourism stand out above the students of the control group. However, no significant difference was found between engineering and social sciences and tourism students. These results differ from some studies that show social career students scoring higher in social skills than engineering students [40].

These results, which demonstrate an improvement in the social skills of university students as a result of participation in service-learning activities, contribute to the need to improve the social and emotional skills associated with the lack of communication of college students [41]. However, of the seven items on the practical communication scale, only one item showed a statistically significant difference; likewise, on the teamwork scale, only one item of the five items showed a significant difference. This finding probably corresponds to the limited sample size used or also to the scale used with four options that do not collect more significant variability, which represents a limitation of this study that can be addressed in future research with larger sample sizes and a scale that allows obtaining more minor differences in the constructs.

Finally, this study underscores the importance of the service-learning methodology for developing social skills in engineering and social sciences and tourism students regarding effective communication and teamwork. The most pertinent practical implication of this research is the recommendation that service-learning should be integrated into university teaching and learning strategies. University decision-makers should incorporate various experiential learning activities into the curriculum, enabling students to engage with community members and apply their knowledge to solve real-life problems. This approach pushes students and faculty members out of their comfort zones, compelling them to collaborate with individuals from different backgrounds and contexts, thereby encouraging them to communicate ideas in innovative and varied ways. Additionally, it is important to ensure that faculty members receive training on how to effectively convey their theories and technical solutions to a broader audience, especially when these concepts may not be easily understood by groups from different backgrounds.

ACKNOWLEDGEMENTS

This research received financial support from ESPOL through the research project 'Assessment of sustainable attitudes and competencies of university students' (FIMCP-04-2023). The authors thank ESPOL and its Outreach Dean and her team for collaborating on this research.

REFERENCES

[1] Tito, B. & Serrano, B., Desarrollo de soft skills una alternativa a la escasez de talento humano. *INNOVA Res. J.*, **1**(12), pp. 59–76, 2016. https://doi.org/10.33890/innova.v1.12.2016.81.

[2] Derco, J. & Tometzová, D., Entry-level professional competencies and skills in tourism: The case of Slovakia. *J. Hosp. Leis. Sport Tour. Educ.*, **32**(February), 2023. https://doi.org/10.1016/j.jhlste.2023.100437.

[3] Carlisle, S., Ivanov, S. & Espeso-Molinero, P., Delivering the European Skills Agenda: The importance of social skills for a sustainable tourism and hospitality industry [Cumplimiento de la Agenda Europea de Competencias: la importancia de las habilidades sociales para una industria turística y hotele]. *Tour. Manag. Stud.*, **19**(3), pp. 23–40, 2023.

[4] Espinoza, M. & Gallegos, D., Habilidades blandas en la educación y la empresa: Mapeo sistemático. *Rev. Científica UISRAEL*, **7**(2), pp. 39–56, 2020. https://doi.org/10.35290/rcui.v7n2.2020.245.

[5]   Fuentes, G., Moreno-Murcia, L., Rincón-Tellez, D. & Silva-Garcia, M., Evaluación de las habilidades blandas en la educación superior. *Form. Univ.*, **14**(4), pp. 49–60, 2021. https://doi.org/10.4067/S0718-50062021000400049.

[6]   Tamayo, M., Besoaín-Saldaña, A., Aguirre, M. & Leiva, J., Teamwork: Relevance and interdependence of interprofessional education. *Saúde Pública*, **51**(39), 2017. https://doi.org/10.1590/s1518-8787.2017051006816.

[7]   Sánchez, R. & Ñañez, M., Percepción del trabajo en equipo y de las habilidades sociales en estudiantes universitarios. *Puriq*, **4**, e265, 2022. https://doi.org/10.37073/puriq.4.265.

[8]   Hernández-Jorge, C. & De la Rosa, C., Habilidades comunicativas en estudiantes de carreras de apoyo frente a estudiantes de otras carreras. **35**(2), pp. 93–104, 2017.

[9]   Gallop, C., Guthrie, B. & Asante, N., The impact of experiential learning on professional identity: Comparing community service-learning to traditional practical pedagogy. *J. Exp. Educ.*, pp. 1–17, 2023. https://doi.org/10.1177/10538259231154888.

[10] Bringle, R. & Hatcher, J., Service learning curriculum for faculty. *Michigan J. Community Serv. Learn.*, pp. 112–122, 1995.

[11] Salam, M., Iskandar, D., Ibrahim, D. & Farooq, M., Service learning in higher education: A systematic literature review. *Asia Pacific Educ. Rev.*, **20**(4), pp. 573–593, 2019. https://doi.org/10.1007/s12564-019-09580-6.

[12] Franklin, K., Halvorson, S. & Brown, F., Impacts of service learning on tourism students' sustainability competencies in conflict-affected Bamyan, Afghanistan. *Int. J. Sustain. High. Educ.*, 2023. https://doi.org/10.1108/IJSHE-04-2022-0112.

[13] Lau, K. & Snell, R., *Service-Learning Outcomes Measurement Scale (S-LOMS): The User Manual*, Office of Service-Learning, Lingnan University, 2020. https://doi.org/10.14793/9789887522201.

[14] Tejada, J., La formación de las competencias profesionales a través del aprendizaje servicio. *Cult. y Educ.*, **35**(3), pp. 285–294, 2013. https://doi.org/10.1174/113564013807749669.

[15] Kandakatla, R., Dustker, S., Bandi, S. & Oakes, W., Achieving Indian National Board of Accreditation engineering graduate attributes through project-based service-learning: Conceptual analysis Surendra Bandi. *Int. J. Serv. Learn. Eng. Humanit. Eng. Soc. Entrep.*, **18**(1), pp. 52–69, 2023.

[16] Schmalenbach, C., Monterrosa, H., Cabrera Larín, A. & Jurkowski, S., The LIFE programme: University students learning leadership and teamwork through service learning in El Salvador. *Intercult. Educ.*, **33**(4), pp. 470–483, 2022. https://doi.org/10.1080/14675986.2022.2090689.

[17] Pinfold, L., Transdisciplinary service-learning for construction management and quantity surveying students. *J. Transdiscipl. Res. South. Africa*, **17**(1), a993, 2021. https://doi.org/10.4102/td.v17i1.993.

[18] Valencia-Forrester, F. & Backhaus, B., Service learning as supported, social learning for international students: An Australian case study. *Int. J. Incl. Educ.*, **27**(3), pp. 403–417, 2020. https://doi.org/10.1080/13603116.2020.1864789.

[19] Keshwani, J. & Adams, K., Cross-disciplinary service-learning to enhance engineering identity and improve communication skills. *Int. J. Serv. Learn. Eng. Humanit. Eng. Soc. Entrep.*, **12**(1), pp. 41–61, 2017. https://doi.org/10.24908/ijsle.v12i1.6664.

[20] Sass, M. & Coll, K., The effect of service learning on community college students. *Community Coll. J. Res. Pract.*, **39**(3), pp. 280–288, 2015. https://doi.org/10.1080/10668926.2012.756838.

[21] Bandi, S., Joshi, G., Shettar, A. & Kandakatla, R., A systematic literature review on faculty learning in service-learning. *2023 IEEE Global Engineering Education Conference (EDUCON)*, pp. 1–10, 2023. https://doi.org/10.1109/EDUCON54358.2023.10125223.

[22] Salam, M., Awang Iskandar, D., Ibrahim, D. & Farooq, M., Technology integration in service-learning pedagogy: A holistic framework. *Telemat. Informatics*, **38**, pp. 257–273, 2019. https://doi.org/10.1016/j.tele.2019.02.002.

[23] Rodríguez-Zurita, D., Jaya-Montalvo, M., Moreira-Arboleda, J., Raya-Diez, E. & Carrión-Mero, P., Sustainable development through service learning and community engagement in higher education: A systematic literature review. *Int. J. Sustain. High. Educ.*, 2024. https://doi.org/10.1108/IJSHE-10-2023-0461.

[24] Queiruga-Dios, M., Santos Sánchez, M.J., Queiruga-Dios, M.Á., Acosta Castellanos, P.M. & Queiruga-Dios, A., Assessment methods for service-learning projects in engineering in higher education: A systematic review. *Front. Psychol.*, **12**(July), 2021. https://doi.org/10.3389/fpsyg.2021.629231.

[25] Kolb, A. & Kolb, D., Experiential learning theory as a guide for experiential educators in higher education. *Exp. Learn. Teach. High. Educ.*, **1**(1), pp. 7–44, 2017. https://nsuworks.nova.edu/elthe/vol1/iss1/7%0Ahttps://eds.b.ebscohost.com/eds/detail/detail?vid=6&sid=ec22dd52-08e4-405f-b976-3e6fe46322f1%40sessionmgr102&bdata=JnNpdGU9ZWRzLWxpdmU%3D#db=a9h&AN=124424435.

[26] Kong, Y., The role of experiential learning on students' motivation and classroom engagement. *Front. Psychol.*, **12**, 771272, 2021. https://doi.org/10.3389/fpsyg.2021.771272.

[27] Kolb, D., *Experiential Learning: Experience as the Source of Learning and Development*, 1984.

[28] Earnest, D., Rosenbusch, K., Wallace-Williams, D. & Keim, A., Study abroad in psychology: Increasing cultural competencies through experiential learning. *Teach. Psychol.*, **43**(1), pp. 75–79, 2016. https://doi.org/10.1177/0098628315620889.

[29] Chan, H., Kwong, H., Shu, G., Ting, C. & Lai, F., Effects of experiential learning programmes on adolescent prosocial behaviour, empathy, and subjective well-being: A systematic review and meta-analysis. *Front. Psychol.*, **12**, 709699, 2021. https://doi.org/10.3389/fpsyg.2021.709699.

[30] Gleason, M. & Rubio, J., Implementación del aprendizaje experiencial en la universidad, sus beneficios en el alumnado y el rol docente. *Rev. Educ.*, **44**(2), 2020. https://doi.org/10.15517/revedu.v44i2.40197.

[31] Furco, A., Service-learning: A balanced approach to experiential education. *Expand. Boundaries Serv. Learn.*, pp. 2–6, 1996. https://digitalcommons.unomaha.edu/slceslgen/128.

[32] Brito, J., Figueroa, A., Mañón, M., Sedano, S., Ramírez, V. & Quintero, M., Community social service: Students away from the classroom, building knowledge in their communities. *Open J. Soc. Sci.*, **5**, pp. 10–24, 2017. https://doi.org/10.4236/jss.2017.51002.

[33] Chiva-Bartoll, O. & Fernández-Rio, J., Advocating for service-learning as a pedagogical model in physical education: Towards an activist and transformative approach. *Phys. Educ. Sport Pedagog.*, **27**(5), pp. 545–558, 2022. https://doi.org/10.1080/17408989.2021.1911981.

[34] Miller, P., Roofe, C. & García-Carmona, M., School leadership, curriculum diversity, social justice and critical perspectives in education. *Cultures of Social Justice Leadership: An Intercultural Context of Schools*, Springer: Cham, pp. 93–119, 2019. https://doi.org/10.1007/978-3-030-10874-8_5.

[35] Armisén, D., Imaz, C., Prieto, C. & Vallecillo, L., Ciudadanía global y aprendizaje-servicio. *Comillas J. Int. Relations*, **19**, pp. 100–106, 2020. https://doi.org/10.14422/cir.i19.y2020.008.

[36] Rose, A., Snyder, M., Murphy-Nugen, A., Maddox, G., MacKusick, C. & Molefe, B., Cultivating cross-cultural learning and collaboration among special educators engaged in international service-learning. *Int. J. Res. Serv. Community Engagem.*, **9**(1), 2021. https://doi.org/10.37333/001C.31307.

[37] Banderas, C. & Quinteros, A., Learning service in evaluating the results of learning: A benefit shared with the community. *13th LACCEI Annual International Conference: 'Engineering Education Facing the Grand Challenges, What Are We Doing?'* pp. 0–6, 2015. https://doi.org/10.18687/LACCEI2015.1.1.141.

[38] Delgado, E., Peralta, J., Quinteros, A., Durazno, G., Calle, A. & Maldonado, F., Enseñanza para el desarrollo de la sostenibilidad energética en el hogar en zonas urbano: marginales de la ciudad de Guayaquil. *Rev. Técnica 'Energía'*, **16**(2), pp. 188–198, 2020. https://doi.org/10.37116/revistaenergia.v16.n2.2020.366.

[39] Oviedo, H. & Campo-Arias, A., Aproximación al uso del coeficiente alfa de Cronbach. *Rev. Colomb. Psiquiatr.*, **34**(4), pp. 572–580, 2005.

[40] Holst, I., Barrera, Y., Gómez, G. & Degante, A., Las habilidades sociales y sus diferencias en estudiantes universitarios. *VERTIENTES Rev. Espec. en Ciencias la Salud*, **20**(2), pp. 22–29, 2018.

[41] Neri, J. & Hernández, C., Los jóvenes universitarios de ingeniería y su percepción sobre las competencias blandas. *RIDE Rev. Iberoam. para la Investig. y el Desarro. Educ.*, **9**(18), pp. 768–791, 2019. https://doi.org/10.23913/ride.v9i18.449.

SECTION 4
CULTURAL, HERITAGE AND GASTRONOMIC TOURISM

DEVELOPING SUSTAINABLE INDIGENOUS TOURISM BASED ON EDUCATION: A COMPARISON BETWEEN JAPAN AND CANADA

LORENZ POGGENDORF, TAKESHI KURIHARA & MIHO HAMAZAKI
Graduate School of International Tourism Management, Toyo University, Japan

ABSTRACT

Since the United Nations recognised the rights of indigenous peoples in 2007, indigenous tourism has received increased attention. This paper compares the situation of the indigenous peoples of northern Japan with that of the indigenous peoples of Canada and related indigenous tourism promotion. For this study, in Japan, citizens of both sexes and all age groups were asked about their knowledge of and interest in the Ainu and their culture. For both countries, academic sources and online information were used to research the handling of settler history, relevant legislation, and the current promotion of indigenous peoples. The results so far show that, despite some recent progress in the targeted promotion of indigenous tourism, Japan is still at the beginning compared to Canada and can learn a lot from Canada in terms of historical reappraisal of its indigenous people.
Keywords: Ainu, Japan, First Nations, Canada, history, government policies, indigenous tourism.

1 INTRODUCTION

What is Japan doing to promote its indigenous culture and associated tourism? In Hokkaido, 'Upopoy' – a symbolic space for coexistence of ethnic groups – opened to the public in July 2020. This is a museum (both indoor and open-air) and cultural meeting place where visitors can experience Ainu culture up close [1]. The promotion of Ainu indigenous tourism is also included in Japan's tourism policy for fiscal year 2022, which calls for the promotion of Ainu as indigenous people [2].

These efforts have been made only in recent years, and Ainu indigenous tourism is not well-known in Japan. While there are organisations dedicated to the preservation and transmission of Ainu culture, there is no organisation that specialises in indigenous tourism, such as the Indigenous Tourism Association of Canada (ITAC) [3]. In this respect, Japan is still lagging behind other countries in the field of indigenous tourism.

While it is still a niche market, indigenous tourism is on the rise worldwide. The culture and lifestyles of native people seem to be gaining acceptance in society as a whole, reflected by international trends such as the 'United Nations Declaration on the Rights of Indigenous Peoples', which was adopted in 2007 by the United Nations General Assembly [4]. It may therefore be argued that the oppressed indigenous people in America, Oceania, and Asia are gradually receiving their human rights and dignity back.

However, how much do non-indigenous people really understand about indigenous people, and how does this relate to the touristic utilisation of indigenous culture?

Curtin and Bird address this question with regard to indigenous tourism in Australia. Based on the Grounded Theory Approach, they conducted interviews with Aboriginal tourism operators to examine the requirements for a sustainable Aboriginal society. In their findings, furthermore, concerns visitors fully engaging with the indigenous people and the location in question. That is why indigenous tour operators are usually the ones who can convey their own culture more authentically than, for example, tourist guides who are not indigenous themselves [5].

The aim of this paper is to point out that indigenous tourism involves more than a smart business model or marketing campaign. In essence, the idea is that indigenous tourism should be closely related to the values and way of life of the indigenous people themselves. It is certainly fair to say that more knowledge about indigenous people is needed among most of the population, stakeholders, and political decision-makers. Therefore, in the first part, this work deals with knowledge transfer about indigenous people, and in the second part with indigenous tourism itself.

In this paper we want to look at the situation of the Ainu people, who were legally recognised as indigenous people of northern Japan since 2008. Initial data was collected on how to arouse interest in the Ainu among contemporary Japanese people. Based on these findings, this paper compares Ainu related educational activities and indigenous tourism with that of Canada. Canada was chosen because it can be seen as a leader in coming to terms with the history of displacement and the development of indigenous tourism.

It may be suggested that Japan is only at an early stage of indigenous tourism, while Canada is at a more mature stage of development. Initial online surveys of contemporary Japanese people about their interest in the Ainu people and the analysis of the responses lead us to this conclusion. Based on this, the question arises as to what needs to be done in Japan to further develop indigenous Ainu tourism in a sustainable way? The paper at hand cannot answer this question conclusively but would like to provide some initial food for thought.

2 GOAL AND METHOD OF THE STUDY

This paper argues that knowledge transfer about the indigenous peoples of one's own country and demand for indigenous tourism are related. Knowledge transfer takes place at various levels, such as in the interpretation of history, political recognition and promotion of indigenous culture, as well as through teaching materials and various cultural activities and events. A comprehensive analysis in this regard would go beyond the scope of this paper, but we will address the most important developments in both countries – Japan and Canada.

The main research questions are as follows:

- What are the requirements for raising Ainu indigenous tourism in Japan to the development stage?
- What can Japan learn from a country like Canada in this regard?

While this paper mainly collected primary data about Japan, we also looked at available information for Canada.

2.1 Indigenous recognition, knowledge transfer, and tourism in Japan

In the case of Japan, we formulated a hypothesis and tested this hypothesis by examining interest in and attitudes towards Ainu tourism by conducting an online survey (primary data – Table 1).

The hypothesis of this study is that successful promotion of Ainu indigenous tourism is reflected by an increase in interest in and consumption of Ainu culture.

Factors that increase interest in Ainu culture relate to knowledge of Ainu culture, respondents' travel preferences, and participation in events, including cultural experiences at school events. Personal attributes such as gender, age, place of residence, occupation, and educational background were also considered.

Table 1: Data collection about Japan.

Data type	Details	Target
Primary data	Online survey	Japanese population (average)
	• Survey subjects	Residents of the Tokyo Metropolitan Area and Hokkaido
	• Survey period	March 2023
	• Survey method	Questionnaire
	• Survey items (content)	Gender and age, residence, marital status, occupation, history of residence in Hokkaido, experience of visiting Upopoy and Ainu-related facilities, intention to purchase Ainu-related products, knowledge of Ainu culture through a quiz, learning about Ainu culture in elementary education
	• Number of responses	603 (Tokyo Metropolitan Area: 301, Hokkaido: 302)
Secondary data	• Government reports • The Foundation for Ainu Culture	Ainu policy and corresponding legal changes in Japan
	• Websites of cultural organisations and activities	Indigenous culture in museums and information centres, indigenous culture outdoors
	• Websites offering indigenous tourism	Tour operators offering tours with the goal of experiencing Ainu culture first-hand

In order to test the hypotheses, a survey on attitudes toward Ainu indigenous tourism was conducted in March 2023 by a web-based survey company. The sample size was 301 for residents in the Tokyo metropolitan area and 302 for residents in Hokkaido, for a totalling 603 participants. Both genders and all age groups were represented in a balanced manner.

Using a five-point assessment similar to the Likert scale, we asked survey participants about their intention to visit Upopoy, the experience of visiting Upopoy and permanent and non-permanent Ainu-related facilities, interest in Ainu culture, and the intention to purchase products related to it. For example, the intention to visit Upopoy was rated as follows: 1 = not at all, 2 = not so much, 3 = undecided, 4 = want to visit, and 5 = definitely want to visit.

The respondents were also asked about the timing of their past Ainu cultural experiences such as eating food, playing musical instruments, and wearing traditional clothes.

Regarding the understanding of Ainu culture, five questions were taken from a quiz provided by the Ainu Culture Foundation, and the number of correct answers was used as a proxy indicator of the level of understanding. Respondents were also asked where they obtained the knowledge used to answer the quiz.

Finally, in order to examine the relationship between attitudes towards Ainu culture and primary education, we asked whether respondents thought that learning about Ainu culture in elementary and junior high school had led to their current cultural understanding and interest.

In addition, we examined the cornerstones of policy towards a better recognition of the Ainu people and corresponding legal adjustments. We also looked at online sources to see what educational offerings are available and to what extent direct experience of Ainu culture is possible in the shape of indigenous tourism (secondary data – Table 1).

2.2 Indigenous recognition, knowledge transfer, and tourism in Canada

In order to compare the situation of the Ainu people in Japan with that of First Nation people in Canada, we first looked at the cornerstones of Canadian policy towards a better recognition of its indigenous people and corresponding legal adjustments (secondary data – Table 2).

Table 2: Data collection about Canada.

Data type	Details	Target
Secondary data	• Government of Canada programs and services for First Nations, Inuit and Métis and related administrations	Policy towards First Nations, Inuit and Métis and corresponding legal changes in Canada
	• Websites of cultural organisations and activities	Indigenous culture in museums and information centres, indigenous culture outdoors
	• Websites offering indigenous tourism	Information provided by ITAC and tour operators offering tours with the goal to experience indigenous culture first-hand

Next, we looked at online sources to see what educational offerings are available and to what extent direct experience of First Nation people is possible in the shape of indigenous tourism. As noted above, in the case of Canada, only secondary data was researched and compared with corresponding information on Japan.

3 RESULTS

3.1 Results for Japan

First, we report on the results of the surveys (primary data), followed by relevant facts concerning the policy towards the Ainu (secondary data).

3.1.1 Online survey's attributes
This section illustrates the characteristics of the survey by presenting the results of each of the survey's attributes. Table 3 shows the results of the basic survey broken down into the residents of Hokkaido and those of the Tokyo metropolitan area.

The decimal points in the table do not always add up to 100%. The gender and age of the targeted respondents was balanced, which enhanced the clarity of the survey results. Most respondents living in Hokkaido have lived in Japan for more than five years. In addition, the respondents and their parents were more likely to be university graduates in the Tokyo area than in Hokkaido.

Table 3: Survey about Ainu, attributes' definition.

Latent variable	Observed variable	Definition
Personal attributes	Gender	Male = 1, female = 0
	Age	20s = 2, 30s = 3, 40s = 4, 50s = 5, 60s = 6
	Residence	Hokkaido = 1, Tokyo, Chiba, Saitama, Kanagawa = 0
	Occupation	Self-employment, professional, student, housemaker, part-time worker, unemployed, retired = 1, office worker, public servant = 0
	Education	University graduate or above = 1, others = 0
	Parents education	University graduate or above = 1, others = 0
Cultural experience	Museum visit	Have visited an Ainu cultural institution or museum other than Upopoy = 1, no = 0
	Event participation	Have participated in non-permanent events, lectures, or exhibitions related to Ainu culture = 1, no experience = 0
	Elementary school	Experienced Ainu culture at an elementary school event = 1, no experience = 0
	Junior high school	Experienced Ainu culture at a junior high school event = 1, no experience = 0
	High school	Experienced Ainu culture at a high school event = 1, no experience = 0
	Museum cultural experience	Experienced Ainu culture at permanent Ainu cultural facilities and museums, including Upopoy = 1, no experience = 0
	Event experience	Experienced Ainu culture through events and exhibitions that are not permanent installations = 1, no experience = 0
	Colleague experience	Personal experience of Ainu culture through acquaintances, etc. = 1, no experience = 0
Travel frequency	Domestic travel	More than one domestic travel in the last year = 1, 0 times = 0
	International travel	More than one travel abroad = 1, never = 0
Educational effect	School education memories	Remember learning about Ainu culture in elementary and junior high school = 1, don't remember = 0
	School education contribution	I believe that learning about Ainu culture in elementary and junior high school has led to my current understanding of and interest in Ainu culture. (5 = pretty, 4 = fairly, 3 = neutral, 2 = not much, 1 = not at all, 0 = don't know, · don't remember)
–	Quiz	Number of correct answers to quiz on Ainu culture (max = 5, min = 0)

Table 3: Continued.

Latent variable	Observed variable	Definition
Cultural interest	Ainu Cultural interest	Interested in Ainu culture (5 = pretty, 4 = fairly, 3 = neutral, 2 = not much, 1 = not at all)
Consumption Intension	Intention to visit Upopoy	Would like to visit Upopoy (5 = pretty, 4 = fairly, 3 = neutral, 2 = not much, 1 = not at all, • don't know)
	Intention to purchase goods	Would like to purchase folk crafts related to Ainu culture (7 = have already purchased and would purchase again, 6 = no experience in purchasing, but would LOVE to, 5 = I have no experience in purchasing, but would LIKE to, 4 = neutral, 3 = experienced purchase but no longer interested in purchasing, 2 = not much, 1 = not at all)

3.1.2 Factor analysis of psychological distance using covariance structure analysis

Covariance structure analysis (CSA) is a statistical method used to examine the relationships between several variables. IBM SPSS AMOS is software specifically designed for such analyses, and for this paper, version AMOS 29 was used. The analysis to understand the factors of psychological distance from the Ainu people is based on the hypotheses set out in Section 2.1 and uses CSA to examine how each item affects people's interest in Ainu culture.

This analysis uses a 'path diagram' to determine the relationship between variables. Fig. 1 shows the results of the analysis visually. The results of the model estimation show that GFI = 0.888 (goodness of fit index), AGFI = 0.857 (adjusted goodness of fit index), CFI = 0.838 (comparative fit index); and RMSEA = 0.073 (root mean square error of approximation).

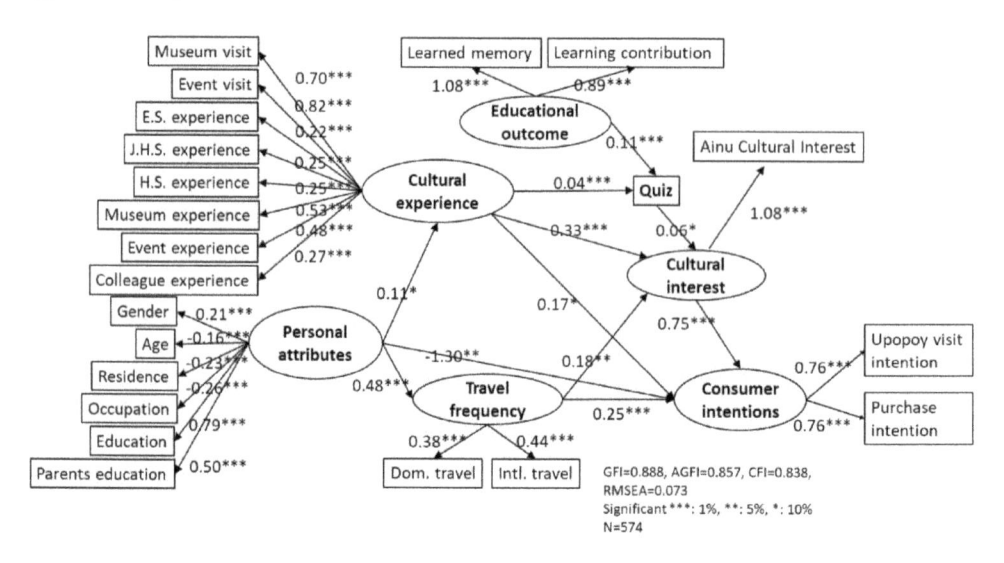

Figure 1: Factor analysis of psychological distance using covariance structure analysis.

The closer the GFI is to 1, the more explanatory power the model has, and a value of 0.9 or higher is considered very good; the closer the AGFI and CFI are to 1, the better the fit to the data, and a value of 0.9 or higher is considered very good. AGFI and CFI are considered to fit the data better if they are close to 1 and very good if they are 0.9 or higher, and RMSEA is considered to fit the data better if it is 0.06 or lower. According to the numbers above in comparison to the target values explained, it can be said that we were able to achieve good results overall in this analysis.

In this estimation, the promotion of Ainu culture is assumed to be formed by two factors: increased interest in culture and increased willingness to consume. The factors that increase interest in Ainu culture are assumed to be 'personal attributes', 'cultural experience', 'cultural knowledge' and 'travel preferences'. The 'intention to consume' is assumed to be 'consumption intention' after visiting Ainu culture-related products and Upopoy. The definitions of the other variables used in the analysis are presented in Table 3. This section summarises the most important results in five statements.

1. Cultural experience is the most significant factor influencing interest in Ainu culture. Among the various cultural experiences, participation in events, participation in permanent exhibitions, and experiences in permanent exhibitions are the most strongly related, in that order.
2. The path from personal attributes to interest in Ainu culture via cultural experiences is also advantageous. However, even if respondents with the most relevant personal attributes have a higher final education level, it is less effective than respondents who experienced Ainu culture at an elementary school event first-hand.
3. Experiencing Ainu culture at an elementary school event and even one trip abroad has about the same effect on the least relevant cultural experience. Although participation in an event is a more probable pathway from cultural experience to cultural knowledge, the effect is greater for respondents who reported remembering their education in elementary and junior high school through cultural knowledge derived from educational outcomes.
4. Although participation in an event is a more probable pathway from cultural experience to cultural knowledge, the effect is greater for respondents who reported remembering their education in elementary and junior high school through cultural knowledge derived from educational outcomes.
5. A higher level of cultural interest has an effect on consumption intention. Notwithstanding the respondent's final educational attainment and personal attributes, the effect is greater when the respondent has attended events and via cultural interest from cultural experiences.

The overall interpretation of the survey results is provided in Section 3.1.5.

3.1.3 Policy towards Ainu people and corresponding legal changes in Japan
Since this paper deals with the role of knowledge transfer, the basic question arises, how can we expect genuine interest in indigenous people and related tourism if these same indigenous people have never really been treated with respect throughout recent history? In most countries, including Japan, it was assumed that the 'savages' had to be civilised and educated according to modern (Western) ideas. In the case of Japan, the colonisation of the Ainu by the Japanese people took place, roughly speaking, in two stages.

The initial phase occurred during the Tokugawa period (1603–1868). Under the leadership of the Matsumae clan, the Japanese or *Wajin* established trading posts along the coasts of Southern Hokkaido (Ezo) and employed the Ainu men in fishing [6]. As we can learn in the

Upopoy museum, trading activities developed from 1821, and as a side effect of increasing encounters with the Ainu, 'smallpox and other infectious diseases broke out among the Ainu. As a result, the population of the Ainu in Hokkaido rapidly decreased' [1]. Traders and first settlers gradually expanded their influence inland, taking control over most of the island from 1856. In other words, the government in Edo (now Tokyo) had already begun to introduce agriculture and push back the traditional Ainu way of life, however, the Ainu were still able to maintain their existence [6].

The second stage took place in the Meiji period (1868–1912) and led to the rapid decline of the Ainu. In 1869, the new Meiji government renamed Ezo as Hokkaido, and officially incorporated the whole territory into the Japanese state. In the same year, the government established the 'Hokkaido Colonization Commission' (*Kaitakushi*) and appointed advisors from the West, particularly the United States, to this commission, to oversee the development and settlement of Hokkaido. In this context, it should be mentioned that the exploitation of the Ainu and the development of the US western frontier, both of which led to the dispossession of indigenous peoples, occurred simultaneously. In short, the Japanese watched what was going on in America and applied it to the colonisation of Hokkaido [6].

In addition, in 1875, the Russian Empire and the Empire of Japan agreed on 'The Treaty of St. Petersburg' (Karafuto-Kuril Exchange Treaty, *Karafuto-Chishima Kōkan Jōyaku*) to resolve territorial disputes in the Far East. The treaty stipulated that Japan would cede all of its claims to Sakhalin Island to Russia. In return, Russia would transfer control of the Kuril Islands to Japan. This political treaty led to the forced resettlement of hundreds of Sakhalin Ainu to Hokkaido and the Kuril Islands. Many Ainu died quickly afterwards.

Also, in 1899, the newly enacted 'Hokkaido Former Aborigines Protection Law' (*Hokkaidō Kyūdojin Hogo Hō*) did not protect the Ainu, as the name suggests, but merely offered them a kind of social assistance due to unemployment and displaced the Ainu from their traditional lands to the mountainous barren area in the island's centre [7].

The name 'Hokkaido Former Aborigines Protection Law' reveals that that at the beginning of the 20th century, the Ainu were already regarded as people of the past. According to estimates, by 1913, only 1% of the total population of Hokkaido remained Ainu. The Ainu language was hardly spoken anymore. With the settlement of hundreds of thousands of new settlers, mainly as farmers, forest was cleared, wilderness was transformed into farmland, and schools and roads were built. The Ainu's way of life as hunters and gatherers in nature was thus finally destroyed. The Ainu became a 'vanishing race' destined for extinction, and remnants of the Ainu culture have been consigned to museums [8].

Even in 1986, Japanese Prime Minister Yasuhiro Nakasone claimed that 'Japan is a mono-ethnic nation', which triggered a lively debate on the Ainu people. Things started to change when Shigeru Kayano became the first Ainu member of the Japanese parliament in 1994. He worked hard to prepare for the 1997 'Ainu Culture Promotion Act' (*Ainubunkashinkōhō*).

Nearly 100 years after the discriminatory 'Hokkaido Former Aborigines Protection Law' of 1899, which was now abolished, the language and culture of the Ainu are now financially supported by the government of Japan. The law also implies that Japan is not an ethnically homogeneous country. However, the new law does not address issues of land use rights or even compensation [8].

In 2007 the United Nations General Assembly declared the basic rights of indigenous people worldwide, and the Japanese parliament followed suit a year later by officially recognising the Ainu as indigenous people of Japan in 2008 (*Ainu senjūmin-zoku nintei ketsugi*). Finally, in 2014, the cabinet decided to create and open up a 'space that symbolizes ethnic symbiosis', which was realised as 'Upopoy' in 2020.

3.1.4 Ainu indigenous knowledge transfer and tourism activities

Historically, with the colonisation of Hokkaido and the displacement of the Ainu culture, the children of the Ainu were transferred to the Japanese school system. At first this happened in mixed schools with the children of the settlers (*Wajin*), later in special schools according to the law of 1899. Due to space constraints, it is not possible to go into detail, but in summary it can be said that from the Meiji period onwards the Ainu culture was not taught in schools, the Ainu were re-educated to become modern Japanese residents, and their own language was successfully eradicated. Around 100 years ago, in the early 1920s, the prefectural government in Sapporo was apparently satisfied to find that hardly anyone was using the Ainu language anymore [8].

What is the state of knowledge transfer about Ainu culture today? In general, it can be said that most Japanese people lack knowledge about the Ainu people and do not learn details about them in school. Makino, who teaches at the prestigious Chuo University, notes that his otherwise well-educated students know little about the Ainu [8]. On a similar note, 'The Foundation for Ainu Culture' (*Ainu minzoku bunka zaidan*), which was established following the 'Ainu Culture Promotion Act' in 1997, states on its homepage: '[W]e must say that the Japanese peoples' understanding of Ainu history and culture remains at a low level' [9].

At the same time, there is also a glimmer of hope. The Foundation for Ainu Culture is active nationwide and, for instance, hosts seminars in both its Sapporo and Tokyo offices. These seminars, designed for school and social educators, feature advanced content on Ainu history and culture. The goal is to spread knowledge and increase awareness about Ainu heritage [10]. In addition, in recent years, schools in Hokkaido, in particular, have been conducting targeted courses to introduce students to Ainu culture. For example, the Midori Elementary School in Chitose City covers a range of topics related to the cultural heritage of the Ainu. Depending on the grade level, the following topics are covered: learning about Ainu songs, dance, food, clothing and shelter, learning how the Ainu people interact with nature (with a guest lecturer), and a summary of Ainu culture studies to date. The school also conducts visits to Upopoy [11]. Other schools in Hokkaido also conduct similar activities.

When it comes to indigenous tourism, which focuses on authentic experiences and encounters with the Ainu, Japan is still at the beginning. Of course, 'Upopoy', which opened in 2020, also includes a park including ethnic cultural experiences. Apart from 'Upopoy', one of the most famous examples of indigenous tourism is 'Akanko Ainu Kotan', an Ainu inhabited settlement located in Akan-Mashu National Park. In this lakeside village visitors can discover traditional Ainu theatre, music, cuisine, and handicraft-making. They even offer an adventure walk in nature around Lake Akan together with an Ainu guide, called 'Anytime, Ainutime!' [12].

On the other hand, we could hardly find any corresponding offers from travel agencies. For instance, the leading travel agency H.I.S. offers the following on its website: 'Learn about Ainu culture and its traditions in 3 days in Hokkaido' *(Dentō o uketsugu Ainu no bunka wo manabu Hokkaidō 3-kakan)*. However, unfortunately below the headline is written in red letters: 'Recruitment is now closed' (*Boshū shūryō shimashita*) [13]. 'Adventure Hokkaido', a smaller travel company specialising in adventure and nature trips in Hokkaido, devotes an interesting blog article to the Ainu and indigenous tourism, but does not offer a trip on the topic [14]. Overall, there does not seem to be enough interest in such offers yet.

3.1.5 Discussion of results for Japan

In the following, we will briefly refer back to the results of our investigation before discussing how the Japanese treat the Ainu and promote indigenous tourism. The survey results show that textbook knowledge or correct answers in the Ainu quiz are not decisive for increased interest in the Ainu. Rather, direct cultural experiences and encounters left a stronger impression on the respondents and aroused interest in the Ainu. Experiences in non-permanent facilities and permanent museums with event-like characteristics had the most significant impact on people.

In addition, as cultural experiences in elementary, junior high, and high schools also lead to an increasing interest in culture, it is necessary to conduct Ainu cultural experiences in elementary and junior high schools not only in Hokkaido but also throughout Japan.

When we look at how the Ainu and their culture were displaced and destroyed by the mainland Japanese, we must conclude that the Ainu and their way of life were neither understood nor respected. The legal regulations and assimilation policies of that time reflect exactly this way of thinking. As other authors observe, this mindset is mainly based on socio-Darwinism, an ideology that applies Charles Darwin's theory of natural selection to human societies. It suggests that certain human groups or races are naturally superior to others and that societal progress occurs through the survival of the fittest. It goes without saying that such thinking promotes ongoing conflict, imperialism, and war, and must soon be overcome if humanity is to survive in the age of nuclear weapons.

It is encouraging to see that in recent years Japan has gradually recognised the Ainu as indigenous people of Japan and is now promoting the Ainu language and culture. However, to truly do justice to the Ainu and their former way of life and to save what can still be saved, more should be done.

Firstly, the Japanese government should openly admit the mistakes it made in the past in dealing with the Ainu. Only then will real understanding and reconciliation with the Ainu descendants become possible. Secondly, cultural transfer should not only involve folklore, everyday objects, music, and clothing. At least as important is how the Ainu understood nature and lived in harmony with it. Centuries before us, they lived sustainably and wisely with nature. Why don't we take a closer look? Indigenous tourism could be well linked to sustainable tourism here. Hokkaido still has rich natural resources and outstanding national parks that would enable such an approach. In the Akan-Mashu National Park, we already see tourist offers that go in this direction.

Adventure travel and nature-based tourism are on the rise. This could be utilised and cleverly combined with indigenous Ainu tourism. However, such an approach requires understanding the values that the Ainu stood for and reflecting on our own attitudes and values, especially on the part of government officials. By contrast, merely commercialising the cultural remnants of the Ainu culture without understanding the core of their way of life will not lead anywhere.

3.2 Results for Canada

3.2.1 Policy towards First Nation people and corresponding legal changes in Canada

Worldwide, including Canada, the reappraisal of the history of the European settlers and of the forced assimilation of indigenous people into the settlers' educational system remains a socially controversial 'hot topic'. As in the previous section about the Ainu policy in Japan, we can only briefly touch on a few key points.

Basically, during the settlement of North America by Europeans, no consideration was given to the indigenous people, who were considered backward. Canada was no exception when it came to such discriminatory thinking. 'Indigenous peoples were not included in the decision making that led to the 1867 creation of the country that settlers named Canada' [15].

This disrespect for the indigenous people also became apparent in the school system. Little describes what happened at Indian Residential Schools (IRS) between the 1880s and 1990s, taking the Blue Quills Indian Residential School as an example [16]. In essence, such boarding schools were government-sponsored but church-run. The aim was to educate the 'Indians' (First Nation people) and assimilate them into the settlers' modern way of life. In reality, however, abuse was the order of the day. It was all about eradication of indigenous culture and values, imposing Christian faith on the children, as well as physical and psychological discrimination and abuse.

Now, why did the scholar choose this particular school for her analysis? On the one hand, this boarding school stands for typical historical discrimination, but on the other hand it also embodies the transformation to a school that is now managed by indigenous people themselves. This is remarkable, as Blue Quills marked the first instance of an educational institution in Canada being fully controlled by indigenous people, representing a significant achievement in the long-standing quest of First Nations for educational autonomy [16].

In a broader sense, however, this example also serves as an illustration of the change in Canada as a whole, and how the Canadian government has dealt with the (unpleasant) issue of settlement history in recent years, from discrimination and repression to respect and reconciliation with the First Nations. As more and more details of discrimination and misconduct in these schools came to light (and continue to this day, as exemplified by many unexplained deaths and hundreds of grave finds of children on former boarding school grounds), Canada took a leap forward and made an impressive policy change. This led to a major nationwide investigation between 2008 and 2015 by 'The Truth and Reconciliation Commission of Canada' and culminated in the opening of the 'National Centre for Truth and Reconciliation' in 2015 [17].

The Canadian government has also officially apologised to the indigenous peoples for the crimes committed [18]. Although the matter is not yet settled and much remains to be resolved, it can be said that Canada is now on a path of reconciliation with its indigenous peoples, which is a remarkable step forward.

3.2.2 First Nation indigenous knowledge transfer and tourism activities
Recognising the mistakes that have been made in dealing with First Nations for more than 100 years made it possible to deal with the topic more openly in schools and universities. After initial research, we can conclude that Canada is making considerable efforts to teach aboriginal culture comprehensively in Canadian schools.

For instance, the National Centre for Truth and Reconciliation (NCTR) offers about 400 teaching resources on boarding schools and other closely related topics. These teaching resources are available free of charge and in a variety of formats, including downloadable apps, books, computer games, films, graphic novels, lesson plans and teaching guides. They are organised by grade level to help school teachers quickly find appropriate materials [19].

Another example is the education toolkit 'It's Our Time' made by the Assembly of First Nations (AFN). Its slogan is as follows: 'A tool to bring together First Nations and non-First Nations people and foster a spirit of cooperation, understanding, and action' [20]. AFN is a national advocacy organisation representing First Nations citizens in Canada, including more than 600 First Nations communities. In this comprehensive toolkit, which is available online free of charge, indigenous people teach the whole story from their own perspective. It includes 21 interactive modules covering topics such as cultural competency, the history of residential schools, treaties, and the First Nations Holistic Lifelong Learning Model. The toolkit is used in schools across Canada, with support from educational bodies such as the

Canadian School Boards Association, the Canadian Education Association, and the Canadian Teachers' Federation [21].

As far as tourism is concerned, Canada has a government-sponsored organisation that takes care of the professional development and marketing of indigenous tourism in Canada, called ITAC, which was mentioned briefly in the introduction [3]. ITAC performs a key position in advertising and marketing indigenous tourism experiences both regionally and internationally. It also offers education and resources to indigenous entrepreneurs and groups to assist them broaden sustainable tourism businesses. This includes workshops, commercial enterprise planning guidance and funding opportunities [3]. In addition to resources on the Internet, we emailed to ITAC and received information and commercial enterprise reviews from the management confirming a dynamic boom of indigenous tourism in Canada since 2015. According to their 2019–2024 'Five-Year Strategic Plan', there were 33,100 jobs in indigenous tourism in 2015, while the target for 2024 is already over 49,000 (despite the slump caused by COVID-19 in 2020–2022) [22].

Particularly impressive are the latest funding initiatives to support Indigenous tourism, such as the 'Micro and Small Business Stream (MSBS)', developed 'to empower indigenous tourism enterprises nationwide'. To be able to apply for financial aid, business must be indigenous majority-owned, operated, or controlled by First Nations, Métis, or Inuit peoples, with a strong connection to the local indigenous community and traditional territory. In short, only companies and tours that offer authentic indigenous culture and experiences are promoted [23].

3.2.3 Discussion of results for Canada

In the 19th century, Canada was just as ruthless in displacing its indigenous peoples and destroying much of their culture as we have seen in the case of Japan. Despite all the differences, the re-education of the indigenous peoples in the boarding schools is similar to the re-education of the Ainu, because in both cases the aim was to eradicate the 'backward' and 'underdeveloped' way of life of the barbarians. All this has been sufficiently described.

Of particular relevance to this paper is how Canada has responded to this historical legacy. As the truth became clearer, particularly about various crimes committed in the residential schools, the Canadian government finally went on the 'offensive' and faced the historic facts as best it could. The establishment of the 'Truth and Reconciliation Commission of Canada' to investigate these human rights issues and the opening of the 'National Centre for Truth and Reconciliation' in 2015 are impressive steps in the change of policy towards Canada's indigenous peoples.

The same applies to the promotion of indigenous knowledge transfer and authentic indigenous tourism. The Canadian state supports extensive activities to reduce prejudices, promote reconciliation through openness, and empower indigenous business start-ups. It is particularly impressive that the indigenous peoples are involved in these social processes, for example by creating their own teaching materials, such as 'It's Our Time!' by AFN, that present history from their own perspective, and not from the perspective of the white settlers.

4 CONCLUSION

In this paper, we compared indigenous history, culture, and tourism between Japan and Canada. Such a comparison entails some difficulties, because despite certain similarities, there are also differences, such as the diversity of indigenous peoples and the size of the two countries. For example, in the case of Canada, we are dealing with a whole range of indigenous people having their own culture and languages, called First Nations, Inuit and Métis.

Furthermore, the data basis is still inadequate. The survey in Japan enabled us to see that, although there is still too little known about the Ainu, cultural encounters have the power to make people more interested. With regard to Canada, we have yet to collect our own data.

However, one thing already seems clear: the comparison of the two countries shows how differently nations can deal with their own settlement histories. Canada has tackled the issue of reconciliation with its indigenous peoples and, building on this, has promoted authentic indigenous tourism. One is not possible without the other. Initially, we asked what Japan could learn from Canada. Of course, it is not always advisable to just imitate others. Japan can and should find its own way. However, this can only be promising if there is an honest reckoning with its own history and a genuine recognition of the values by which the Ainu have lived. Then there is certainly potential for a more successful indigenous tourism industry in Japan.

ACKNOWLEDGEMENTS

We thank everyone who contributed to the success of this work. Reports from the Indigenous Tourism Association of Canada (ITAC) were particularly helpful. We would also like to express our sincere gratitude to Alice Freeman, Oxford, for her excellent proofreading.

REFERENCES

[1] Upopoy National Ainu Museum and Park. https://ainu-upopoy.jp/en/. Accessed on: 6 Jun. 2024.

[2] Ministry of Land, Infrastructure, Transport and Tourism, Hokkaido Branch, Promotion of Ainu culture [*Ainu bunka no shinkō-tō ni tsuite*]. 2022. https://www.mlit.go.jp/policy/shingikai/content/001521617.pdf. Accessed on: 2 Jun. 2024.

[3] Indigenous Tourism Association of Canada (ITAC). https://indigenoustourism.ca/. Accessed on: 6 Jun. 2024.

[4] UN Declaration on the Rights of Indigenous Peoples, Office of the High Commissioner for Human Rights, 13 September 2007. https://www.ohchr.org/en/indigenous-peoples/un-declaration-rights-indigenous-peoples. Accessed on: 2 Jun. 2024.

[5] Curtin, N. & Bird, S., 'We are reconciliators': When Indigenous tourism begins with agency. *Journal of Sustainable Tourism*, 2021. https://doi.org/10.1080/09669582.2021.1903908.

[6] Hirano, K., Settler colonialism as encounter, on the question of racialization and labor power in the dispossession of Ainu lands. *Race and Migration in the Transpacific*, eds Y. Takezawa & A. Tanabe, Routledge: New York, 2023.

[7] Cobb, E., Japan's forgotten indigenous people, BBC, 21 May 2020. https://www.bbc.com/travel/article/20200519-japans-forgotten-indigenous-people. Accessed on: 27 Jun. 2024.

[8] Makino, U., *Die Ainu – Begegnung mit den japanischen Ureinwohnern* [*The Ainu – Encounter with the Japanese Natives*], BoD – Books on Demand: Norderstedt, 2015.

[9] The Foundation for Ainu Culture, Dissemination of knowledge about Ainu traditions. 2024. https://www.ff-ainu.or.jp/web/english/details/dissemination-of-knowledge-about-ainu-traditions.html. Accessed on: 29 Jun. 2024.

[10] The Foundation for Ainu Culture, Ainu no dentō-tō ni kansuru fukyū keihatsu [Raising awareness of Ainu traditions]. Seminar in Sapporo and Tokyo offices, 2024. https://www.ff-ainu.or.jp/web/overview/business/details/post-193.html. Accessed on: 29 Jun. 2024.

[11] The Midori Elementary School, a UNESCO associated school in Chitose City. https://www.unesco-school.mext.go.jp/schools/list/midori-primary-school/. Accessed on: 29 Jun. 2024.

[12] Akanko Ainu Kotan, Experience. https://www.akanainu.jp/en/experience/. Accessed on: 29 Jun. 2024.

[13] H.I.S., Dentō o uketsugu Ainu no bunka wo manabu Hokkaidō 3-kakan [Learn about Ainu culture and its traditions in 3 days in Hokkaido]. https://eco.his-j.com/eco/tour/TF-SPK0001-ECO. Accessed on: 29 Jun. 2024.

[14] Yoshikawa, A., 'Adventure Hokkaido', 23 Apr 2020. Ainu Indigenous Cultural Tourism. https://www.adventure-hokkaido.com/blog/hokkaido-culture/ainu-indigenous-cultural-tourism. Accessed on: 29 Jun. 2024.

[15] Bear, L.C., Indian status as the foundation of justice. *Bucking Conservatism: Alternative Stories of Alberta from the 1960s and 1970s*, eds L.C. Bear, L. Hannant & K.R. Patton, Athabasca University Press, 2021. https://doi.org/10.15215/aupress/9781771992572.01.

[16] Little, T.D., Teaching it our way: Blue Quills and the demand for Indigenous educational autonomy. *Bucking Conservatism: Alternative Stories of Alberta from the 1960s and 1970s*, eds L.C. Bear, L. Hannant & K.R. Patton, Athabasca University Press, 2021. https://doi.org/10.15215/aupress/9781771992572.01.

[17] National Centre for Truth and Reconciliation. https://nctr.ca/. Accessed on: 19 Jun. 2024.

[18] Parrott, Z., Government apology to former students of residential schools. The Canadian Encyclopedia, 14 Jul. 2014. https://www.thecanadianencyclopedia.ca/en/article/government-apology-to-former-students-of-indian-residential-schools. Accessed on: 19 Jun. 2024.

[19] National Centre for Truth and Reconciliation, Reconciliation through education. https://nctr.ca/education/. Accessed on: 24 Jun. 2024.

[20] Assembly of First Nations, It's our time: The AFN education toolkit. https://education.afn.ca/afntoolkit/. Accessed on: 24 Jun. 2024.

[21] Assembly of First Nations, Assembly of First Nations launches digital resource for teachers it's our time First Nations education toolkit on iTunes U. 28 Jun. 2017. https://afn.ca/all-news/news/assembly-of-first-nations-launches-digital-resource-for-teachers-its-our-time-first-nations-education-toolkit-on-itunes-u/. Accessed on: 24 Jun. 2024.

[22] Indigenous Tourism Association of Canada (ITAC), Accelerating Indigenous tourism growth in Canada: Five-year strategic plan update 2019–2024. Unpublished strategy plan. https://indigenoustourism.ca/plans-reports/. Accessed on: 24 Jun. 2024.

[23] Indigenous Tourism Association of Canada (ITAC), Indigenous tourism fund micro and small business stream. https://indigenoustourism.ca/programs-services/indigenous-tourism-fund-micro-and-small-business-stream/. Accessed on: 24 Jun. 2024.

IMPACT ASSESSMENT OF URBAN HERITAGE SITES: THE CASE OF KHOR DUBAI, UAE

EMAN ASSI
American University of Ras Al Khaimah, UAE

ABSTRACT

This research questions the efficiency of impact assessment as a tool for the holistic management of urban living heritage sites, considering the evolving understanding of urban heritage presented in the 2011 UNESCO Recommendation on the Historic Urban Landscape and the Sustainable Development Goals. The research focuses on Khor Dubai in the United Arab Emirates, a site nominated for World Heritage since 2014, as a case study to identify the potential of such a tool to maintain the outstanding universal values embedded in the site. Drawing on UNESCO, ICCROM, ICOMOS, and IUCN resource manuals on impact assessment, the study identifies critical elements and proposes mitigation strategies for urban development adjacent to Khor Dubai. Ultimately, the research underscores that impact assessment is a complex process essential for safeguarding and enhancing these culturally and historically significant assets.
Keywords: impact assessment, world heritage, historic urban landscape, sustainable tourism development, Dubai.

1 INTRODUCTION

Khor Dubai is situated along a natural seawater inlet on the Arabian side of the Gulf, at the heart of Dubai in the United Arab Emirates. The creek (khor in Arabic) divides the city into two parts, Bur Dubai and Deira, and has played a crucial role in the Emirate's economic development throughout history. The natural shape of the creek significantly influenced Dubai's urban layout. The settlement grew organically on both banks of the creek from an early stage, distinct from the desert hinterland. Rather than limiting urban expansion, the creek served as the focal point of a maritime-dependent urban ensemble connected to a broader network of Gulf ports and settlements. In the early 19th century, the creek was essential to Dubai's establishment and early growth as a trading and fishing port. For over a century, it remained the city's primary port, crucial in establishing Dubai's commercial significance. The creek's morphology, including its port facilities and associated traditional markets, has been preserved through ongoing modifications to the site's geomorphology and commercial infrastructure, ensuring its continuity as a historical and economic landmark.

Khor Dubai, a traditional merchant's harbour, was nominated to the World Heritage List in 2014 under criteria ii, iii and iv. Its outstanding universal value (OUV) lies in its preservation of the original port and urban structure connected by the creek, and its status as the last remaining example of a neighbourhood with traditional wind-tower houses on the Arabian Gulf coast. Today, Khor Dubai remains an active port and living community, maintaining continuity with its historical origins [1]. The nominated property spans approximately 2.5 km of the waterway from its historic mouth to the Al Fahidi historic neighbourhood. However, the nomination process faced setbacks, as it was changed in 2014, referred to in 2016, and eventually withdrawn in 2018 [2].

The property includes the waterway itself, specialised traditional markets, and surrounding quarters that form the urban context of the port, all encompassed by a large buffer zone containing additional sections of the creek harbour. Concerns were raised in ICOMOS' 2018 evaluation about proposed developments around Khor Dubai, such as the Marsa Al Seef project in the southern buffer zone and the Deira Enrichment waterfront across the creek, including the infinity bridge at the mouth of the Khor. These developments were seen as potentially altering the urban characteristics and setting of Khor Dubai, posing threats to its OUV, integrity, and authenticity.

This paper aims to evaluate the measures implemented by Dubai Municipality (DM) to mitigate the impacts of these new developments before their implementation. The goal is to determine whether these measures effectively prevent adverse effects on the OUV and other values of the site. The analysis is based on the impact assessment guidance toolkit provided within the World Heritage Convention context by UNESCO, ICOMOS, ICCROM, and IUCN.

2 LITERATURE REVIEW

The present-day concept of cultural heritage is shaped by the ongoing evolution of contemporary society, its values, and its needs [3], [4]. Ricca notes that in the 1990s, a new cultural approach emphasising the appreciation of heritage emerged alongside the growing importance of local values and traditions [4]. In her work on the uses of heritage, Smith explores heritage as a cultural practice rather than a static entity. She argues that heritage is a social process involving acts of remembering that help us understand and engage with the present. Culture at the national level is a fundamental aspect of everyday life, serving as a dynamic space for knowledge production, innovation, and reconstruction [5]. The significance of urban heritage gained prominence during the mid-20th century with documents like the Athens Charter of 1933 and subsequent works by Le Corbusier in the 1950s, 1970s and 1986 [6]–[8]. These documents, arising from the Fourth International Congress of Modern Architecture, stressed the importance of safeguarding architectural treasures amidst rapid urban development and threats to socio-cultural values.

The Stockholm Declaration of 1972 responded to environmental concerns during a period of global urbanisation and development [9], [10]. Concurrently, the establishment of the US Environmental Protection Agency in 1970 and the National Environmental Policy Act of 1969 underscored the integration of environmental impact assessments in development processes, influenced by early ecological advocates such as Ian McHarg's principles of 'designing with nature' [11], [12]. The approach to impact assessment evolved significantly after 2011 with the introduction of the UNESCO Recommendation on the Historic Urban Landscape and the UN-Habitat New Urban Agenda in 2016 [13], [14]. These initiatives expanded the scope of cultural heritage to encompass living historic cities, reflecting a broader understanding of sustainability that integrates environmental considerations.

Several key initiatives have contributed to this evolution, including the European Union's Sustainable Development of Urban Historical Areas through Active Integration within Towns (SUIT) in 2004 [15], the URBACT Heritage as Opportunity network in 2008 [16], and the United Nations Office for Disaster Risk Reduction's Sendai Framework and Resilient Cities Campaign in 2017 [17]. These efforts introduced frameworks like the 'Ten Essentials for Resilient Cities' and aligned with the United Nations' 2030 Sustainable Development Goals [18].

The attention to threats to urban heritage developed later, with a predominant focus on architectural and monumental cultural heritage. Reporting on World Heritage sites in danger drew significant attention to the necessity of conducting impact assessments for any upcoming interventions that could adversely affect the site's OUVs. ICOMOS urged state parties to undertake impact assessments for future projects proposed near World Heritage site boundaries. ICOMOS's toolkit, a joint publication by UNESCO, ICCROM, ICOMOS and IUCN, provides guidance on impact assessment for World Heritage properties [19]. This toolkit explains how impact assessments can safeguard the OUV of World Heritage properties, facilitating informed decision-making to manage continuity and change effectively.

The cases of Dresden Elbe Valley and Liverpool Maritime Mercantile City are extreme examples of World Heritage properties, with the former being delisted in 2009 and the latter confirmed on the List of World Heritage in Danger continuously since 2012 [20]. In Dresden's case, a limited-focus visual impact study was applied to the proposed Waldschlößchen Bridge crossing the River Elbe, which ignored broader considerations such as environmental, economic, and transportation management within the city, as well as alternative, less obtrusive design options for the bridge itself [21].

In Liverpool, three inconsistent impact assessments were conducted for the major Liverpool Waters development project along the waterfront north of the city centre. These assessments predominantly focused on visual impacts on the World Heritage Site, while neglecting potentially significant socio-economic impacts and relationships across the wider city [22].

The concept of 'sustainable development' gained prominence with the Brundtland Report in 1987, solidifying environmental impact assessment as a well-established tool [23], [24]. However, its focus has evolved to incorporate the social and economic dimensions of sustainability, primarily as a reactive instrument when applied at the project level [25]. The emerging concept of strategic environmental assessment aims to be more proactive and comprehensive, addressing broader strategic impacts and involving a spectrum of stakeholders [26], [27]. This approach encourages the participation of various disciplines and emphasises that the impact assessment process is not solely about immediate outcomes or resulting statements, but also about the broader value it brings through fostering stakeholder dialogue.

3 RESEARCH METHODOLOGY

The study is structured into two main sections. The first section examines the evolution of approaches to urban heritage impact assessment within the international framework and explores how this issue has been addressed at World Heritage Sites globally.

The second section focuses on analysing the impacts of new urban developments implemented since 2014, specifically assessing their effects on Khor Dubai as a historic urban site. It also seeks to propose alternative mitigation strategies to minimise negative impacts on the site's significance. The assessment will adhere to the guidance toolkit and follow the steps outlined below:

1. Identify the significance of the site based on the OUV and other values.
2. Identify attributes that reflect the values of the site.
3. Identify potential negative and positive impacts on OUV and other values.
4. Identify a range of reasonable alternatives and assess their potential impact.

4 DISCUSSION

Since 2014, during the preparation of the nomination file for Khor Dubai, three major new developments have been undergoing approval by DM. These developments are situated within the buffer zone of the nominated property and are owned by different sectors.

4.1 The Marsa Al Seef project

The Marsa Al Seef project is owned by a semi-private entity, while the Deira Enrichment waterfront and Infinity Bridge are owned by the Dubai government but implemented by a private developer. Marsa Al Seef, a waterfront development initiated by Meraas, a semi-private developer, was proposed in 2014 to replace a public open space utilised by the nearby community. Completed in 2017, it is strategically located at the border of the Al Fahidi historic district within the buffer zone of the nominated property of Khor Dubai, which was submitted to the World Heritage Centre in 2014. This site was historically known for hosting cultural festivals.

The development is characterised by distinct architectural styles. One section faithfully emulates traditional architecture, while another features a more modern aesthetic with shops, cafes, and underground parking facilities. The primary aim of Marsa Al Seef is to establish a recreational destination for visitors, offering an array of attractions such as an open-air market for handcrafted artifacts, cafes, restaurants, hotels, and boutiques. Despite its low-rise profile, this development introduces elements of traditional Dubai architecture, including multiple new wind towers, in proximity to the historic Al Fahidi neighbourhood [25].

4.2 Deira Waterfront Development project

The Deira area stands as one of Dubai's oldest and most densely populated communities, renowned for its role as a trading hub for spices, textiles and jewellery with destinations across Asia and Africa. The recently launched Deira Waterfront Development aims to preserve Deira's rich tradition and culture while revitalising its waterfront area. Encompassing the entire northern section of the current Deira district, the project is situated opposite the Gold Souq and overlooks the Dubai creek, adjacent to the proposed World Heritage Site of Khor Dubai. The development includes the construction of new residential blocks ranging from 7 to 12 storeys high, accommodating more than 31,000 residents. It also introduces new community amenities such as plazas, parks, bicycle routes, and transportation hubs, along with refurbishing existing shops, hotels, commercial zones, parking facilities, and storage areas. Construction commenced in 2017 and concluded in 2023.

In terms of its impact on the urban skyline, Deira Waterfront Development LLC focuses on structures up to six stories tall, aiming to provide housing, offices, and commercial spaces along the northern banks of the creek, from the mouth of Khor Dubai to its bend. Emphasising traditional architectural elements, the development falls entirely within the Deira Bank buffer zone and is situated close to historic merchant houses in Al-Ras. The new urban fabric of the project seamlessly extends the existing one, preserving key visual corridors to the water and enhancing community access with ample parking and open public areas for communal enjoyment.

4.3 Infinity Bridge

A new Infinity Bridge has been recently completed along the historic Shindagha shoreline, featuring a futuristic steel design. On the opposite shore, the Deira Enrichment project nears completion, adding another contrast to the historic context with its modern grandeur. Spanning the Dubai creek, the 295 m long bridge connects the Al Shindagha and Al Ras districts, standing 15.5 m above the water. It boasts 12 lanes of traffic, six in each direction, along with pedestrian crossings, and is distinguished by a 42 m high steel arch symbolising infinity.

Announced in 2018 and completed in 2022, the Infinity Bridge is a pivotal component of the AED 5.3 billion Al Shindagha Corridor Project. This extensive corridor, spanning nearly 13 km, aims to enhance connectivity to developments such as the Dubai Seafront, Port Rashid, Deira Islands and Dubai Maritime City. According to the RTA, the bridge's opening has significantly reduced travel times during the morning rush hour, cutting the journey between Sheikh Khalifa Bin Zayed Street and Al Mamzar Intersection to just 13 minutes, marking a substantial 73% improvement.

5 RESULTS

Approval for these projects requires issuance from the Architectural Heritage Department (AHD) of DM to ensure they do not compromise the OUV of the nominated property. The review process involved extensive discussions with developers and led to specific alternative actions being mandated for each project to mitigate potential negative impacts on the site's values. See Table 1 for an assessment of values, their attributes, potential impacts and identified alternative measures.

In the case of Marsa Al Seef, the AHD approved the project's general concept but expressed concerns about specific issues that could adversely affect the site's OUV. The department recommended the following alternatives:

1. Relocate some project masses southward to allow direct contact between the nominated site and the water.
2. Maintain the original boundaries along Khor Dubai without any land extension or reclamation.
3. If developers wish to extend beyond the site boundaries, utilise reversible floating structures.
4. Change the building colours on the site from beige to a distinct colour to differentiate them from the traditional architectural character of the Al Fahidi area.
5. Reconstruct the Al Seef watchtower in its original location.
6. Relocate the proposed mosque to the south to position it centrally within the site.

These measures were prescribed to ensure that Marsa Al Seef and similar projects align with the preservation and enhancement objectives of the nominated property's OUV (Table 2).

Regarding the Deira Enrichment Waterfront Development, the AHD has raised significant concerns about its potential negative impact on the urban landscape of the creek, particularly at its mouth (Table 3). The project involves reclaimed land currently used for parking, which blocks direct access of the original urban fabric to the water and reduces the presence of traditional cargo activities along the Khor. Additionally, the proposed tall building at the creek's mouth poses a threat to the visual experience. In response, the AHD has requested that the developer undertake the following actions to mitigate the project's potential impact on the OUV of the nominated property:

1. Relocate the tall building to a position outside of the visual corridor.
2. Maintain public access to the water.
3. Reduce the height of the structures facing the creek.

In the case of the Infinity Bridge, the AHD considers it a significant intervention that could dramatically alter the urban fabric and character of the creek, potentially diminishing the importance of the simple, low-traditional buildings in historic Shindagha. The department has requested specific actions from the developer to prevent any negative impact on the OUV of the nominated property, notably emphasising the need to relocate the bridge's ascending portion away from historic Shindagha (Table 4).

Table 1: Values and attributes of Khor Dubai.

Category	Values	Attributes
Urban landscape	Unique morphology of traditional trade settlements composed of creek traffic, port activities, souk features Khor Dubai a living urban heritage	• The geomorphology of the creek and its continuous adaptation. • The port quays facilities for cargo activities and passenger traffic. • The structure and evolution of the traditional souks. • Urban fabric around the creek and the souks including merchants' housing, Indian quarter, ruler. • At the large scale: the preserved traditional landscapes from the creek with the specific landmark signs of the wind-towers.
Historical	Historic port since 19th century developed as a trade and fishing port and become the core of global trade in the 20th century	• The structure and evolution of the traditional souks. • The geomorphology of the creek and its continuous adaptation to permit boat traffic. • The continuing evidence of the traditional urban fabric around the creek and the souks. • Appealing to a large multi-cultural and multi-religious population.
Architectural	Outstanding technical and architectural solutions adapted to harsh environment Unique architectural synthesis of Arab, Persian and Indian traditions	• The presence of religious buildings belonging to different communities. • The reconstructed neighbourhood of Shindagha, traditional seat of the rulers. • Ruler's family, materialising the physical 'protective' role of the Ruler over trade in the city. • The architectural details showing intercultural exchanges reflected in wind tower, gypsum decoration panels and imported decorated wood doors.
Socio economic	Place where encourage interchanged of human values and unique multi culture multi-ethnic environment	• Diversity of exchanges of Dubai cosmopolitan mercantile society. • Wind tower houses. • The political and religious openness of Dubai that while cherishing and preserving its Arab and Islamic traditions, has been able to provide an urban and social environment. • The presence of an active multi-ethnic population continuing to actively trade in Khor Dubai.
Economic	Unique active economic entity based upon free trade principles	• Traditional boats. • Traditional souq on both side of the khor. • Custom building at the mouth of Shindagha. • Merchants' houses. • Rulers' houses. • Cargo activities.

Table 2: Impact assessment for Project 1: Marsal Al Seef project.

Category	Attributes	Nature of impact	Potential impact on values
Urban landscape	• The geomorphology of the creek and its continuous adaptation. • The port quays facilities for the cargo activities and the passenger traffic. • The structure and evolution of the traditional souks. • Urban fabric around the creek and the souks including merchants' housing, Indian quarter, ruler. • At the large scale: the preserved traditional landscapes from the creek with the specific landmark signs of the wind-towers.	The project is cutting the visual and physical access to the creek.	Negative minor impact No positive impact
Historical	• The structure and evolution of the traditional souks. • The geomorphology of the creek and its continuous adaptation to permit boat traffic. • The continuing evidence of the traditional urban fabric around the creek and the souks. • Appealing to a large multi-cultural and multi-religious foreign population.	Historical function of the area will change to be touristic oriented rather than community and traditional trade function.	Negative moderate impact No positive impact
Architectural	• The presence of religious buildings belonging to different communities. • The reconstructed neighbourhood of Shindagha, traditional seat of the Ruler's family, materialising the physical 'protective' role of the Ruler over trade in the city. • The architectural details showing intercultural exchanges reflected in wind tower, gypsum decoration panels and imported decorated wood doors.	Misconception of traditional architectural affect its authenticity. Fake copied and insertion of wrong interpretation of traditional architecture.	Moderate negative impact No positive impact
Social	• Wide diversity of exchanges of Dubai cosmopolitan mercantile society. • Wind tower houses. • The political and religious openness of Dubai that, while cherishing and preserving its Arab and Islamic traditions, has been able to provide an urban and social environment. • The presence of active multi-ethnic population continuing to actively trade in Khor Dubai.	Erase memory of the place as being a public open space for the community.	Major negative impact No positive impact
Economic	• Traditional boats. • Traditional souq on both side of the Khor. • Custom building at the mouth of Shindagha. • Merchants' houses. • Rulers' houses. • Cargo activities.	Might bring some economic improvement to Al Fahidi historic district.	No negative impact Minor positive impact

Table 3: Impact assessment for Project 2: Deira Enrichment Waterfront.

Category	Attributes	Nature of impact	Potential impact on values
Urban landscape	• The geomorphology of the creek and its continuous adaptation. • The port quays facilities for the cargo activities and the passenger traffic. • The structure and evolution of the traditional souks. • Urban fabric around the creek and the souks including merchants' housing, Indian quarter, ruler. • At the large scale: the preserved traditional landscapes from the creek with the specific landmark signs of the wind-towers.	The project is cutting the visual and physical access to the creek.	Negative moderate impact No positive impact
Historical	• The structure and evolution of the traditional souks. • The geomorphology of the creek and its continuous adaptation to permit boat traffic. • The continuing evidence of the traditional urban fabric around the creek and the souks. • Appealing to a large multi-cultural and multi-religious foreign population.	Historical function of the area will change to be touristic oriented rather than community and traditional trade function.	Negative minor impact No positive impact
Architectural	• The presence of religious buildings belonging to different communities. • The reconstructed neighbourhood of Shindagha, traditional seat of the Ruler's family, materialising the physical 'protective' role of the Ruler over trade in the city. • The architectural details showing intercultural exchanges reflected in wind tower, gypsum decoration panels and imported decorated wood doors.	Misconception of traditional architectural affect its authenticity. Fake copied and insertion of wrong interpretation of traditional architecture.	Minor negative impact No positive impact
Social	• Wide diversity of exchanges of Dubai cosmopolitan mercantile society. • Wind tower houses. • The political and religious openness of Dubai that, while cherishing and preserving its Arab and Islamic traditions, has been able to provide an urban and social environment. • The presence of active multi-ethnic population continuing to actively trade in Khor Dubai.	Erase memory of the place as being a public open space for the community.	Minor negative impact No positive impact
Economic	• Traditional boats. • Traditional souq on both side of the Khor. • Custom building at the mouth of Shindagha. • Merchants' houses. • Rulers' houses. • Cargo activities.	Might bring some economic improvement to Al Fahidi historic district.	No negative impact Moderate positive impact

Table 4: Impact assessment for Project 3: Infinity Bridge.

Category	Attributes	Nature of impact	Potential impact on values
Urban landscape	• The geomorphology of the creek and its continuous adaptation. • The port quays facilities for the cargo activities and the passenger traffic. • The structure and evolution of the traditional souks. • Urban fabric around the creek and the souks including merchants' housing, Indian quarter, ruler. • At the large scale: the preserved traditional landscapes from the creek with the specific landmark signs of the wind-towers.	The project is cutting the visual and physical access to the creek.	Major negative impact No positive impact
Historical	• The structure and evolution of the traditional souks. • The geomorphology of the creek and its continuous adaptation to permit boat traffic. • The continuing evidence of the traditional urban fabric around the creek and the souks appealing to a large multi-cultural and multi-religious foreign population.	Historical function of the area will change to be touristic oriented rather than community and traditional trade function.	Major negative impact No positive impact
Architectural	• The presence of religious buildings belonging to different communities. • The reconstructed neighbourhood of Shindagha, traditional seat of the Ruler's family, materialising the physical 'protective' role of the Ruler over trade in the city. • The architectural details showing intercultural exchanges reflected in wind tower, gypsum decoration panels and imported decorated doors.	Misconception of traditional architectural affect its authenticity. Fake copied and insertion of wrong interpretation of traditional architecture.	Minor positive impact No positive impact
Social	• Wide diversity of exchanges of Dubai cosmopolitan mercantile society. • Wind tower houses. • The political and religious openness of Dubai that, while cherishing and preserving its Arab and Islamic traditions, has been able to provide an urban and social environment. • The presence of active multi-ethnic population continuing to actively trade in Khor Dubai.	Erase memory of the place as being a public open space for the community.	No negative impact Minor positive impact
Economic	• Traditional boats. • Traditional souq on both side of the Khor. • Custom building at the mouth of Shindagha. • Merchants' houses. • Rulers' houses. • Cargo activities.	Might bring some economic improvement to Al Fahidi historic district.	No negative impact Minor positive impact

6 CONCLUSIONS

Heritage conservation is viewed as a socio-cultural endeavour rather than solely a technical discipline, encompassing a range of activities that precede and follow any material intervention. It is a complex process shaped by the evolving values and contemporary needs of society. Historically, the focus was often on individual artworks or monumental structures. However, the widespread destruction of world wars and the rapid industrialisation from the 1950s onwards underscored the profound connection between people's lives and their environments. This realisation emphasised the role of cultural heritage in shaping identities and providing a spiritual and mental foundation for a balanced quality of life.

UNESCO's recommendations emphasise that protecting cultural heritage requires a clear understanding of the resource and its social and cultural dimensions. This understanding is crucial in fostering an appreciation of heritage as an integral part of modern society. It involves developing frameworks to assess the value of resources, defining management objectives, and crafting policies for preservation and interpretation. This holistic approach aims to ensure that heritage conservation not only preserves physical artifacts but also sustains their socio-cultural significance for future generations.

Impact assessment is a process of thinking before acting. Effective impact assessment involves a comprehensive approach that considers various dimensions and engages stakeholders to ensure the protection and enhancement of these valuable cultural and historical assets. It informs the decision-making process by exploring the consequences that proposed actions may have on the environment, or in the case of World Heritage properties, on their OUV. It should always be carried out before any irreversible decisions or actions are taken, so that any findings can genuinely inform a final decision.

The threats encompass not only environmental, social, and economic aspects but also cultural dimensions in their broadest sense, including tangible heritage and the legacies of our cities. The methodology for impact assessment of urban heritage is more complex and addresses different interconnected relationships compared to the impact assessment of monuments. Identifying alternatives to proposed actions at an early stage means considering several options while it is still possible to influence planning decisions and even avoid negative impacts. There are multiple stages in the development and implementation of a proposed action. Although the existing management regulations set by DM permit monitoring and controlling not only the physical elements of the property but also the commercial and economic processes essential for its sustainability and long-term preservation, there is still a need to enforce a more comprehensive management and monitoring system that will address the complexity of the site.

REFERENCES

[1] Assi, E., Layers of meaning and sustainability of cultural identity: The case of wind tower in Dubai. *Conservation*, **2**(1), pp. 38–50, 2022. https://doi.org/10.3390/conservation2010004.
[2] UNESCO World Heritage Convention, Khor Dubai. https://whc.unesco.org/en/tentativelists/5662/.
[3] UNESCO, The operational guidelines for the implementation of the World Heritage Convention, p. 49, 2022. https://whc.unesco.org/en/guidelines/.
[4] ICOMOS, 2018 Addendum: Evaluations of nominations of cultural and mixed properties – ICOMOS report for the World Heritage Committee 42nd ordinary session, Manama, 24 Jun.–4 Jul. 2018. https://whc.unesco.org/archive/2018/whc18-42com-inf8B1.Add-en.pdf.

[5] Smith, L., *Uses of Heritage*, Routledge: London, 2006. https://doi.org/10.4324/9780203602263.
[6] Le Corbusier, C., *La Charte d'Athènes*, Éditions de Minuit: Paris (original French text of the Charter), 1955.
[7] Le Corbusier, C., *Athens Charter* (English translation of the 1933 Charter), Grossman: New York, 1973. https://modernistarchitecture.wordpress.com/2010/11/03/ciam%E2%80%99s-%E2%80%9Cthe-athens-charter%E2%80%9D-1933/.
[8] Cevat, E., English Translation of the 1933 Athens Charter. *Our Architectural Heritage: From Consciousness to Conservation*, ed. C. Erder, UNESCO: Paris, pp. 219–220, 1986. http://unesdoc.unesco.org/images/0007/000714/071433eo.pdf.
[9] Matthias, R. & Rodwell, D The geography of urban heritage. *The Historic Environment: Policy and Practice*, **6**(3), pp. 240–276, 2015.
[10] Matthias, R. & Rodwell, D The governance of urban heritage. *The Historic Environment: Policy and Practice*, **7**(1), pp. 81–108, 2016.
[11] Ricca, S., Urban heritage in the Arabian Peninsula: The experience of Jeddah and Dubai. *Built Heritage*, **2018**(2), pp. 108–122, 2018.
[12] Teaiwa, K.M., *Implementing, Monitoring and Evaluating Cultural Policies: A Pacific Toolkit*, Secretariat of the Pacific Community: Suva, Fiji, 2012.
[13] US Environmental Protection Agency, The guardian: Origins of the EPA. EPA Historical Publication-1. 1992. https://www.epa.gov/archive/epa/aboutepa/guardian-origins-epa.html
[14] UNESCO, Recommendation on the Historic Urban Landscape, 2011. https://whc.unesco.org/en/hul/. Accessed on: 16 Dec. 2018.
[15] European Commission, Directorate-General for Research and Innovation, Teller, J., Ruelle, C. & Dupagne, A., SUIT, sustainable development of urban historical areas through an active integration within towns. Research report no. 16, Publications Office, 2004.
[16] URBACT, HerO Results, 2012. http://urbact.eu/hero. Accessed on: 16 Dec. 2018.
[17] UNISDR, *How to Make Cities More Resilient: A Handbook for Local Government Leaders – A Contribution to the Global Campaign 2010–2020 'My City is Getting Ready!'*, 2017. https://www.unisdr.org/campaign/resilientcities/assets/documents/guidelines/Handbook%20For%20Local%20Government%20Leaders_WEB_May%202017.pdf. Accessed on: 16 Dec. 2018.
[18] UNISDR, The ten essentials for making cities resilient. 2017. http://www.unisdr.org/files/26462_13.tenessentialschecklist.pdf. Accessed on: 16 Dec. 2018.
[19] Court, S., Jo, E., Mackay, R., Murai, M. & Therivel, R., *Guidance and Toolkit for Impact Assessment in a World Heritage Context*, ICCROM: Italy, 2018.
[20] Patiwael, R., Groote, P. & Vanclay, F., Improving heritage impact assessment: An analytical critique of the ICOMOS guideline. *International Journal of Heritage Studies*, 2018.
[21] Ringbeck, B. & Mechtild, R., Between international obligations and local politics: The case of the Dresden Elbe Valley under the 1972 World Heritage Convention. *Denkmalschutz und Stadtentwicklung. Informationen zur Raumentwicklung*, **3**(4), pp. 205–211, 2011.
[22] Liverpool City Council, Nomination of Liverpool – Maritime Mercantile City for Inscription on the World Heritage List, Liverpool City Council, 2003.

[23] Gaillard, B. & Rodwell, D., A failure of process? Comprehending the issues fostering heritage conflict in Dresden Elbe Valley and Liverpool – Maritime Mercantile City World Heritage Sites. *The Historic Environment: Policy and Practice*, **6**(1), pp. 16–40, 2015
[24] Hinchliffe, J. & Burns, R., Heritage impact assessment of Liverpool waters on the outstanding universal value of Liverpool Maritime Mercantile City World Heritage Site. Liverpool City Council: Liverpool, 2012.
[25] Sheate, W.R. & Partidário, M.R., Strategic approaches and assessment techniques: Potential for knowledge brokerage towards sustainability. *Environmental Impact Assessment Review*, **30**(4), pp. 278–288, 2010.
[26] United Nations, The Sustainable Development Agenda. 2016. http://www.un.org/sustainabledevelopment/development-agenda/. Accessed on: 16 Dec. 2018.
[27] United Nations, Framework Convention on Climate Change. 2017. http://unfccc.int/2860.php. Accessed on: 16 Dec. 2018.

CONVERTING A LOCAL MARKET INTO A TOURIST DESTINATION: THE CASE OF PLAZA DE MERCADO LAS FERIAS, BOGOTÁ, COLOMBIA

MARICELA I. MONTES-GUERRA, NATALIA ZAPATA-CUERVO, MARIA PAULA DEAZA,
FELIPE CASTILLA CORZO, MARIA CATALINA GONZALEZ FORERO
& ANNAMARIA FILOMENA-AMBROSSIO
Universidad de La Sabana, Escuela Internacional de Ciencias Económicas y Administrativas,
Grupo de Investigación Alimentación, Gestión de Procesos y Servicio, Bogotá, Colombia

ABSTRACT

Local markets function as nexuses for historical narratives, gastronomic heritage, cultural practices and traditional customs. Recent initiatives have focused on revitalising and increasing visibility of these elements through gastronomic offers for tourists. Gastronomical tourism is considered an engine of economic development for societies. Many tourists travel specifically to try restaurants and local cuisine, experiences that can be accomplished at local markets. Moreover, buying food is the third general cost of any trip. For these reasons, this research characterises the local market 'Las Ferias' in Bogotá, Colombia, through the perception of its visitors and information from vendors, with the aim of proposing strategies that transform this local market into a touristic and gastronomic destination. This research employed a mixed methodology approach. To collect information, vendors from various business types at the local market were interviewed. Additionally, surveys were administered to visitors to understand their motivations for visiting, perceptions, intentions to revisit and likelihood of recommending the local market to others. The results show that this local market is not yet considered a tourist destination or a place of gastronomic interest. It is visited mainly by people living in nearby areas, primarily for their personal supply. Visitors appreciate the variety of products, quality and prices, as well as the cleanliness of the place. Among the strategies that can be proposed to transform local market 'Las Ferias' into a tourist destination are organising gastronomic festivals, implementing promotional strategies through social media using storytelling. The improvement of security in the surrounding areas and expanding parking facilities is necessary.

Keywords: local market, tourist destination, gastronomic tourism, visit motivators, revisit intention.

1 INTRODUCTION

The local markets known in Spanish as *plazas de mercado*, are informal working spaces for families and/or farmers in Latin America [1]. Local markets constitute an important economic axis, being the main form of income and living of families [2]. In Colombia, marketplaces have been designated as tangible cultural heritage by Mincultura (Ministry of Culture). The way of obtaining food in Latin American countries used to be based on the purchase of food in the marketplaces, however, over time this has been changing, starting to buy food, vegetables and fruits in shops or retail shops. In addition, *plazas de mercado* are meeting places of *convivium*, where besides buying fresh and healthy products, families also find knowledge from the vendors and farmers, who know the properties and uses of food, which have been historically used as medicinal and healthy solutions, likewise in the marketplaces culture can be preserved, transmitted, and created, since in these spaces the regions can be recognised by their crops, products, and their uses.

Also, travellers are attracted by cultural background through tasting local food finding *plazas de mercado* as a destination. There they learn about endemic foods, regional cuisine, and recipes, therefore, they become closer to the national culture and ancestral knowledge [3].

According to Thompson [4], interest in farmers' markets has been increasing since the 1970s. This rise in interest highlights the value of agricultural production and enhances food tourism experiences. In 2013, the World Tourism Organization recognised gastronomy and culinary arts as a touristic product and declared them part of intangible cultural heritage, a decision supported by UNESCO [5], [6]. As a result, many places have seen an opportunity to boost tourism by transforming authenticity and heritage into commodities, leading to the prominence of all actors involved in the process, which in turn promotes economic growth, sustainability, and empowerment [5].

Considering the reasons stated above, it is important to highlight marketplaces *plazas de mercado* as places of tourist interests, essential to enhance the economic development of families working in this sector and strengthen their promotion of this places to both local and foreigner tourists. In this study researchers will focus on Las Ferias local market which is located in the northwest of Bogotá, Colombia. The aim of the study was to explore the perception of visitors to the Las Ferias local market, as well as to investigate whether this local market currently receives visits from national and international tourists, also to propose strategies to promote this local market as a tourist destination.

2 LITERATURE REVIEW

2.1 Influence of gastronomy in destination image

Destination image refers to the perception tourists have of a travel destination, encompassing cognitive, emotional, and overall impressions that influence their decision-making process [7]–[9] Previous studies focus on the importance of understanding destination image formation, which impacts tourists' behaviour, satisfaction, and intentions to recommend a place [10]. In addition, destination image involves considering tourists' experiences, perceptions, and sense of place, which can vary between domestic and international visitors [11]. Payel et al. [12] explore destination image through factors such as hygiene, attractions and value for money which significantly influences tourists' choices when selecting tourist attraction, those elements are present when visiting a local market.

Gastronomical destination image can be defined as a place where food plays a central role in shaping overall image and identity of the location [13], [14]. Indeed, gastronomical destination image plays a crucial role in tourism, influencing travellers' decisions and satisfaction levels. Previous studies emphasise the significance of gastronomic experiences in shaping tourists' perceptions of a destination [15], [16]. Kaur and Kaur [17] highlighted the importance of local cuisine in attracting both domestic and international tourists.

2.2 Local market as a tourism destination

Local market can be defined as a marketplace where local producers and consumers interact to exchange goods, services, and resources within a specific region, fostering economic, social, and cultural development [18], [19]. Local markets play a vital role in tourism destinations by showcasing local products and enhancing the overall tourist experience [20]. The local food culture is recognised as a key factor in destination marketing and development, highlighting the importance of local culinary experiences in attracting tourists [21].

To transform a local's market into a tourist destination, it should offer a unique experience by showcasing local produce, local cuisine, local and organic foods, promoting events and create a regional food identity, serving as a distribution channel, enabling direct interaction between farmers and consumers, and providing educational opportunities [22]. In addition, To become a tourist destination, a local's market should forming a region's food identity and provide entertaining experiences and as entertainment factor significantly impacts visitor experience value and satisfaction, enhancing its appeal [22], [23].

2.3 Gastronomic tourism

Gastronomy in the field of tourism can be understood as a representation of the culture of a community, which can be tasted and experienced [24]. The relationship between gastronomy and tourism is developed through the recognition of gastronomy as a cultural expression. This means that food and its scope of production and consumption comprise geographical, social, political, and economic elements [25], [26]. Furthermore, consumption of local and authentic food contributes to the sustainability of a region, supports local agriculture and local food production, improves destination incentive, and in particular, are strong agents for the development of a local destination brand [27].

2.4 Strategies to potentialise local markets as tourism destination

Previous studies developed strategies to potentiate local markets and gastronomy in tourism [28]. Those strategies include developing emotional marketing plans to enhance the visibility of local markets [29], promoting interactions between tourists and home producers, providing information about gastronomic heritage and regional products and regional meals [30], [31], providing cultural experiences, trough histories related to heritage, and developing eco-friendly tourism [32], [33].

Previous research highlights the importance to develop branding and destination image in enhancing the competitiveness of local markets ad a tourist destination, with social media acting as a moderator in this process [34]–[36]. By effectively communicating sustainability of local foods, tourism can enhance local markets, attracting consumers through engaging product features and emotional attributes [37].

3 METHODOLOGY

This research developed a mixed methodology by integrating different methodologies, researchers can explore beyond traditional boundaries, enhance the depth of analysis, and address wicked problems effectively [38], [39]. The aim of this research was to explore the perception of visitors to the Las Ferias local market, as well as to investigate whether this local market currently receives visits from national and international tourists.

Initially, 618 questionnaires were collected from Las Ferias local market visitors. Following a rigorous data cleaning process to ensure quality and reliability, the final sample consisted of 516 valid questionnaires. This data refinement step eliminated incomplete or inconsistent responses, resulting in a more robust dataset for analysis. The questionnaire was administered in person by students belonging to a research incubator who were previously trained to perform the task. Tablets were used, and the data was collected using QuestionPro. To ensure data quality, the information was gathered on different days of the week and during peak visitor hours.

The questionnaire was structured in four sections: demographics, visit motivators, perception of the market square, and finally, revisit intention and recommendation. Previous studies that have developed these elements were used as input for its development [22], [23], [40]–[46].

To complement and validate the questionnaire findings, semi-structured interviews were conducted with a representative vendor from each type of sales stand. These interviews were recorded with explicit consent from the participants and subsequently transcribed verbatim for thorough analysis.

4 RESULTS AND DISCUSSION

This section presents the findings from our mixed-method data collection approach. We will first discuss the results obtained from questionnaires administered to visitors of the Las Ferias local market, followed by insights gathered from semi-structured interviews conducted with vendors at this local market.

The demographic profile of the surveyed population reveals diverse characteristics. The largest age group of visitors (22.48%) falls within the 31–40 years range, closely followed by those aged 51–60 years (21.32%). There is a slight gender imbalance, with females comprising 52.23% of visitors and males 47.48%. Marital status data shows that 41.47% of respondents are married, while 29.26% are single. Occupationally, there is an even split between employed and self-employed individuals, each accounting for 34.69% of respondents. Educational attainment varies, with 29.26% having completed a professional degree and 26.55% having finished high school. Notably, while the majority of respondents (63.37%) reside in various Bogotá neighbourhoods, a significant proportion (36.05%) are local residents of the Las Ferias neighbourhood, where the market square is situated (see Table 1).

Analysis of the survey responses revealed diverse motivations for visiting the Las Ferias local market. The overwhelming majority (86.24%) of respondents cited personal consumption as their primary reason for visiting. Commercial purposes accounted for a smaller but significant portion of visits, with 5.81% of respondents coming to stock their mini-markets or convenience stores, and 5.62% sourcing supplies for their restaurants. Interestingly, only a marginal 2.33% of visitors reported tourism or leisure as their main purpose (see Fig. 1).

To assess the factors motivating visitors to Las Ferias local market. The study examined eleven variables: product quality, price, product variety, hygiene, hours of operation, culinary offerings, security, location, access, parking options, and bathroom facilities. The results revealed that product quality was the strongest motivator, with 84.5% of respondents strongly agreeing on its importance. Price followed closely, with 82.56% strongly agreeing it influenced their decision to visit. Product variety ranked third, as 80.43% strongly agreed it was a motivating factor. Hygiene also played a significant role, with 76.36% of respondents strongly agreeing it motivated their visit (see Fig. 2).

When asked the visitors about the perceptions at Las Ferias local market, eight variables were considered: handicrafts, cultural experience, exclusive regional products, good service, culinary preparations, product variety, product quality and price. The findings revealed high levels of satisfaction, with 77.13% of respondents strongly agreeing that Las Ferias local market offered a wide variety of products. Additionally, 72.48% strongly agreed that the service was excellent, while 70.74% strongly endorsed the quality of the products available (see Fig. 3).

When asking visitors to Las Ferias local market about their likelihood to recommend various aspects of their experience. Overall, 73.64% of respondents indicated they would be highly likely to recommend the local market in general. Breaking down the specific offerings, 77.52% of surveyed visitors expressed a high likelihood of recommending the fruits and

Table 1: Demographics.

Variable	N	%
Age		
Under 18 years old	10	1.94
18–30 years old	102	19.77
31–40 years old	116	22.48
41–50 years old	104	20.16
51–60 years old	110	21.32
Over 60 years old	74	14.34
Gender		
Feminine	270	52.33
Masculine	245	47.48
Other	1	0.19
Marital status		
Single	151	29.26
Married	214	41.47
Not married but living with partner	99	19.19
Divorced	25	4.84
Widowed	27	5.23
Occupation		
Student	34	6.59
Employee	179	34.69
Self-employed	179	34.69
Housewife/house husband	63	12.21
Retired	58	11.24
Unemployed	3	0.58
Education level		
Elementary school	34	6.59
High school	137	26.55
Associate degree	135	26.16
Bachelor's degree	151	29.26
Postgraduate degree	39	7.56
Master's degree	19	3.68
Doctoral degree	1	0.19
Place of residence		
Las Ferias neighbourhood	186	36.05
Other neighbourhood	327	63.37
Other Colombian city	3	0.58
Abroad	0	0.00

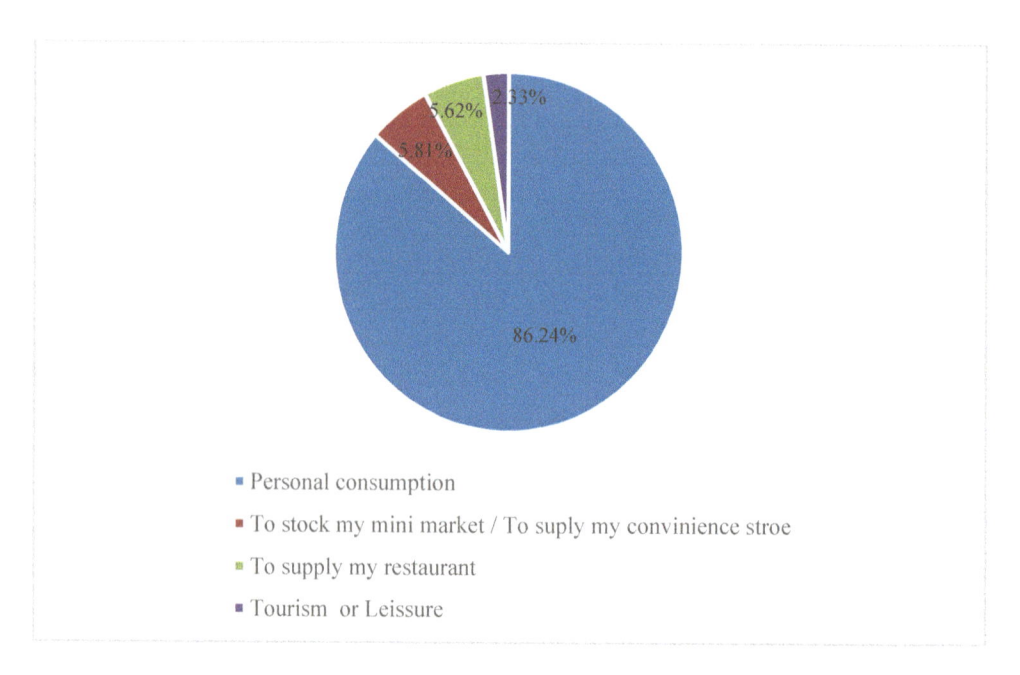

Figure 1: Reason of visit.

vegetables available. However, the recommendation rate for meals was notably lower, with only 42.25% of respondents indicating they would be highly likely to recommend the food options (see Fig. 5).

When asking to visitors to Las Ferias local market, their answers revealed strong intentions for return visits. 82.75% of respondents indicated that they would be highly likely to revisit, while an additional 15.5% stated it was likely. This suggests an overwhelmingly positive reception, with a total of 98.25% of visitors expressing a probable or highly probable intention to return (see Fig. 4).

To complement and validate the survey results, in-depth interviews were conducted with vendors at the Las Ferias local market. These interviews revealed several key insights: Firstly, the market offers a diverse array of products that are both representative and native to the region, presenting a unique selling point for potential tourism promotion. The vendors emphasised the cultural and gastronomic significance of these local offerings, which could serve as a cornerstone for marketing strategies. Secondly, the market's strategic location within the city was highlighted as a major advantage. Vendors consistently noted that the market's accessibility makes it not only convenient for regular shoppers but also positions it as an easily reachable destination for tourists exploring Bogotá.

Vendors see strong tourism potential in the market, emphasising its cultural heritage, history, and gastronomic offerings. They note that foreign tourists particularly value local agricultural products, more so than locals. This insight could be key for tourism strategies. However, currently few tourists visit the market, with most visitors being Bogotá residents, as confirmed by survey data. This gap between the market's tourism potential and its current visitor profile indicates an opportunity for focused tourism development and marketing efforts to attract more diverse visitors and capitalise on the market's unique appeal.

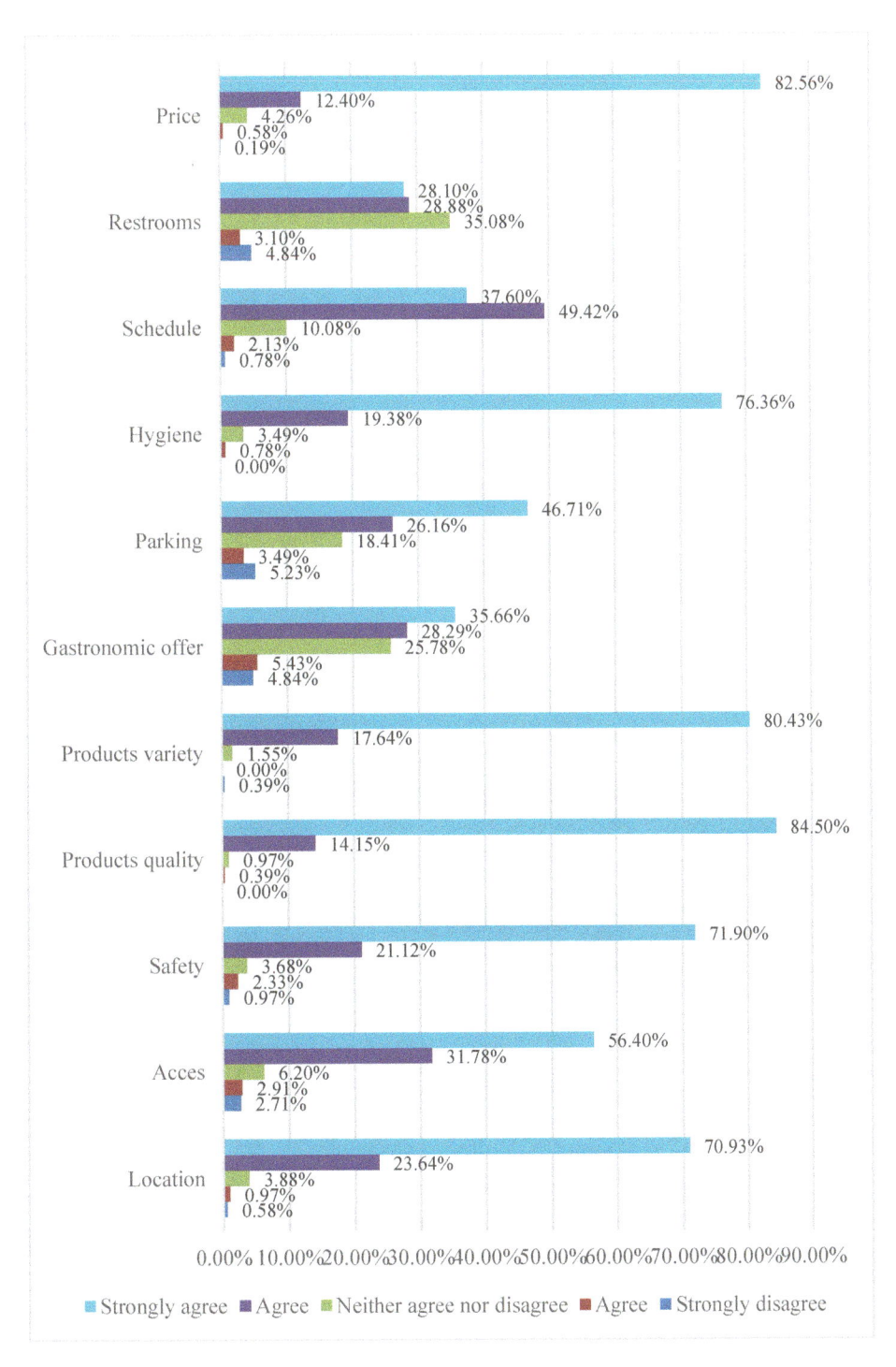

Figure 2: Visit motivators.

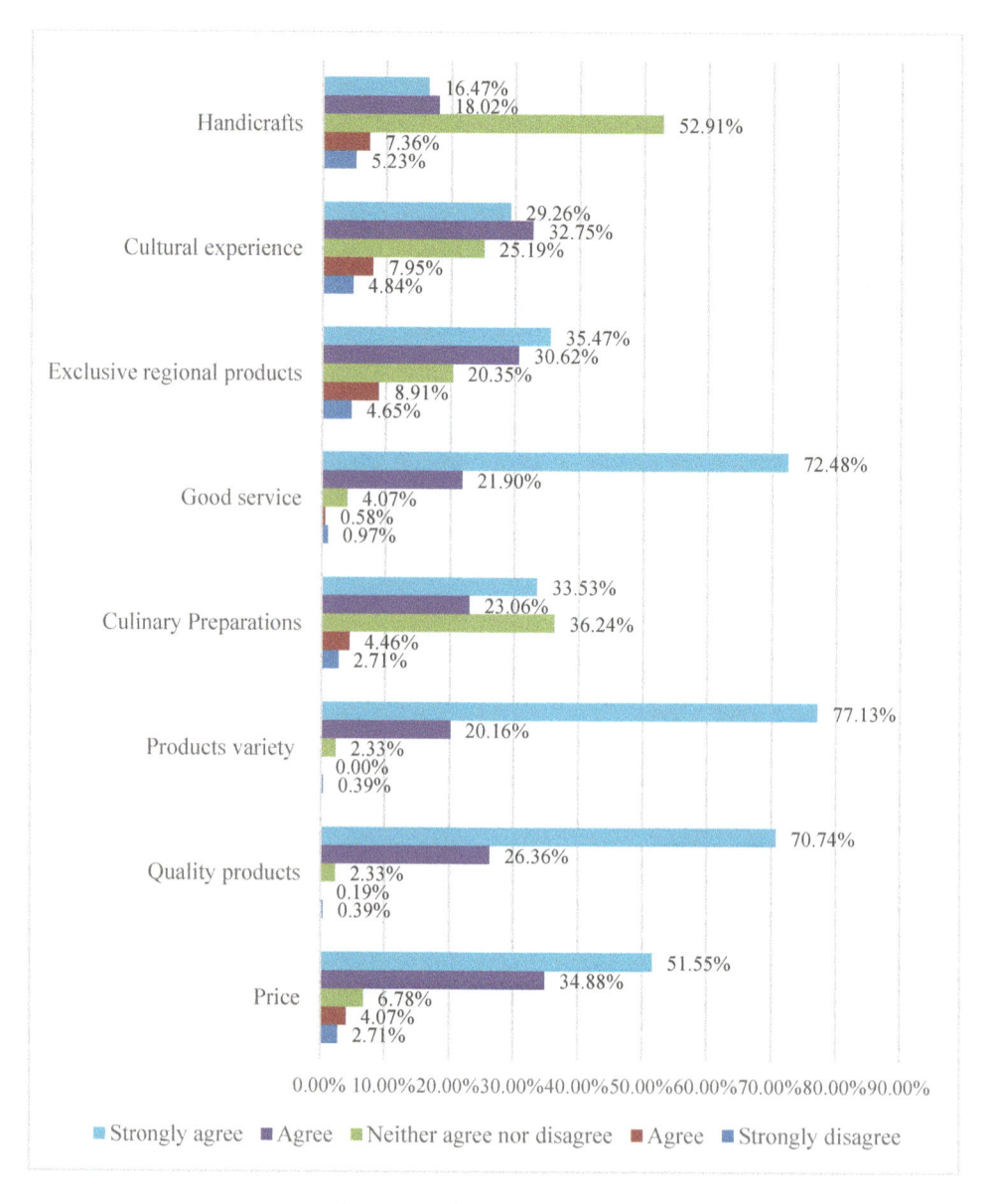

Figure 3: Visitors' perceptions.

The market's potential as a tourist attraction lies in showcasing its product origins. A significant portion of products comes directly from farmers in nearby municipalities, while others are sourced through Corabastos, Bogotá's major wholesale market. Finally, vendors note minimal promotional activities for the market, citing only the 'Fritanga fest' as memorable. They advocate for increased advertising across diverse media channels to boost the market's appeal as a tourist destination. Crucially, vendors identify improving security in the market's vicinity as a critical issue that must be addressed to successfully transform the market into a tourist attraction.

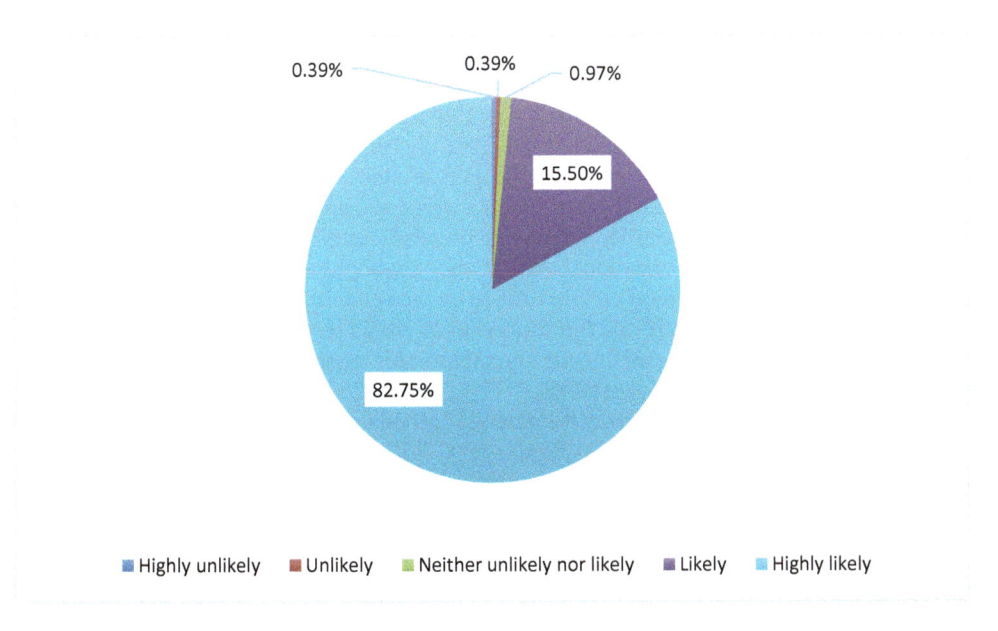

Figure 4: Revisit intention.

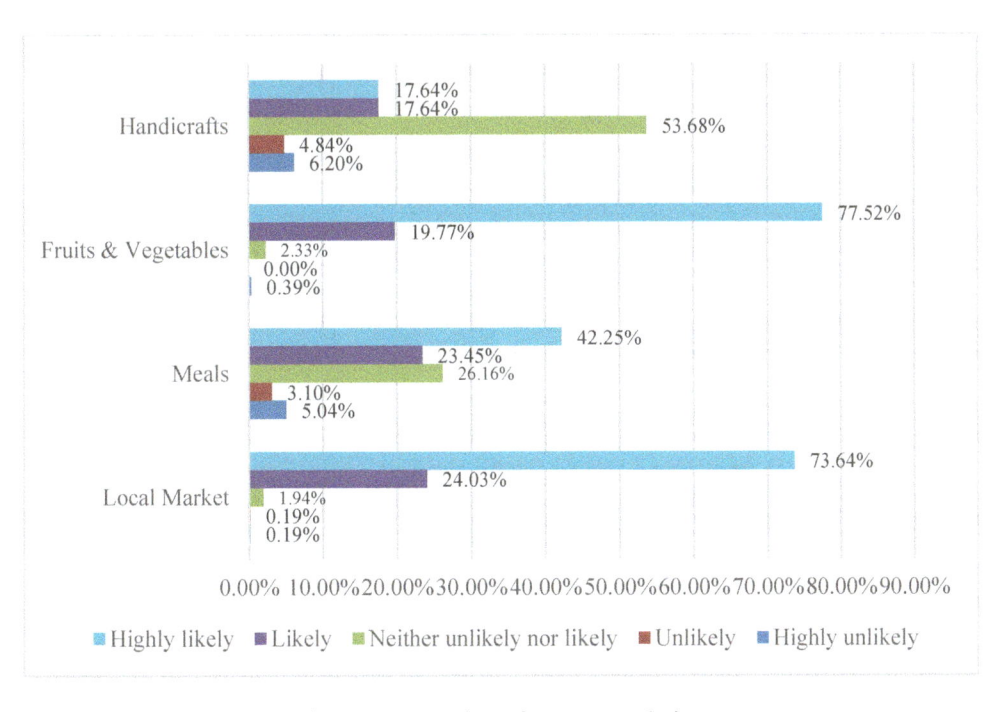

Figure 5: Intention of recommendation.

5 CONCLUSIONS

Currently, the Las Ferias local market is visited mostly by people from different neighbourhoods in the city of Bogotá. Of the 100% surveyed, only 2.33% are domestic tourists, indicating that this local market is not currently considered a tourist destination. The vast majority of visitors come to this local market to stock up on products for their own consumption. Likewise, the main motivators for visiting are product quality, prices, product variety, facility cleanliness, security within the premises, and its location. When studying visitors' perceptions of Las Ferias local market, they highlight the high quality and variety of its products, as well as the good service offered by the vendors. Finally, 82.75% of visitors have a strong intention to revisit, and the vast majority would recommend this market square to friends and family, emphasising that the main reason for recommending the market square would be to purchase fruits and vegetables.

According to Björk and Kauppinen-Räisänen [47] food is an important element that gives relevance and recognition to any place around the world. Highlighting that nowadays food is a new tourism attraction, and that places that lack of natural resources to boost tourism rely on their food and local gastronomy to promote itself as a tourist destination.

Results of this research indicates that transforming a local market into a tourist destination requires the strategic use of promotional tools, particularly social media. This method has proved effective in educating potential visitors about local markets and encouraging them to explore these vibrant spaces. Storytelling, in particular, is a powerful technique employed by established tourist-oriented local markets to vividly portray the life, culture, and societal nuances of their region.

Future studies should focus on developing comprehensive strategies to promote local market as tourist attractions across Latin America. This approach should emphasise preserving the authenticity and cultural significance of regional cuisines and local products, which are often central to these markets' appeal. Additionally, researchers could focus on compiling detailed information about local products, including their origins, cultural importance, and health benefits. This knowledge can then be effectively communicated to visitors, enhancing their understanding and appreciation of the market's offerings and the broader regional heritage.

ACKNOWLEDGEMENTS

The authors would like to thank the Alliance Network and Universidad de La Sabana for the financial support provided with the project 'Comprendiendo La Relación Entre La Gastronomía Regional y Los Productos Locales y La Intención De Visitar Un Mercado En Diferentes Ciudades. Estrategias Turísticas Para Salvaguardar La Gastronomía Local' (Project code EICEA-151-2022) and the Institut LYFE for its support.

REFERENCES

[1] Balslev, H. & García, M.A., Re-writing the Sustainable Development Goals from marketplaces in Argentina, Chile, Colombia and Mexico. *Dialogos Latinoamericanos*, **20**(28), pp. 77–88, 2019.

[2] Bromley, R.J. & Symanski, R., Marketplace trade in Latin America. *Latin American Research Review*, **9**(3), pp. 3–8, 1974.

[3] Pinto Dussan, L. & Rodríguez Uribe, L.M., Valorización de la plaza de mercado La Concordia de Bogotá a través del turismo, 2017.

[4] Thompson, M., Farmers' markets and tourism: Identifying tensions that arise from balancing dual roles as community events and tourist attractions. *Journal of Hospitality and Tourism Management*, **45**, pp. 1–9, 2020.

[5] Medina, F.X. & Tresserras, J. (eds), *Food, Gastronomy and Tourism: Social and Cultural Perspectives*, Universidad de Guadalajara, 2018
[6] OMT (Organización Mundial del Turismo), *Turismo y Patrimonio Cultural Inmaterial*, OMT: Madrid, 2013.
[7] Hu, T. & Geng, J., Research on the perception of the terrain image of the tourism destination based on multimodal user-generated content data. *Peer J. Computer Science*, **10**, e1801, 2024.
[8] Fjelldal, I.K., Kralj, A. & Moyle, B., Profanity in viral tourism marketing: A conceptual model of destination image reinforcement. *Journal of Vacation Marketing*, **28**(1), pp. 52–63, 2022.
[9] Montes-Guerra, M.I., Zapata-Cuervo, N. & Jeong, M., Colombia as a future tourism destination from US travelers' perspective. *Innovar.*, **34**(93), e98406, 2024.
[10] Castro Analuiza, J.C., Palacios Pérez, J.M. & Plazarte Alomoto, L.V., Imagen del destino desde la perspectiva del turista [Destination image from the tourist's perspective]. *Turismo y Sociedad*, **26**, 2020.
[11] Wibisono, N., Destination image: Perception, experience, and behavioural intention: In the context of West Java, Indonesia as a tourist destination. *Asia Tourism Forum 2016: The 12th Biennial Conference of Hospitality and Tourism Industry in Asia*, Atlantis Press, 2016.
[12] Payel, D., Mandal, S., Dixit, S.K., Patra, S.K. & Chandran, A., Reconceptualizing destination image. *Anatolia*, **35**(2), pp. 359–373, 2023. https://doi.org/10.1080/13032917.2023.2213713.
[13] Čavić, S., Ćurčić, N., Radivojevic, N., Živanov, J.G. & Lakićević, M., Gastronomic manifestation in the function of branding a tourist destination. *Marketing Intelligence and Planning*, **42**(3), pp. 749–770, 2024.
[14] Pappas, N., Michopoulou, E., Farmaki, A. & Leivadiotaki, E., Chaordic destination image formulation through gastronomy perspectives: Evidence from Greece. *International Journal of Contemporary Hospitality Management*, **34**(9), pp. 3459–3481, 2022.
[15] Ademoğlu, A. & Şahan, M., The effects of gastronomic experience and food image towards the gastronomic products of local tourism on the intention to eat local foods: The case of Hatay. *Journal of Multidisciplinary Academic Tourism*, **8**(2), pp. 129–140, 2023.
[16] Kovalenko, A., Dias, Á., Pereira, L. & Simões, A., Gastronomic experience and consumer behavior: Analyzing the influence on destination image. *Foods*, **12**(2), p. 315, 2023.
[17] Kaur, S. & Kaur, M., Image of local cuisine in emerging gastronomic destinations: Scale review, development, and validation. *International Journal of Hospitality and Tourism Administration*, **25**(1), pp. 153–201, 2024.
[18] Petrović, M.D., Ledesma, E., Morales, A., Radovanović, M.M. & Denda, S., The analysis of local marketplace business on the selected urban case: Problems and perspectives. *Sustainability*, **13**(6), p. 3446, 2021.
[19] Ustyugova, I.E., Trineeva, L.T. & Kolesova, E.Y., The concept of formation and development trends of the local food industry market in the context of intensifying the integration interaction of its participants. *Proceedings of the Voronezh State University of Engineering Technologies*, **81**(3), pp. 276–280, 2019.

[20] Vuksanović, N., Demirović Bajrami, D., Petrović, M.D., Radovanović, M.M., Malinović-Milićević, S., Radosavac, A., Obradović, V. & Ergović Ravančić, M., The role of culinary tourism in local marketplace business: New outlook in the selected developing area. *Agriculture*, **14**(1), p. 130, 2024.
[21] Stalmirska, A.M., Local food in tourism destination development: The supply-side perspectives. *Tourism Planning and Development*, **21**(2), pp. 160–177, 2024.
[22] Garner, B. & Ayala, C., Regional tourism at the farmers' market: Consumers' preferences for local food products. *International Journal of Culture, Tourism and Hospitality Research*, **13**(1), pp. 37–54, 2019.
[23] Tseng, S.C., Wang, D., Shen, C.C. & Chung, H.P., A study on the relationship between tourists' experience and experience value and satisfaction in Taiwan's farmer's markets. *Sustainability*, **15**(10), p. 8347, 2023.
[24] Mejía, M.O., Franco, W.C., Franco, M.C. & Flores, F.Z., Perfil y preferencias de los visitantes en destinos con potencial gastronómico: Caso 'Las Huecas' de Guayaquil (Ecuador). *Rosa dos Ventos*, **9**(2), pp. 200–215, 2017.
[25] Davidova, E. & Dudkina, O., Gastronomic culture as a factor of intercultural communication in tourism. *BIO Web of Conferences*, **113**, 06028, 2024.
[26] Lopes, T.H., Klein, W.L. & de Fatima Fontana, R., Gastronomy as a tool for rural tourism development: The case of Casa Carnasciali Winery. *Applied Tourism*, **8**(1), pp. 63–73, 2023.
[27] Royo Vela, M. & Serarols Tarrés, C., El turismo rural-cultural: un modelo de gestión del marketing turístico a nivel local basado en la medida de la imagen del destino. *Cuadernos de Turismo*, **16**, pp. 197–222, 2005.
[28] Kuhn, V.R., dos Anjos, S.J. & Krause, R.W., Innovation and creativity in gastronomic tourism: A bibliometric analysis. *International Journal of Gastronomy and Food Science*, 100813, 2023.
[29] Carbache Mora, C., Zambrano Zambrano, J.L. & Lemoine Quintero, F.A., Estrategia de marketing emocional para la promoción de locales de servicios gastronómicos en la ciudad de Bahía de Caráquez. Ecuador. *Económicas cuc*, **41**(1), pp. 203–216, 2020.
[30] Rivza, B., Foris, D., Foris, T., Privitera, D., Uljanova, E. & Rivza, P., Gastronomic heritage: A contributor to sustainable local tourism development. *Geo Journal of Tourism and Geosites*, **44**(4), pp. 1326–1334, 2022.
[31] Mwangi, G. & Mwalongo, J., Exploring the role of communication in enhancing the gastronomic tourism experience. *Journal of Digital Marketing and Communication*, **3**(1), pp. 28–35, 2023.
[32] Okhee, K. & Woo-Jun, M., An exploratory study on local oral history-based tourism as an alternative cultural experience model: A theoretical discussion on the transboundary values of local history. *Jiyeog sahoehag*, **24**(1), pp. 137–163, 2023.
[33] Dzhabarova, Y. & Ruseva, M., Tourist destination development through reviving and promotion the local identity. *Scientific Works*, pp. 60–71, 2023.
[34] Kuswardani, D.C., Nurhidayati, N., Wibisono, T. & Santoso, A., Local branding: Imperative strategy towards competitiveness of sustainable destinations through the role of social media. *Kontigensi: Jurnal Ilmiah Manajemen*, **11**(1), pp. 281–293, 2023.
[35] Gordin, V. & Trabskaya, J., The role of gastronomic brands in tourist destination promotion: The case of St. Petersburg. *Place Branding and Public Diplomacy*, **9**, pp. 189–201, 2013.
[36] Sultan, M.T., Sharmin, F., Badulescu, A., Gavrilut, D. & Xue, K., Social media-based content towards image formation: A new approach to the selection of sustainable destinations. *Sustainability*, **13**(8), p. 4241, 2021.

[37] Savelli, E., Gregory-Smith, D., Murmura, F. & Pencarelli, T., How to communicate typical–local foods to improve food tourism attractiveness. *Psychology and Marketing*, **39**(7), pp. 1350–1369, 2022.

[38] Brocklesby, J., Mixing methods in systems practice. *Journal of Systems Thinking*, pp. 1–16, 2023.

[39] Denton, J., Mixing methodologies: A sliding continuum or an iterative cycle? *Research Anthology on Innovative Research Methodologies and Utilization Across Multiple Disciplines*, IGI Global, pp. 222–242, 2022.

[40] Ab Karim, S. & Chi, C.G., Culinary tourism as a destination attraction: An empirical examination of destinations' food image. *Journal of Hospitality Marketing and Management*, **19**(6), pp. 531–555, 2010.

[41] Annes, A. & Bessiere, J., Staging agriculture during on-farm markets: How does French farmers' rationality influence their representation of rurality? *Journal of Rural Studies*, **63**, pp. 34–45, 2018.

[42] Hall, C.M. & Wilson, S., Scoping paper: Local food, tourism and sustainability. Academia.edu, 2009.

[43] Kastenholz, E., Eusébio, C. & Carneiro, M.J., Purchase of local products within the rural tourist experience context. *Tourism Economics*, **22**(4), pp. 729–748, 2016.

[44] Kim, K.H. & Park, D.B., Factors influencing rural tourists' purchasing behaviour: Four types of direct farm markets in South Korea. *Tourism Economics*, **20**(3), pp. 629–645, 2014.

[45] Li, X., Kong, W.H. & Yang, F.X., Authentic food experiences bring us back to the past: An investigation of a local food night market. *Journal of Travel and Tourism Marketing*, **38**(3), pp. 233–246, 2021.

[46] Skuras, D., Dimara, E. & Petrou, A., Rural tourism and visitors' expenditures for local food products. *Regional Studies*, **40**(7), pp. 769–779, 2006.

[47] Björk, P. & Kauppinen-Räisänen, H., Local food: A source for destination attraction. *International Journal of Contemporary Hospitality Management*, **28**(1), pp. 177–194, 2016.

SECTION 5
TOURISM AND THE ENVIRONMENT

ENVIRONMENTAL IMPACT OF CRUISE TOURISM: EXPLORING MITIGATION CASE STUDIES IN MAJOR PORTS

ALEXANDRA ALEXANDROPOULOU, NATALIA CHATZIFOTI, KONSTANTINA K. AGORAKI,
ANDREAS FOUSTERIS & DIMITRIOS A. GEORGAKELLOS
Department of Business Administration University of Piraeus, Greece

ABSTRACT

Cruise tourism has transformed into a separate industry with unique characteristics and has contributed to developing a new tourism product clearly distinguished from passenger maritime transportation. This new product has led to new economic benefits not only for the operating shipping firms, but also for the local communities at the ports of call along the travel/cruise itinerary driving socio-economic growth. Despite these beneficial effects, cruise tourism has raised many concerns among local communities due to the inflicted environmental pressures on resources and ecosystems. Energy and water consumption, waste management, marine pollution, traffic and noise burden are the main topics of dispute that ports have to consider in their development strategies. To allay these concerns, major ports around the world, mainly in cruise intensive destinations, have implemented strategies, policies, plans and measures to alleviate or pre-empt any negative effects that could impose not only on the natural environment, but also on the well-being of residents. This review explores case studies of the measures undertaken to mitigate environmental impact due to cruise tourism around the ports and highlights some common practices. While ports are still testing measures and technologies more investment is necessary to create a positive impact.
Keywords: cruise tourism, environmental impact, cruise impact mitigation, case studies, ports.

1 INTRODUCTION

An intriguing post at the *Guardian* newspaper arguing that 'A good cruise is one that doesn't come: Europe's ports bear brunt of ship pollution' [1] has triggered the initiation of this research around the cruise ports realm. It seeks to unveil case studies and best practices that major ports around the world are implementing to offset the negative effects of cruise tourism.

The cruise industry has long been under debate for its positive or negative impacts. Frequently accused of not complying with regulations for environmental protection cruise lines, have often been the subject of related fines. At the same time, local economies may argue that they unfold economic benefits from the cruise operations (direct or indirect economic effects) and the near port economic activity that is being developed through a wide nexus of supporting services.

Today, cruise is an integrated sector that shapes, promotes and delivers a very distinct product: cruise tourism [2]. The sector has managed to bounce back since the COVID era and is expected to reach new heights by 2029 [3]. Fig. 1 shows that in 2023, it has already reached the 107% of the 2019 levels counting over 31 million passengers [4] with a special focus on routes sailing in the Caribbean and the Mediterranean Sea [5].

Most studies in the industry have been mainly concentrated on the impacts of cruise on local and regional economies [6], [7]. Cruising plays an important role in the social and economic growth of both host countries and cruising centres. As ports of call are the centre of the cruise industry, local economies are most affected by its operation. Local economic activity is greatly stimulated by the expenses cruise passengers are producing during land

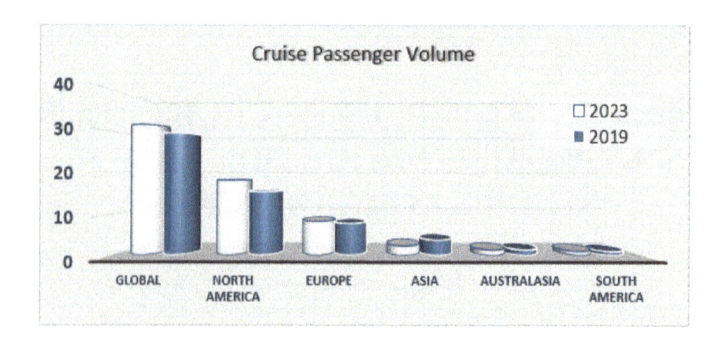

Figure 1: Cruise passenger volume evolution 2019–2023 (in millions of passengers). *(Source: CLIA 2023 Global Passenger Report.)*

activities and excursions, shopping, eating, and various complementary services. Klein [8] argues that cruise ports can create value not only to passengers but also to the local communities by leveraging economic advantage for local markets, tourism operators as well as to the wider ecosystem of services that evolves around them. Ports of call benefit from the large numbers of visitors, resulting in the demand and hereafter creation of jobs and expansion of local businesses to supply a wide range of services. As more and more travellers select cruise as their holiday option and cruise ship traffic rises, the industry often acts as a catalyst for infrastructure development in many destinations.

In port cities, cruise tourism is a fast-growing part of the tourism industry with significant benefits, including economic, environmental and social challenges for both the city and the surrounding area. During a cruise, tourists spend both on board and ashore. Total spending on land is often closely linked to the time spent on land and the attractions of the port city. Tourist resources in port cities are the main factor determining the attractiveness of cruise ports. Cruise tourists add value to economies before, during and after their cruise. On a typical 7-day cruise, guests spend an average of €660 in port towns and 24 cruise guests help create a full-time equivalent job. Forecasts for the total cruise industry revenue are quite optimistic (Fig. 2) as there seems to be a positive trend until 2029 (last year of forecast).

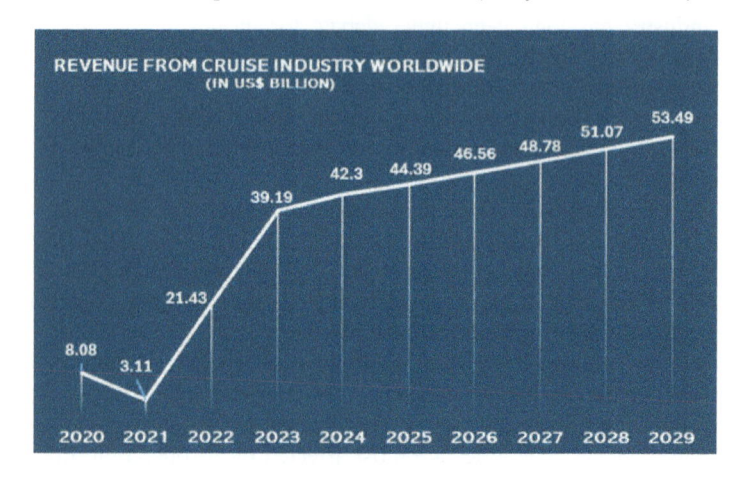

Figure 2: Cruise industry revenue 2020–2029 (in billion US$) [3].

These benefits do not stop there, as 60% of people who have cruised admit returning to a destination which have visited during a cruise in the past, thus multiplying the economic benefit for the host communities [9], [10].

Brida and Zapata-Aguirre [11] argue that cruising represents the paradigm of globalisation: physical mobility, international capital that can be moved anywhere and anytime, multi-national crews on a single ship, no national or international regulations, optimal ship registries.

The growth of the cruise tourism industry has been accompanied by the development of new cruise passenger terminals in many port cities to support the goals of land use planning and urban regeneration [12]. Although, local benefits fail to materialise when cruise tourism is undertaken without investment in, and involvement of, destination communities [13].

Concerns arise as cruise ships are now larger and perform most of the functions of a small resort: accommodation, catering, transport and tourism activities, and recreation, reducing in-destination spending.

The most valued economic benefits are now under scrutiny whether the income generated exceeds direct and indirect costs (including environmental costs) and whether income distribution is responsible. As the popularity and geographical reach of cruising grows so does its environmental, social and economic impacts.

2 IMPACT OF THE CRUISE TOURISM ON THE ENVIRONMENT

Port development is a driver for economic growth from local to national and regional scale but has been proved to raise significant challenges for the environment. Focusing on sustainability, several strategies can be used to help ensure that port development is environmentally sound. Responsible tourism has three broad areas of concern: (a) tourism's impact on the environment; (b) the equitable distribution of economic benefits to all segments of a tourist destination; and (c) minimising negative sociocultural impacts [8]. This review explores only the environmental pillar and, in particular, focuses on the mitigation efforts trialled and/or adopted by large cruise ports around the world.

Cruise tourism can have adverse environmental impacts, including increased air and water pollution, habitat destruction and disruption of marine ecosystems. These environmental risks can have socio-economic consequences, such as negative impacts on public health, reduced attractiveness for tourism and damage to local industries dependent on natural resources.

In their research, Lloret et al. [14] summarise the effects cruise tourism can have both on the environment and human health: 'cruising, despite technical advances and some surveillance programmes, remains a major source of air, water (fresh and marine) and land pollution affecting fragile habitats, areas and species, and a potential source of physical and mental human health risks'. Estimating the impact of the entire life cycle of a cruise ship on both the environment and human health is a really challenging task.

In this point we should state that all shipping traffic produces environmental impacts, but the cruise ships create disproportionate impacts because they carry thousands of passengers who produce their own personal waste streams [15].

The environmental impacts from the cruise industry can be upstream (concerning the ship construction phase) or downstream (pollution generated by the operation of cruise tourism. In this paper we only examine the downstream impacts which are more relevant to the operations of the cruise ships, the mere service of cruise tourism. A brief overview of the main impacts of cruising involves the following.

2.1 Air pollution

The shipping sector is one of the leading sources of greenhouse gas (GHG) emissions, air and water pollution. The sector still relies almost entirely on fossil fuels full of toxic substances including sulphur [16].

Port operations and logistics activities are often accompanied by an increase in energy demand and subsequently pollutant emissions [17], they bring a certain degree of impact on the surrounding environment, especially carbon dioxide (CO_2), a GHG that has a significant impact on the ecosystem [18]. Even though all ship types have an environmental and climate impact, air pollution from cruise ships is particularly worrying [16], [19].

2.2 Water/sea pollution

Wastewaters, including 'blackwater' (contaminated wastewater from toilets) and 'grey water' (greywater is wastewater generated from domestic, non-industrial processes, including drainage from dishwasher, galley taps, laundry facilities, showers, bath and washbasin drains, etc.), are a growing problem for sea pollution. Wastewater can result in a decrease of available dissolved oxygen in the marine ecosystem and can potentially cause algae bloom especially in shallow or enclosed waters [20]. Greywater is usually kept separate from blackwater to reduce the amount of water that gets heavily polluted and represents the greater percentage liquid waste produced by a cruise ship (50%–80%).

The discharge of bilge water (i.e. the water that collects in the bilges of a vessel that contains fluids from machinery spaces and internal drainage systems, among other sources) is a source of hydrocarbon discharge, even when treated to reduce the oil content to levels meeting international regulations for release into the environment [14]. Ballast water (used for the ships stability and manoeuvrability during a voyage) can contain wastewaters, oil and other hydrocarbons, microbes, microplastics and invasive species [14], [20], [21].

2.3 Solid waste

Cruise ships are bound to answer to a multitude of needs and desires and provide respective services like 24-hour food service, living accommodations, transport and leisure activities [22]. Cruise liners generate large amounts of non-hazardous solid waste (plastic, paper, wood, cardboard, food waste, cans, glass) and other waste discarded by passengers. [8]. In particular, they produce large amounts of food- and cabin-related waste, contributing 25% of waste from ships despite only making up <1% of the global shipping fleet [23].

2.4 Biodiversity

Cruise ships and maritime transport in general, have been associated with the transfer of alien species from one part of the world to another. This has often resulted in the introduction of vector borne diseases in new regions where they were not previously endemic [24]. The introduction of invasive aquatic species to new environments is a major threat to the world's oceans and to the conservation of biodiversity. Carried either in ships' ballast water or on ships' hulls, many transported species may establish a reproductive population in the host environment, becoming invasive, out-competing native species and multiplying into pest proportions thus threatening local biodiversity [25].

2.5 Traffic, noise and visual pollution

When a cruise port is located near a city and port traffic mixes with city traffic, road traffic, especially cars/coaches and lorries, may increase. Local negative effects include increased travel time, reduced efficiency and additional pollution from increased travel [26].

Noise from cruise ships is also considered as a pollutant. Noise pollution in the marine environment is a significant issue that is often neglected in marine pollution assessments, yet low frequency noise has doubled every decade since 1950 [27]. Research by Caric et al. [28] found noise can displace both fish and predators. Noise sensitive marine organisms are more prone to suffer adverse effects.

Seldom does visual pollution get accounted for when researching about cruise tourism impacts on the environment. Especially in large ports of call the aesthetic impact of cruise ships can have a toll for the residents in the vicinity.

2.6 Dredging (during port development)

While cruise ships come in all sizes, there is an eminent trend towards larger vessels, which may require ports to increase the frequency and depth of dredging projects in order to accommodate them, which can destroy local (marine) habitats. Even without dredging, the passage of cruise ships can affect bottom dwellers and cause severe turbidity by stirring up sediment.

3 METHODOLOGY

This literature review is based on internationally published studies on the effects of cruises on both the environment and human health. Our study used the following resources: peer-reviewed journals and books in scientific databases related to the research field (e.g. Science Direct, PubMed, Web of Science) and grey literature (e.g. papers, reports, technical notes and congress contributions). Online sources were also exploited, especially information provided by the selected port authorities' websites.

This study should not be considered a systematic review given that only key documents providing examples of the issues identified were selected. This kind of exploratory analysis allowed us to address the specifics of the cruise industry and study these particular examples/case studies. The aim of this review was to improve the understanding of cruise tourism in coastal areas, to present practices that enhance the environmental footprint of cruise tourism and to look forward to future research directions. Therefore, it only focuses on the environmental effects' mitigation measures in cruise ports.

4 MITIGATION MEASURES FROM THE CRUISE LINES

Greening of the cruise tourism industry is an endeavour that requires all stakeholders aboard a common cause. The major stakeholders are the cruise lines and the port that host the cruise ships. Both have an equal responsibility to design, adopt and implement integrated strategies to soften their environmental footprint.

Some of the promoted measures to be undertaken by the cruise ships companies are the following.

4.1 Onshore power supply (OPS)

OPS or cold ironing – in maritime jargon – involves using shoreside electricity that allows ship engines to be switched off at birth. This infrastructure can help reduce emissions by up to 98%, depending on the mix of energy sources used to produce this electricity. Under the

Fit for 55 package, from January 2030 ships staying for more than 2 hours in a port would have to connect to OPS, unless they used another zero-emission technology.

In Europe most OPS are situated in ports in northern Europe while Mediterranean ports are funded to incorporate such facilities in the immediate future. Fig. 3 illustrates OPS geographical distribution around the world and stage of implementation. A study conducted with data from 714 major ports in the European Economic Area and the UK showed that significant annual reductions in local air pollution can be achieved by using OPS amounting to 86,431t NO_x, 4,130t SO_x, 1,596t PM_{10}, 4,333t CO, 94t CH_4, 4,818t NMVOC, and 235t N_2O [29].

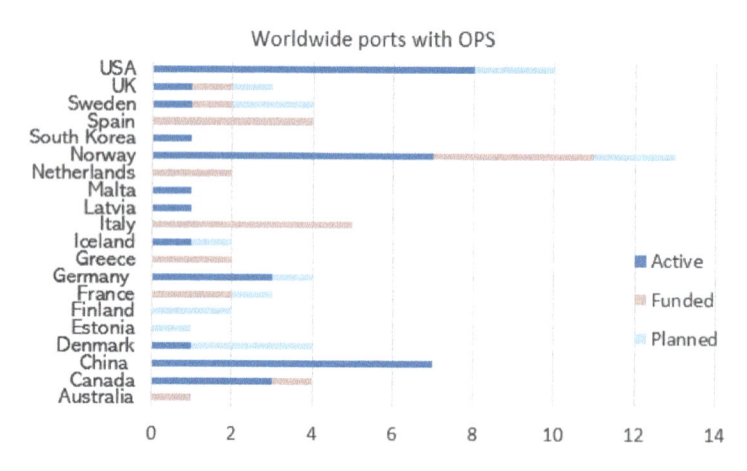

Figure 3: World ports with at least one cruise berth with OPS [9].

4.2 Wastewater management

Many technological advances have been applied to cruise ships to help with the management of the wastewater produced during voyage or in port. As part of their overarching sustainability focus, cruise lines have committed to not discharging untreated sewage anywhere in the world, during normal operations and are bound to incorporate advanced treatment systems.

4.3 Solid waste management

A cruise ship produces a large volume of non-hazardous solid waste, including huge volumes of plastic, paper, wood, cardboard, food waste, cans, glass, and the variety of other wastes disposed of by passengers [8]. A CLIA report [30] states that some ships are able to repurpose 100% of waste, transfer surplus heat from machinery to heat water for showers and pools, and significantly reduce food waste by using bio-digesters.

4.4 Use of renewable fuels and alternative energy sources

Various cruise lines are testing and using into new ships the capability to run on renewable fuels, including biofuels and synthetic carbon fuels [30]. Ships designed with LNG engines and fuel supply systems are able to switch to bio or synthetic LNG in the future, with little or no modifications. Zhang et al. (2023) have estimated that the use of alternative fuels in cruise ships will reach economic competitiveness comparable to conventional fossil fuels by 2040.

5 MITIGATION ACTIVITIES FROM PORTS

Fit for 55 provides ports with a unique opportunity to implement key mitigation measures and create infrastructure for shore power or zero-emission technologies. Failure to comply with the new will become a factor contributing to loss of competitiveness for some. Cruise ports around the world are on the frontline in supporting and promoting the sustainability of the industry. They act as the critical interface between cruise ships, ports and port cities.

5.1 Europe

5.1.1 Port of Barcelona, Spain

Barcelona is a principal cruise port in Europe, with numerous marinas and ferry terminals. In 2023, the Barcelona Cruise Port handled 3.6 million passengers, but Barcelona was the most sulphur polluted cruise port in Europe in 2022, with cruise ships emitting 18,277 kg of sulphur dioxide (SO_x) [31]. In their research, Ruiz-Guerra et al. [32] observed a linear relationship between passenger volume and air pollution in Barcelona port while Perdiguero and Sanz's [33] simulations showed that the effect of one cruise entering, staying or leaving the port affects the air quality even as far as 7–10 km away. This implies that the whole city of Barcelona, and some localities around the city are affected by it. To mitigate the impact of air pollution, the port of Barcelona has created an Air Quality Improvement Plan with the aim to reduce emissions as much as possible, specifically of particulate matter (PM_{10}), nitrogen oxides (NO_x) and other polluting gases resulting from the Port's activity. The measures to achieve this goal include among others environmental discounts for vessels with good environmental performance. The Port is also working on bringing about a change in legislation so that such environmental discounts can be increased up to 40% of the boat's fee, in order to attract cleaner boats and reduce emissions.

5.1.2 Port of Venice, Italy

Venice, one of Europe's most overcrowded cities from tourists, was also Europe's most polluted cruise port in 2019. To alleviate this impact, in 2021, Italian law banned cruise ships and other large vessels from the Venice Lagoon [34]. This had an impressive result as it led air pollutants' concentrations from cruise ships in Venice to fall roughly by 80% (SO_x) between 2019 and 2022.

5.1.3 Port of Le Havre, France

Since 1993 the port of Le Havre, has claimed to be one the most environmentally conscious cruise port [35]. Today, France's leading eco-responsible port, has defined a range of ecological services that may be technological or technical in nature, for provision of clean ship reception services at ports. Among other initiatives, the Port has joined SEREP in a common effort to develop a collection and treatment of scrubber waste industry to offer concrete solutions to shipping companies that choose to use scrubbers. Furthermore, has decided to cover 30% of the cost of the waste collection and disposal with the aim to encourage ship lines to deposit their liquid waste and scrubber residues on site.

5.1.4 Port of Dubrovnik

In 2019, Dubrovnik signed a Memorandum of Understanding with Cruise Lines International Association (CLIA) to promote sustainable tourism management. The number of visitors in Dubrovnik's Old Town – a UNESCO World Heritage site – in a relatively limited city area, had a great toll not only for the pleasure of the tourists but for the local community as well. It was deemed important to improve communications with cruise companies and introduce more efficient organisation. Adopted measures included careful planning of cruise arrivals and departures resulting in better tourism flows for the benefit of residents and visitors and the protection of the heritage site [4].

5.1.5 Port of Stockholm
A leading port in environmental initiatives, Stockholm has developed a closed-loop system to manage greywater and blackwater from cruise ships. Wastewater from cruise ships is collected, treated, and then reused or safely discharged. The port also connects to the city's central sewage treatment facility, allowing ships to pump their waste directly to the plant for treatment, preventing the dumping of untreated sewage into the Baltic Sea [36].

5.2 The Americas

5.2.1 Port of Miami, USA
The Port of Miami in Florida is the busiest port in the world based on cruise passenger traffic. Miami claims to be the cruise capital of the World and welcomes the biggest passenger ships on its nine modern cruise terminal – in 2023, the port received 7.3 million cruise passengers [37]. Miami has taken a big step to reduce pollution from cruise ships. It spent $125 million to build and launch a shore power program. That allows cruise ships to turn off their engines and plug into the grid while docked, reducing emissions by more than 95%. Onshore electricity capacity covers three cruise ships simultaneously plugged in.

5.2.2 Nassau Cruise Port, Bahamas
Nassau Port is situated on New Providence Island near the coast of Florida. It is the main seaport of the Bahamas, and in 2023, it handled 4.49 million passengers. Nassau has developed an integrated Environmental Management Plan to ensure minimum adverse impacts to the environment. A major measure to safeguard the marine environment concerns a coral relocation plan. These marine organisms are very sensitive to the changes of their environment. To protect the local population for the cruise port development, 500 corals will be moved. The proposed site for translocation is the western tip of Paradise Island and was selected in order to meet the environmental requirements of the coral, ensuring they are outside of any impact from construction activities at the Port.

5.3 Australasia

5.3.1 Port of Shanghai, China
Situated at the estuary of the Yangtze River in eastern China, the port of Shanghai is famous for being the busiest in the world. But it also has the sixth largest cruise terminal in the world. In 2023, Shanghai Cruise Terminal welcomed 1.2 million cruise guests. The Port of Shanghai has the ambition to become carbon neutral by 2060. The government of the city has outlined incentives to promote the use of land-based power. Some of the proposed incentives include subsidising construction fees, setting minimum usage requirements for vessels to be connected to the power, subsidising the cost of electricity for users, and ensuring that costs are affordable in line with international oil prices.

5.3.2 Port of Sydney, Australia
Sydney has two dedicated cruise passenger terminals – the Overseas Passenger Terminal and the White Bay Cruise Terminal, where smaller ships typically berth. The two terminals

collectively house four berths. To mitigate possible environmental effects due to air pollution from incoming cruise ships, the Australian Maritime Safety issued a Direction to use either low sulphur (maximum 0.10% m/m) fuel or an alternative measure that achieves an equivalent outcome. Cruise ships are required to changeover to low sulphur fuel or an alternative measure within one hour of arrival and changeover back to heavy fuel oil is only permitted up to one hour prior to departure of the vessel.

6 LIMITATIONS AND CHALLENGES TO OVERCOME

Aware of their impact on the environment, cruise ports are beginning to try and adopt a series of measures to help mitigate this impact. Up to now, these efforts are promising but not yet sufficient as only large ports have the capacity to implement such breakthrough measures. Ports are experimenting with new technologies and try to incorporate them in their daily operation.

As ports are starting to move towards sustainability, they are encountering a series of challenges that might hinder their transition in becoming green ports. A major challenge is the need for substantial infrastructure upgrades. Extensive investments will be required to both refurbish their already existing facilities and to build new clean energy infrastructure. Another major challenge for EU ports is overcoming technological barriers to the adoption of green technologies. A great percentage of ports still relies on equipment powered by fossil fuels. All this equipment will need to be replaced sooner or later and the technological transition path is not yet obvious.

EU ports must adopt a more proactive approach to guarantee that adequate regulatory frameworks are in place to lift all the limitations and that all competent stakeholders (ports, cities, local community, cruise operators) are aligned and work together for a 'greener' cruise industry. Incentives and funding will also be required to accelerate action especially because there is an urgency in confronting the environmental impacts of cruise tourism. To this end, cooperation with the cruise lines is also a prerequisite for an integrated solution to environmental protection.

7 CONCLUSION

This review only focuses on the environmental effects of mitigation measures in cruise ports presenting diverse case studies and the efforts ports are making towards environmental sustainability. The cases presented in this review reveal that although many efforts are being implemented there is still a great amount of work to be done. The environmental challenges to cruise tourism are multiple and pose great limitations in the transition of the cruise industry to sustainability. Ports around the world are faced with the same dilemma: economic benefits vs environmental costs. Nevertheless, common issues do not mean common solutions. Each port initiates, promotes and supports different measures, different solutions considering its unique characteristics or problems that is confronting.

ACKNOWLEDGEMENTS

This work has been partly supported by the University of Piraeus Research Center.

REFERENCES

[1] Wizenberg, D., Europe's ports bear brunt of ship pollution. *Guardian*, 19 Oct. 2023. https://www.theguardian.com/travel/2023/oct/19/europe-ports-bear-brunt-of-cruise-ship-pollution. Accessed on: 18 Aug. 2024.

[2] Logunova, N., Kalinkina, S., Lazitskaya, N. & Tregulova, I., Specifics of cruise tourism and features of creating a cruise tourism product. *E3S Web Conf.*, **217**, 05005, 2020. https://doi.org/10.1051/e3sconf/202021705005.
[3] Statista, Revenue of the cruises industry worldwide 2020–2029, 25 Jul. 2024. https://www.statista.com/forecasts/1258061/revenue-cruises-worldwide. Accessed on: 18 Aug. 2024.
[4] CLIA, Charting the future of sustainable cruise travel. 2023. https://cruising.org/-/media/CLIA-Media/StratCom/Charting-the-Future-of-Sustainable-Cruise-Travel_October-2023?mc_cid=ac83e132e1&mc_eid=65b2d83c2f. Accessed on: 16 Aug. 2024.
[5] Sanchez, V.M.L. et al., Management of cruise ship-generated solid waste: A review. *Marine Pollution Bulletin*, **151**, 110785, 2020. https://doi.org/10.1016/j.marpolbul.2019.110785.
[6] Gabe, T., Gayton, D., Robinson, P., Mcconnon, J. & Larkin, S. Economic impact of cruise ship passengers visiting Bar Harbor (Maine) in 2016. University Library of Munich, Germany, 2017.
[7] Penco, L. & Di Vaio, A., Monetary and non-monetary value creation in cruise port destinations: An empirical assessment. *Maritime Policy and Management*, **41**(5), pp. 501–513, 2014.
[8] Klein, R.A., Responsible cruise tourism: Issues of cruise tourism and sustainability. *Journal of Hospitality and Tourism Management*, **18**(1), pp. 107–116, 2011. https://doi.org/10.1375/jhtm.18.1.107.
[9] CLIA, The importance of cruise to the economy, 2024. https://europe.cruising.org/the-importance-of-cruise-to-the-economy/. Accessed on: 14 Aug. 2024.
[10] CLIA, We are #SailingSustainably, 2024. https://cruising.org/en-gb/environmental-sustainability. Accessed on: 14 Aug. 2024.
[11] Brida, J.G. & Zapata-Aguirre, S., Cruise tourism: Economic, socio-cultural and environmental impacts. *International Journal of Leisure and Tourism Marketing*, **1**, 2009. https://doi.org/10.1504/IJLTM.2010.029585.
[12] McCarthy, J.P. & Romein, A., Cruise passenger terminals, spatial planning and regeneration: The cases of Amsterdam and Rotterdam. *European Planning Studies*, **20**(12), pp. 2033–2052, 2012.
[13] MacNeill, T. & Wozniak, D., The economic, social, and environmental impacts of cruise tourism. *Tourism Management*, **66**, pp. 387–404, 2018. https://doi.org/10.1016/j.tourman.2017.11.002.
[14] Lloret, J., Carreño, A., Carić, H., San, J. & Fleming, L.E., Environmental and human health impacts of cruise tourism: A review. *Marine Pollution Bulletin, Part A*, **173**, 2021, 112979, 2021. https://doi.org/10.1016/j.marpolbul.
[15] Jones, P., Hillier, D. & Comfort, D., The environmental, social and economic impacts of cruising and corporate sustainability strategies. *Athens Journal of Tourism*, **3**(4), 2016. https://www.athensjournals.gr/tourism/2016-3-4-2-Jones.pdf.
[16] Dijkstra, C. & Simon, V., *The Return of the Cruise: How Luxury Cruises are Polluting Europe's Cities*, Transport and Environment, 2023. https://www.transportenvironment.org/uploads/files/2023-Cruise-ship-study.pdf. Accessed on: 24 Jul. 2024.
[17] Styhre, L. & Winnes, H., Emissions from ships in ports. *Green Ports*, eds R. Bergqvist & J. Monios, Elsevier, pp. 109–124, 2019. https://doi.org/10.1016/B978-0-12-814054-3.00006-2.

[18] Chen, L. et al., Green construction for low-carbon cities: A review. *Environmental Chemistry Letters*, **21**(3), pp. 1627–1657, 2023.
[19] Transport and Environment, One corporation to pollute them all, 2019.
[20] Randone, M., Bocci, M., Castellani, C., Laurent, C. & Piante, C., Safeguarding marine protected areas in the growing Mediterranean blue economy: Recommendations for the maritime transport sector. *International Journal of Design and Nature and Ecodynamics*, **14**(4), pp. 264–274, 2019.
[21] Copeland, C., Cruise ship pollution: Background, laws and regulations, and key issues. CRS report for Congress, Library of Congress, Congressional Research Service, 2008
[22] Fugita, D.M. & de Andrade, H.F., Cruises ships: History, evolution and typology oriented for hospitality management. *Revista Acadêmica Observatório de Inovação do Turismo*, Rio de Janeiro, pp. 1–30, 2014. https://doi.org/10.12660/oit.v8n2.48185.
[23] Merk, O., The competitiveness of global port-cities: Synthesis report. OECD Regional Development Working Papers, No. 2013/13, OECD Publishing: Paris, 2013. https://doi.org/10.1787/5k40hdhp6t8s-en.
[24] Wilson, M.E., The traveller and emerging infections: Sentinel, courier, transmitter. *Journal of Applied Microbiology*, **94**, pp. 1–11, 2003. https://doi.org/10.1046/j.1365-2672.94.s1.1.x.
[25] IMO, Biofouling, 2024. https://www.imo.org/en/OurWork/Environment/Pages/Biofouling.aspx. Accessed on: 14 Aug. 2024.
[26] Geerlings, H., Kuipers, B. & Zuidwijk, R., *Ports and Networks: Strategies, Operations and Perspectives*, Routledge: New York, 2017.
[27] ASCOBANS, Agreement on the conservation of small cetaceans of the Baltic, North East Atlantic, Irish and North Seas, 2009.
[28] Caric, H. et al., Safeguarding marine protected areas in the growing Mediterranean blue economy: Recommendations for the cruise sector. PHAROS4MPAs project, 48 pp., 2019.
[29] Stolz, B., Held, M., Georges, G. & Boulouchos, K., The CO_2 reduction potential of shore-side electricity in Europe. *Applied Energy*, **285**, 116425, 2021. https://doi.org/10.1016/j.apenergy.2020.116425.
[30] CLIA, State of the cruise industry report. 2024. https://cruising.org/-/media/clia-media/research/2024/2024-state-of-the-cruise-industry-report_updated-050824_web.ashx. Accessed on: 19 Aug. 2024.
[31] Statista, Top cruise ship polluted ports in Europe in 2022. Statista Research Department, June 2023.
[32] Ruiz-Guerra, I., Molina-Moreno, V., Cortés-García, F.J. & Núñez-Cacho, P., Prediction of the impact on air quality of the cities receiving cruise tourism: The case of the Port of Barcelona. *Heliyon*, **5**(3), 2019.
[33] Perdiguero, J. & Sanz, A., Cruise activity and pollution: The case of Barcelona. *Transportation Research Part D: Transport and Environment*, **78**, 2020.
[34] Figueroa, D., Italy: Cruise ships banned from Venice Lagoon, waterways declared national monument. 2021. https://www.loc.gov/item/global-legal-monitor/2021-11-01/italy-cruise-ships-banned-from-venice-lagoon-waterways-declared-national-monument/.
[35] Velter, G., Ports and their environment: The Port of Le Havre, a proactive port for environmental protection. *Transactions on the Built Environment*, vol. 1, WIT Press: Southampton and Boston, 1993.

[36] Wilewska-Bien, M. & Anderberg, S., Reception of sewage in the Baltic Sea: The port's role in the sustainable management of ship wastes. *Marine Policy*, **93**, pp. 207–213, 2018. https://doi.org/10.1016/j.marpol.2018.04.012.
[37] MarineInsight, 10 largest cruise ports in the World. https://www.marineinsight.com/ports/10-largest-cruise-ports-in-the-world. Accessed on: 6 Aug. 2024.

AIR POLLUTION FROM CRUISE SHIPS DURING HOTELLING IN PORTS: A CASE STUDY IN ANCONA HARBOUR, ITALY

SIMONE VIRGILI[1], UMBERTO RIZZA[2], MARTINA TOMMASI[1],
SILVIA DI NISIO[1] & GIORGIO PASSERINI[1]
[1]Department of Industrial Engineering and Mathematical Science, Marche Polytechnic University, Italy
[2]Institute of Atmospheric Sciences and Climate, National Research Council of Italy, Italy

ABSTRACT

Air pollution caused by cruise ships during the hotelling phase in ports represents a significant source of emissions. The hotelling phase refers to the period during which ships remain docked and keep their main and auxiliary engines running to supply power to onboard systems. Numerous studies have shown that this practice significantly contributes to emissions of nitrogen oxides (NO_x), sulphur oxides (SO_x), particulate matter (PM), and carbon dioxide (CO_2), degrading air quality in port areas and surrounding urban zones. Cruise ships, equipped with powerful internal combustion engines, release substantial amounts of pollutants even during hotelling. Emissions of NO_x and SO_x are particularly concerning due to their adverse health effects, associated with respiratory and cardiovascular diseases. Additionally, CO_2 emissions significantly contribute to global greenhouse gas emissions, exacerbating the issue of climate change. The scientific literature has explored various solutions to mitigate these impacts. Among these, the implementation of cold ironing (shore power supply) and the installation of exhaust gas cleaning systems, such as scrubbers, have been identified as effective technologies. However, the adoption of these solutions is uneven globally, influenced by economic and infrastructural factors. In the case study conducted at Ancona Harbour, the analysis focused on a period during the COVID-19 pandemic when a cruise ship carrying COVID-positive passengers was docked in the port for over a month (Central Adriatic Ports Authority, https://porto.ancona.it/). This period was compared with the average pollutant levels of SO_2, NO_x, and PM10 during the same timeframe in 2019. The results showed that during the 2020 hotelling, the average concentrations of NO_x were 63 µg/m^3, PM10 was 15 µg/m^3, and SO_2 was 4.5 µg/m^3. In contrast, during the same period in 2019, the average concentrations were significantly lower: NO_x at 25 µg/m^3, PM10 at 12 µg/m^3, and SO_2 at 2.5 µg/m^3. These findings indicate a substantial increase in pollutant levels during the prolonged hotelling of the cruise ship in 2020, underscoring the environmental impact of such events. The case highlights the critical need for implementing effective emission reduction strategies, particularly in scenarios involving extended docking periods.
Keywords: cruise ship emissions, hotelling, cold ironing, covid, lockdown.

1 INTRODUCTION

Urban ports present a significant challenge in terms of atmospheric pollution due to maritime activities taking place in densely populated areas. Cruise ships are among the main contributors to harmful emissions in ports, significantly increasing the concentration of nitrogen oxides (NO_x), sulphur oxides (SO_x), and fine particulate matter (PM10) [1], [2], substances known for their detrimental effects on both human health and the environment. Numerous studies have highlighted how maritime traffic and port operations are responsible for a substantial portion of atmospheric emissions in port cities, exacerbating existing air quality problems caused by other pollution sources such as road traffic and industrial activities [3]. Specifically, cruise ships emit large amounts of pollutants during the hotelling phase, when they remain docked with auxiliary engines running to power onboard systems, causing significant localised emission peaks [4].

The issue of emissions due to the hotelling phase has been widely documented. During docking, ships keep their auxiliary engines running to maintain vital systems, such as lighting, air conditioning, and hotel services, requiring fuel consumption that leads to continuous emissions. This phenomenon is particularly relevant in urban ports, where the proximity between the pier and residential areas directly exposes local populations to pollutants [5]. Further studies conducted in different European ports, showed that cruise ships contribute a substantial portion of the total SO_x and PM10 emissions in the urban area, significantly contributing to the exceedance of air quality limits set by European regulations [6], [7].

Another crucial aspect concerns European regulations on marine fuel quality, which have recently undergone significant revisions to improve air quality in port areas. Directive (EU) 2016/802 has set stricter limits on the sulphur content of fuels used by ships, reducing the maximum sulphur content to 0.50% by mass from 2020 for international waters, and further reduced to 0.10% for Emission Control Areas, such as the Mediterranean Sea (Marpol Annex VI, IMO, 2020). This measure has direct implications for the hotelling phase, as ships are required to use low-sulphur fuels while docked, significantly reducing SO_x emissions and helping to improve air quality in port surroundings. However, despite regulatory advancements, emissions from low-sulphur fuels do not eliminate the environmental impact of hotelling, as other pollutants, such as NO_x and particulate matter, continue to be emitted in significant quantities.

The Port of Ancona, located on Italy's Adriatic coast, serves as a crucial hub for commercial and passenger traffic, acting as a point of connection between Italy and numerous ports in Eastern Europe and the Mediterranean. With a long history as a mercantile port, Ancona has expanded in recent decades to include an increasing number of cruise ships, which now represent a significant component of the local economy. The port is located adjacent to the urban centre, with residential and commercial areas directly surrounding the docks (Fig. 1).

This proximity between the port and the city makes atmospheric pollution from port activities a central concern for the quality of life of Ancona's population [8]. The port infrastructure includes a network of air quality monitoring stations, with a specific focus on tracking pollutants such as NO_x, SO_2, and PM10, due to their relevance to public health and the obligation to comply with European air quality regulations.

During the lockdown imposed by the COVID-19 pandemic in 2020, global maritime traffic drastically decreased, with many ships remaining docked for extended periods without engaging in the usual loading and unloading operations. This exceptional scenario provided a unique opportunity to assess the impact of cruise ships in prolonged hotelling on atmospheric pollutant concentrations in port areas.

The objective of this study is to analyse how the prolonged docking of a cruise ship in hotelling mode at the Port of Ancona during the COVID-19 lockdown may have affected the air pollutant measurements recorded by an air quality monitoring station located near the port in an elevated position. In particular, the study will focus on the concentrations of NO_x, SO_2, and PM10, three of the most relevant pollutants for urban air quality and linked to naval emissions. The lockdown offered a unique context to isolate the impact of the cruise ship in hotelling mode, as many other industrial and vehicular traffic activities were minimised, allowing for a more accurate attribution of pollutant variations to the ship's activity. The data collected by the monitoring station during the extended docking period will be analysed and compared with the historical average values of the same pollutants in similar periods of previous year.

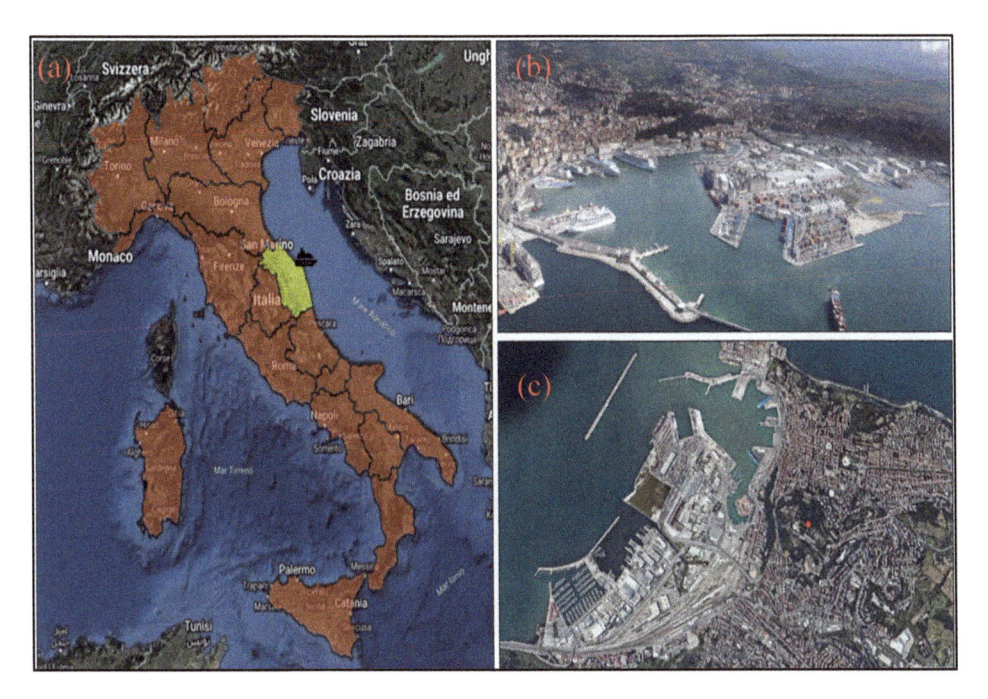

Figure 1: (a) Italy in orange, Marche region in yellow and Ancona Harbour is identified with a cruise ship icon; (b) Front view of Ancona Harbour; and (c) Aerial view of port, red pin denotes the position of measuring point.

This study is part of the broader discussion on strategies to reduce the environmental impact of ships in urban ports, with a particular focus on measures that can be implemented to minimise emissions during the hotelling phase, such as shore-side electricity (cold ironing) and the use of cleaner fuels. The results obtained may provide useful insights for local and national policies aimed at mitigating the effects of atmospheric pollution in ports and coastal cities, contributing to promoting more sustainable practices in the maritime sector.

2 METHODS

To evaluate NO_x, SO_2, and PM10 concentrations, data was collected from the Ancona-Cittadella urban monitoring station (ARPAM, https://aria.arpa.marche.it/), located about 1 km from the cruise ship dock. Italy's Phase 1 COVID-19 lockdown began on 9 March 2020, ending on 3 May 2020, followed by Phase 2 from 4 May to 14 June. The cruise ship, which docked on 28 April 2020, remained in 'hotelling' mode until 4 June with auxiliary engines running. Pollutant average concentrations were analysed for two periods: 9 March–27 April (hard lockdown, no cruise ship) and 28 April–4 June (partial lockdown, cruise ship present), compared with the same periods in 2019 (Table 1).

Table 1: Summary table with the characteristics of the periods analysed.

Periods	Date	Pollutants	Lockdown	Cruise ship hotelling
Period 1	9 March–27 April	NO_x–SO_2–PM10	Hard	No
Period 2	28 April–4 June	NO_x–SO_2–PM10	Partial	Yes

3 RESULTS

During the COVID-19 lockdown, various sources reported a positive impact on air quality due to the reduction in vehicular traffic and industrial activities. However, there was also an increase in domestic emissions, primarily due to the heightened use of heating systems and electricity as people were forced to stay at home. Several studies confirm this trend. For instance, a report by the European Environment Agency (EEA, https://www.eea.europa.eu/) highlighted that the drop in transport-related emissions was counterbalanced by a rise in emissions from residential heating systems during the lockdown. Furthermore, an analysis by ISPRA (Italian Institute for Environmental Protection and Research, https://www.isprambiente.gov.it/) noted that the demand for heating and energy use at home led to an increase in pollutants such as NO_x, PM10, and SO_2, particularly in urban areas with high population density.

The time series reported in Fig. 2, display the concentrations of PM10, NO_x, and SO_2 pollutants from 9 March to 4 June. A marked increase in concentrations is noted during Period 2 of 2020 compared to the same period in 2019. Preliminary analysis suggests that, on average, pollutant levels in 2020 are higher in both Period 1 and Period 2 (All periods) than those recorded in 2019, except for PM10, which shows a comparable trend.

Analysing the average concentrations of PM10 (Tables 2 and 3), it is immediately evident that the percentage variation in 2020 compared to 2019 is only −2.7%. Upon closer examination, it is noted that 2020 Period 1 shows a reduction of +8.7% compared to 2019 Period 1. Moreover, 2020 Period 2 shows a +28.6% reduction compared to 2020 Period 1. This decrease does not appear to be influenced by cruise ship extended hotelling but seems to be more affected by the reduced use of domestic heating systems, particularly biomass devices, due to the rise in spring temperatures.

Analysing the average concentrations of NO_x (Tables 2 and 3), it becomes immediately evident that the percentage variation in 2020 compared to 2019 is significant, reaching +111.9%. Specifically, the Period 1 in 2020 shows an increase of +104.2% compared to 2019 Period 1, with this upward trend intensifying in 2020 Period 2, which records a +152% rise compared to the same period in 2019. This increase may be attributed to the heightened use of domestic gas heating systems during the lockdown. Unlike PM10, there is no reduction in 2020 Period 2 due to the seasonal temperature rise. Additionally, 2020 Period 2 shows a +28.6% increase compared to 2020 Period 1, which, in this case, could be influenced by cruise ship extended hotelling.

The average concentration data of SO_2 (Tables 2 and 3) indicate a significant percentage increase of +51.9% in 2020 compared to 2019. A more detailed analysis shows that 2020 Period 1 experienced a +33.3% rise compared to 2019 Period 1, with the growth trend further intensifying in 2020 Period 2, showing an +80% increase over the same period in 2019. Additionally, 2020 Period 2 recorded a +12.5% increase compared to 2020 Period 1. This rise could be attributed to cruise ship hotelling. Given that SO_2 is a typical pollutant from combustion in ship engines, which use fuels containing sulphur, even in small percentages, this trend is particularly significant.

4 CONCLUSIONS

This study emphasises the significant impact of cruise ships on air quality, particularly during the hotelling phase, when ships are docked but continue to run their engines to power onboard systems. The data collected at the Port of Ancona during the COVID-19 lockdown demonstrate a clear increase in the concentrations of NO_x, SO_2 when a cruise ship was docked

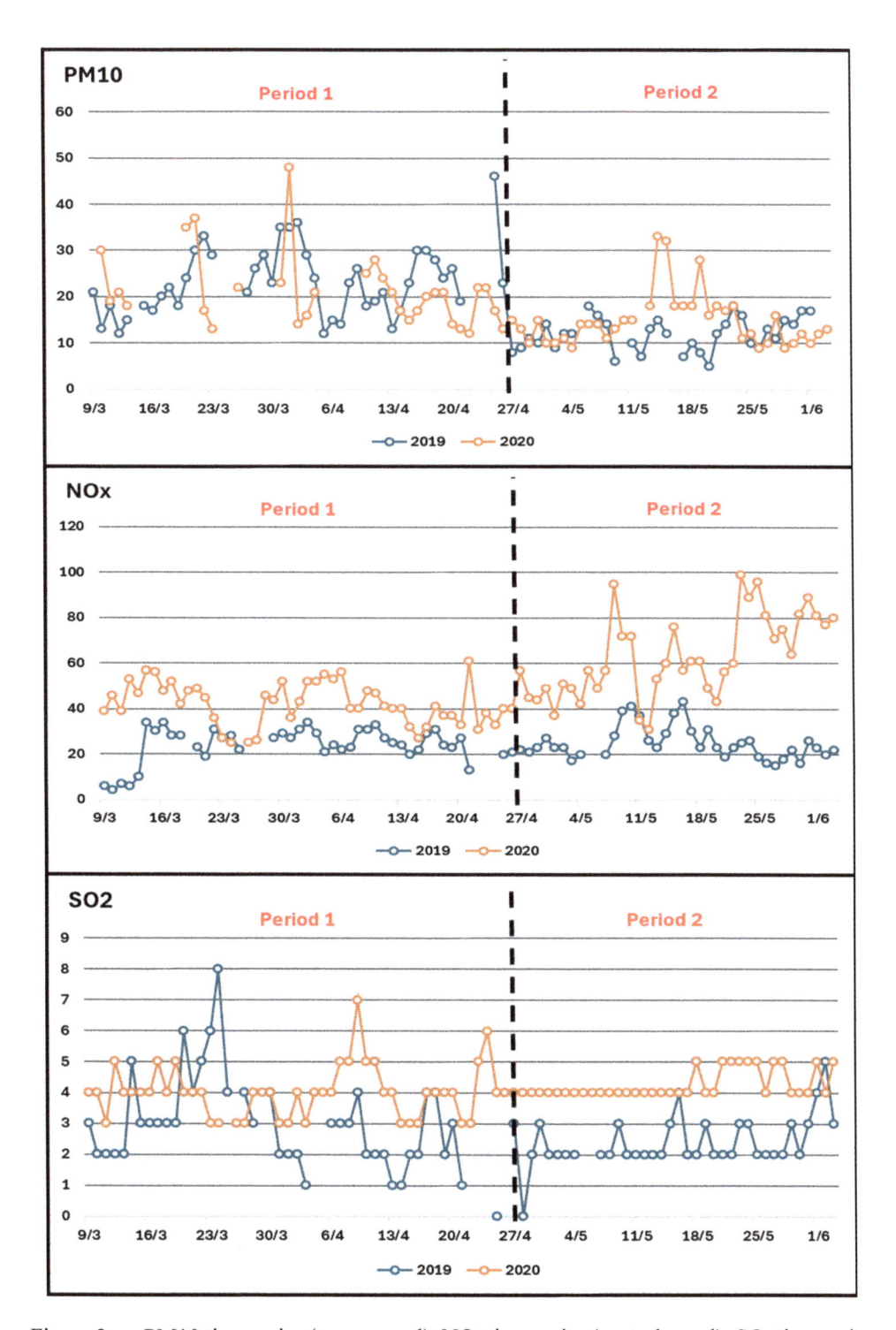

Figure 2: PM10 time series (upper panel); NO$_x$ time series (central panel); SO$_2$ time series (lower panel).

Table 2: Average concentration (AC) ($\mu g/m^3$) for each pollutant in different periods analysed.

	2019 AC Period 1	2019 AC Period 2	AC All periods 2019	2020 AC Period 1	2020 AC Period 2	AC All periods 2020
PM10	23	12	18.2	21	15	17.7
NO_x	24	25	24.3	49	63	51.5
SO_2	3	2.5	2.7	4	4.5	4.1

Table 3: Ratio (%) for each pollutant in different periods analysed.

Pollutant	Ratio % (2020 Period 1)/ (2019 Period 1)	Ratio % (2020 Period 2)/ (2019 Period 2)	Ratio % (2020 Period 1)/ (2020 Period 2)	Ratio % (ALL periods 2020)/ (ALL periods 2019)
PM10	−8.7	25	−28.6	−2.7
NO_x	104.2	152	28.6	111.9
SO_2	33.3	80	12.5	51.9

for an extended period. This highlights the pressing environmental challenge posed by the hotelling phase, particularly in urban ports, where the proximity to residential areas exacerbates the effects of emissions on local populations.

Cruise ships are equipped with large auxiliary engines that burn fossil fuels contributing significantly to the emission of pollutants such as nitrogen oxides (NO_x), sulphur oxides (SO_2), particulate matter (PM), and carbon dioxide (CO_2). These emissions have well-documented effects on public health, contributing to respiratory and cardiovascular diseases [3]. Furthermore, they contribute to the broader issue of climate change, with CO_2 being a major greenhouse gas [9].

One of the most effective strategies to mitigate emissions during the hotelling phase is the use of cold ironing, also known as shore-side power. This technology allows ships to connect to the local electrical grid while docked, enabling them to shut down their engines entirely. By switching to grid electricity, ships can reduce their emissions of NO_x, SO_2, and CO_2 to near-zero levels while in port, significantly improving local air quality [6].

However, despite its clear environmental benefits, the adoption of cold ironing remains limited due to several factors. First, the cost of retrofitting existing ships with the necessary infrastructure can be prohibitively high. Additionally, ports must invest in significant infrastructure upgrades to provide the necessary electrical power, which can be challenging in regions with limited resources or less stringent environmental regulations [10]. Moreover, the effectiveness of cold ironing depends on the cleanliness of the local electrical grid. In areas where the grid relies heavily on fossil fuels, the overall reduction in emissions may be less significant.

Despite these challenges, the increased awareness of maritime emissions and tightening environmental regulations, particularly in the European Union and Emission Control Areas, are likely to drive broader adoption of cold ironing and similar technologies. The results of this case study underscore the urgency of implementing such measures to reduce the environmental footprint of cruise ships, particularly in urban ports where the health and environmental impacts of emissions are most pronounced. As the global maritime industry moves toward more sustainable practices, cold ironing represents a critical tool in reducing emissions and protecting air quality.

REFERENCES

[1] Zis, T., North, R., Angeloudis, P., Ochieng, W. & Bell, M., Evaluation of cold ironing and speed reduction policies to reduce ship emissions near and at ports. *Maritime Economics and Logistics*, **16**(4), pp. 371–398, 2014.

[2] Saxe, H. & Larsen, T., Air pollution from ships in three Danish ports. *Atmospheric Environment*, **38**(24), pp. 4057–4067, 2004.

[3] Corbett, J.J., Winebrake, J.J., Green, E.H., Kasibhatla, P., Eyring, V. & Lauer, A., Mortality from ship emissions: A global assessment. *Environmental Science and Technology*, **41**(24), pp. 8512–8518, 2007.

[4] Pandolfi, M. et al., Source apportionment of PM10 and PM2.5 at multiple sites in the Strait of Gibraltar by PMF: Impact of shipping emissions. *Environmental Science and Pollution Research*, **18**(2), pp. 260–269, 2011.

[5] Murena, F., Mocerino, L., Quaranta, F. & Toscano, D., Impact on air quality of cruise ship emissions in Naples, Italy. *Atmospheric Environment*, **187**, pp. 70–83, 2018.

[6] Tzannatos, E., Ship emissions and their externalities for the port of Piraeus – Greece. *Atmospheric Environment*, **44**(3), pp. 400–407, 2010.

[7] Maragkogianni, A. & Papaefthimiou, S., Evaluating the social cost of cruise ships air emissions in major ports of Greece. *Transportation Research Part D: Transport and Environment*, **36**, pp. 10–17, 2015.

[8] Fileni, L., Mancinelli, E., Morichetti, M., Passerini, G., Rizza, U. & Virgili, S., Air pollution in Ancona harbour, Italy. *WIT Transactions on The Built Environment*, vol. 187, WIT Press: Southampton and Boston, pp. 199–208, 2019.

[9] Eyring, V., Köhler, H.W., Van Aardenne, J. & Lauer, A., Emissions from international shipping: 1. The last 50 years. *Journal of Geophysical Research: Atmospheres*, **110**(D17), 2005.

[10] Burel, F., Taccani, R. & Zuliani, N., Improving sustainability of maritime transport through utilization of liquefied natural gas (LNG) for propulsion. *Energy*, **57**, pp. 412–420, 2013.

GREEN DREAMS IN URBAN BORDERLAND: THE ECOTOURISM DEVELOPMENT TRANSFORMATION UNDER THE CONTEXT OF POLICY IN XISHUANGBANNA, YUNNAN PROVINCE, CHINA

MIN LIU & THANAPAUGE CHAMARATANA
Faculty of Humanities and Social Sciences, Khon Kaen University, Thailand

ABSTRACT

This research evaluates the current status of ecotourism development and proposes strategic measures for sustainable growth in border urban areas. The motivation behind this research stems from the region's rich biodiversity and cultural heritage, offering substantial potential for ecotourism, coupled with the strategic significance of Xishuangbanna as a key node in China's Belt and Road Initiative (BRI). The primary research question addresses how ecotourism can be effectively developed in this region, leveraging the opportunities and navigating the challenges presented by policy. Using a qualitative research approach, the study employs documentary research, observation and in-depth interviews with 20 key stakeholders, including local government officials, tourism operators, and community members. Content analysis is utilised to interpret the collected data, highlighting key themes and patterns related to ecotourism development. Findings indicate that Xishuangbanna possesses significant potential for ecotourism, attributed to its rich biodiversity, cultural heritage and strategic location along the BRI route. However, challenges such as inadequate infrastructure, limited community involvement and environmental concerns must be addressed. The study concludes with recommendations for enhancing ecotourism development in urban borderlands, emphasising the importance of integrated planning, stakeholder collaboration, and sustainable practices to ensure long-term benefits for the local community and the environment.
Keywords: ecotourism, sustainable tourism, urban tourism, sustainable development, policy.

1 INTRODUCTION

Urban areas worldwide are experiencing rapid growth and development, leading to significant environmental, social, and economic challenges. Tourism is a crucial tool for enhancing and supporting environmental conservation [1]. As cities expand, integrating ecotourism into urban planning emerges as a critical approach to achieving sustainable development goals. Urban ecotourism, which combines the principles of ecotourism with the unique characteristics and needs of urban environments, offers a pathway to promote sustainability while enhancing the quality of life for urban residents and visitors.

Ecotourism, traditionally associated with natural and rural areas, focuses on responsible travel to natural areas, conserving the environment, and improving the well-being of local communities [2]. The concept gained prominence in the late 20th century as a response to the negative impacts of mass tourism on natural and cultural resources. It was globally identified as a means of achieving biodiversity conservation and sustainable development [3]. Initially, ecotourism initiatives were primarily concentrated in remote and rural areas, where pristine environments and indigenous cultures could be showcased and preserved. However, as urbanisation intensifies, there is a growing recognition of the need to adapt ecotourism principles to urban settings. Urban ecotourism seeks to balance the demands of urban development with the preservation of natural and cultural resources, providing opportunities for environmental education, cultural exchange, and economic benefits [4].

Consequently, the growth of urban ecotourism is driven by the increasing appreciation of nature and heritage sites and the recognition of tourism's role in promoting environmental conservation and socio-economic benefits [5].

In China, the rise of ecotourism took root in the 1990s, evidenced by the designation of 'China Ecotourism Year' by the China National Tourism Administration in 1999 and the subsequent declaration of 'China Ecotourism Year' in 2009 [6]. The significance of ecotourism was further underscored in the 'Outline of the Thirteenth Five-Year Plan for National Economic and Social Development of the People's Republic of China' published in March 2016, where explicit support for the development of ecotourism was outlined. Furthermore, the central government's reiterated emphasis on the development of ecotourism, as highlighted in the annual government work reports, has emphasised the need to align ecological civilisation with economic, political, cultural, and social development. This enriched perspective aligns with the concept that 'Lucid waters and lush mountains are invaluable assets' and underscores the importance of both tourism development and the preservation of natural environments [7].

Xishuangbanna Dai Autonomous Prefecture, as the border urban area in China, is strategically positioned at the station of the Belt and Road initiatives land-based routes. Its proximity to Southeast Asia and its role as a major transportation hub makes it a linchpin in China's efforts to strengthen economic ties with neighbouring countries [8]. The region's rich biodiversity, cultural heritage, and strategic location offer substantial potential for ecotourism development. The integration of ecotourism into urban planning in Xishuangbanna provides a unique opportunity to balance urban growth with the conservation of natural and cultural resources.

The objective of this research is to explore the integration of ecotourism into urban planning, particularly in the urban borderlands. The study seeks to understand how urban ecotourism can balance urban development with the preservation of natural and cultural resources, promoting sustainability in rapidly growing urban areas within the context of policies and strategy in the borderlands.

2 METHODOLOGY

The study employs a qualitative research approach to deeply understand the context of ecotourism and the situation of tourism development in Xishuangbanna. Data collection methods include documentary research, in-depth interviews, and observation, with content analysis conducted using Atlas.ti software.

2.1 Research design

The research design is structured to generate knowledge about ecotourism in Xishuangbanna through a qualitative lens. The specific methods employed are documentary research, in-depth interviews and observation.

1. In the documentary research part, this research employs a systematic review of peer-reviewed journals, governmental reports, case studies published, and relevant policy documents between 2000 and 2024 to identify the situation of ecotourism development in urban borderlands. This documentary research provides a solid theoretical foundation and background to support and contrast the data gathered from in-depth interviews method and observation method.
2. In the in-depth interviews research part, interviews are conducted with 20 key informants selected through purposive sampling. These interviews focus on gathering in-depth

information about experiences and perspectives related to ecotourism development. While these perspectives are subjective, they offer valuable insights that, when compared with documentary research, can reveal meaningful patterns and themes [9].
3. In the observation research part, systematic field observations are employed in selected ecotourism areas to collect qualitative data on the ground realities of ecotourism practices and the environmental, socio-cultural context. These observations are recorded to supplement the insights gained from interviews and documentary research.

2.2 Key informants

To gain a comprehensive understanding of tourism and ecotourism development in Xishuangbanna, key informants are carefully selected from different sectors through purposive sampling [10]. According to Marshall [10] and Babbie [11] about the qualitative methodology and key informants criteria, the key informants are divided into three main sectors:

1. Community sector: informants include residents, five people who have lived near ecotourism sites for over 2 years; and a community leader, one person involved in ecotourism projects, because they have deeper insights into the long-term impacts of ecotourism on the community [12].
2. Government sector: informants comprise central government tourism official, one person with experience in national policy-making; and local government tourism bureaus, four people responsible for implementing tourism policies. Because central government officials provide insights into national tourism strategies, while local bureaus offer perspectives on the practical implementation and challenges of these policies at the local level [13].
3. Private sector: informants include tour operators, five people with at least 5 years of experience in providing diverse ecotourism experiences; as well as tourists, five people who have visited ecotourism sites multiple times. Experienced tour operators can offer insights into the evolving trends and best practices in ecotourism, while repeat tourists provide valuable feedback on the quality and sustainability of ecotourism experiences [14].

This selection ensures a multi-faceted view of the tourism ecosystem, with a total of 20 key informants.

2.3 Research area

Xishuangbanna Dai Autonomous Prefecture, located in Yunnan Province, China (see Fig. 1), is notable for its rich ethnic diversity and biological resources, making it an example of ecotourism destination within the Greater Mekong Subregion. As an autonomous prefecture, Xishuangbanna has the authority to preserve and promote local culture, making it an ideal location to study the integration of ecotourism into urban planning.

The region is known for its tropical rainforests, which are recognised as a UNESCO Man and Biosphere Reserve enhancing its appeal as an ecotourism destination. The ethnic minority communities, especially the Dai people, maintain cultural traditions and sustainable living practices linked to the natural environment.

As a border region, Xishuangbanna serves as a confluence for diverse cultural influences and cross-border dynamics, adding complexity to its ecotourism development. This study

Figure 1: Location of Xishuangbanna Dai Autonomous Prefecture in Yunnan Province, China.

selects Xishuangbanna to explore how ecotourism can support conservation efforts, promote cultural heritage, and stimulate local economies. The established ecotourism industry, coupled with ongoing development pressures, makes Xishuangbanna an ideal model for studying the balance required for sustainable ecotourism.

The population of Xishuangbanna is 1,196,000 people, covering an area of 19,124.5 km^2 [15]. The region comprises two counties (Menghai and Mengla) and one county-level city (Jinghong).

2.4 Data collection

The data collection process includes the following methods:

1. Documentary research, sourcing information from relevant governmental reports, and peer-reviewed journals about ecotourism development, between 2000 and 2024. By covering more than two decades, the research can identify long-term trends and patterns in urban ecotourism development.
2. In-depth interviews are conducted with 20 key informants from the community, government, and private sectors to extract qualitative data on their experiences and perceptions. The in-depth interviews were conducted over a period from December 2023 to May 2024 in Xishuangbanna, Yunnan Province, China.
3. Field observations are carried out in selected areas to collect qualitative data on the environmental conditions and socio-cultural practices related to ecotourism.

2.5 Data analysis

Content analysis is employed for the study. The data undergoes qualitative analysis using Atlas.ti software, which aids in coding the data, identifying themes, and drawing patterns and relationships from the information [16]. The findings from documentary research, interviews, and observations are triangulated to ensure reliability and validity.

3 CONTEXT OF TOURISM DEVELOPMENT IN THE URBAN BORDERLAND

Xishuangbanna, located in the southern part of Yunnan Province, is renowned for its rich ethnic culture and biodiversity. Historically, it has been the homeland of the Dai ethnic group, with a long-standing cultural tradition and a distinctive way of life [17]. As early as the 1980s, Xishuangbanna began attracting both domestic and international tourists, primarily due to its unique natural landscapes and minority cultures [18]. With the development of China's tourism industry, Xishuangbanna has gradually become an important tourist destination. The early development of tourism largely relied on the allure of its natural scenery and cultural attractions [19].

3.1 Historical background of tourism development in Xishuangbanna

Initially, in the 1960s, Xishuangbanna started to gain attention due to its unique tropical landscapes and cultural diversity. However, limited infrastructure and accessibility meant that early tourism was primarily limited to adventurous travellers and researchers [20].

The 1980s marked a turning point with the implementation of China's reform and opening-up policies. These policies led to significant improvements in transportation infrastructure, such as the construction of highways and airports, facilitating easier access to Xishuangbanna [18]. The establishment of the Xishuangbanna National Nature Reserve in 1986 highlighted the area's ecological importance, attracting ecotourists and researchers [21].

The 1990s and 2000s saw rapid expansion driven by further infrastructure developments and increased marketing efforts. The promotion of the region's natural and cultural attractions solidified Xishuangbanna's status as a major tourism destination in China [22]. During this period, large-scale rubber plantations were also established, significantly impacting the local ecosystems and the traditional agricultural practices of ethnic minorities [23].

The 2010s brought a focus on sustainable tourism, with efforts to balance development with environmental conservation [18]. Xishuangbanna has become a key destination for both domestic and international tourists, contributing significantly to the local economy. The integration of technology, such as digital tourism platforms and smart tourism initiatives, has further enhanced the visitor experience, making Xishuangbanna a modern hub for sustainable tourism [24].

For the timeline of tourism development in Xishuangbanna, see Fig. 2.

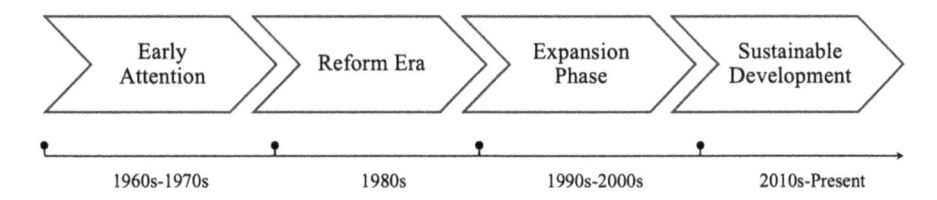

Figure 2: The timeline of tourism development in Xishuangbanna.

3.2 Current tourism landscape in Xishuangbanna

3.2.1 Theoretical information of current tourism landscape in Xishuangbanna

Xishuangbanna's tourism landscape is diverse and can be categorised into several main types of attractions (see Fig. 3): Natural attractions include the Xishuangbanna Tropical Botanical

Garden and the Wild Elephant Valley, which are renowned for their lush tropical rainforests and a wide variety of plant and animal species [19]. Cultural attractions feature the Dai Minority Park and the Manting Park [17], showcasing the unique cultural practices and traditional lifestyles of the Dai and other ethnic groups. Historical attractions are highlighted by the Xishuangbanna Primitive Forest Park and the Jinuo Ethnic Village, offering insights into the region's historical development and cultural evolution [18]. Ecotourism activities in the region encompass the scenic Nannuo Mountain Tea Plantation for hiking and the Bird Island for wildlife viewing, attracting nature enthusiasts from around the world. Modern amenities include luxury resorts like the Anantara Xishuangbanna Resort and the use of digital tourism platforms such as the Xishuangbanna Travel Guide app, enhancing the visitor experience by providing easy access to information and services [25]. This diverse array of attractions ensures that Xishuangbanna continues to be a popular destination for various types of tourists, from nature lovers to cultural enthusiasts.

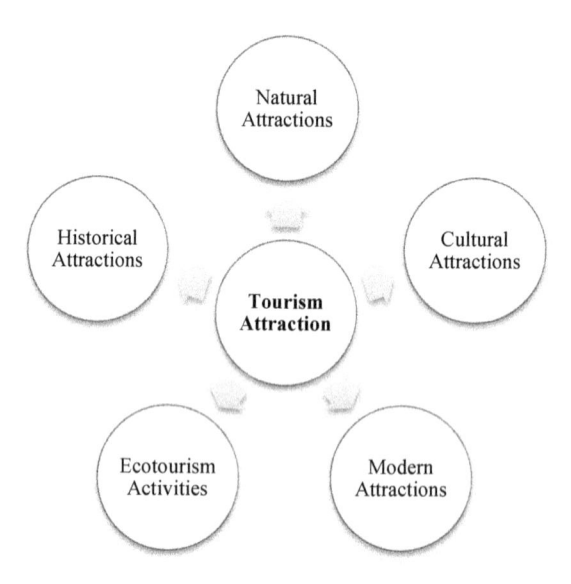

Figure 3: Current types of tourism attractions in Xishuangbanna.

Currently, tourism in Xishuangbanna primarily revolves around ecotourism and cultural tourism [26]. The region's tropical rainforests, rare flora and fauna, and unique Dai culture attract a large number of visitors. However, the rapid development of the tourism industry has also brought about several challenges, such as inadequate infrastructure and increased environmental pressure. Rapid mass tourism expansion often outpaces the development of essential infrastructure and leads to significant environmental degradation, including habitat loss, pollution, and resource depletion [27].

3.2.2 Perceptions from key informants about landscape in Xishuangbanna
Residents expressed a mix of satisfaction and concern regarding the current state of tourism. In terms of infrastructure, Xishuangbanna has made some progress, but further improvements are still needed. For instance, one resident mentioned, 'There have been some infrastructure improvements compared to before, but there are still many issues, such as the lack of public

restrooms and parking spaces. It's difficult to park when I want to go to the night market, I feel like I'm competing for territory with the tourists.' This comment underscores the persistent challenges in infrastructure, despite the region's popularity among tourists and expresses frustration over the competition for resources with tourists, particularly in crowded areas like the night market, where parking has become increasingly difficult. These perceptions highlight ongoing tensions between tourism growth and local needs. This indicates that while there have been advancements, more investment, and improvements are necessary to address these ongoing issues.

3.3 Policy in Xishuangbanna

The development of tourism in Xishuangbanna is supported and regulated by various policies aimed at promoting ecological tourism and sustainable development. As an important ecological tourism demonstration area, Xishuangbanna has received significant policy attention from the Chinese government. Policies are designed to balance economic development with environmental protection, ensuring the healthy growth of ecological tourism [27].

3.3.1 Local policy in Xishuangbanna
Local policies in Xishuangbanna focus on the preservation of cultural and natural resources while fostering community involvement in tourism activities. National policies emphasise sustainable development, aligning with broader environmental goals and promoting green tourism initiatives [28]. Locally, these provisions enforce conservation laws within the Xishuangbanna National Nature Reserve and introduce zoning laws to minimise environmental disruptions [29]. Additionally, they focus on empowering the community by funding local artisan cooperatives and establishing training centres that impart knowledge on hospitality and conservation practices [21].

3.3.2 National policy in Xishuangbanna
Nationally, the provisions prioritise environmental protection by banning single-use plastics in key tourist areas and advocating for renewable energy in hospitality facilities [30]. They also support sustainable development through incentives for businesses that achieve carbon neutrality and incorporate sustainable practices into national tourism recognition programmes.

3.3.3 International policy in Xishuangbanna
Internationally, Xishuangbanna benefits from China's Belt and Road Initiative (BRI), which enhances infrastructure, connectivity, and tourism opportunities through cross-border collaboration with neighbouring countries. The BRI plays a crucial role in Xishuangbanna's tourism landscape. By improving infrastructure and facilitating easier access, the BRI aims to boost tourism and economic development in the region [31]. The initiative encourages the development of new tourism routes and partnerships with countries along the Belt and Road, enhancing Xishuangbanna's attractiveness as a tourist destination.

3.3.4 Specific policy in Xishuangbanna
Specific policies include ecological tourism policies, the environmental protection regulations that enforce strict guidelines on waste management, pollution control, and conservation of natural habitats to minimise environmental impact [23]. Protected areas management policies establish and maintain protected areas, set the Xishuangbanna National Nature Reserve to conserve biodiversity and promote ecotourism. Sustainable development

policies include green tourism initiatives that promote eco-friendly tourism practices [28]. Sustainable infrastructure development policies invest in sustainable infrastructure projects that support tourism while reducing environmental degradation. Local community involvement policies include community-based tourism programmes that encourage local communities to participate in and benefit from tourism activities through training programmes and financial incentives [17]. Additionally, China's Five-Year Plans incorporate tourism development goals into the national Five-Year Plans, focusing on sustainable and inclusive growth. Tourism development plans develop specific tourism development plans that outline strategic priorities, investment areas, and regulatory frameworks [20].

Despite these policies, there are specific phenomena and negative impacts. Environmental degradation remains a significant issue as the rapid growth of tourism has led to deforestation, habitat loss, and pollution in some areas [32]. Cultural erosion is another concern, with the influx of tourists and commercialisation of cultural sites sometimes resulting in the erosion of traditional customs and practices. Economic disparities have emerged, as tourism has boosted the local economy but also led to rising living costs and income disparities, affecting the affordability of goods and services for local residents. Safety and management issues are highlighted by incidents like the falling accidents near the Lancang River, reflecting gaps in safety management and infrastructure maintenance.

4 ECOTOURISM DEVELOPMENT IN THE URBAN BORDERLAND

4.1 Ecotourism potential in Xishuangbanna

Xishuangbanna, with its rich natural and cultural resources, is an ideal location for ecotourism. Its tropical rainforests and biodiversity offer visitors a unique tourism experience, while the cultures of ethnic minorities such as the Dai add to the attraction [25]. As one government official stated, 'We hope to promote local economic development through ecotourism while protecting our natural resources.' Another local resident echoed this sentiment, saying, 'We hope more people will realise that "clear waters and green mountains are as valuable as gold and silver." The environment is very good now, with greenery everywhere. We hope tourists are attracted here but do not destroy our vegetation.'

The architectural style in Xishuangbanna also reflects the concept of ecotourism. In Meng Xing community, traditional stilted houses have been modernised while retaining their ecological features, using environmentally friendly materials in construction and showcasing the blend of ecology and culture. One interview excerpt mentioned, 'The third generation of stilted houses uses reinforced concrete but still retains the traditional design.'

4.2 Existing ecotourism initiatives in Xishuangbanna

Currently, Xishuangbanna has implemented a series of ecotourism initiatives (see Fig. 4), including the establishment of nature reserves and the promotion of ecotourism projects. According to local tourism practitioners, 'We have many environmental projects here, where tourists can participate in tree planting and wildlife protection activities.' These activities not only allow tourists to personally experience the importance of protecting the environment but also increase their engagement and satisfaction. As one scholar noted, 'Xishuangbanna's ecotourism projects not only attract a large number of tourists but also bring economic benefits to the local community.' This indicates that the implementation of ecotourism projects is beneficial not only for environmental protection but also for the economic development of the area.

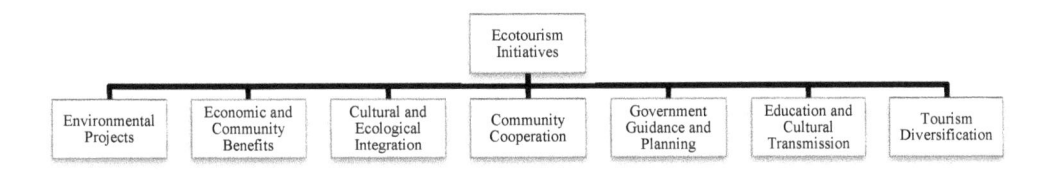

Figure 4: Existing ecotourism initiatives in Xishuangbanna.

In further interviews, local residents mentioned that although many tourism projects are led by external teams, local residents are gradually beginning to participate. For example, one resident stated, 'Local people rarely participate, but as ecotourism develops, more local residents are starting to get involved, boosting the local economy.' The involvement of local residents is also a crucial part of the development of ecotourism. Another resident noted, 'These ecotourism projects not only increase our income but also create job opportunities.' This active participation helps enhance the community's support and recognition of ecotourism, thereby promoting the sustainable development of the projects.

Xishuangbanna places a strong emphasis on the integration of culture and ecology in promoting ecotourism. One local remarked, 'When promoting ecotourism, we incorporate local cultural elements such as traditional dances and handicraft displays.' This approach not only attracts more tourists but also enhances cultural heritage and protection. Many tourism projects in Xishuangbanna adopt a community cooperation model, where residents jointly operate and share the profits. For instance, a tour guide mentioned, 'Residents here operate tourism projects collectively, and the income is distributed collectively.' This model not only fosters community cooperation but also improves overall management efficiency.

The government plays a pivotal role in the development of ecotourism. Certain villages in Xishuangbanna are designated as 'Centennial Villages' or 'Millennial Villages' and are protected and developed accordingly. This approach not only preserves the original landscape but also promotes tourism development. One interviewee noted, 'Through planning and regulation, the government designates villages with original landscapes as heritage sites and protects them accordingly.'

Xishuangbanna also emphasises education and cultural heritage. Schools and temples provide bilingual education to promote Dai culture. One interviewee mentioned, 'Our schools and temples offer bilingual education to protect and pass on Dai culture.' This educational model not only helps with cultural heritage but also improves residents' cultural literacy. The ecotourism in Xishuangbanna not only stresses ecological protection but also considers economic development. One interviewee noted, 'Tourism in Xishuangbanna primarily focuses on ecology, with cultural elements. In recent years, the government has vigorously developed the tourism industry, and infrastructure has gradually improved.' Achieving this dual goal helps improve local residents' living standards while protecting the natural environment.

4.3 Ecotourism impacts from environmental, socio-cultural, and economic dimensions in Xishuangbanna

While tourism has promoted economic development and cultural exchange, it has also introduced environmental pressures, cultural homogenisation, and income distribution disparities. Effective management and planning are crucial for achieving sustainable development in the tourism industry.

In the environmental dimension, ecotourism in Xishuangbanna has enhanced environmental awareness but also created environmental stress. Xishuangbanna boasts excellent ecological conditions, with a resident describing, 'Xishuangbanna is a place where one could grow a plant by just sticking a chopstick into the ground, indicating its excellent ecological environment.' However, despite its favourable natural environment, infrastructure shortcomings remain a significant issue. According to a local driver, 'The traffic planning within the scenic areas is chaotic, and tourists often complain about not being able to find their way.' These issues not only affect the visitor experience but also negatively impact the overall image of Xishuangbanna. A local doctor also pointed out, 'This is one of the few places in Yunnan with a relatively humid climate …. In recent years, the increase in tourists has led to a noticeable rise in population, causing traffic congestion and increased waste.' Another resident added, 'The traffic planning is inadequate, especially around scenic spots where roads are frequently congested. Despite the improved environmental awareness brought about by ecotourism, challenges remain. Although we strive to keep the environment clean, the management pressure is significant.' Additionally, some tourists have complained, 'Some areas in the scenic spots have unclear signage, causing tourists to get lost, which is also a management issue.'

In the socio-cultural dimension, ecotourism has facilitated cultural exchange but also led to the commercialisation and homogenisation of culture. A local resident remarked, 'Tourism is massively commercialising our own culture. I switched to being a driver because the government pushed for tourism development.' This suggests that tourism might alter local lifestyles, making them more commercialised. Furthermore, tourism has impacted the local cultural life. A local doctor observed, 'As the number of people increases, businesses need to make money, which causes price increases. Cultural conflicts have also increased …. There are more instances of tourists fighting with each other and with locals.' A tour guide added, 'Many tourists are very interested in Xishuangbanna's culture, such as the Dai matrilineal society. However, tourists' behaviour sometimes disrupts local culture, and there is an increase in Han cultural influences.' A community leader noted, 'We strive to preserve Dai culture through tourism, but commercialisation sometimes brings cultural impacts.' Additionally, some tourists mentioned, 'The development of tourism in some areas has lost its original charm and become more commercialised, which is not what I expected.' Additionally, there remain the lack of management problem. Key informants provided critical reflections on the efficacy of policies in Xishuangbanna. A local resident, Mr. Dong, noted, 'Last year, 2022, tourism here just recovered. Over there by the Lancang River, you see those signs? There used to be only three because someone fell into the river, and then it happened again, so now there are more signs.' This account illustrates ongoing challenges in safety management within the tourism sector. Additionally, a tourism bureau employee commented on the disconnect between policy and practice, stating, 'The initiatives are good, but the capabilities of the local government leadership are really limited. They fail to meet targets every year. I think the local government's practice level is still not enough.' This critique highlights the difficulties in local implementation of central government policies, despite their well-intentioned design.

In the economic dimension, ecotourism is a crucial economic pillar for the region but has also led to issues of income inequality. One resident stated, 'If you are not involved in tourism, there are not many other industries here. Rubber production seems unfeasible, and fruit farming is even less viable.' Additionally, it has been noted that 'Local participation in ecotourism development is minimal, with most operations handled by outsiders.' This reflects a problem where, despite the economic benefits brought by tourism, locals are unable to fully participate and benefit. An interviewee described the shift in Xishuangbanna's industrial structure, 'Xishuangbanna has traditionally relied on sugar, rubber, and tea as its economic pillars. Now, the order has reversed because tea culture has become a major attraction for ecotourism,' illustrating the impact of changing economic pillars on local industries. A local doctor further mentioned, 'Prices in this place are also rising …. There are more conflicts between people due to cultural collisions and economic competition.' A driver added, 'After tourism development, there are more tourists, but local people benefit very little. Most of the operations and profits are controlled by outsiders. The government should intervene to allow locals to participate and enjoy the benefits of tourism.' A tour guide noted, 'The development of tourism in Xishuangbanna has brought significant economic income, particularly with the promotion of small cooperative models, which has increased village income. However, issues of unfair distribution remain, especially during peak tourist seasons when hotel prices soar, leading to dissatisfaction among both tourists and locals.' Community leaders also pointed out, 'We have boosted village economies through tourism, but issues of distribution still exist and require a fairer mechanism.' Moreover, some tourists noted, 'Although tourism has brought economic development, it has also made locals increasingly dependent on tourism, lacking other economic sources.'

4.4 Existing ecotourism challenges and opportunities

Ecotourism in Xishuangbanna, while promoting economic development and cultural exchange, has also brought about several challenges. Environmental pressures are a significant issue, as the influx of tourists has led to traffic congestion, waste management problems, and infrastructure development that disrupts natural habitats. Socially, ecotourism has facilitated cultural exchange but also caused cultural commercialisation and conflicts. The traditional lifestyle of locals is being altered, and there are rising instances of cultural conflicts between tourists and residents. Despite efforts to preserve and promote Dai culture, commercialisation has diluted some of the cultural authenticity. Economically, while tourism has become a crucial pillar, it has also highlighted income disparities. Many locals are not fully benefiting from the tourism boom, with much of the industry controlled by outsiders. The rising cost of living and economic reliance on tourism are growing concerns. Despite these challenges, ecotourism presents significant opportunities for sustainable development. By addressing environmental, social, and economic issues through effective management and planning, Xishuangbanna can enhance its ecotourism model to benefit both its residents and the natural environment.

5 RECOMMENDATIONS FOR THE ECOTOURISM DEVELOPMENT IN URBAN BORDERLAND UNDER THE CONTEXT OF POLICY

To ensure the sustainable development of ecotourism in Xishuangbanna, the following measures need to be implemented:

- Improve the quality of tourism infrastructure, especially transportation and sanitation facilities, to enhance the residents and visitor experience.
- Encourage and support local community participation in tourism to ensure they benefit from tourism development.
- Promote green tourism certification and eco-labels, encouraging tourism businesses to adopt sustainable practices.

- Support and fund cultural activities and traditional crafts to avoid cultural commodification and preserve their original value.
- Leverage the Belt and Road Initiative and the construction of the China-Laos Railway to actively pursue international tourism cooperation, attracting more international tourists.
- Strengthen cooperation with neighbouring countries in ecological protection and tourism development to jointly promote regional sustainable development.

Xishuangbanna is poised to become a global model for ecotourism development in urban borderlands, achieving harmonious economic, social, and environmental development, and providing valuable experiences and lessons for other regions. As a local official stated, 'The future of Xishuangbanna is full of hope. As long as we adhere to the path of sustainable development, we can certainly realise the beautiful vision of ecotourism.'

6 CONCLUSIONS

Through the study of ecotourism development in Xishuangbanna, it is evident that despite numerous challenges, the region has tremendous potential for ecotourism development due to its unique natural and cultural resources. Government, businesses, and communities need to strengthen cooperation to address the environmental and social issues brought about by tourism development and to promote sustainable ecotourism. Community participation is crucial in ecotourism, but development activities must be carefully managed to avoid negatively impacting the community's way of life. Furthermore, in developing ecotourism in urban borderlands, it is essential to focus on cultural heritage preservation to prevent the cultural homogenisation that often accompanies over-commercialisation. Culture is a significant asset, and it is crucial to protect cultural heritage while promoting tourism development. In conclusion, urban borderlands unique position and resources present a valuable opportunity for establishing a sustainable ecotourism.

ACKNOWLEDGEMENTS

This paper constitutes a significant part of the doctoral dissertation in the Development Science programme, Faculty of Humanities and Social Sciences, Khon Kaen University, Thailand, entitled 'Ecotourism Development in the Border Urban Areas of the Greater Mekong Subregion within the Context of China's Belt and Road Initiative.'

REFERENCES

[1] Baruah, P., Potential of urban wetlands for ecotourism development: A case of Deepor Beel, Guwahati. *NEPT*, **19**(2), pp. 611–625, 2020. https://doi.org/10.46488/NEPT.2020.v19i02.016.

[2] Reimer, J.K. & Walter, P., How do you know it when you see it? Community-based ecotourism in the Cardamom Mountains of southwestern Cambodia. *Tourism Management*, **34**, pp. 122–132, 2013. https://doi.org/10.1016/j.tourman.2012.04.002.

[3] Aversa, R. et al., Modern transportation and photovoltaic energy for urban ecotourism. *TRAS*, Special Issue, pp. 5–20, 2017. https://doi.org/10.24193/tras.SI2017.1.

[4] Cheshmehzangi, A. et al., From eco-urbanism to eco-fusion: An augmented multi-scalar framework in sustainable urbanism. *Sustainability*, **13**(4), 2373, 2021. https://doi.org/10.3390/su13042373.

[5] Antweiler, C., Urbanization and urban environments. *The International Encyclopedia of Anthropology*, 1st ed., ed. H. Callan, Wiley, pp. 1–10, 2008. https://doi.org/10.1002/9781118924396.wbiea1585.

[6] De Jong, M., From eco-civilization to city branding: A neo-Marxist perspective of sustainable urbanization in China. *Sustainability*, **11**(20), 5608, 2019. https://doi.org/10.3390/su11205608.

[7] Busbarat, P., Bunyavejchewin, P. & Suporn, T., China and Mekong regionalism: A reappraisal of the formation of Lancang-Mekong cooperation. *Asian Politics and Policy*, **13**(2), pp. 193–211, 2021. https://doi.org/10.1111/aspp.12575.

[8] Yang, G., Gong, G., Luo, Y., Yang, Y. & Gui, Q., Spatiotemporal characteristics and influencing factors of tourism–urbanization–technology–ecological environment on the Yunnan–Guizhou–Sichuan region: An uncoordinated coupling perspective. *IJERPH*, **19**(14), 8885, 2022. https://doi.org/10.3390/ijerph19148885.

[9] Thomas, J. & Harden, A., Methods for the thematic synthesis of qualitative research in systematic reviews. *BMC Med. Res. Methodol.*, **8**(1), p. 45, 2008. https://doi.org/10.1186/1471-2288-8-45.

[10] Marshall, M.N., Sampling for qualitative research. *Family Practice*, **13**(6), pp. 522–526, 1996.

[11] Babbie, E.R., *The Practice of Social Research*, 12th ed., Wadsworth Cengage: Belmont, CA, 2010.

[12] Álvarez-García, J., Durán-Sánchez, A. & Del Río-Rama, M., Scientific coverage in community-based tourism: Sustainable tourism and strategy for social development. *Sustainability*, **10**(4), 1158, 2018. https://doi.org/10.3390/su10041158.

[13] Palmer, N.J. & Chuamuangphan, N., Governance and local participation in ecotourism: Community-level ecotourism stakeholders in Chiang Rai province, Thailand. *Journal of Ecotourism*, **17**(3), pp. 320–337, 2018. https://doi.org/10.1080/14724049.2018.1502248.

[14] Larhsoukanh, S. & Wang, C., Public–private partnership in land compensation for an eco-cultural park: Game theoretical analysis. Presented at the *SDP 2018*, Siena, Italy, Sep. 2018, pp. 459–467. https://doi.org/10.2495/SDP180411.

[15] Yang, M., Van Coillie, F., Liu, M., De Wulf, R., Hens, L. & Ou, X., A GIS approach to estimating tourists' off-road use in a mountainous protected area of northwest Yunnan, China. *Mountain Research and Development*, **34**(2), pp. 107–117, 2014. https://doi.org/10.1659/MRD-JOURNAL-D-13-00041.1.

[16] Asian Development Bank, *Greater Mekong Subregion Atlas of the Environment*, 2nd ed., ADB: Manila, 2012.

[17] Shen, S. et al., Agrobiodiversity and in situ conservation in ethnic minority communities of Xishuangbanna in Yunnan Province, Southwest China. *J. Ethnobiology Ethnomedicine*, **13**(1), p. 28, 2017. https://doi.org/10.1186/s13002-017-0158-7.

[18] Liu, Y., Xu, W., Hong, Z., Wang, L., Ou, G. & Lu, N., Assessment of spatial-temporal changes of landscape ecological risk in Xishuangbanna, China from 1990 to 2019. *Sustainability*, **14**(17), 10645, 2022. https://doi.org/10.3390/su141710645.

[19] Du, Y., Chen, J. & Xie, Y., The impacts of the Asian elephants damage on farmer's livelihood strategies in Pu'er and Xishuangbanna in China. *Sustainability*, **15**(6), 5033, 2023. https://doi.org/10.3390/su15065033.

[20] Jin, Y., Liu, Y., Liu, J. & Zhang, X., Energy balance closure problem over a tropical seasonal rainforest in Xishuangbanna, southwest China: Role of latent heat flux. *Water*, **14**(3), p. 395, 2022. https://doi.org/10.3390/w14030395.

[21] Jianchu, X., The political, social, and ecological transformation of a landscape: The case of rubber in Xishuangbanna, China. *Mountain Research and Development*, **26**(3), pp. 254–262, 2006.
https://doi.org/10.1659/0276-4741(2006)26[254:TPSAET]2.0.CO;2.

[22] Ling, Z. et al., Estimation of applicability of soil model for rubber (*Hevea brasiliensis*) plantations in Xishuangbanna, southwest China. *Water*, **14**(3), p. 295, 2022.
https://doi.org/10.3390/w14030295.

[23] Wen, Z., Li, X. & Li, T., Comprehensive study on freshwater ecosystem health of Lancang river basin in Xishuangbanna of China. *Water*, **12**(6), 1716, 2020.
https://doi.org/10.3390/w12061716.

[24] Yang, Y., Bai, K., Li, G., Jarvis, D.I. & Long, C., Assessment of the resilience in SEPLS (socio-ecological production landscapes and seascapes) in Yanuo Village, Xishuangbanna, southwest China. *Sustainability*, **12**(9), 3774, 2020.
https://doi.org/10.3390/su12093774.

[25] Xiong, Q., Sun, Z., Cui, W., Lei, J., Fu, X. & Wu, L., A study on sensitivities of tropical forest GPP responding to the characteristics of drought: A case study in Xishuangbanna, China. *Water*, **14**(2), p. 157, 2022.
https://doi.org/10.3390/w14020157.

[26] Shi, Y., Hu, H., Xu, Y. & Liu, A., An ethnobotanical study of the less known wild edible figs (genus Ficus) native to Xishuangbanna, southwest China. *J. Ethnobiology Ethnomedicine*, **10**(1), p. 68, 2014. https://doi.org/10.1186/1746-4269-10-68.

[27] Yan, M. et al., Construction of the ecological security pattern in Xishuangbanna tropical rainforest based on circuit theory. *Sustainability*, **16**(8), 3290, 2024.
https://doi.org/10.3390/su16083290.

[28] Corne, P. & Zhu, V., Ecological civilization and dispute resolution in the BRI. *Chin. J. Environ. Law*, **4**(2), pp. 200–216, 2020.
https://doi.org/10.1163/24686042-12340058.

[29] Yan, Z. et al., Spatio-temporal variations and socio-economic driving forces for wetland area changes: Insights from 2008–2017 data of Yunnan Province, China. *Water*, **14**(11), 1790, 2022. https://doi.org/10.3390/w14111790.

[30] Liu, X., Zhang, S. & Ji, M., Mobility dilemmas: Conflict analysis of road constructions in a Tibetan tourism community in China. *Journal of Sustainable Tourism*, **28**(2), pp. 284–304, 2020. https://doi.org/10.1080/09669582.2019.1665055.

[31] Lu, M., Corporate environmental responsibility: Another road to achieve ecological civilization and green BRI. *Chin. J. Environ. Law*, **4**(2), pp. 182–199, 2020.
https://doi.org/10.1163/24686042-12340057.

[32] Sattar, A., Hussain, M.N. & Ilyas, M., An impact evaluation of Belt and Road Initiative (BRI) on environmental degradation. *SAGE Open*, **12**(1), 215824402210788, 2022.
https://doi.org/10.1177/21582440221078836.

INTEGRATED COASTAL MANAGEMENT IN EMERGING TOURIST DESTINATIONS ON THE MEXICAN CARIBBEAN COAST

MÓNICA ARIADNA CHARGOY ROSAS[1*], ÓSCAR FRAUSTO MARTÍNEZ[1†]
& JOSÉ ALFREDO CABRERA HERNÁNDEZ[2‡]
[1]Universidad Autónoma del Estado de Quintana Roo, México
[2]Universidad de Matanzas, Cuba

ABSTRACT

Mexico's Caribbean coast is known for its large tourist centres, such as Cancun, Playa del Carmen and Tulum. In 2023, they generated revenues of more than $20.5 billion, continuously recovering after the COVID-19 pandemic. As a result of new regional development policies (for example, investment in infrastructure such as the Tulum airport and the Mayan Train), the model of expansion of tourist activity along the entire coast continues. The main goal of this study is to present the progress in identifying the key issues and actors described in the State Coastal Policy to recognise areas of opportunity and advance their application at the local level. To do this, we identified key issues (opportunities and threats) by examining the institutional instruments of coastal policy. The results show 11 central themes, 19 focal topics and four key issues: (a) urbanisation and provision of services; (b) integrative vision with diverse actors; (c) environmental or ecosystem connectivity; and (d) management of government agencies. We concluded that these critical issues build the strategies and actions necessary for adopting integrated coastal management in the southern Mexican Caribbean.
Keywords: policy, sustainable development, tourism, integrated diagnostics.

1 INTRODUCTION

The Caribbean coast of Mexico is known for its large tourist centres such as Cancun, The Riviera Maya (from Playa del Carmen to Tulum), Cozumel and Isla Mujeres. Despite the challenges posed by the COVID pandemic, the tourism industry has shown remarkable resilience, with revenues continuously recovering. In 2020, the tourism destinations generated revenues of more than 15.4 billion dollars and closed the year 2023 with revenues over $20.5 billion [1].

In Mexico, there is a broad regulatory and institutional framework related to the sustainable management of the country's seas and coastal resources. According to Rivera-Arriaga and Azuz-Adeath [2], there are 14 institutions under the Intergovernmental Commission for the Sustainable Management of the Coasts and Seas of Mexico (CIMARES). Each of these institutions, including those represented by our audience, plays a crucial role in addressing the different issues related to the governance of the coastal zone, conferring to the competencies of each institution member.

In the National Policy of Seas and Coasts of Mexico, Quintana Roo is identified as one of the coastal states of the country bordering the Caribbean Sea, thus known as the Mexican Caribbean (Fig. 1). Othón P. Blanco is the southern coastal municipality of the Mexican Caribbean, bordering Central America through Belize, ranked as the third municipality in the state with the most significant number of inhabitants (233,648) according to INEGI [3].

---

*ORCID: https://orcid.org/0000-0001-8849-2545
†ORCID: https://orcid.org/0000-0002-6610-5193
‡ORCID: https://orcid.org/0000-0002-2723-3619

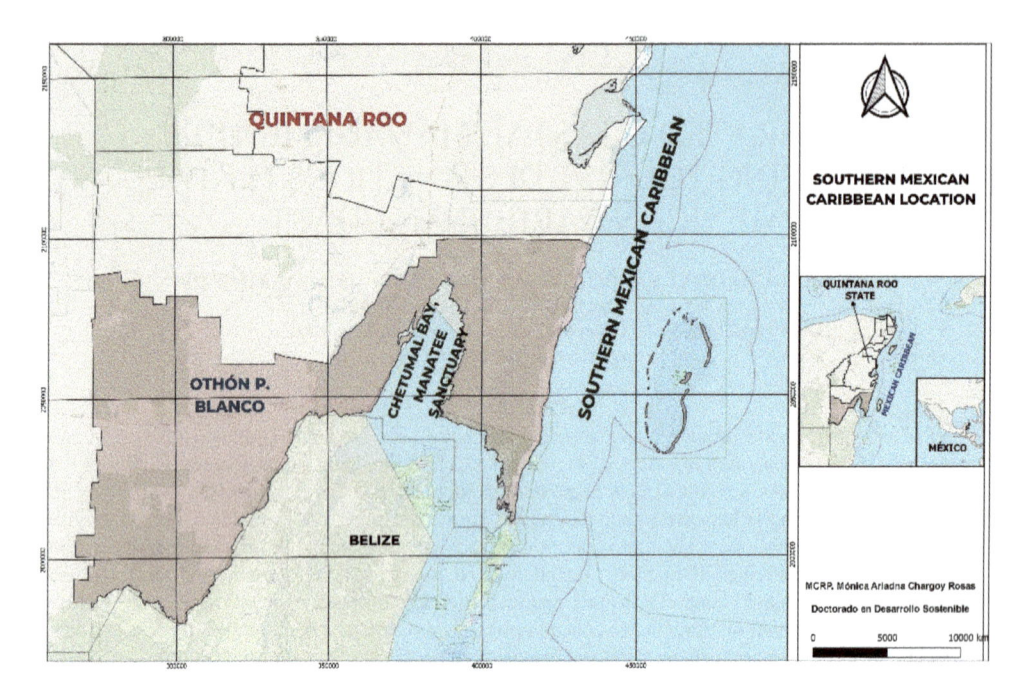

Figure 1: Map of the Southern Mexican Caribbean location at Quintana Roo State.

2 THEORETICAL FRAMEWORK

As part of the scope of Agenda 21, the Integrated Coastal Management (MIC) was presented at the Conference on Development and Environment in Rio 1992 as the most promising means to move towards more sustainable human activity on the coasts. However, the challenges are political, as much or more than technical and scientific. The MIC must be transparent and convincing that a set of explicit values constitutes the basis for practice [4].

Integrated Coastal Zone Management (MIZC) is a dynamic and continuous, multifactorial, and complex process [5]–[7]. It is relevant to identify its spatial and temporal scales, as well as the different levels of analysis and dimensions that compose it, as a way of 'establishing the most urgent areas of attention with regard to the spatial and temporal adequacy of inputs and needs among the different actors involved' [8].

In Mexico, the development of coastal areas is relatively recent; according to Rivera-Arriaga et al. [7], it was from the sun and beach industry that coastal paradises such as Acapulco, Cancun or Los Cabos were revealed to the world. However, coastal zone management is even more recent and less common since it is understood as a regional planning task, similar in perspective to marine and coastal ecological arrangements. According to the authors, some issues that need to be addressed in coastal areas in Mexico are:

1. The capacities of local governments are constructed by inequitable decentralisation processes.
2. Planning instruments are underutilised for decision-making.
3. The bases of the areas under legal or illegal use are poor, and the income generated should be adequately labelled so that it is used for environmental and development purposes.

4. Participation is required to be expressed as effective involvement in the decision-making process with co-responsibility for implementing control and surveillance measures that can replace the passive reception of information on the environmental challenges of coastal areas.
5. The MIZC in Mexico is based on a legal structure that needs to be strengthened in its financial and operational capacity.
6. An integrated coastal management perspective is required. Ecosystem-based management of mangrove wetlands, coral reefs, seagrasses, and coastal dune systems, among other coastal natural ecosystems, is necessary to reduce their vulnerability and increase their resilience to the effects of climate change.

Although Mexico has a broad regulatory and institutional framework related to the sustainable management of the country's seas and coastal resources [9], regional or state indicators (for example, territorial regulations, risk atlases, and fisheries management plans) continue to be replicated for the coastal zone. This continues to inform general situations but does not report progress or setbacks in the context of the sustainability of the municipalities and their localities.

Vázquez Sosa et al. [10] indicate that the challenge to face is the transition from the elaboration of characterisations and diagnoses of coastal ecosystems and conflicts to the formation and implementation of MIZC programs, particularly at the local level, agreed with governments and authorities, and above all with broad participation of all the actors involved. Through a comparative critical analysis of different models for the implementation of the MIZC, the authors oriented the work towards the elaboration of a proposal for its implementation in Akumal, located in the middle of the Mexican Caribbean Coast. Conclusions indicate that the adoption of a model based on the methodological conceptions of Olsen–ECOCOSTAS–LOICZ, combined with the methodology of Barragan's *Decalogue*, would serve as an initial framework for multiscale MIZC analysis, as a convenient condition for moving towards a local approach to MIZC.

Quintana Roo, the only state bordering the Mexican Caribbean, published on August 26, 2022, the 'Política de Costas del Estado de Quintana Roo' (Coastal Policy of the State of Quintana Roo, referred to henceforward as Coastal Policy or Policy). With this, it became the first state at the national level to have an instrument aligned with the National Policy of the Seas and Coasts. By presenting itself as the first state in the country to have a coastal policy, it became a pioneer and example for the rest of the states with coastal zones. Such achievement also becomes a challenge to ensure the success of its implementation.; with the added pressure of being the number one state nationally in coastal tourism visits, generating an economic spill of over $15,400 million, according to SEDETUR data for 2020 [11].

Given this situation, the need arises to analyse this Policy within the Integrated Coastal Zone Management framework and find areas of opportunity to advance in its application at the local (municipal) level. This document aims to answer the following questions: What are the key issues, problems, trends, and conflicts found and defined in Quintana Roo State's Coastal Policy Southern Mexican Caribbean? Who are the identified actors and stakeholders? How to build the strategies and actions necessary for implementing integrated coastal management in emerging tourism destinations in the southern Mexican Caribbean?

The objective is to identify the key issues and actors described in Coastal Policy for the Southern Mexican Caribbean to design strategies and actions necessary to implement integrated coastal management programs in emerging tourism destinations in the region.

3 METHODOLOGY

The research was developed using qualitative research methods and techniques in two stages. The first stage consisted of the review of secondary sources to define the state of the art. For this, various sources were used, such as indexed and refereed articles, as well as books and book chapters. These were obtained through searches in electronic databases and internet search engines using keywords. In the same way, the information on the Internet pages of official institutions was reviewed and used, registering all the sources for inclusion in the bibliography. The literature review focused on the topics of integrated coastal management, sustainable development, and publications on the Mexican Caribbean particularly the southern localities and emerging tourism destinations. In this first stage, different working meetings were attended, with the German cooperation agency (GIZ) and institutions of the three levels of government as participating observers. There was also attendance at the presentation event of the Coastal Policy and the installation of the Intersectoral State Commission for Sustainable Coastal Management as an observer.

For the second stage of this work, the methodology proposed by Olsen and Ochoa [12] was used, particularly regarding the identification and evaluation of key issues. These are understood as the problems or opportunities on which action is going to be taken and are better visualised when it is possible to graph the expected changes in a trend or opportunity on which you want to act.

In this methodology, five sections correspond each to a step in the coastal management cycle. Each section is subdivided into topics, and for each of these, a series of questions are identified, and each question focuses on some aspect associated with what is known as best practices [6]. For the identification and evaluation of key issues, Olsen and Ochoa [12] indicate that management issues are at the heart of the design of a management effort: the goals, the identification of key actors, the extension of the field of action, the delimitation of the context, the characteristics of the governance system, etc. depend on the management issues (Fig. 2).

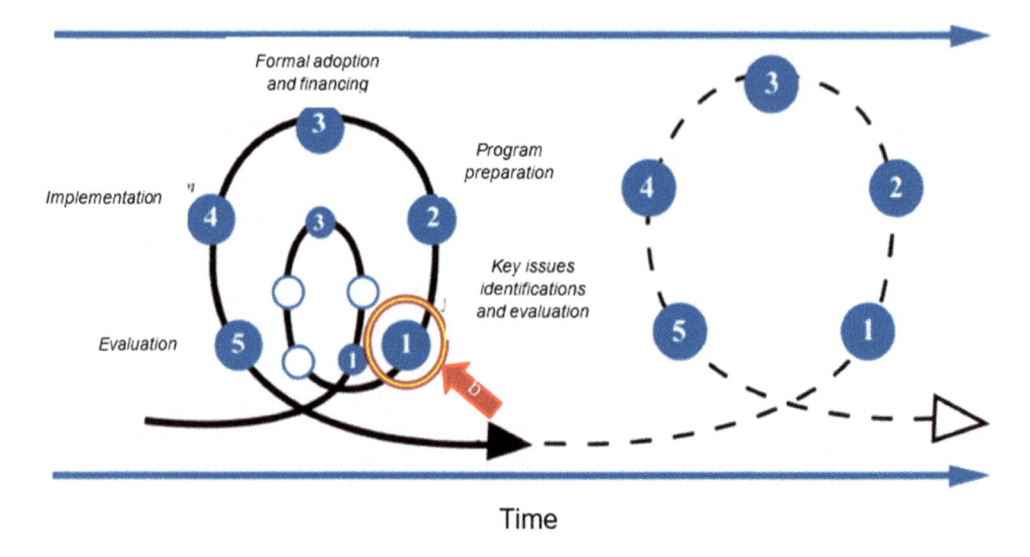

Figure 2: Stage of identification and evaluation of key actors within the sequence of stages along each successive cycle of an integrated coastal zone management programme. *(Source: Adapted from GESAMP, 1996; Olsen, et al. [6].)*

The identification and evaluation of crucial issues require the following essential actions [6]:

a. Identify and assess critical environmental, social, and institutional issues and their implications.
b. Identify the main actors and their interests.
c. Verify feasibility and governmental and non-governmental leadership on selected issues.
d. Select the issues on which the management initiative will focus its efforts.
e. Define the goals of the MC initiative.

The activities listed above are implemented as an external evaluation, in which the questions form a frame of reference for discussions that lead to recommendations [6]. These questions were transcribed in a guide to structure and answer through a critical review of the publication of the Coastal Policy in the Official Newspaper of the State of Quintana Roo on 26 August 2022. To identify the following key issues, understand these as '...the problems or critical situations to be solved, potentialities and aspects that stand out of interest for the development of the future scenario that has been raised' [13]. Below are the results.

4 RESULTS

In this first stage, the environmental, social, and institutional issues are described as the basis of the Coastal Policy published in the Official Gazette. Through the critical analysis of contents, the problems identified for each theme and the defined actors. The initiative is divided into 11 main themes. These themes lay the basis for the definition of the problem and the key issues. Tables 1–3 present the main themes and problems described in the Coastal Policy Decree, organised by socio-environmental, environmental, institutional, legal, governance, and planning themes and problems.

Although all the themes and problems described in the previous table are presented within the Coastal Policy, it is from the Policy's Integrated Diagnosis that the following key issues could be identified:

1. There are essential delays regarding the development of (a) Basic housing services; (b) Adequate urbanisation (streets and public services); (c) proper land use in areas with highly fragile ecosystems and natural resources.
2. Regulation enforcement often faces deficiencies, mainly due to legal and administrative gaps or overlaps between the three levels of government.
3. Institutions regularly act under a sectorial vision instead of synergic or comprehensive, resulting in a lack of inter-sectorial coordination and a lack of comprehensive vision that incorporates the participation of interdisciplinary actors linked to academia and society.
4. Regarding project implementation, private interest usually comes before common interest and short-term investments are privileged over long-term investments.
5. Technical and scientific information is either lacking or limited in availability in planning or decision-making.
6. There is a lack of continuity, capacities, or performance in the human resources of the government agencies responsible for territorial management, resulting in effective governance with institutional leadership.
7. Coordination of actions in the Caribbean Sea and its connectivity to the Gulf of Mexico and the Atlantic Sea.
8. Environmental or ecosystem connectivity as a basis for coastal planning.

Table 1: Socio-environmental themes and problems described in the Coastal Policy Decree.

Themes	Problems
Trends in the coast	Socio-territorial conflicts
	Disorderly urbanisation
	Deterioration of coastal ecosystems
	Tourism activities
	Contamination of soils, aquifers, and sea
	Agriculture with the use of agrochemicals
	Loss of biodiversity
	Loss of environmental services
	Forest fires
	Land use change
Environmental current features and trends	Deforestation processes, causes, and effects
	Pollution: Surface and groundwater quality (causes)
	Agrochemicals and pig farming
	Sunscreen pollution
	Pollution and affectation from maritime transport
	Contamination by black water and runoff by waterproofing
	Municipal solid waste
	Saline intrusion
	Sargasso
Oceanographic dynamics and their socio-environmental influence	Direct impacts on fishery resources and ecosystem services
	Facilitate intensive fishing
	Projected temperature increase by 2050 of up to 2°C
	Planning processes should aim to reduce precipitation caused by torrential rain events
	Potential generation of extreme wave events capable of damaging reefs
	Potential increased hurricane intensity and strength
	Karstification of the aquifer implies rapid infiltration from the surface and transport of pollutants

9. Follow-up of agreements and regional cooperation with the countries of Central America and the Caribbean.
10. Inclusion of Indigenous communities in territorial planning.
11. Proper management of beaches as public spaces (access, facilities, and services).
12. Integration of local uses with associated tourism.
13. Incorporation of human rights and the gender perspective in integrating the policy.
14. Implement governance strategies and methods to achieve objectives.

As for the actors in the Policy Decree, the Governor of the State of Quintana Roo, the Secretary of Government, the Secretary of Ecology and Environment, the Secretary of Sustainable Urban Territorial Development, the Secretary of Economic Development, the Secretary of Agricultural, Rural and Fisheries Development and the Secretary of Tourism signs it. These same actors comprise the State Intersectional Commission for Sustainable Coastal Management (Fig. 3).

Table 2: Environmental themes and problems described in the Coastal Policy Decree. *(Source: Own elaboration from Política de Costas del Estado de Quintana Roo [11].)*

Themes	Problems
'Flagship species'	The Strategy for the Conservation and Sustainable Use of Biodiversity of the State of Quintana Roo (ECUSBEQRoo) is 'the environmental policy instrument that defines biodiversity priorities'.
	Provide an overview of the conservation status of ecosystems in the coastal marine zone and a framework for decision-making.
	Sea turtles are a species with a high degree of vulnerability exposed to various threats; they provide a fruitful economy around tourism.
	Inadequate tourism management in the Whale Shark Biosphere Reserve can reduce abundance and sightings in the aggregation area.
	The manatee remains vulnerable to various threats.
	The jaguar is an endangered species under the species umbrella and flag. It requires efforts to conserve biological corridors.
Ecosystems	Coastal dunes. Highly vulnerable to climate change due to various threats shared with other coastal ecosystems, such as land use change, pollution, and invasion of exotic species.
	Reef system of the Mexican Caribbean. Various stressors that cause its decrease: climate change, overfishing, excessive tourism and diseases. Massive arrival of Sargasso as a stressor and factor of affectation of the reef system. Decline in the quality of coral reef health. Accounting for the blue carbon stock.
	Seagrasses. Protection is required for its conservation.
	Mangroves. Threats of degradation or loss due to anthropogenic use include deforestation, road construction, and tourism infrastructure. Fragmentation.
	Islands and cays. There is no conceptual legal differentiation. This differentiation is essential for their territorial and ecological management.

Table 3: Institutional, legal, governance and planning themes and problems described in the Coastal Policy Decree. *(Own elaboration from Política de Costas del Estado de Quintana Roo [11].)*

Themes	Problems
Institutional, legal framework	They provide an overview of the conservation status of ecosystems in the coastal marine zone and a framework for decision-making.
	Sea turtles are a species with a high degree of vulnerability exposed to various threats; they provide a fruitful economy around tourism.
	Inadequate tourism management in the Whale Shark Biosphere Reserve can reduce abundance and sightings in the aggregation area.
	The manatee remains vulnerable to various threats.
Ports and merchant marine	The jaguar is an endangered species under the species umbrella and flag. It requires efforts to conserve biological corridors.
Energy	Electricity production deficit.
	High transmission costs.
	High prices for end users.
	Reduction in productive competitiveness.
Governance and cross-sector aspects	Integration of policies, processes, and programs towards the MIZC. Definition of short, medium, and long-term strategies at a local level. Synergy with the actions of civil society organisations. Incorporation of available scientific and technological information. Promotion of research actions and social and environmental monitoring. Alignment to the National Policy of Seas and Coasts and the precepts of the High-Level Panel for a Sustainable Ocean Economy. Coordination and concurrence of actions between the three levels of government.
	High-Level Panel for a Sustainable Ocean Economy. Endorsement of Mexico in 2018. Commitment to the development of a Sustainable Ocean Plan. Opportunity for the development of the Coastal Policy of the Mexican Caribbean.
	The efforts of various institutions and civil society organisations require attention and greater coordination.

Table 3: Continued.

Themes	Problems
	Diagnosis by SWOT analysis. The higher percentage in strengths and opportunities.
	Strategic scenarios to meet the needs observed by specialists.
	Success pairs (strengths and opportunities).
	Border status and experience in general planning opportunities for regional and international technical and financial cooperation for the MIZC in Quintana Roo.
	Leaders in environmental management, fisheries organisations, research institutions, and academic and civil society groups to generate innovative local governance models.
	A cosmopolitan society that includes Mayan ancestral knowledge.
	Opportunities for implementing commercial strategies focused on green markets.
	Implementation of climate change mitigation and adaptation actions.
Strategic planning based on integrated coastal zone management	Adaptation pairs (weaknesses and opportunities).
	Lack of transversely and comprehensiveness in planning and operation.
	Lack of continuity in programs and projects that transcend administrative changes.
	Lack of internalisation of costs of degradation and loss of natural resources.
	There is a lack of scientific support for evaluating environmental services to influence economic policy.
	Reaction pairs (strengths and threats).
	Accelerated population growth triggers:
	Irregular settlements, deforestation, habitat fragmentation, a deficit of urban services, conditions of poverty, uprooting, unhealthy, and other factors of socioeconomic impact.
	Monitoring and enforcement mechanisms need to be improved.

Figure 3: Installation of the State Intersectional Commission for Sustainable Coastal Management. *(Source: Mónica Chargoy, taken on 21 September 2022.)*

Throughout the document, however, the following actors are mentioned as related to the themes and problems of the diagnosis:

1. Federal, state, or municipal government entities

    a. Federal government (seven secretaries)
    b. State government (three secretaries, two institutions and one committee)
    c. Municipal governments (eight coastal municipalities)

2. Business groups

    a. One entrepreneurial group

3. Social groups

    a. Rural population
    b. Fisheries and aquaculture communities
    c. *Punta Allen* Fisheries Cooperative
    d. Research institutions
    e. NGOs

4. International

    a. Commission For Environmental Cooperation (CEC) of the North American Agreement on Environmental Cooperation (NAAEC)
    b. High-Level Panel for a Sustainable Ocean Economy (Ocean Panel)

As shown in Fig. 4, most of the actors identified are in the political-administrative sphere, in the category of government entities, since they are primarily federal, municipal, or state agencies.

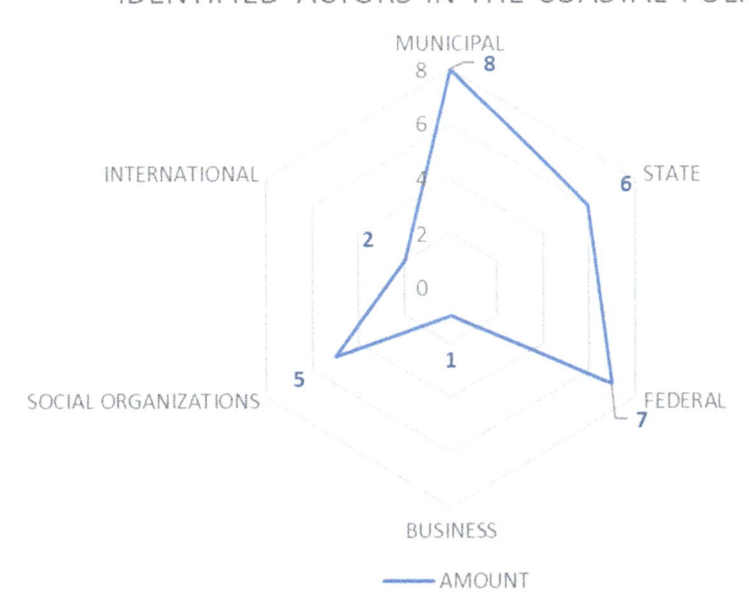

IDENTIFIED ACTORS IN THE COASTAL POLICY

- MUNICIPAL: 8
- STATE: 6
- FEDERAL: 7
- BUSINESS: 1
- SOCIAL ORGANIZATIONS: 5
- INTERNATIONAL: 2

Figure 4: Action area of the actors identified in the coastal policy.

Finally, because of the Strategic Planning based on Integrated Coastal Zone Management, three objectives were developed, with their respective strategies and lines of action, namely: five strategies for objective one, with 26 lines of action; five strategies for objective two, with 27 lines of action; and three strategies for objective three with 15 lines of action. However, these objectives, strategies, and lines of action are written as infinitive actions without a specific subject, or a key actor designated for their execution. At the end of the strategies the document indicates, as a manner of acknowledgment, that the operation of the policy will be based on the attributions and competencies of each institution responsible on the three levels of government through coordination, communication, the concurrence of actions, and acts of authority, as well as annual operational programming and institutional planning [11].

5 CONCLUSIONS AND IMPLICATIONS

Not all previously identified actors translate into key actors for the implementation of the Policy. Similarly, in the Strategic Planning section, there is talk of an inclusive design that involved holding two workshops, the first for SWOT analysis and the second for the design of strategic lines. It is mentioned that in these workshops, it was possible to concentrate the perception of specialists from different research institutions, civil society organisations and dependencies of the three levels of government, but the decree does not mention details or identify these specialists. Undoubtedly, this lack of identification of key actors for the execution of the Policy has direct repercussions on its progressive progress to the next stages and its implementation at the local level, which will be analysed in the following stages of the research.

This is the first part of a broader analysis of Coastal Policy. It is limited to identifying and evaluating key issues in the Coastal Policy Decree according to the proposed methodology. The following steps are to evaluate the current situation of the MIZC in the emerging tourism destinations at the southern Mexican Caribbean in Quintana Roo, with respect to what is defined in the Coastal Policy, taking this identification of critical issues and identified actors as a base for the next level of analysis, completing the following steps on the methodology proposed by Olsen and Ochoa [12] and the methodological conceptions of Olsen–ECOCOSTAS–LOICZ, combined with the methodology of Barragán's *Decálogo*.

The expected outcome would be a proposal of a set of strategic and operational guidelines to move towards the adoption and implementation of a MIZC model that adequately responds to the new Coastal Policy of the State of Quintana Roo, which:

1. would fulfil the function of a framework model for the MIZC in the territorial intermediate scale: level of the State of Quintana Roo, in response to its pioneering Coastal Policy in the country, which at the same time:
2. also corresponds to the country's Seas and Coasts Policy.
3. serves as a starting point for initiatives and programs at the local level.

This will have direct repercussions on the way activities are carried out in the coastal zone, highlighting all the uses identified in the Policy, particularly tourism, the state's main economic activity.

REFERENCES

[1] Secretaría de Turismo del Estado de Quintana Roo, Quintana Roo: How are we doing in tourism? February 2024 vs February 2023. Chetumal, Quintana Roo, pp. 3–21, 2024. https://sedeturqroo.gob.mx/ARCHIVOS/comovamos/como_vamos_202402.pdf. (In Spanish.)

[2] Rivera-Arriaga, E. & Azuz-Adeath, I.A., Implementing the SDG14 in Mexico: Diagnosis and ways forward. *Costas*, 1(1), pp. 219–242, 2019. https://doi.org/10.26359/costas.0112.

[3] INEGI, Consultation systems: Space and data of Mexico. https://www.inegi.org.mx/app/mapa/espacioydatos/. (In Spanish.)

[4] Milanés Batista, C., Lastra Mier, R.E. & Sierra-Correa, P.C., Case studies on integrated management of coastal zones in Latin America: Management, risk and good practices. Corporación Universidad de la Costa: Barranquilla, Colombia, p. 10, 2019.

[5] Barragán Muñoz, J.M., *Politics, Management and Coastline: A New Vision of Integrated Management of Coastal Areas*, Tébar Flores, S.L.: Madrid, 2014. (In Spanish.)

[6] Olsen, S., Lowry, K. & Tobey, J., *A Manual for Assessing Progress in Coastal Management*, Coastal Resources Center, University of Rhode Island, Graduate School of Oceanography: USA, pp. 6, 9, 10, 1999. https://pdf.usaid.gov/pdf_docs/Pnach693.pdf.

[7] Rivera-Arriaga, E. et al., Global review of ICZM in Mexico. *Costas*, 1, pp. 133–154, 2020. https://doi.org/10.26359/costas.e107.

[8] Azuz Adeath, I. & Rivera Arriaga, E., Spatial and temporal scales of coastal management. *Coastal Management in Mexico*, eds E. Rivera Arriaga, G.J. Villalobos, I. Azuz Adeath & F. Rosado May, Centro de Ecología, Pesquerías y Oceanografía del Golfo de México (EPOMEX), Universidad Autónoma de Campeche: Campeche, pp. 27–37, 2004. http://etzna.uacam.mx/epomex/pdf/Manejo_Costero.pdf. (In Spanish.)

[9] Frausto-Martínez, O. & Colín-Olivares, O., Sustainability indicators of the Seas and Coasts Policy: Mexico. *Costas*, 1(2), pp. 41–58, 2019. https://hum117.uca.es/wp-content/uploads/2020/05/1203.pdf. (In Spanish.)

[10] Vázquez Sosa, A., Frausto Martínez, O. & Cabrera Hernández, J.A., Models of integrated coastal zone management: Comparative analysis and adoption proposal in the case of Akumal (Mexico). *Costas*, **2**(1), pp. 25–50, 2020. https://doi.org/10.26359/costas.0202. (In Spanish.)
[11] Política de Costas del Estado de Quintana Roo, *Periódico Oficial del Estado de Quintana Roo*, **Tomo II**(142 Extraordinario), Novena Época, pp. 58,70, 82, 2022.
[12] Olsen, S.B. & Ochoa, E., *The Why and How of a Baseline for Governance in Coastal Ecosystems.* ECOCOSTAS, CRC Rhode Island, AVINA, LOICZ, USAID: Guayaquil, p. 24, 2007. https://pdf.usaid.gov/pdf_docs/pnaeb386.pdf. Accessed on: 18 Apr. 2023. (In Spanish.)
[13] Rojas Giraldo, X., Sierra Correa, P.C., Lozano Rivera, P. & López Rodríguez, Á.C., *Methodological Guide for the Integrated Management of Coastal Zones in Colombia. Manual 2: Coastal Zone Planning.* INVEMAR: Bogotá, Colombia, 2010. https://www.cbd.int/doc/meetings/mar/mcbem-2014-04/other/mcbem-2014-04-co-manual-2-es.pdf. (In Spanish.)

THE END OF A WAR = THE EXPLORATION OF UNTOUCHED LANDS: AN INVESTIGATION INTO HOW ECOTOURISM CAN PLAY A KEY ROLE IN BUILDING A LASTING PEACE IN COLOMBIA

RACHEL GERMANIER[1*] & SOFIA VARGAS SOURDIS[2]
[1]Les Roches Global Hospitality Education, Switzerland
[2]UN Tourism, Spain

ABSTRACT
In 2016, a peace treaty was signed in Colombia which was intended to signal the end of more than 100 years of conflict in the country. As a result, it was possible to enter lands which had been inaccessible and untouched by human development during the war and the potential to exploit these for ecotourism became apparent. The aim of this study was to see how, through sensitively interviewing 12 actors in the field of Colombian ecotourism, Colombia could use this form of tourism to its advantage in a meaningful way, preserving the phenomenal diversity of the country's nature and cultures, and moving towards a peaceful resolution of the war. The interviewees' pride for Colombia's natural and cultural treasures was evident as they expressed a clear desire to see ecotourism boom while respecting these assets. The picture the participants painted is a nuanced one with the unrivalled ecotourism potential of the country balanced against many challenges including a population uneducated in hospitality and a perceived lack of infrastructure and strategy. Several recommendations are made including marketing, preferably digitally, to specific niches, educating locals, improving national security and infrastructure and creating a solid strategy for ecotourism so that the Colombian population may finally benefit from its virgin lands.
Keywords: ecotourism, peacebuilding, reconciliation, Colombia, tourism development, post-conflict, environmental conservation, social cohesion, community empowerment.

1 INTRODUCTION
The signing of the peace treaty in 2016 marked a turning point in Colombia's history, opening new opportunities and instigating transformations in a land marked by internal conflict. Ecotourism is one of the areas significantly affected by this historic agreement. This paper explores the evolving relationship between the peace treaty and the subsequent development of Colombia's ecotourism industry through in-depth interviews with a wide range of stakeholders, including investors in ecotourism, politicians, a traveller and ecotourism providers. Their perspectives shed light on the potential of ecotourism to contribute to post-conflict reconciliation and the establishment of meaningful and enduring peace in Colombia. The participants' recommendations offer valuable guidance for the tourism industry with a view to leveraging the huge potential of ecotourism as a catalyst for sustainable peacebuilding.

Colombia, one of the world's largest countries [1] located in northwestern South America, is home to an enormous variety of ecosystems ranging from the Amazon rainforest and the Andes Mountains to coastal plains and Caribbean and Pacific coastlines. Labelled as one of the world's 'megadiverse' countries with close to 10% of the planet's biodiversity [2], its population is no less varied with an ethnic diversity of around 85 different groups [3].

---

*ORCID: http://orcid.org/0000-0002-5629-0882

Through an examination of interview data from a rich variety of stakeholders in the Colombian tourist industry, this work aims to explore the impact of the Colombian Peace Treaty of 2016 on ecotourism and analyse the role ecotourism could play in the future of the peacebuilding process in Colombia.

2 HISTORICAL CONTEXT

2.1 The establishment of a peace treaty

Colombia's war history is marked by three significant conflicts: La Guerra de los Mil Días (1899–1902), La Violencia (1948–1958) and the Armed and Drug Conflict which, fuelled by land reform, economic inequality, and political representation, escalated due to drug cartels and paramilitary groups. This conflict, which saw the birth of The Revolutionary Armed Forces of Colombia (FARC) and the National Liberation Army (ELN), resulted in severe human rights abuses and displaced over 5 million people [4]–[6]. In 2012, President Santos initiated peace negotiations, culminating in a peace treaty signed on 26 September 2016. The Final Agreement to End the Armed Conflict and Build a Stable and Lasting Peace focused on rural reform, political participation, conflict resolution, drug control, and implementation [4], [7]. This treaty offered hope to Colombians after a century of strife, addressing the underlying social and economic issues that had fuelled the war [8].

2.2 Consequences of the war and the peace treaty

2.2.1 Environmental impact
While the stereotype of Colombia focused on drug cartels [9] and a resulting considerable use of land to grow coca [10], the reality was that the whole of the Colombian environment was affected during the conflict. Indeed, Rettberg et al. [11] demonstrated that conflict over legal crops such as bananas, coffee, coal, flowers, gold, ferronickel, emeralds, and oil were all linked to crime during this period, causing environmental damage. A surprising positive outcome of the conflict era was that violence also protected ecosystems by making certain areas 'off limits' to development [12], [13]. The peace treaty established a National Land Fund to support rural land reform and promote sustainable land use, recognising the importance of traditional knowledge and community participation in conservation efforts [14], [15].

2.2.2 Tourism impact
Colombia exemplifies how war negatively impacts tourism, with mass media portraying the country as unsafe and tourism agencies blacklisting it [16], [17]. Despite this, tourism can mitigate the impact of conflicts, as demonstrated by post-conflict increases in the number of visitors to the country which increased from 1.3 million per annum in 2006 [18] to almost 6 million in 2023 [19].

2.3 Ecotourism as means to build a lasting peace

2.3.1 Sustainability and ecotourism
Sustainability's three pillars, established in the Brundtland Report in 1987 [20] are well known: the environment, the society and the economy. The UN Tourism definition of sustainable tourism logically follows this lead as 'tourism that takes full account of its current and future economic, social and environmental impacts, addressing the needs of visitors, the industry, the environment and host communities' [21].

Ecotourism has been described as a 'complex tourism phenomenon' [22] since its conception in the 1960s and its description of a type of pure tourism where one could travel to 'uncontaminated natural areas' to 'enjoy the scenery' [23]. The definition has evolved with Diamantis and Ladkin proposing, in 1999 [24], a simple but seemingly little-used four-layer, very weak to very strong cline, depending on the emphasis of the offering including nature, education and economic and socio-cultural sustainability. Two years later, a content-analysis of 85 definitions of ecotourism [25] showed that the key terms employed were 'conservation, education, ethics, sustainability, impacts and local benefit'. The themes of conservation, education and support, involvement and development of local populations was reiterated in a review of definitions in 2016 [26]. Finally, the definition which UN Tourism created in 2001 [27] will be used in this work. Its key elements are: nature, education, provision of services by locals to small groups, preservation of the natural and socio-cultural environment and ensuring locals benefit from tourism.

2.3.2 Promoting ecotourism for peace building

There is evidence that the Colombian government prioritised tourism as a peacemaker by creating the campaign Tourism for Peace Building from 2014–2018, aiming to rebuild the country's culture, improve the value chain and improve quality of life through responsible and sustainable practices [28]. While this campaign helped war-ravaged urban areas achieve sustainable development [29], the extent to which this could be described as ecotourism is unclear. The scant research carried out on Colombian ecotourism shows that locals believe ecotourism will promote environmental conservation in their area and that they should be involved in those enterprises [30]. Indeed, ecotourism projects which involve local communities, foster empowerment and participation and attract international visitors have been found to aid reconciliation [16]. However, infrastructure, security concerns, and the influence of popular culture and media complicate these efforts [17], [31], [32]. Bearing in mind Crisis Group's recent statement that 'levels of violence remain high' in the country [33], the aim of this research was therefore to ask how could ecotourism contribute to building lasting peace in Colombia?

3 METHODOLOGY

The research employed the technique of semi-structured interviews in English or Spanish with 12 purposively chosen ecotourism stakeholders: investors in ecotourism, both Indigenous and outsiders, a traveller and politicians whose accounts were recorded and translated by the interviewer, and subsequently analysed thematically [34] and for salience [35] using MAXQDA in order to understand the individuals' 'stories' [36]. Informed consent was obtained from all interviewees, ensuring they knew the study's purpose and rights once ethical clearance had been provided by the academic institution's research committee. Individuals were anonymised and identifiers used, as shown in Table 1.

The interviewer's identity as a Colombian positioned her as an insider which facilitated access to the participants who were potentially more open and trusting [37] with her than if she had been an outsider. Separate interview schedules including themes of perception of the country's ecotourism provision, the challenges faced and potential strategies for the future were created for each group of interviewees and were used as guides rather than a rigid framework as the interviewer deliberately maintained a conversational 'loose' style during the discussions.

Table 1: Stakeholders of ecotourism in Colombia.

Role	Identifier	Gender
Indigenous investors	Ind. Inv. 1	Male
	Ind. Inv. 2	Male
Outsider investor	Out. Inv. 1	Male
Traveler	Trav. 1	Male
Ecotourism providers	Eco. Prov. 1	Male
	Eco. Prov. 2	Male
	Eco. Prov. 3	Female
	Eco. Prov. 4	Male
Politicians	Pol. 1	Female
	Pol. 2	Male
	Pol. 3	Male
	Pol. 4	Female

4 RESULTS AND DISCUSSION

4.1 Colombia as a Phoenix rising from the embers

Positivity regarding the future after the incredibly difficult years of the war was a strong theme. Tourism is seen by Pol. 1 as a 'vehicle for peace' and a 'huge opportunity' with Colombia ready to be reborn (Pol. 2). Pol. 3 specifically mentioned that the Colombian people could benefit from tourism as the 'most powerful vehicle Colombia has'. Ecotourism providers, and the traveller, all referred more specifically to the potential of ecotourism in their analysis with Eco. Prov. 4 alluding to 'green tourism' being 'what people are looking for' and Trav. 1 describing Colombia as having 'absurd potential' for ecotourism.

4.2 Ecotourism post peace-treaty

Since the signing of the peace treaty in 2016, large swathes of the country which were previously unreachable and perceived as 'dangerous' (Ind. Inv. 2) are now becoming accessible. These lands are described in poetic language as 'magical' (Pol. 3), 'unexplored treasures' (Ind. Inv. 2), 'spectacular' (Trav. 1) and 'virgin' (Eco. Prov. 4). Trav. 1 even shares his gratitude to the guerillas who participated in maintaining the fauna of these spaces as some of them 'had very strong rules. You couldn't traffic animals, macaws, because whoever did it was killed. That, you have to thank them [for]'. Notably, the Indigenous leader, Ind. Inv. 1, takes a less positive view, describing his people as being 'violently displaced' from regions which were subsequently turned into 'nature disaster' zones. The opening up of these previously inaccessible lands has resulted in ecotourism in the form of 'glamping' (Ind. Inv. 2) flourishing in these areas with visitors coming to see 'birds and cave paintings' (Trav. 1) but tourist provision there is 'little known and of low quality' (Ind. Inv. 2).

In order to answer the research question, Colombian tourism stakeholders' perspectives are mapped onto the UN Tourism's definition of ecotourism in the following subsections.

4.2.1 Natural environment and its preservation
Undeniably, and mentioned by all the participants, the remarkable biodiversity in the untouched gems which were off-limits and where destructive activities such as cattle

ranching were not possible (Eco. Prov. 2) during the conflict years are phenomenal natural assets for the country. Preventing subsequent deforestation and biodiversity loss are worries expressed by Pol. 3 and Eco. Prov. 3 who is concerned that 'the whole world is already arriving' which is leading to 'a very strong environmental crisis' including deforestation. Although the general and tourist economy suffered as a result of the COVID pandemic, Pol. 3 articulates the need for individuals 'to look for quieter places, where they could connect with nature, to look for places of nature and adventure' and find this solace in Colombia's ecotourist provision. Alluding to the fossil fuel industry and its economic and environmental impact on society, Eco. Prov. 4 comments that ecotourism is, 'the new oil, we pollute less and we do not need huge investments the oil industry might need'.

4.2.2 Education

The second theme UN Tourism includes in its ecotourism definition is the provision of 'educational features', presumably to the visitors, but, in line with Nash [38], locals can benefit from training and education as an element of sustainable ecotourism. As a result, both aspects are developed below.

Colombians are unaware of the biodiversity on their doorstep (Pol. 3) or of the wonders they take for granted, as Trav. 1 explained in his account of a farmer being astounded that tourists would pay to see the toucans 'he sees every day'. They also lack training in hospitality but do not want to be 'only left as waiters and employees of cleaning services' (Eco. Prov. 4), instead, they are trained to become executives. This notion was echoed by Pol. 1 who talked of a long-term vision where education would 'empower young people' as 'we need to … pay back to society', implying that there is a debt due to those who had suffered through the conflict.

Aligning with UN Tourism's view of education, the local Indigenous leader, Ind. Inv. 1, spoke movingly of showing the wonders of the Colombian resources to 'the world, to the tourists, [so] we can send a clearer message of how to live in peace with nature'.

4.2.3 Local involvement in ecotourism

This section combines the third element of UN Tourism's definition which attends to the locals providing services to small groups with the last element which deals with locals benefitting from such tourism.

The theme of working in close harmony with locals (Pol. 1) was strongly represented in the stakeholders' accounts with Eco. Prov. 4 articulating, 'If the Koguis do not want to receive tourists in the Sierra Nevada in their territory, it must be respected'. Tourist numbers and their accommodation must, he insisted, be agreed with locals before implementing any ecotourism programmes. Ind. Inv. 1 mentioned that, as the native peoples 'have all the wisdom', they must be worked with in a 'responsible way'.

One of the repercussions of the peace treaty was the 'wonderful' (Trav. 1) conversion of guerillas into tourism actors. Ind. Inv. 1 spoke proudly of educating guerillas about sustainable living in remote jungle areas and these individuals now acting as 'even better tour guides than an outsider' as they have learnt how to 'live in harmony with nature, traditions, how to be safe, even how to find and identify wild animals that at that time were a great threat to them but today tourists pay millions to go and see even a trace of them'. The harmony the Indigenous leader mentioned not only concerned nature but between individuals. Pol. 2 recounted touchingly the time when he was being taken to a tourist destination driven and accompanied by two former guerillas from different gangs who each had family members killed by the other's gang – and here they were, working together, tourism uniting them.

Pol. 1 explored the possibility of extending gender equality by empowering local women to provide sensitive tourism packages to their area, ensuring they receive fair payment for their contributions and are then promoted in the tourist organisations.

The aim of many of the stakeholders was to see tourism replace drugs as the economic driving force of the local populations with one of the providers, Pol. 3, dreaming of his company having more competition as a reflection of this growth. Eco. Prov. 1 explained, 'If people don't have anything to eat, they start to commit crimes and cut trees for coca… then they realised that tourism was a catalyst. If they have something to eat, they will not do these things'. Trav. 1 pointed out that this realisation can emanate from a simple observation, as a farmer relayed to him, 'I am realising that there are people who want to sleep in my house, without electricity, see toucans, drink water from the river, instead of cutting down half the jungle to grow coca'.

4.2.4 The socio-cultural environment

The fourth part of UN Tourism's definition covers the preservation of the natural and socio-cultural environment. As nature was attended to in Section 4.2.1, this last subsection focuses on the importance given to the socio-cultural aspects mentioned by the participants.

The theme of spirituality resonated through the accounts of the interviewees with expressions such as, 'a country that … is in communion with the earth' (Eco. Prov. 4), 'we have to be at peace with nature…to gain inner peace' (Ind. Inv. 1) and nature being able to 'nourish your body, mind and spirit' (Eco. Prov. 3) peppering the narratives. Music contributes to both the spiritual side of tourism with Colombian spiritual traditions being spread through a festival of sacred music (Eco. Prov. 4) and Colombian culture becoming known worldwide through musicians such as Shakira, Maluma and Karol G (Trav. 1, Pol. 2). Eco. Prov. 1 recounted how tourists leave Colombia 'transformed, because you can't imagine that there is so much beauty or so much human quality in a territory, the way you can connect to these places, they can't imagine it'.

Two overarching communities, native and the Afro-Colombian populations, were referenced repeatedly as assets needing to be valued and safeguarded in the same way the participants referred to the biodiversity of flora and fauna. Ind. Inv. 1 described how native peoples in 32 different regions 'could easily explain part of their culture' and Eco. Prov. 3 said that 'they are one of the most important things that our country has'. The benevolence of the stakeholders towards these communities and the high regard they held them in was powerfully portrayed in the stakeholders' accounts.

Finally, other socio-cultural components of ecotourism which the participants mentioned were the ancestral element (Eco. Prov. 3), folklore (Eco. Prov. 4), gastronomy (Eco. Prov. 4) and the diversity of ethnicities and languages (Trav. 1).

Returning to the four-level definition of ecotourism, Diamantis and Ladkin [24] mentioned earlier, it is clear that the participants' perception of Colombia's ecotourism provision aligns with the 'strong' definition, one which places an equal emphasis on nature, education and socio-cultural and economic elements.

4.3 Setting the Phoenix free: Recommendations for the future

The stakeholders' levels of optimism about Colombia's future were hugely divergent. Eco. Prov. 4 estimated that a rise from 3 million to 12 million tourists over the next 8 years as per the president's vision 'is not something unreasonable', while Eco. Prov. 2 bemoaned the room for improvement in the industry: 'We do not have good products; we do not have a good offer developed. We do not have a good presence; we do not have good distribution'.

Eco. Prov. 4 offers somewhat of a middle ground, stating that sustainable tourism is 'like a win–win, the tourist is happy, there is no pollution, neither cultural, nor environmental, nor visual'. The participants' responses when asked about how they saw the future of Colombian ecotourism are grouped thematically in the following eight subsections. They act as recommendations to enable Colombia to fully embrace ecotourism so that it may contribute to a sustainable peace.

4.3.1 Luxury provision
The traveller interviewee was cognisant of the fact that Colombia is currently underselling its ecotourism offerings commenting, 'There is a market that wants to pay to be very comfortable in the middle of nowhere'. Developing this idea, he mentioned the ultra-luxury market where individuals pay between US$10,000–15,000 to experience a safari in Casanare while Ind. Inv. 2 draws attention to the fact that currently the average nightly Colombian hotel room revenue is no more than $100. There is therefore a market and a possibility to move away from the 'very ugly…low quality glamping' (Ind. Inv. 2) towards a much more upmarket offering in the ecotourism field.

4.3.2 Experiential provision
Especially post-COVID, tourists 'are looking for experiences, they want to connect with people, but they want to understand the stories behind the people' (Pol. 2). This statement underpins the findings of Packer and Ballantyne [39] which referred to providing experiences enabling the visitor to actively reflect and lead not only to more environmentally sensitive behaviour but also to customer satisfaction.

4.3.3 Security
The optimism expressed earlier regarding Colombia's ecotourism potential, post-peace treaty ceded to a much greater degree of morosity regarding the current state of national security. All of the stakeholders referred to the current return to violence in certain areas as being hugely problematic. The challenges are complex, as articulated by Eco. Prov. 3 who described complicated communication in the post-FARC era as there is 'no clear leader'. Trav. 1, an influencer who shares his travel adventures regularly on social media, 'cannot post in real time for security reasons'. Such feelings of insecurity are problematic 'because as long as they [violent movements] are there, successful ecotourism will not be possible' (Ind. Inv. 1). Ind. Inv. 2 provided a rather disheartening but potentially realistic commentary demonstrating the challenges faced by wishing to replace coca with tourism: 'I don't think the drug traffickers want these projects to be developed in certain places. There are many places that drug traffickers use to transport drugs and this is very convenient for them because these areas are alone, so I do not think this can improve'.

4.3.4 Digitalisation
A stronger contrast between the untouched, pristine natural world underpinning Colombia's ecotourism sector and the use of digital tools to market it to potential customers worldwide would be hard to find but digitalisation was seen as the way forward for many of the participants in this study. Politicians (Pol. 3) and ecotourism providers (Eco. Prov. 2) through their accounts, and Trav. 1, the social media traveller/influencer through his actions, all aligned with Vukasović and Očko [40] in their understanding that digital marketing is the way to expand demand for ecotouristm offerings.

4.3.5 Infrastructure

A second contradiction becomes apparent when considering the co-existence of ecotourism and infrastructure. Eco. Prov. 2, with his experience on the ground, explained,

> For tourism to exist, everything has to be working. There is no tourism where something is missing, where connectivity is missing, where training is missing, where public services are missing, where health is missing. All these are elements that are missing, you cannot bring foreign tourists if you do not have the capacity to ensure their wellbeing in every sense.

This sentiment was echoed by Eco. Prov. 3 who commented that most travellers like to 'travel to…destinations that work'. Providing a counter-argument, Eco. Prov. 4 stated that with hotel occupancy of 52%, 'we have infrastructure…we have half of the infrastructure still to be filled', although he acknowledged that there is scope for gently building on what already exists.

4.3.6 Marketing

As mentioned in Section 4.3.4, using digital tools to market the ecotourism offerings was deemed primordial. Additionally, participants stressed the notion of security 'projecting the image of a pacified country' (Eco. Prov. 4), marketing to both the foreign (Eco. Prov. 4) and to the domestic markets (Eco. Prov. 1 and 2) and using storytelling to get people to 'fall in love with other types of products' (Pol. 3). They recommended creating packages (Eco. Prov. 2) with experiences and marketing Colombia's diversity to Europeans and Americans (Eco. Prov. 3). Several niche markets were suggested, including backpackers as they are the executives of the future and could bring a convention here in 20 years (Eco. Prov. 4), 20–40 year olds who have seen the change from 'the most dangerous place in the world' and whose 'perception has shifted' to 'one of the trendiest destinations in the world' (Pol. 3) and bird-watchers (Pol. 2, Pol. 3, Eco. Prov. 2, Eco. Prov. 3 and Trav. 1) as they are very sophisticated and have a large spending power although Eco. Prov. 2 wonders about the size of this market realistically. Sports tourists interested in activities such as rafting (Pol. 3), fishing in 'rivers that are absolutely virgin' (Ind. Inv. 2) and solo female trekkers was a surprising suggestion from Pol. 2. Those attracted by specific flora and fauna could be targeted (Eco. Prov. 4) as could the well-being tourism market specifically linked to ancestral medicine (Pol. 3) or with a high level of comfort (Eco. Prov. 3). The last niche to be suggested was the Afro-American population 'because they are people who are today looking for their roots and one of the most important diasporas in the world of Afro people is Colombia' (Pol. 2). The stakeholders in the Colombian ecotourist field have clearly considered a wide range of natural and socio-cultural elements in their quest for new markets to target.

4.3.7 Education

Training of locals was mentioned above and was considered a vital part of the future of Colombian ecotourism (Eco. Prov. 2) to ensure not only a quality of service and related guest satisfaction but economic growth for the local communities.

4.3.8 Strategy

Politicians expressed a desire to see a bottom-up approach where communities 'create tourist packages' (Pol. 1) while ecotourism provider Eco. Prov. 3 would prefer more government involvement. Eco. Prov. 1 held a more balanced view with 'local, regional and national entities' working together. Planning was considered vital by Eco. Prov. 2 while Pol. 1 would like to see a professionalisation of the tourist industry, potentially overlapping with the area of education mentioned above. Finally, both the outsider investor and Eco. Prov. 3 perceived the decriminalisation of drugs as being the only way to move forward into a lasting peace.

5 CONCLUSION

This work had, as its aim, to answer the research question: How could ecotourism contribute to building lasting peace in Colombia? Following an in-depth analysis of the accounts of 12 Colombian ecotourism stakeholders, it can clearly be seen that the country has the potential to turn to ecotourism to contribute to building a sustainable peace through its bountiful and unique untouched lands and its natural and cultural diversity. However, the path to lasting peace does not appear to be straightforward and several recommendations including marketing, specifically digitally, to particular niches, educating locals and improving national security and infrastructure and creating a solid ecotourism strategy have been put forward as suggestions for action by politicians and invested stakeholders in ecotourism.

REFERENCES

[1] Statista Research Department, Colombia: Statistics and facts. *Statista*, 2024. https://www.statista.com/topics/3506/colombia/. Accessed on: 21 Jun. 2024.

[2] Convention on Biological Diversity, Colombia: Country Profile – Biodiversity facts. https://www.cbd.int/countries/profile?country=co. Accessed on: 21 Jun. 2024.

[3] Sawe, B.E., Ethnic groups of Colombia. *WorldAtlas*, 2019. https://www.worldatlas.com/articles/ethnic-groups-of-colombia.html. Accessed on: 21 Jun. 2024.

[4] Kline, H.F., *Between the Sword and the Wall*, The University of Alabama Press, 2020. https://www.uapress.ua.edu/9780817359911/between-the-sword-and-the-wall/. Accessed on: 21 Jun. 2024.

[5] Thoumi, F.E., Illegal drugs in Colombia: From illegal economic boom to social crisis. *The Annals of the American Academy of Political and Social Science*, **582**, pp. 102–116, 2002.

[6] Torres Del Río, C.M., *Colombia siglo XX: Desde la guerra de los mil días hasta la elección de Álvaro Uribe*, 2nd ed., Pontificia Universidad Javeriana, 2015. https://doi.org/10.2307/j.ctv893gth.

[7] Gomez-Suarez, A. & Newman, J., Safeguarding political guarantees in the Colombian peace process: Have Santos and FARC learnt the lessons from the past? *Third World Quarterly*, **34**, pp. 819–837, 2013.

[8] Muñoz Cardona, A.E., The justice and the Colombia peace talks. *Open Journal of Political Science*, **6**, pp. 261–273, 2016.

[9] Caro, A.J., Colombia behind the scenes: A country swallowed by a stereotype. *DecipherGrey*, 2021. https://www.deciphergrey.com/post/colombia-behind-the-scenes-a-country-swallowed-by-a-stereotype. Accessed on: 21 Jun. 2024.

[10] Isacson, A., Crisis and opportunity: Unraveling Colombia's collapsing coca markets. *WOLA*, 2023. https://www.wola.org/analysis/crisis-opportunity-unraveling-colombias-collapsing-coca-markets/. Accessed on: 21 Jun. 2024.

[11] Rettberg, A., Leiteritz, R.J., Nasi, C. & Prieto, J.D. (eds), *Different Resources, Different Conflicts? The Subnational Political Economy of Armed Conflict and Crime in Colombia*, Ediciones Uniandes, 2020. http://doi.org/10.30778/2019.116.

[12] Ross, M.L., How do natural resources influence civil war? Evidence from thirteen cases. *International Organization*, **58**, pp. 35–67, 2004.

[13] Le Billon, P., *Fuelling War: Natural Resources and Armed Conflicts*, Routledge, 2005.

[14] Álvarez, M.D., Forests in the time of violence: Conservation implications of the Colombian war. *Journal of Sustainable Forestry*, **16**, pp. 47–68, 2003.
[15] Anderson, J.L., Out of the jungle. *The New Yorker*, pp. 28–33, 2017.
[16] Ospina, G.A., War and ecotourism in the National Parks of Colombia: Some reflections on the public risk and adventure. *International Journal of Tourism Research*, **8**, pp. 241–246, 2006.
[17] Guilland, M.-L. & Naef, P., Tourism challenges facing peacebuilding in Colombia. *Via Tourism Review*, **15**, 2019. https://doi.org/10.4000/viatourism.4046.
[18] Colombia Reports, Tourism statistics. *Colombia Reports*, 2019. https://colombiareports.com/amp/colombia-tourism-statistics/. Accessed on: 21 Jun. 2024.
[19] Ventanilla Unica de Inversion, Colombia, Colombia breaks tourism records in 2023. https://vui.gov.co/news/colombia-rompe-records-turisticos-en-2023-mas-de-5-86-millones-de-viajeros-descubren-el-pais-de-la-belleza. Accessed on: 21 Jun. 2024.
[20] World Commission on Environment and Development, *Our Common Future*, 1987. https://www.are.admin.ch/are/en/home/medien-und-publikationen/publikationen/nachhaltige-entwicklung/brundtland-report.html. Accessed on: 23 Jun. 2024.
[21] United Nations, Department of Economic and Social Affairs, Sustainable tourism. https://sdgs.un.org/topics/sustainable-tourism. Accessed on: 23 Jun. 2024.
[22] Higham, J., Ecotourism: Competing and conflicting schools of thought. *Critical Issues in Ecotourism*, ed. J. Higham, Butterworth-Heinemann: Oxford, pp. 1–19.
[23] Ceballos-Lascurain, H., The future of ecotourism. *Mexico Journal*, 1987. https://cir.nii.ac.jp/crid/1570854175499121408. Accessed on: 23 Jun. 2024.
[24] Diamantis, D. & Ladkin, A., The links between sustainable tourism and ecotourism: A definitional and operational perspective. *Journal of Tourism Studies*, **10**, pp. 35–46, 1999.
[25] Fennell, D.A., A content analysis of ecotourism definitions. *Current Issues in Tourism*, **4**, pp. 403–421, 2001.
[26] Chandel, A. & Mishra, S., Ecotourism revisited: Last twenty-five years. *Czech Journal of Tourism*, **5**, pp. 135–154, 2019.
[27] World Tourism Organization, *The British Ecotourism Market*, WTO, 2001. https://www.e-unwto.org/doi/book/10.18111/9789284404865. Accessed on: 23 Jun. 2024.
[28] Salcedo Ribero, G., What makes Colombia the next ecotourism hotspot. *TradeArabia*, 30 November 2021. https://www.tradearabia.com/news/TTN_390312.html. Accessed on: 21 Jun. 2024.
[29] Oxford Business Group, The report: Colombia 2017, 18 June 2017. https://oxfordbusinessgroup.com/reports/colombia/2017-report. Accessed on: 21 Jun. 2024.
[30] Pineda, F. et al., Community preferences for participating in ecotourism: A case study in a coastal lagoon in Colombia. *Environmental Challenges*, **11**, 100713, 2023.
[31] Wood, A.G., *The Business of Leisure: Tourism History in Latin America and the Caribbean*, University of Nebraska Press: Lincoln, NE, 2021. https://muse.jhu.edu/pub/17/edited_volume/book/78620. Accessed on: 21 Jun. 2024.
[32] Bocarejo, D. & Ojeda, D., Violence and conservation: Beyond unintended consequences and unfortunate coincidences. *Geoforum*, **69**, pp. 176–183, 2016.
[33] Crisis Group, Colombia: Is 'total peace' back on track? 2023. https://www.crisisgroup.org/latin-america-caribbean/andes/colombia/colombia-total-peace-back-track. Accessed on: 22 Jun. 2024.

[34] Braun, V. & Clarke, V., Thematic analysis. *APA Handbook of Research Methods in Psychology, Vol 2: Research Designs: Quantitative, Qualitative, Neuropsychological, and Biological*, eds H. Cooper et al., American Psychological Association: Washington, pp. 57–71, 2012.

[35] Buetow, S., Thematic analysis and its reconceptualization as 'saliency analysis'. *Journal of Health Services Research and Policy*, **15**, pp. 123–125, 2009.

[36] Veal, A.J., *Research Methods for Leisure and Tourism*, 5th ed. Pearson Education: Harlow, 2018.

[37] Clark, T. et al., *Bryman's Social Research Methods*, 6th ed., Oxford University Press, 2021.

[38] Nash, J., Eco-tourism: Encouraging conservation or adding to exploitation? *PRB*, 2001. https://www.prb.org/resources/eco-tourism-encouraging-conservation-or-adding-to-exploitation/. Accessed on: 23 Jun. 2024.

[39] Packer, J. & Ballantyne, R. (eds), Encouraging reflective visitor experiences in ecotourism. *International Handbook on Ecotourism*, Edward Elgar Publishing, pp. 169–177, 2013.

[40] Vukasović, T. & Očko, K., The importance of digital marketing in the sale and promotion of tourist accommodation. *IJMKL*, **13**. https://doi.org/10.53615/2232-5697.13.1-12.

ARE OCEAN USERS OCEAN LITERATE? A CASE STUDY OF RECREATIONISTS AND TOURISTS IN CAPE TOWN, SOUTH AFRICA

SERENA LUCREZI
TREES, North-West University, Potchefstroom, South Africa

ABSTRACT

Non-consumptive recreation and tourism in or by the ocean, from scuba diving to snorkelling, have been regarded as generating memorable wildlife interactions, place attachment, nature connectedness, awareness of environmental problems, concern for environmental degradation and ocean literacy. The latter is the understanding of the influence of the ocean on people and of people on the ocean. Ocean literacy can foster environmental stewardship, and more responsible use of blue spaces for tourism and recreation, including fragile ecosystems. However, it is not guaranteed that marine tourists will be adequately ocean literate. This study evaluated levels of ocean literacy among 83 ocean-based recreationists and tourists in Cape Town, South Africa. This location offers numerous opportunities for ocean recreation and tourism such as scuba diving, free diving and snorkelling. A semi-structured interview was used to collect data at a tourism organisation offering these activities between January 2023 and January 2024. The participants' narratives, audio-recorded with their consent, were coded and analysed using thematic analysis and descriptive statistics. The participants were generally ocean literate, although some principles of ocean literacy were more familiar than others. Participants were mostly aware of provisioning ecosystem services of the ocean and human impacts on the ocean. The results of this study demonstrate that while ocean-based recreationists and tourists acknowledge the general importance of the ocean, more education is required to generate awareness about the inextricable link between the ocean and humankind, with a focus on the total dependence of people on the ocean and the need to be a part of strategies to mitigate damage to the ocean, its features, and ecosystems.

Keywords: environmental knowledge, eco-tourism, marine ecosystems, ecosystem services, ocean threats, environmental education, ocean stewardship.

1 INTRODUCTION

The oceans and coastal environments are a vital source of food and home to a great proportion of the earth's biodiversity but are facing several threats and problems that need to be acknowledged, from climate change to overfishing, pollution and tourism [1]–[3]. The oceans, seas and marine life need to be recognised as a conservation concern, and ocean conservation through the mitigation of human impacts is paramount to preserving biodiversity, ensuring food security, and maintaining carbon storage, among other ecosystem services provided by the ocean [4]. In line with this impinging need, in 2021 the United Nations (UN) announced the Decade of Ocean Science for Sustainable Development (hereon referred to as the UN Ocean Decade) to ensure that oceans are restored by the end of 2030 and that major efforts are implemented to address the decline in ocean health, create awareness about ocean issues and improve the relationship between people and the ocean in terms of attitude, awareness and behaviour [5], [6]. Part of the UN Ocean Decade's goals and objectives include identifying required knowledge for sustainable development, generating comprehensive knowledge and understanding of the ocean, increasing the use of ocean knowledge and also a deeper understanding of the relationship between people and the ocean [6]. If users view the ocean, seas and marine life as valuable and recognise the many negative impacts that affect the ocean, their emotional involvement, attitudes towards marine sustainability and pro-environmental behaviour can change positively, fostering ocean stewardship [7].

The ocean literacy movement [8] is closely connected to the UN Ocean Decade and is critical to its success [9]. First developed in 2004 by ocean scientists and educators in the USA, ocean literacy is generally defined as 'an understanding of the ocean's influence on you, and your influence on the ocean' [10]. The movement began to endorse the introduction of the ocean sciences in formal education [11]. Ocean literacy is characterised by seven principles [8]:

- The Earth has one big ocean with many features (OL1);
- The ocean and life in the ocean shape the features of Earth (OL2);
- The ocean is a major influence on weather and climate (OL3);
- The ocean made the Earth habitable (OL4);
- The ocean supports a great diversity of life and ecosystems (OL5);
- The ocean and humans are inextricably interconnected (OL6);
- The ocean is largely unexplored (OL7).

Ocean-literate people would be considered people capable of understanding the importance of the ocean for humankind, meaningfully communicating about the ocean, and embracing pro-ocean behaviours [12]. The ocean literacy movement is now recognised globally and targets all levels of society, with the assumption that ocean-literate people ought to have strong relationships with the ocean and embrace ocean stewardship through respectful and responsible behaviours [13], [14]. Recently, authors have developed new ocean literacy models shifting away from a knowledge-centric paradigm to include other concepts such as ocean connectedness, perceptions, and active participation in ocean stewardship [13]. These shifts highlight the importance of ensuring that ocean literacy is not simply understood to underpin enhanced awareness of the connection between people and the ocean and that its complexity and multi-dimensionality are properly addressed to create truly ocean-literate societies [13], [15].

As previously stated, there has been a growing call to ensure that ocean literacy is accessible to various groups of society, from indigenous communities to tourists [14]. For instance, people who participate in ocean-based recreation, such as snorkellers, scuba divers and surfers, can be important advocates for ocean conservation [16]. However, tapping the potential of ocean-based recreation groups requires a thorough investigation of these groups to evaluate awareness, attitudes and ultimately, pro-ocean behaviours, since these cannot be guaranteed based on the simple use of or proximity to the ocean [14]. Studies have revealed different levels of knowledge-based ocean literacy among ocean-based recreationists, who may be more familiar with certain principles than others, resulting in varying degrees of pro-ocean attitudes and behaviours [14], [17], [18]. Although ocean literacy is complex and requires the consideration of different constructs [13], an evaluation of awareness and knowledge of ocean literacy principles among ocean-based recreationists can represent the foundation for work to improve and deepen connections with the ocean, as well as foster true ocean stewardship through pro-environmental behaviour. Additionally, there is a call to increase research into the relationship between blue spaces and society, considering that ocean-based recreation is a major ecosystem service [14] and that this type of research is still scant compared to research evaluating relations between people and green spaces [19].

Based on the above, this study aimed to assess the awareness and knowledge of ocean literacy principles among ocean-based users including recreational and tourist groups, to guide strategies to create ocean-literate communities among ocean users and to support pathways towards ocean stewardship among these groups. The location selected for this study was Cape Town in South Africa. The coastlines of South Africa present many recreation and tourism opportunities supporting economic growth [20], [21]. The coastlines around Cape Town offer different types of ocean-based recreation and tourism, including activities like surfing, snorkelling, scuba diving, freediving, and kayaking; and eco-tourism, edu-tourism and scientific tourism [22], [23]. Based on this scenario, it was assumed that ocean-based recreation and tourism experiences in the area would be stimulating enough to foster good connections with the ocean and a basic understanding of ocean facts through education, interpretation, briefings and experiential learning, possibly resulting in decent levels of basic ocean literacy.

2 METHOD

This study used qualitative research and a phenomenology approach. According to Sokolowski [24], phenomenology is 'the study of human experiences and of the way things present themselves to us through such experiences'. A semi-structured interview (Table 1) was used to collect the data. The interview guide was developed by the researcher and validated by the scientific and ethics committees of the researcher's institution, as well as one marine biologist based at an international academic institution. It included basic demographic questions (e.g. gender, age, ocean-based activities practised by the participants); and one generic question (the core of the interview guide) asking the participants to describe the relationship between humankind and the ocean. To extract as much information as possible from the participants in answer to this question, probes were used to stimulate the conversation. The interview guide ended with a question asking the participants whether they wished to add anything to the conversation.

Table 1: Semi-structured interview guide.

Category	Question
Demography	1. What is your gender?
	2. What is your age?
	3. What is your country of origin?
	4. Are you local to this area?
	5. What is your highest level of education?
	6. What kinds of ocean-based activities do you regularly partake in?
Ocean literacy	7. Can you describe the relationship between human beings and the ocean?
	Probes:
	What is the influence that the oceans have on people?
	What is the influence that people have on the oceans?
	Can you describe some ocean ecosystems?
Final thoughts	8. Do you wish to add anything about people and the ocean, or these questions?

The population in this study included people engaging in ocean-based recreational and tourism activities recruited in Simon's Town, Cape Town. Recruitment took place at an eco-tourism establishment offering day and overnight visitors scuba diving and snorkelling trips on both the Indian Ocean and Atlantic Ocean sides of Cape Town. The establishment had a Memorandum of Understanding with the researcher formalising the research collaboration. Interviews were conducted once every two months from January 2023 to January 2024, for a total of six 4-day sampling trips. On each sampling day, the researcher randomly approached visitors at the eco-tourism centre, normally after they had participated in snorkelling or scuba diving and invited them to take part in the study. Agreeing participants were invited to sit with the researcher in a comfortable environment at the centre, where they could feel relaxed and free to speak. Before the start of the interview, the participants were provided with a letter explaining the purpose of the study and asked to provide informed consent to be interviewed and audio recorded. The interviews were conducted according to the ethical guidelines of the researcher's institution. The interviews lasted 20–40 minutes, with the participants being free to speak as much as they wanted or leave the research at any moment without having to explain why (although this never happened during the study). After conducting 25 interviews, the researcher began to analyse the data to look for data saturation, which was achieved when approximately 70 people were interviewed. To ensure that data saturation had been achieved, the researcher conducted another 13 interviews, after which sampling was interrupted. The final sample size was 83 participants.

The recordings were transcribed verbatim into Microsoft Excel. The participants were coded using pseudonyms (Participant 1–Participant 83). Numerical and categorical answers, including demographic ones, were analysed with TIBCO Statistica (Version 14, 2020) using basic statistics including frequency tables and averages. The transcribed data (mainly the narratives in answer to Questions 7 and 8 in Table 1) were first analysed using manual thematic analysis, which is a method used in research to identify, sort, and get meaning from patterns or themes that are found when doing qualitative research [25]. The analysis was first performed deductively, with the researcher using the seven principles of ocean literacy (OL1–OL7) as themes to assess whether these would emerge in the participants' narratives. The analysis was also performed inductively, to assess whether additional themes emerged from the narratives (ocean threats, and ecosystem services provided by the ocean). These themes were also coded to establish response frequencies for every theme among the participants. The data were thus reported both numerically and as rich-text quotes by the participants.

3 RESULTS

3.1 Demographic profile and ocean-based activities

The participants (N = 83) included 59% females and 41% males, aged 37 years on average (min–max = 18–77, SD = 13.48, SE = 1.48). A large proportion (39%) were local to the area and South African citizens, while 3% were South Africans from outside the area and the remaining 58% came from overseas, mainly from Europe and the USA. The highest level of education for most participants (87%) was tertiary (28% having a STEM qualification), while 13% possessed the equivalent of a high school diploma. The participants enjoyed mainly non-consumptive ocean-based activities including snorkelling and free diving (52%), surfing, kite surfing and kayaking (43%), scuba diving (41%), swimming (24%), walking on the beach (22%) and boating (13%).

3.2 Ocean literacy

In answer to the question of what the relationship between people and the ocean is, the participants provided answers which were coded to assess if, what, and with what frequency principles in ocean literacy were mentioned and described. As indicated in Fig. 1(a), all principles in ocean literacy were mentioned by more than one participant. The most mentioned principle (81% of participants) was OL6: The oceans and humans are inextricably interconnected. The main narrative associated with this principle was that humankind is severely and negatively affecting ocean environments and ecosystems through a series of impacts (Fig. 1(b)). For example, Participant 6 explained: 'I think we don't have the best influence on the ocean. I know there are so many different instances of harm that we do to it. Whether it's the emissions from the vehicles we drive or things we use that have been produced with carbon-emitting technologies.' Participant 45 elaborated: 'Humanity is not good for ocean life. The way we fish, the way we mine, the way we drill for oil, the way we do business with the boats and everything, it's all very bad and there are ways to do it better but it's not easy, so I think the immediate danger is people just breaking the ocean without really realising it.'

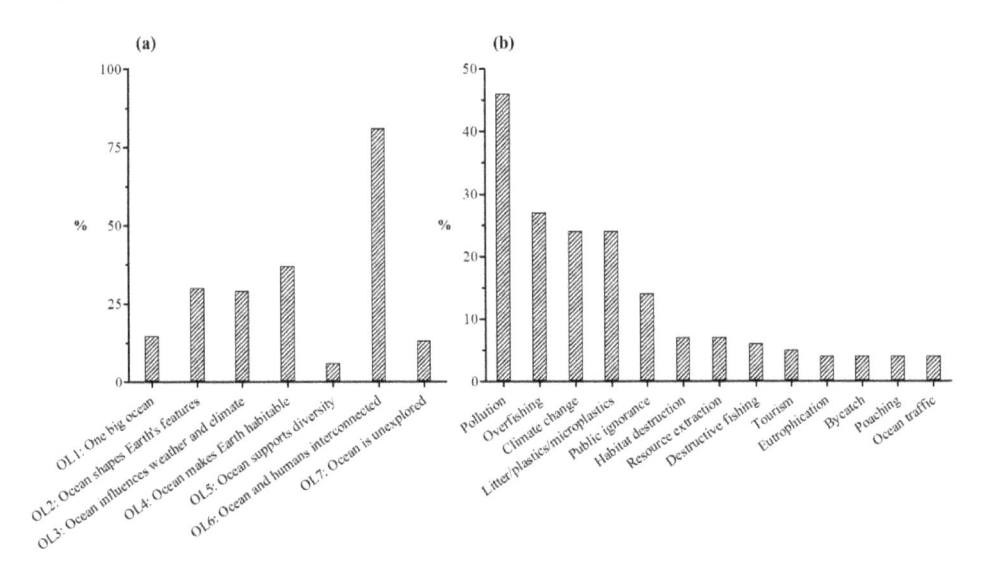

Figure 1: (a) Frequency distribution of ocean literacy principles mentioned by the participants; and (b) Frequency distribution of human impacts on ocean environments.

Human impacts on the ocean were described in detail including pollution (46% of participants), overfishing (27%), climate change (24%) and litter/plastics/microplastics (24%), among others (Fig. 1(b)). Some participants (14%) also explained that public ignorance and abstraction should be considered to have an indirect negative impact on the ocean, as it can result in support for bad environmental policies and practices, or inaction to endorse ocean conservation. For example, Participant 32 explained: 'Public ignorance is a problem. Just think of sharks, false beliefs are the reason why we're losing them. Shark culling and finning are driven by false beliefs and ignorance about them. If people have the right knowledge, they'll understand that they're doing damage.' Participant 39 added: 'Unless you live by the ocean and are connected to it every day, you ignore it. I think that people think of the oceans as vast but not functional in their lives. So they ignore it.' Another, more positive narrative associated with OL6 was that the ocean provides many ecosystem services (e.g. food, livelihood, transport) (Fig. 2). This narrative also underpinned awareness of other ocean literacy principles, as later described.

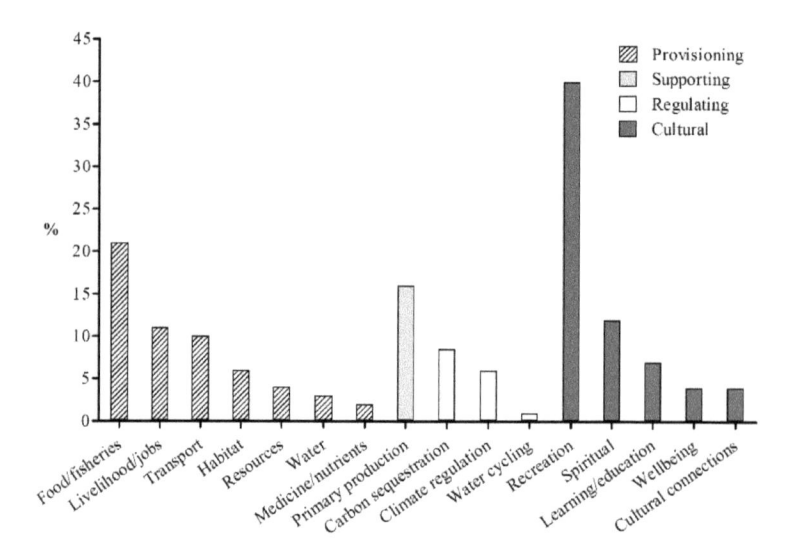

Figure 2: Frequency distribution of ecosystem services provided by the ocean per category.

The second most mentioned principle (37% of participants) was OL4: The ocean makes Earth habitable, with the participants mainly describing how the ocean is responsible for most of the primary production generating oxygen. Participant 18, for example, explained: 'People always consider the rainforests, for instance. They don't realise the importance of the oceans, most of the air we breathe comes from the algae there.' Participant 32 also stated: 'The ocean is considered the lungs of the planet. It's impossible to think of human life without the ocean. Human life started in the ocean. Even to this day, we are highly dependent on it.'

The third most mentioned principle (30% of participants) was OL2: The ocean and life in the ocean shape the features of the Earth. Here, however, the participants were not able to provide specific elaborations and explanations, and their narratives stayed generic. For example, Participant 17 claimed: 'Let's consider that the planet is made almost entirely of water and it's necessary to get that understanding that without the ocean, we cannot survive.' Participant 45 also stated: 'The world is one big machine and if one thing stops working such as the oceans everything just starts. I think the best example is the polar ice caps, they are one major part of the ocean and as soon as we see changes there you know that we will see changes everywhere.'

Concerning the fourth most mentioned principle (29% of participants), which was OL3: The ocean is a major influence on weather and climate, all that the participants could say was that the ocean plays a role in climate regulation but could not further elaborate with any specific narratives; only a small percentage (<10%) mentioned carbon sequestration as an important process carried out by the ocean. The least familiar principles were OL1: Earth has one big ocean with many features (14.5% of participants), OL7: The ocean is largely unexplored (13% of participants), and OL5: The ocean supports a great diversity of life and ecosystems (6% of participants). In support of OL1 and OL7, Participant 30 stated: 'It's something so vast and there is still so much to learn about it and from it.' Participant 37 added: 'There's a lot of mystery around the ocean that sparked a lot of curiosity and research into it. There are ecosystems that we probably haven't even come across yet underneath, like within water that's been sitting without sunlight for millions of years, like within the Mariana

Trench.' While only a small number of participants mentioned OL5 when asked to list ocean ecosystems they were familiar with they were able to mention several including coral reefs (25%), kelp forests (22%), rocky shores (13%), sandy beaches (10%), mangroves (9%), the pelagic zone (8%), seagrass (6%), and others like thermal vents, the surf zone and ice ecosystems.

As previously mentioned, when asked to describe the relationship between humankind and the ocean, the participants focused a large part of their descriptions on the ecosystem services of the ocean, which are listed in Fig. 2. The participants (70%) listed 16 ecosystem services, especially cultural and provisioning ones. Concerning cultural ecosystem services, the participants mainly acknowledged how the ocean is a place of recreation (40%), although some also explained that humans have spiritual and cultural connections with the ocean and that the ocean contributes to human wellbeing and learning. Regarding provisioning ecosystem services, the participants mostly explained that the ocean provides food and supports fisheries (21%), but some added livelihood and jobs, transport, habitat, resources, water, medicine, and nutrients. Participant 5 stated: 'I think we get a lot of enjoyment out of the ocean. For us, it brings food and jobs. Recreationally we've got scuba diving, all the water sports.' Participant 71 added: 'I think for many people it's like a sort of healing because not only do you get some exercise, but you also feel refreshed, it clears your mind, it makes you happier.' Participant 78 claimed: 'The ocean means a lot to humankind. We have a spiritual connection with the ocean because a lot of people go to the ocean for a sense of calm and peace, and many indigenous communities have cultural, religious and spiritual bonds with the ocean. Most people live by the ocean and get work from the ocean, through tourism for example. The ocean is a source of food and supports the fisheries, especially for countries that heavily rely on fish.'

The only supporting ecosystem service mentioned by the participants (16%) was primary production, while regulating ecosystem services included carbon sequestration (8.5%), climate regulation and water cycling. For example, Participant 9 stated: 'The ocean takes in so much carbon and provides oxygen; we always talk about the forest and deforestation, but more attention should be paid to the ocean and what happens if its functions are compromised.'

4 DISCUSSION AND RECOMMENDATIONS

The results of this study depict a profile typical of ocean-based recreational and tourist groups visiting both the area of study and South Africa in general, to engage in 'soft' adventure including also eco-tourism and edu-tourism [26], [27]. The participants' origin (mainly international but in large part also South African) mirrors a recovering recreation and tourism reality following the travel and movement restrictions associated with the COVID-19 pandemic.

The results of this study concerning the basic level of ocean literacy among ocean-based recreation and tourist groups in the case study are not easily comparable to previous work, since similar research is presently scanty [14], [19]. However, Fox et al. have recently started measuring ocean literacy among groups including surfers [17], yielding findings that can help with the interpretation of the outcomes of this research. The participants generally possessed some basic awareness of the seven principles of ocean literacy, however, there was more familiarity with certain principles (OL6, OL4, OL2 and OL3) compared with others (OL1, OL7, OL5). These results are partly aligned with work done on surfers, where principles including OL6 and OL3 were better known compared with principles including OL1 and OL7 [17].

Narratives related to OL6 were primarily connected to the awareness that human beings are severely damaging ocean environments through a series of impacts. These narratives are recurrent in several studies of ocean users' perceptions of the ocean, and it is understood that ocean connectedness, which in this case is offered by recreational and tourism activities, has a strong influence on these perceptions [17], [27], [28]. Additionally, the level of awareness of different human impacts mirrors that encountered in other studies of ocean users' understanding of marine environmental problems, where pollution, overfishing, climate change and litter (particularly plastics and microplastics) are normally ranked most relevant [27], [28]. Some participants believed public ignorance is indirectly a threat to the ocean and an impediment to conservation, a result that has been encountered in similar research on perceptions of ocean threats, also in South Africa [29]. Although the participants provided passionate narratives about the negative impacts of human activities on the ocean, only a small number acknowledged tourism to be a part of these impacts. Similar work has suggested that ocean and coastal users may generally underestimate the potential damage caused by recreation and tourism activities on ocean environments, which is an oversight calling for particular attention [28]–[30].

Narratives linked to OL6 also revolved around the ecosystem services offered by the ocean, particularly recreation. This finding is not new in the literature, particularly in studies of ocean users' perceptions of the benefits of the ocean to humankind [17], [29], [31]. Tourists tend to value intangible ocean ecosystem services supporting their wellbeing, including the scenery, peace, and setting to engage in their preferred activities (e.g. walking, swimming, diving, and relaxing) [31], [32]. In line with the positive narratives regarding OL6, the participants were aware of supporting ocean ecosystem services, specifically primary production (OL4). Other research, including work conducted around Cape Town, has highlighted how recreational ocean users can perceive the role of the ocean and ocean ecosystems in carrying out essential processes that make life on Earth possible [27], [29]. This result is also positive in comparison with previous work done on surfers, who were unable to describe the characteristics of OL4 in much detail [17].

While a third of the participants in this study could mention that the ocean and life within it shape the features of the Earth (OL2), they could not pinpoint exactly how nor provided concrete examples. This result concurs with the research by Fox et al. [17] who demonstrated a lack of basic knowledge of OL2 among surfers and suggests that recreational ocean users do not yet possess a sophisticated understanding of how visible processes like erosion and waves, or intangible ones like tectonic movement and geochemical cycles, are governed or controlled by the ocean. Similarly, although a third of the participants were aware of OL3, they could not go beyond stating that the ocean has a role in climate regulation, with a few people mentioning carbon sequestration. This result is in slight contrast with research showing that surfers could better elaborate on OL3, for example, describing the ocean's power to regulate the atmospheric temperature, pressure and wind [17]. The least mentioned principles were OL1, OL7 and OL5, partly in line with previous research on surfers [17]. These results suggest that recreational ocean users may take for granted certain ocean characteristics, such as how it covers most of the planet and supports a vastity of ecosystems and life forms. This is indicated by how the participants, when probed, were able to list several ocean ecosystems. Therefore, possibly the participants did not see certain ocean characteristics as signifying the relationship between humankind and the ocean or being instrumental to supporting human life on Earth.

Generally, the results of this study suggest that recreational ocean users possess basic knowledge of the principles of ocean literacy. Considering that they attached intrinsic and extrinsic values and benefits to the ocean, especially connected to recreational activities, it can be argued that these activities constitute a mechanism for ocean literacy development. However, Fox et al. [17] stated that it is debatable whether this mechanism is reliable and consistent enough to produce truly ocean-literate communities. Ocean-based recreation activities like scuba diving, snorkelling, and surfing have the potential to increase knowledge of the ocean by improving the connection between people and the sea through experiential engagement and learning, as well as increasing awareness of global environmental problems [14], [16], [17]. However, for ocean literacy to be truly incorporated into ocean-based recreational experiences, more efforts are required [16]. For example, considering mass tourism forms such as scuba diving or marine wildlife watching, the challenge would be to ensure that educational aspects are present in the operational environment, from posters and information sheets to pre- and post-activity briefings and interpretation. The work of tourist centres alone may also be insufficient to guarantee shifting mindsets among tourists and recreational groups, thus the involvement of different stakeholders is required to support knowledge acquisition. For instance, in marine protected areas, where recreational ocean-based activities are popular, governing bodies and researchers ought to support education aimed at improving ocean literacy as part of their conservation mandate. The support of external entities like meta-governance bodies, non-governmental organisations and academic/research institutions can foster education interventions and promote public participation in conservation and scientific activities, like marine restoration and citizen science, which are known to promote reflections on the ocean and how it is affected by human activities [26]. In this context, tourist centres offering scientific tourism, eco-tourism and edu-tourism activities have a particular responsibility to deliver the goals of raising awareness and educating tourists, as well as engage them proactively in activities that can stimulate reflection and intentions towards pro-environmental behaviours. Guaranteeing shifting mindsets and meaningful transitions towards a mentality of ocean stewardship remains a challenge to attain and measure, especially when long-term changes in attitude and behaviour are considered [33]. It is important, however, to strive for partnerships to support efforts toward ocean literacy among recreational ocean users, and to conduct research that will measure the long-term effects of specific interventions and initiatives on people's awareness, knowledge, attitudes and behaviours.

The results of this study highlight limited awareness and understanding of ocean literacy principles, as well as specific facts about the ocean underlying some of these principles. This lack of awareness and understanding can be addressed in communication, education, interpretation and experiential engagement as part of tourism activities or through the channels normally used to disseminate facts about the ocean (e.g. social media, television programmes). Overall, there should be a better emphasis on several aspects underpinning the inextricable connection between people and the ocean, such as overlooked ecosystem services; the dynamics of the ocean shaping the features of the Earth; and the importance of ocean exploration and science. More generically, the narratives revolving around ocean literacy should be well connected with various global agendas, such as the UN Ocean Decade, Sustainable Development Goals, Aichi Biodiversity Targets, and the Ocean Panels and Sustainable Ocean Plans. More specifically, narratives should be well connected with local ocean landscapes and ecosystems; especially in contexts of eco-tourism and edu-tourism, ocean users should be able to use their experiences with local environments and species as a channel for a greater understanding of how the ocean works and provides for humankind. An overarching goal of improving ocean literacy, at least among recreational ocean users, should be to establish and strengthen bonds between people and the ocean, or ocean connectedness [9], to the point where people would feel compelled to commit to ocean stewardship as a way to safeguard the activities they hold dear and contribute to their wellbeing. Reducing the level of abstraction felt even by ocean users towards the ocean would be key to removing the perception that human lives would be unaffected if ocean ecosystem services were compromised [34]. One way to do so would include specific campaigns aimed at demonstrating how human life on Earth would not be possible without the ocean.

5 CONCLUSION AND STUDY LIMITATIONS

This study aimed to shed light on the basic awareness and knowledge of ocean literacy principles among ocean-based users including recreational and tourist groups, to guide strategies to create ocean-literate communities among ocean users and to support pathways towards ocean stewardship among these groups. The results show that while recreational ocean users possess some basic understanding of ocean literacy principles, more work is required to improve ocean literacy, with the expectation that this will result in positive behaviour towards ocean protection and ocean stewardship. The tourism and recreation sector is in an advantageous position to support strategies to create ocean-literate communities. People can better understand the connection between the ocean and humankind, the complex dynamics underpinning this connection, and the vulnerability of the ocean to human impacts, through experiential engagement and learning-by-doing experiences. These experiences can allow ocean users to observe ocean environments and acknowledge the diversity of ecosystems and species and human impacts threatening the functioning of the ocean (e.g. pollution, and habitat degradation). It is acknowledged that this study has several limitations. For example, it was conducted in a specific geographical area and targeted only some ocean-based recreation and tourist groups. Additionally, this study only focused on the measurement of basic awareness and knowledge of ocean literacy principles, not considering the greater complexity of the ocean literacy construct. Nevertheless, the results presented here offer some valuable insight into the opportunities to be exploited and gaps to be filled concerning the creation of ocean-literate societies, starting with ocean-based users.

ACKNOWLEDGEMENTS

Special thanks go to the participants in the study, and to Mike Barron (Cape RADD) and Michael du Plessis for their assistance. The research was approved by the Research Ethics Committee of the Faculty of Economic and Management Sciences at the North-West University, South Africa, under the ethics code NWU-00559-23-A4. This paper reflects only the author's view. The North-West University accepts no liability in this regard.

REFERENCES

[1] Campbell, L.M. et al., Global oceans governance: New and emerging issues. *Annual Review of Environment and Resources*, **41**, pp. 517–543, 2016. https://doi.org/10.1146/annurev-environ-102014-021121.

[2] Lincoln, S. et al., Marine litter and climate change: Inextricably connected threats to the world's oceans. *Science of The Total Environment*, **837**, 155709, 2022. https://doi.org/10.1016/j.scitotenv.2022.155709.

[3] Sumaila, U.R. & Tai, T.C., End overfishing and increase the resilience of the ocean to climate change. *Frontiers in Marine Science*, **7**, 523, 2020. https://doi.org/10.3389/fmars.2020.00523.

[4] Sala, E. et al., Protecting the global ocean for biodiversity, food and climate. *Nature*, **592**(7854), pp. 397–402, 2021. https://doi.org/10.1038/s41586-021-03371-z.

[5] Ryabinin, V. et al., The UN decade of ocean science for sustainable development. *Frontiers in Marine Science*, **6**, 470, 2019. https://doi.org/10.3389/fmars.2019.00470.

[6] UNESCO, The Ocean Decade. https://oceandecade.org/. Accessed on: 6 May 2024.
[7] Pecl, G.T., Alexander, K.A., Melbourne-Thomas, J., Novaglio, C., Villanueva, C. & Nash, K.L., Future seas 2030: Pathways to sustainability for the UN Ocean Decade and beyond. *Reviews in Fish Biology and Fisheries*, **32**(1), pp. 1–7, 2022. https://doi.org/10.1007/s11160-022-09705-y.
[8] UNESCO, The seven principles of ocean literacy. https://oceanliteracy.unesco.org/principles/. Accessed on: 6 May 2024.
[9] Kelly, R. et al., Connecting to the oceans: Supporting ocean literacy and public engagement. *Reviews in Fish Biology and Fisheries*, **32**(1), pp. 123–143, 2021. https://doi.org/10.1007/s11160-020-09625-9.
[10] UNESCO, Ocean literacy for all. https://www.unesco.org/en/node/82173. Accessed on: 6 May 2024.
[11] Santoro, F., Selvaggia, S., Scowcroft, G., Fauville, G. & Tuddenham, P., *Ocean Literacy for All: A Toolkit*, UNESCO Publishing, 136 pp., 2018.
[12] Cava, F., Schoedinger, S., Strang, C. & Tuddenham, P., Science content and standards for ocean literacy: An ocean literacy update. National Geographic Society, 2005. https://www.coexploration.org/oceanliteracy/documents/OLit2004-05_Final_Report.pdf. Accessed on: 6 May 2024.
[13] McKinley, E., Burdon, D. & Shellock, R.J., The evolution of ocean literacy: A new framework for the United Nations Ocean Decade and beyond. *Marine Pollution Bulletin*, **186**, 114467, 2023. https://doi.org/10.1016/j.marpolbul.2022.114467.
[14] Worm, B. et al., Making ocean literacy inclusive and accessible. *Ethics in Science and Environmental Politics*, **21**, pp. 1–9, 2021. https://doi.org/10.3354/esep00196.
[15] Stoll-Kleemann, S., Feasible options for behavior change toward more effective ocean literacy: A systematic review. *Frontiers in Marine Science*, **6**, 273, 2019. https://doi.org/10.3389/fmars.2019.00273.
[16] Garcia, O. & Cater, C., Life below water; challenges for tourism partnerships in achieving ocean literacy. *Journal of Sustainable Tourism*, **30**(10), pp. 2428–2447, 2022. https://doi.org/10.1080/09669582.2020.1850747.
[17] Fox, N., Marshall, J. & Dankel, D.J., Ocean literacy and surfing: Understanding how interactions in coastal ecosystems inform blue space user's awareness of the ocean. *International Journal of Environmental Research and Public Health*, **18**(11), 5819, 2021. https://doi.org/10.3390/ijerph18115819.
[18] Holland-Smith, D., Love, A. & Lorimer, R., British surfers and their attitudes and values toward the environment. *Ecopsychology*, **5**(2), pp. 103–109, 2013. https://doi.org/10.1089/eco.2013.0020.
[19] Gascon, M., Zijlema, W., Vert, C., White, M.P. & Nieuwenhuijsen, M.J., Outdoor blue spaces, human health and well-being: A systematic review of quantitative studies. *International Journal of Hygiene and Environmental Health*, **220**(8), pp. 1207–1221, 2017. https://doi.org/10.1016/j.ijheh.2017.08.004.
[20] Gounden, R., Munien, S., Gounden, D. & Perry, N., Visitor profiles of coastal and marine tourism sites in the Eastern Cape, South Africa. *African Journal of Hospitality, Tourism and Leisure Geography and Planning*, **9**(6), pp. 1060–1075, 2020. https://doi.org/10.46222/ajhtl.19770720-68.
[21] Saayman, A. & Saayman, M., Forecasting tourist arrivals in South Africa. *Acta Commercii*, **10**(1), pp. 281–293, 2010. https://hdl.handle.net/10520/EJC11382.

[22] Munien, S., Gumede, A., Gounden, R., Bob, U., Gounden, D. & Perry, N.S., Profile of visitors to coastal and marine tourism locations in Cape Town, South Africa. *Geo Journal of Tourism and Geosites*, **27**(4), pp. 1134–1147, 2019. https://doi.org/10.30892/gtg.27402-421.
[23] Pfaff, M.C. et al., A synthesis of three decades of socio-ecological change in False Bay, South Africa: Setting the scene for multidisciplinary research and management. *Elementa: Science of the Anthropocene*, **7**, 32, 2019. https://doi.org/10.1525/elementa.367.
[24] Sokolowski, R., *Introduction to Phenomenology*, Cambridge University Press: New York, 238 pp., 2000.
[25] Braun, V., Clarke, V. & Terry, G., Thematic analysis. *Qualitative Research on Clinical and Health Psychology*, eds P. Rohleder & A.C. Lyons, Palgrave Macmillan: New York, pp. 95–113, 2014.
[26] Cilliers, C.D., A critical assessment of marine wildlife voluntourism in Southern Africa. Doctoral dissertation, North-West University, 2022.
[27] Lucrezi, S. & Du Plessis, M.J., Cold-water recreational diving experiences: The case of kelp forests. *WIT Transactions on Ecology and the Environment*, vol. 256, WIT Press: Southampton and Boston, pp. 27–38, 2022.
[28] Lucrezi, S., Public perceptions of marine environmental issues: A case study of coastal recreational users in Italy. *Journal of Coastal Conservation*, **26**(6), 52. https://doi.org/10.1007/s11852-022-00900-4.
[29] Lucrezi, S., Characterising potential participants in kelp monitoring in the recreational diving community: A comparative study of South Africa and New Zealand. *Global Ecology and Conservation*, **28**, e01649, 2021. https://doi.org/10.1016/j.gecco.2021.e01649.
[30] Gkargkavouzi, A., Paraskevopoulos, S. & Matsiori, S., Public perceptions of the marine environment and behavioral intentions to preserve it: The case of three coastal cities in Greece. *Marine Policy*, **111**, 103727, 2020. https://doi.org/10.1016/j.marpol.2019.103727.
[31] De Juan, S., Gelcich, S. & Fernandez, M., Integrating stakeholder perceptions and preferences on ecosystem services in the management of coastal areas. *Ocean and Coastal Management*, **136**, 38–48, 2017. https://doi.org/10.1016/j.ocecoaman.2016.11.019.
[32] Wood, L.E., Vimercati, G., Ferrini, S. & Shackleton, R.T., Perceptions of ecosystem services and disservices associated with open water swimming. *Journal of Outdoor Recreation and Tourism*, **37**, 100491, 2022. https://doi.org/10.1016/j.jort.2022.100491.
[33] Brennan, C., Ashley, M. & Molloy, O., A system dynamics approach to increasing ocean literacy. *Frontiers in Marine Science*, **6**, 360, 2019. https://doi.org/10.3389/fmars.2019.00360.
[34] Schuldt, J.P., McComas, K.A. & Byrne, S.E., Communicating about ocean health: Theoretical and practical considerations. *Philosophical Transactions of the Royal Society B: Biological Sciences*, **371**(1689), 20150214, 2016. https://doi.org/10.1098/rstb.2015.0214.

Author index

Agoraki K. K. 39, 209
Aguilar-Aguilar M. 93
Alexandropoulou A. 39, 209
Anastasopoulos I. 23
Assi E. 181

Bahadir Kalipçi M. 119
Bevilacqua D. 107
Briones-Bitar J. 127

Cabrera Hernández J. A. 243
Carrión-Mero P. 93, 127
Casares J. 63
Castilla Corzo F. 193
Chamaratana T. 229
Chargoy Rosas M. A. 243
Chatzifoti N. 209
Chiappini A. 107

de la Calle M. 63, 77
de Mingo F. 63, 77
Deaza M. P. 193
Di Nisio S. 221
Didaskalou E. 39
Dujmović M. 3

Espinel R. 127

Facoetti V. 139
Filomena-Ambrossio A. 193
Fousteris A. 209
Frausto Martínez Ó. 243

Galluzzo L. 139
Gálvez-Pérez D. 63, 77
Georgakellos D. A. 39, 209
Georgopoulos N. 23
Germanier R. 257
Ghimire N. 49
Gonzalez Forero M. C. 193
Guirao B. 63, 77

Hamazaki M. 167

Jaya-Montalvo M. 93, 127

Katsanakis I. 23
Klada N. 23
Konstantopoulou C. 23
Kopanaki E. 23
Kurihara T. 167

Liu M. 229
Lucrezi S. 269

Mahler R. L. 49
Mayes I. 49
Mendoza de Miguel S. 63
Mohíno I. 77
Montes-Guerra M. I. 193
Morán-Rodríguez H. 153

Ortuño A. 63, 77

Passerini G. 107, 221
Pattanaro G. 13
Poggendorf L. 167

Rizza U. 107, 221
Rodríguez-Zurita D. 153

Saladié Ó. 93
Soto-Navarrete L. 93, 127
Stokes B. 49
Stroumpoulis A. 23

Tommasi M. 221
Tsoupros G. 23

Valenzuela P. 63, 77
Varelas S. 23
Vargas Sourdis S. 257
Villar Navascués R. 63
Virgili S. 221
Vitasović A. 3

Zapata-Cuervo N. 193